A/C HIS

D1255140

Patterns of Episcopal Leadership

MAKERS OF THE CATHOLIC COMMUNITY

The Bicentennial History of the Catholic Church in America
Authorized by the National Conference of Catholic Bishops

Patterns of Episcopal Leadership

Gerald P. Fogarty, S.J., Editor

The Bicentennial History of the Catholic Church in America
Authorized by the National Conference of Catholic Bishops
Christopher J. Kauffman, General Editor

MACMILLAN PUBLISHING COMPANY
NEW YORK

Collier Macmillan Publishers
LONDON

Macmillan Publishing Company
866 Third Avenue, New York, NY 10022

Collier Macmillan Canada, Inc.

Library of Congress Catalog Card Number: 88-18095

Printed in the United States of America

printing number
1 2 3 4 5 6 7 8 9 10

Library of Congress Cataloging-in-Publication Data

Patterns of Episcopal leadership / Gerald P. Fogarty, editor.
        p.   cm. — (The Bicentennial history of the Catholic Church in America)
    ISBN 0-02-910611-7
    1. Catholic Church—United States—Bishops—History. 2. United States—Church history.   I. Fogarty, Gerald P.   II. Series.
BX1406.2.P39 1989
282'.092'2—dc19
[B]   88-18095
                                                                          CIP

To Archbishop William Donald Borders
Twelfth successor to John Carroll

Contents

List of Contributors

PETER CLARKE, a priest and pastor in South Carolina, has served on the Board for the National Federation of Priests' Councils. He was the editor for the *Fides* News Service of the Congregation for Evangelization from 1978–1979.

CLYDE F. CREWS, a native of Louisville, chairs the department of theology at Bellarmine College. He has published six books on theology and church history, including *An American Holy Land*, and has written extensively on Louisville and Kentucky history.

ROBERT EMMETT CURRAN, S.J., an associate professor of history at Georgetown University, is the author of *Michael Augustine Corrigan and the Shaping of Conservative Catholicism in America, 1878–1902* (1978), *American Jesuit Spirituality: The Maryland Tradition, 1634–1900* (1988), and the forthcoming *Georgetown University: A Bicentennial History* (1989).

JOHN TRACY ELLIS, a professorial lecturer in church history at The Catholic University of America, is the premier historian of American Catholicism. Among his hundreds of publications is the highly praised and prize-winning two-volume biography of Cardinal James Gibbons.

GERALD P. FOGARTY, S.J., teaches church history at the University of Virginia. Among his many works is *The Vatican and the American Hierarchy from 1870 to 1965*.

JAMES P. GAFFEY, pastor of Saint Eugene's Cathedral in Santa Rosa, California, took his doctorate in history under John Tracy Ellis in 1965. His articles have appeared in *Church History* and *The Catholic Historical Review*, and his books include biographies of Patrick W. Riordan and Francis Clement Kelley. In 1983 he occupied the chair endowed by the Catholic Daughters of America for American history at The Catholic University of America.

JAMES HENNESEY, S.J., teaches the history of Christianity and serves as rector of the Jesuit community at Canisius College, Buffalo, New York. His publications include *American Catholics: A History of the Roman Catholic Community in the United States* (Oxford, 1981), several other books, and more than 150 articles in the field of church history.

M. EDMUND HUSSEY is pastor of Saint Paul Church in Yellow Springs, Ohio, adjunct professor of historical theology at Mount Saint Mary Seminary in Cincinnati, and president of the Association of Catholic Diocesan Archivists. He is the author of several studies of the Catholic church in Cincinnati.

EDWARD R. KANTOWICZ, formerly a professor of history at Carleton University, Ottawa, Canada, is now a free-lance historian in Chicago. He is the author of *Corporation Sole: Cardinal Mundelein and Chicago Catholicism*.

ANNABELLE M. MELVILLE, Commonwealth professor emerita, Bridgewater State College, Bridgewater, Massachusetts, is the author of *Elizabeth Bayley Seton, 1774–1821* (New York, 1951); *John Carroll of Baltimore* (New York, 1955); *Jean Lefebvre de Cheverus* (Milwaukee, 1958); and *Louis William DuBourg* (Chicago, 1986).

MARVIN R. O'CONNELL teaches history at Notre Dame University. His biography of John Ireland was published in 1988.

JAMES M. O'TOOLE, an assistant professor of history and archives at the University of Massachusetts at Boston, is the author of the *Guide to the Archives of the Archdiocese of Boston* (1982) and co-editor of *Catholic Boston: Studies in Religion and Community, 1870–1970*. He is currently at work on a full-length biography of Cardinal William Henry O'Connell.

THOMAS J. SHELLEY teaches church history at Saint Joseph's Seminary, Dunwoodie, New York. He is the author of *The Vital Center: Archbishop Paul J. Hallinan and Forces of Change in Twentieth-Century American Catholicism* (1988).

THOMAS W. SPALDING, a Xaverian brother and professor of history at Spalding University in Louisville, is the author of *Martin John Spalding: American Churchman* (1973) and a number of articles in historical journals.

General Editor's Preface

The Second Vatican Council developed a new apologetic, a fresh articulation of faith suitable to the diverse peoples of the world. The Council also marked the turn from the atemporal transcendental character of the neoscholastic theological synthesis to a historical approach to the role of culture in the development of dogma, an approach influenced by the historical-literary methodology fostered by Catholic biblical exegetes. Implicit in the Council Fathers' call to discern the "signs of the times" is the need of the historian to provide a lens to improve our vision of the signs of past times. New models of the church, such as the "pilgrim people" or the "people of God," stressed not the institutional structures but rather the people's religious experiences.

Concurrent with these general trends in apologetics, systematic theology, and ecclesiology was the dramatic rise in consciousness of the ethnic particularities throughout the world. Just as the movements in the Catholic church were based upon a dynamic of historical consciousness, so the rise in ethnic awareness was steeped in the historical dynamic of national and regional identities.

Of all the students of American Catholicism, James Hennesey, S.J., stands out for his singular contribution to the dialogue between theologians and historians. In several studies he has focused on the role of the Christian historian in the process of discerning the authentic tradition of the church. To sharpen our focus on that tradition he juxtaposes a quotation from John Henry Newman with a text from the conciliar decree on Divine Revelation.
Newman in 1859:

> I think I am right in saying that the tradition of the Apostles, committed to the whole Church in its various constituents and functions *per modum*

unius [as one unit], manifests itself variously at various times, sometimes by the mouth of the episcopacy, sometimes by the doctors, sometimes by the people, sometimes by liturgies, rites, ceremonies and customs, by events, disputes, movements, and all those other phenomena which are comprised under the name of history. It follows that none of these channels of tradition may be treated with disrespect; granting at the same time fully that the gift of discerning, discriminating, defining, promulgating, and enforcing any portion of that tradition resides solely in the Ecclesia Docens [the teaching Church].

The Council Fathers in 1965:

What was handed on by the apostles [the tradition] comprises everything that serves to make the People of God live their lives in holiness and increase their faith. In this way the Church in her doctrine, life and worship, perpetuates and transmits to every generation all that she herself is, all that she believes.

Of course this implied religious task of the church historian must be grounded in the rigorous principles and scholarly methodology of the profession. Writing religious history is by its very nature different from writing, say, economic history. Both must avoid a priori reasoning and evaluate the sources of their discipline with a precise analysis. Just as the economic historian must be conscious of the biases embedded in her or his social-class perspective, so the church historian must explore her or his place at the intersection of faith and culture. Without such a hermeneutical exercise of self-exploration one can neither adequately struggle against biases nor develop clear principles for understanding the past. During several group meetings with the six primary contributors to this work such a hermeneutical process developed. Since all of us have been influenced by recent trends in ecclesiology and historiography, each has a sense of her or his place at the intersection of faith and culture. Though some focus on the institutional church and others analyze the movement of peoples, all are professionally trained historians and are sensitive to Newman's notion of the diverse manifestations of tradition.

We conceived this topical approach of the six-volume history as the most effective means of dealing with an enormous amount of material. In a sense this project was an attempt to weave the American fabric of tradition into distinctive patterns. Although I designed the overall project, each of the primary contributors, either author or editor-author, was responsible for the particular design of his or her book. We seven historians met several times over a three-year period. In this case the term "community of scholars" is no exaggeration; a remarkable climate of honesty, candor, civility, and humor prevailed in our discussions. Though each volume stands on its own, the six achieve an unusual unity. There is a common beginning in most of the books. Commemorating the bicentennial of the appointment of John Carroll, each of the books opens during the federal period when Catholics achieved some semblance of ecclesiastical organization. We anticipate that a fresh synthesis of colonial Catholic history will be published at the quincentennial in 1992 of Columbus's arrival in the New World.

Throughout these volumes one reads about the persistent need for Catholics to forge their religious identities within the ethos of the new nation. In its origins the nation tended toward enlightenment and toleration; Catholics in Maryland and Pennsylvania reflected an open cosmopolitanism symbolized by the leadership of John Carroll. There was a conscious effort to embrace religious liberty and pluralism as positive factors; a denominational civility characterized the era. Subsequently, periodic outbursts of militant anti-Catholicism and nativism during the periods of immigration led Catholics to identify their loyalty to the United States in terms of good citizenship, but they retreated from the culture into ethnic enclaves; these were the preservationists who nurtured their particular Old World cultures in defense against this hostility. Isaac Hecker and the Americanists, such as John Ireland, forged a transformationist identity, one that was derived from the Carroll era and was based upon the spiritual compatibility of Catholicism and American culture.

Preservationist and transformationist are more appropriate concepts than ideological terms such as conservative and liberal because they are rooted in the religious and social contexts. Though today the lines are blurred between these identities, they are still viable conceptually. Today's preservationists are defensive against what they perceive as the antireligious tendencies of the culture and are searching for a wholeness in their view of the past. Transformationists tend to mediate religion in the terms of the culture and, like Isaac Hecker, see the movement of the Spirit not in opposition to modern society but within strands of the larger national ethos.

The "Romanness" of the American Catholic identity has seldom been a problem. During periods of conflict and controversy leaders in both camps have appealed to Rome as symbolic of their general loyalty to the papacy. American notions of religious liberty, denominationalism, pluralism, and voluntarism were not legitimated by Rome until the Second Vatican Council. While many Americans have consistently held that this attitude by the Vatican represents the inherent conflict between Roman authority and American democracy, Catholics have tended to consider the assumption that there is such a conflict to be another malicious manifestation of the anti-Catholic animus. While very loyal to Rome, Catholics have shared with other

Americans a pragmatic sense, a sense that Martin E. Marty refers to as a kind of experimentalism. While Catholics articulated a loyalty to Rome as the center of their changeless religion, paradoxically many had derived from their American experience a spirituality and a religious worldview that accept change as a fact of life. Marty quotes Jacques Maritain on American experimentalism: "Americans seem to be in their own land as pilgrims, prodded by a dream! They are always on the move—available for new tasks, prepared for the possible loss of what they have. They are not settled, installed. . . . In this sense of becoming and impermanence one may discern a feeling of evangelical origin which has been projected into temporal activity." In a sense this Catholic insistence on changeless faith, while their religious behavior is protean, allowed many leaders to hold to an Americanist vision and even a modernist methodology (applied not to Scripture but to evangelization) after the condemnations of Americanism and modernism.

Catholic identities derived from race, gender, and non-European ethnic groups are distinctive from the Roman, transformationist, and preservationist identities. Black Catholics were so marginalized that there was no sizable number of black clergy until the mid-twentieth century. The general periodization, particularly "immigrant church," is simply meaningless to their experience. The racism of the vast majority of people was reflected in the church. Many black Catholics now identify with Afro-American culture and the exodus experience basic to liberation theology. French Canadians and many Hispanic people also have developed their distinctive identities. Their non-European origins marginalized them in a church dominated by assimilationists of the more affluent classes. As with the black Catholics, their identities are deeply influenced by their historically rooted outsider status.

These six volumes struggled against exclusivism based on race, ethnicity, and gender. While chapters in these books deal with race and major non-European ethnic groups, an entire volume focuses on gender. I consulted with several Catholic feminists before deciding on a separate book on women in the Catholic community. Some might ask why not each of the other five books deals with this subject. Because there are so few secondary works on Catholic women and because not each historian could do ground-breaking research in women's studies, it became evident that an entire book should be devoted to this topic. As a consequence of a corollary decision, specialists in particular areas wrote separate chapters in the book because one author could not do justice to a general history of Catholic women. Of course, many Catholic women were drawn into the issues discussed in the other five volumes, but many behaved in a countercultural manner and opposed the dominant ecclesiastical identity represented by the conventional notion of the "ideal Catholic woman." In the shadow of patriarchy many women formed spiritual identities that did not fit religious and social categories.

Dolores Liptak, R.S.M., and Karen Kennelly, C.S.J., help us to understand the varieties of ethnic and female identities; David O'Brien and Gerald P. Fogarty, S.J., elaborate on the public forms of Catholicism and episcopal leadership; Margaret Mary Reher and Joseph P. Chinnici, O.F.M., locate various Catholic identities on the intellectual, spiritual, and devotional planes.

These six historians have been sensitive to regional variations, to differing contexts of urban development, and to the need to expand beyond the boundary of the stated theme of each volume into such frontiers as the micro-history of neighborhoods and parishes, the rural Catholic experience, meanings of the Catholic rites of passage and of Catholic "habits of the heart." The design of the project and the bicentennial deadlines limited the historians' range to the broad national contours of their topics. Though there is unavoidable overlapping in the treatment of persons and movements, the particular points of view preclude redundancy. More significantly, these books focus on the distinctive character of the American aspect of the Catholic community and represent various blends of original research and a unique rendering of topics derived from secondary literature.

From design to production I have had the good fortune to work with excellent historians and other fine people. To Justus George Lawler, the literary editor, to Charles Buggé, our liaison with the United States Catholic Conference, to Elly Dickason and Charles E. Smith of Macmillan Publishing Company, to Virgil C. Dechant and the late John M. Murphy of the Knights of Columbus, to Archbishop William D. Borders of Baltimore and Archbishop Oscar H. Lipscomb of Mobile, chairmen of the bicentennial committees of the National Conference of Catholic Bishops, and to John Bowen, S.S., Sulpician archivist and consultant, I am exceedingly grateful for their participation in making this six-volume set an appropriate tribute to John Carroll and to all those people who formed the Catholic tradition in the United States. I am particularly indebted to the inspiration of John Tracy Ellis in this the fifty-first year of his priesthood. May we always cherish his tradition of scholarship, honesty, and civility.

Christopher J. Kauffman

Acknowledgments

The National Conference of Catholic Bishops in 1981 established an ad hoc committee to plan for an appropriate observance of the 200th anniversary of the appointment in 1789 of John Carroll of Baltimore as the first Roman Catholic bishop for the United States of America. It was quickly determined that an important component of that observance should be a serious and substantial effort to shed added light on the growth and development of the Catholic church in Carroll's native land for these two hundred years. A subcommittee for publications was formed and the six volumes, *Makers of the Catholic Community*, are the result of its initiatives.

Grateful acknowledgment is made to the Knights of Columbus and their Supreme Knight, Virgil C. Dechant, who provided a generous grant that underwrote the scholarly efforts necessary to such a venture. For more than a century the work of the Knights of Columbus has epitomized much of the Catholic life that fills these volumes just as their presence and spirit have given discernible form to the faith and external witness of the Catholic church in the United States.

The Order has a rich tradition of fostering historical studies. In 1921 the Fourth Degree established the K of C Historical Commission. It presented its awards to Samuel Flagg Bemis and Allan Nevins, historians who later became notable figures. The commission also sponsored the publication of the K of C Racial Contribution Series: W. E. B. DuBois, *The Gift of the Black Folk;* George W. Cohen, *The Jews in the Making of America;* and Frederick F. Schrader, *The Germans in the Making of America.* Coincidentally, these books were also published by Macmillan. The K of C microfilm collection of the manuscripts of the Vatican archives, which resides at Saint Louis University, is a remarkable testimony to the Knights' promotion of scholarship. In 1982 a scholarly history of the Order, *Faith and Fraternalism*, by

Christopher J. Kauffman, was published, a book that has been widely noted as a solid contribution to social and religious history. Hence, *Makers of the Catholic Community* is a significant mark on the long continuum of the Knights' role in historical scholarship.

For six years the NCCB Ad Hoc Committee for the Bicentennial of the U.S. Hierarchy has given consistent and affirmative support for this series, and the Subcommittee for Publications has provided the technical insights and guidance that were necessary to the finished work. All who have thus contributed time and talent deserve recognition and gratitude. The members of the committee were: Archbishop William D. Borders, chairman; Archbishops Eugene A. Marino, S.S.J., Theodore E. McCarrick, and Robert F. Sanchez; and Bishops John S. Cummins, F. Joseph Gossman, Raymond W. Lucker, and Sylvester W. Treinen. The staff consisted of Rev. Robert Lynch and Mr. Richard Hirsch. Members of the subcommittee were: Rev. William A. Au, Ph.D.; Msgr. John Tracy Ellis, Ph.D.; Sister Alice Gallin, O.S.U., Ph.D.; Msgr. James Gaffey, Ph.D.; Rev. James Hennesey, S.J., Ph.D.; and Msgr. Francis J. Lally.

Most Reverend Oscar H. Lipscomb
Chairman, Subcommittee for Publications

Foreword

The appointment of John Carroll as the first bishop of the new republic occurred in 1789, the year of the ratification of the federal Constitution. Just as the latter marks the passage of a significant phase in the political organization of the United States, so Carroll's appointment represents the origin of the official organization of the institutional church. This study of sixteen bishops who played significant leadership roles in the Catholic community is the only book in this multi-volume work that specifically deals with the American hierarchy on the bicentennial of its foundation.

Some leading historians of the Catholic church disparage traditional historiography with its emphasis upon institutions as opposed to local communities and upon the elite rather than the people in the pews. This book is institutional history but it departs from tradition in focusing on the intersection between human and institutional experience.

Patterns of Episcopal Leadership is a prism through which the reader may perceive the general trends in the shaping of the American Catholic community such as Enlightenment Catholicism, the frontier experiences, the conditions of nativism and anti-Catholicism, ethnic diversity and the Americanization of the immigrant, and the self-understanding of the United States church in light of its relationship with the papacy and its own American experiences.

These biographical portraits focus on the personal characterstics and administrative styles of the various bishops and on how they dealt with issues on local and national levels. The lives of American bishops tend to reflect the developments of American-Catholic identities, while the leaders of the church frequently articulated the meaning of being Catholic and American. Hence, this study of the episcopacy is in the "life and times" genre, to illuminate the Catholic historical landscape from the point of view of the cathedrals. In the process the reader will appreciate the human element and the distinctively American character of the Catholic experience.

Christopher J. Kauffman

Introduction

On May 18, 1788, the clergy of the United States elected John Carroll as their first bishop. Carroll had insisted that the bishop be elected by the priests, but his insistence was not due to his being enamored with American republicanism. He was quite conscious of a more ancient Catholic tradition—the election of bishops by cathedral chapters. After American independence, he had, in fact, organized the clergy, all of whom had been Jesuits before the order's suppression in 1773, into the "General Chapter." Election of bishops by chapters had been the standard method of choosing bishops, except where the Holy See transferred that right to monarchs.[1] The United States had been offered that right but rejected it, and so the American church was now free to conduct its own affairs. Over the next century and a half, however, this freedom from government interference led to episcopal absolutism, both in the manner in which bishops were chosen and in the way in which dioceses were governed.

The mode of election of bishops went through a series of changes in the nineteenth century. In May 1789, after Pius VI confirmed Carroll's appointment, the General Chapter provided for a series of delegated electors for future bishops.[2] The First Synod of Baltimore in 1791 requested the establishment of a senate of fifteen priests, ten who had served the longest on the mission and five chosen by the bishop, who would advise the bishop and elect his successor.[3] This seems to have been the group Carroll consulted in nominating as his coadjutor first Laurence Graessl, who died before he could be consecrated, and then Leonard Neale.

When Carroll sought candidates for his suffragan sees in 1808 he seemed willing to accept the Holy See's appointees, as James Hennesey notes, at least in the case of Richard L. Concanen, O.P., who died before reaching his see city of New York. Gone was the tiny American church centered in Maryland and Pennsylvania and the general ethnic homogeneity of Anglo-Maryland colonial Catholicism. Louisiana, with its Spanish and French culture, was already part of the republic. Louis William DuBourg, S.S., the subject of Dr. Annabelle Melville's essay, was at home with the French language but faced so many challenges to his authority that he could not remain in his see city of New Orleans. Because of a lack of qualified American-born priests Carroll had to look for non-natives for bishops even for his suffragan sees. Clyde Crews studies the missionary career of the French Sulpician Benedict Flaget, S.S., first bishop of Bardstown.

Between 1808 and 1833, the manner of selecting bishops varied. In some instances, individual bishops vied with one another to have their own candidates appointed, and, in others, the Holy See directly chose its own candidates. In 1810, Carroll met with his suffragans, in preparation for a provincial council that they hoped could meet in 1812. They petitioned that the Holy See "allow the nomination for the vacant Dioceses to proceed solely from the Archbishop & Bishops of this Ecclesiastical Province."[4] For the time being, however, Rome preferred to take a more direct hand in appointing American bishops.

The Roman appointees were a mixed group. On the one hand, there was Henry Conwell, appointed to Philadelphia after he failed to become archbishop of Armagh—his successful rival in Armagh said he could not have been more surprised if Conwell had been named emperor of China.[5] Conwell was a disaster, especially in his handling of lay trusteeism. In 1830, Propaganda (the Sacred Congregation for the Propagation of the Faith) appointed Francis P. Kenrick as his coadjutor, with the understanding that Conwell would retire to Ireland. Conwell, however, first sought the assistance of Charles Bonaparte, Napoleon's nephew, next hinted that he might seek the intervention of the president of the United States, and then broke his agreement with Propaganda and returned to Philadelphia, where he repudiated Kenrick's authority.[6] On the other hand, Propaganda also appointed the dynamic Irishman, John England, as the first bishop of Charleston in 1820. His would be the guiding hand that developed a sense of collegiality among the American bishops and, in the process, developed a more regular method of nominating bishops. He also was more deft in handling trusteeism, and he developed a constitution for his diocese that provided for lay involvement in administering church temporalities—a theme treated here by Peter Clarke.[7]

Upon his arrival in the United States, England began putting pressure on Archbishop Ambrose Maréchal of Baltimore to hold a provincial council to provide uniform legislation on such issues as lay trusteeism. Only after Maréchal's death did he prevail on the new archbishop, James Whitfield, to convoke the First Provincial Council in 1829. England based his canonical demand for councils on the legislation of the Council of Trent, which had prescribed that metropolitans should convoke such councils every three years. The first council of Baltimore, therefore, called for a second council, "unless for grave reason it seemed good to the archbishop to defer it."[8] Whitfield found a "grave reason" for not holding a council and he revealed it to Nicholas Wiseman, then the rector of the English College in Rome and later the cardinal archbishop of Westminster. England and Kenrick, wrote Whitfield,

> are both warm headed Irishmen, & have, it seems, strong predilections in favour of Irish Bishops & Irish discipline for the U. States. . . . They both have united in using every effort, even by publications in their newspapers, to make me hold another Provincial Council, which, notwithstanding all they have exposed before the public, I have not consented to convoke, because such is the agitating disposition of Dr. England, that he would be restless in proposing changes in our discipline until it were reduced to the standard of Ireland or reformed according to his republican notions.

Whitfield knew England was then in Rome, attempting to have Propaganda order him to convoke the council. "I am sorry that any more Irish Bishops are added to our hierarchy," Whitfield wrote, "as I fear their increase in number will have power to have others of their countrymen nominated hereafter & bring over to this country a great number of Irish Priests whilst I wish, with a few exceptions, they would all stay at home."[9] The English-born Whitfield would have been appalled had he lived to see the gradual Irish domination of the hierarchy.

Despite Whitfield's reservations, on August 6, 1833, Propaganda ordered him to convoke the Second Provincial Council on October 22 of the same year. This time, England and the other bishops took no chances that the archbishop would find a "grave reason" to defer other councils. The final decree of the council stated "that the next council is to be held on the third Sunday after Easter in the year of our Lord 1837."[10] In each of the councils from 1837 through the Sixth Provincial Council in 1846, the final decree set the date of the next council without giving the metropolitan any power to defer it.[11] The Second Provincial Council also decreed the method of nominating bishops that would prevail until 1852. The bishops of the province were now to submit a list of three names, a *terna*, for vacant sees or for coadjutors.[12] Giving the right of nomination to the bishops as a body was but the practical expression of the collegiality that, as will be seen, was developing among the American bishops.

At the Seventh Provincial Council of Baltimore in 1849, there were already two new metropolitan sees, Saint Louis and Oregon City. Archbishop Peter Richard Kenrick of Saint Louis attended the council. The council decreed that the bishops of each province should still submit a *terna* for vacant sees but that the metropolitan should also seek the opinion of the other archbishops. Further they legislated that, with the approval of the Holy See, a national council be held in Baltimore in 1850.[13] Such a council was necessary because they had petitioned that the new metropolitan provinces of New Orleans, Cincinnati, and New York be established. To preserve their practical experiment in collegiality, they requested that the "Metropolitan See of Baltimore enjoy primacy of honor."[14]

A primate at that time had the canonical right to preside over plenary or national councils.[15] This privilege, however, the Holy See denied to Baltimore. In 1852, it convoked the First Plenary Council and delegated Archbishop Francis P. Kenrick of Baltimore (the brother of Archbishop Peter Richard Kenrick of Saint Louis) to preside over the council—a right he would have had *ex officio* as primate. His successors, Martin J. Spalding, in 1866, and James Gibbons, in 1884, were similarly delegated to preside over the Second and Third Plenary Councils, respectively. The council of 1852 was important for introducing the first innovations in diocesan structure. First, each bishop was to appoint consultors, whose opinion he should seek in the administration of his diocese. Second, every bishop was to appoint a chancellor "for the easier administration of ecclesiastical affairs, and for achieving a stable norm of acting in those matters."[16] The bishops had thus passed legislation that widened the deliberative voice in diocesan governance but still preserved their authority, for both consultors and chancellor were to be appointed directly by the bishop alone and not in a diocesan synod, as was the case for a vicar general. The chancellor in the common law of the church, was moreover, merely the archivist and keeper of the records. The American church transformed the office into a governing one, but always subject to the bishop.[17]

By the mid-nineteenth century, the American bishops were receiving the first signs of Roman disapproval, but were still strengthening their authority. And the church and the nation were still ex-

panding. After the Mexican War, the United States annexed the former
Mexican territories of the Southwest, Texas and California. The
American hierarchy now included Bishop Joseph Sadoc Alemany,
O.P., of Monterey, who was named the first archbishop of San Francisco in 1853. New York, which had emerged as the nation's largest
city, was the recipient of the largest waves of immigrants to enter
the nation. It was also the scene of anti-Catholicism, controlled by
the militant defender of Catholic rights, John Hughes, the third bishop
and first archbishop of New York. The expanse and rapid growth of
the nation, combined with the independent spirit of the American
bishops, may have motivated the Holy See in refusing any prerogatives
that would have strengthened that spirit.

In June 1853, Archbishop Gaetano Bedini, on his way to Brazil as
nuncio, made an official visitation of the Church in the United States.
The American bishops were loyal to Rome, he reported, but the "ocean
that divides them" and the "unbridled liberty of their civil institutions" could "later form some pretext for independent action." Because of this, he continued, "the Holy See has very wisely refused to
grant them their request for a Primatial See." Bedini acknowledged
that the bishops were motivated by a desire to preserve their unity,
but he thought a nuncio appointed to the government was a better
way to "bring about their complete unity."[18] Quite clearly Bedini's
vision of how to preserve episcopal unity was diametrically opposed
to that of the Americans.

In 1858, the Congregation of Propaganda compromised on the issue
and conferred on the archbishop of Baltimore the title of "prerogative
of place"—a title that enabled him to have seniority over other archbishops, but not cardinals. In 1859, the congregation also decreed
that, when a metropolitan see was vacant, the other metropolitans
were to be consulted on the *terna*.[19] Later in the century, as will be
seen, this decree led the archbishops to attempt to draw up their own
ternae for metropolitan sees.

Behind the frequent councils of the American bishops and their
desire to preserve their unity was a theology of collegiality. John Carroll had already articulated it in 1811, when he wrote: "[The] center
of Catholic unity must be found in the steadfast, public, avowed doctrine, confession and authority of the Successor of St. Peter, united
in language and belief with all (I mean morally all) the Bishops of
the Catholic world."[20] The Second Plenary Council approached collegiality more directly in its pastoral letter. Speaking of the relationship between the church and Scripture, the bishops said that the "inspired page" of Scripture came to life through "the recorded testimony
of those ancient and venerable witnesses, who in every nation and
every age, proclaimed in the name of the Catholic church, and with

its approbation, the interpretation of the Holy Bible, whether they were assembled in their councils or dispersed over the surface of the Christian world."[21]

The author of the pastoral was most probably John England, but the theology showed the influence of Francis P. Kenrick, who at that time was completing his *Theologia Dogmatica*. There he stated that the teaching authority of the church was under divine guidance from the Apostolic age up to his own time in such a way that one or even many bishops could fall into error, but that "infallibility" or the "privilege of inerrancy" resided "in the body of the bishops, under the presidency of the Roman Pontiff."[22]

This theology of collegiality underlay the conciliar practice. In 1866, the bishops at the Second Plenary Council stated it even more strongly:

> Bishops, therefore, who are the successors of the Apostles, and whom the Holy Spirit has placed to rule the Church of God, which He acquired with His own blood, agreeing and judging together with its head on earth, the Roman Pontiff, whether they are gathered in general councils, or dispersed throughout the world, are inspired from on high with a gift of inerrancy, so that their body or college can never fail in faith nor define anything against doctrine revealed by God.[23]

Even though this decree received Roman approbation, within three years the American hierarchy would find its cherished tradition sorely tried at the First Vatican Council.

Vatican I was the first ecumenical council that Americans attended. As a group, they were opposed to any definition of infallibility of the pope independent of the traditional authority of the bishops. Some held that the definition was inopportune. Others, like Martin John Spalding, as Thomas Spalding explains in this study, shifted to support of the doctrine. Still others, like Kenrick of Saint Louis and Richard Purcell of Cincinnati, opposed the definition outright. Papal infallibility, argued Peter Kenrick, was merely a theological opinion, which theologians were free to debate. In his estimate, bishops were to reflect and preserve the faith but not take sides on theological opinions. In fine, he stated: "I boldly declare that the opinion, as set down in the schema, is not a doctrine of faith, and that it cannot become such by any definition whatsoever, even of a council."[24]

With others of the opposition, Kenrick received the permission of Pius IX to absent himself from the solemn definition of papal infallibility on July 18, 1870. For the next year, he was a *cause célèbre* as the Holy See sought, unsuccessfully, to gain a full retraction of what he had said at the council. It finally contented itself with his economic public statement that "simply and singly on that authority [of the church] I yield obedience and full and unreserved submission to the definition the character of which there can be no doubt as emanating from the Council, and subsequently accepted by the greater part of those who were in the minority on that occasion." One reason for his resistance to a retraction of what he had said during the council was that this would restrict the freedom of discussion of bishops at any future session of the council.[25]

Vatican I, with its definitions of papal primacy and infallibility, had seemed to sound the death knell for American episcopal collegiality. Bishop Bernard McQuaid of Rochester put it well to the people of his diocese gathered in his cathedral to welcome him home. "I have now no difficulty in accepting the dogma of papal infallibility," he said, "although to the last I opposed it; because somehow or other it was in my head that the Bishops ought to be consulted."[26] While the Holy See issued a clear statement that the definition of papal primacy did not detract from the ordinary jurisdiction of bishops,[27] American bishops now began to lose their earlier sense of collegiality, in part because of other issues.

There was an anomaly in the American church. While there was a regularly constituted hierarchy with ordinary bishops—a point on which Carroll had been so insistent—there were not canonically established parishes with proper pastors, except in a few sections of the country. Though Carroll had insisted on the participation of priests in episcopal nominations, in the nineteenth century, priests were without rights. Of the bishops, only John England recommended that some priests be canonically recognized as pastors. At the First Provincial Council, he linked the establishment of canonical parishes with the solution to the trustee problem (i.e., lay authority in parish corporations), and on this point he received the support of Francis Kenrick, then a theologian at the council. Rejecting this, however, the other bishops were insistent that the only canonical parish in the United States was one church in New Orleans.[28] American priests, therefore, were not canonical pastors of parishes, but "rectors" of "missions," transferable throughout the diocese at the will of the bishop.

This canonical anomaly would lead to conflict in the former Mexican territory. In Taos, New Mexico, for example, the colorful and popular Father Antonio José Martínez claimed that he had been named an irremovable pastor by the bishop of Durango. He therefore resisted the authority of Bishop Jean Baptiste Lamy of Santa Fe, who first suspended him in 1856 and then excommunicated him.[29] This was the type of situation envisioned in the legislation of the Metropolitan Province of Saint Louis, of which Lamy was a suffragan. In 1855, the First Provincial Council of Saint Louis provided a form of trial of priests who protested their transferral or removal from their mission. In such an instance, the priest was to be suspended, and the bishop or vicar general was to appoint two of the diocesan consultors to hear the case. If both consultors disagreed with the bishop, he was to appoint a third consultor. If the consultors still rejected the bishop's sentence, the case was to be appealed to the metropolitan or, if it originated in a metropolitan see, to the senior suffragan, whose decision was final, except for appeal by either the bishop or the priest to the Holy See.[30] In 1866, the Second Plenary Council extended this form of discipline to the entire American church.[31] Several priests, with journalistic assistance, now began registering their complaints at Rome.[32]

Paradoxically, in 1855, the same year that the Provincial Council of Saint Louis passed its restrictive legislation on clerical discipline, the Eighth Provincial Council of Baltimore reintroduced the voice of priests into the selection of bishops—a factor missing since John Carroll's early episcopacy. In implementing the First Plenary Council, the council of 1855 decreed that there should be between ten and twelve consultors, who should also, in the event of a vacancy, give their opinions to the metropolitan or senior suffragan.[33] Probably reflecting this legislation as he prepared for the Second Plenary Council, Archbishop Spalding strongly recommended that consultors have an actual vote in nominating bishops, much as cathedral chapters did in Europe. On this proposal it was not surprising that he met the opposition of Kenrick of Saint Louis.[34] The Second Plenary Council did, however, include in its decrees a letter from Propaganda in 1861 requiring that each bishop send to both his metropolitan and Rome a triennial list of those priests he thought worthy of the episcopate.[35] It also introduced another change in diocesan administration. Repeating the legislation of the council of 1852 on appointing chancellors, it described the authority of a vicar general—he was to take precedence over all other priests, but was not to exercise the extraordinary faculties delegated to him unless the bishop was absent from the diocese for a full day.[36] To a great extent, the office of vicar general was largely ceremonial, while the chancellor became the bishop's actual delegate. It would remain for the Holy See to intervene, as will be seen, for priests finally to receive canonical rights as irremovable rectors and episcopal electors.

In the meantime, despite the hesitance of so many of the American bishops to accept papal infallibility and their increasingly strong concept of their episcopacy, the Holy See acknowledged the growing importance of the American church in 1875 by appointing the first American cardinal, Archbishop John McCloskey of New York. At the same time, it established new metropolitan provinces. From New

York, it created the provinces of Philadelphia and Boston. From Saint Louis, it carved out the provinces of Milwaukee and Santa Fe.[37]

Still, the Holy See expressed its reservations about the general independence of the American bishops. In 1878, it sent Bishop George Conroy of Ardagh, Ireland, then on a mission to Canada, to visit the United States. The memorial of his visitation was a devastating critique of the American hierarchy. He said that, frequently, "the most valued gifts of a candidate proposed [for the episcopacy] to the Holy See were properly those of a banker, and not a Pastor of Souls." He mentioned that one bishop had gone so far as to open a diocesan bank—an allusion to Purcell's disastrous venture, narrated here by M. Edmund Hussey.

Conroy feared that some American Catholics were too eager to prove that they were "good Americans": "[They] affect a kind of ecclesiastical independence which, if faith were to fail among the clergy or the people, would not be without damage to the very unity of the Church." The secrecy surrounding the nomination of bishops, he continued, led priests to say that "of the total number of 68 Bishops, there are hardly ten distinguished in talent of any kind. The others hardly approach a decent mediocrity, and in theological knowledge they do not reach even mediocrity!" In regard to clerical discipline, he stated, both priests and bishops appealed only to those parts of the existing legislation that supported their cases. Priests, in his mind, were not rejecting episcopal authority, but were demanding that a bishop not remove them from their missions without showing cause. Conroy, therefore, recommended that Propaganda devise practical procedures for clerical discipline.[38]

Before receiving Conroy's report, the Congregation of Propaganda had already promulgated a new method of clerical discipline. In an *Instructio*, it decreed that every bishop was to appoint, preferably in a diocesan synod, an investigating commission of five or at least three priests, trained in canon law, who were to analyze the evidence against a priest, collect testimony, examine witnesses, and assist the bishop in making a decision. To remove the rector of a mission against his will, the bishop had to have the advice of at least three members of the commission. In the event of an appeal, the metropolitan or senior suffragan was to proceed in the same manner, and his investigating commission was to have all the records of the trial in the first instance.[39] In retrospect, this instruction on clerical discipline was the first in a series of direct Roman interventions into the domestic affairs of the American church.

Five years after the instruction, Propaganda summoned the American metropolitans to Rome for discussions preparatory to holding the Third Plenary Council—the last national council of the American bishops and the only one whose convocation was due to Roman initiative. In preliminary discussions with the cardinal members of the congregation, Cardinal Johann Baptist Franzelin, S.J., had at hand Conroy's report on the American church as he drafted proposals for the meeting with the archbishops. He recommended that the council would be a good opportunity for appointing a permanent apostolic delegate, who could perhaps be an American bishop, favorable to Rome. To preside over the council itself, Leo XIII approved the appointment and elevation to the rank of archbishop of Bishop Luigi Sepiacci, an Augustinian consultor to the congregation—a departure from the practice of the First and Second Plenary Councils, over which the archbishops of Baltimore had been delegated to preside.[40]

At the preliminary meetings and at the council itself, the American bishops succeeded in altering the Roman agenda. At the meetings in Rome, they had Sepiacci's appointment withdrawn and Archbishop James Gibbons of Baltimore named delegate. They rejected the Roman proposal of cathedral chapters but did acquiesce in the appointment of irremovable rectors and in the requirement that a bishop have the advice of his consultors in financial matters. Of greater significance for the appointment of bishops was the Holy See's request that irremovable rectors and consultors of the diocese were now to draw up a *terna* for vacant sees. This was then to be submitted to the bishops of the province, who were to give reasons for rejecting any name on the priests' list. The bishops, seeking further to strengthen their authority, also decreed that religious orders were to vest in the bishop the title to any property purchased or building erected with funds raised from the faithful, but this decree failed to receive Roman approval.[41]

In retrospect, the last legislative assembly of the American bishops did little to settle some of the issues then surfacing in the American church. As reward for his work as delegate, Gibbons received the red hat of a cardinal in 1887 and would dominate the hierarchy for the next thirty years. But within a few years, the bishops were sharply divided on such issues as parochial schools, ethnic tension, and suspect secret societies. One result of the council, however, was to evoke a new form of collegiality. The council had decreed that cases of suspect secret societies were to be submitted to all the metropolitans. In addition, the archbishops had been consulted since 1859 about the candidates for vacant metropolitan sees. In order to exercise these two prerogatives, the archbishops began holding annual meetings in 1890. Gradually, their discussions expanded to include any issue then of concern to the American church—a development that led Bishop McQuaid of Rochester to remark: "We are not interested in the doings of the Archbishops at their annual meetings outside the question of secret societies. . . . It is about time for us bishops to begin to hold annual meetings and have a banquet."[42]

McQuaid did have a valid point and one with which the Holy See agreed. In 1890, Archbishop John Ireland of Saint Paul, whose vibrant character is captured here by Marvin R. O'Connell, influenced the archbishops to move beyond their right to be consulted on vacant metropolitan sees to draw up a separate *terna* for the vacant Archdiocese of Milwaukee. His intention was to exclude Bishop Frederick Katzer of Green Bay, a strong opponent of his Americanizing efforts. But this attempt met with a sharp Roman rejection.[43] The Milwaukee succession was but one of the issues that evoked tension between German-Americans and the dominant Irish-Americans. Of even greater import, however, was the controversy over Archbishop Ireland's praise of public schools, his support of the right of the state to demand English as the language of instruction in all schools, and the arrangement he made with two public school boards to lease his parochial schools during school hours. To German-Americans, he seemed to be seeking to remove the German language, which they saw as crucial for preserving the faith. For his conservative opponents, such as Archbishop Michael A. Corrigan of New York (the subject of R. Emmett Curran's study), he was surrendering to the state the right to educate. Although Ireland won toleration of his school plan from Propaganda, his victory had its price.[44] For one thing, he alienated friends like Bishop John Lancaster Spalding of Peoria and, as James Gaffey notes, Archbishop Patrick J. Riordan. Moreover, the division in the hierarchy that ensued ushered in what John Ireland had sought to avoid—increased Roman supervision of the American church through a permanent papal representative to the American hierarchy.

Archbishop Ireland and Monsignor Denis J. O'Connell, then rector of the American College in Rome and a protégé of Gibbons, both agreed to the establishment of a delegation because they were led to believe that the American church would then be removed from the increasingly conservative supervision of Propaganda and placed directly under the Secretariat of State. Archbishop Francesco Satolli had been designated to discuss the education of Catholic children attending public schools with the archbishops at their annual meeting in November, 1892, but Ireland and O'Connell knew that he would probably remain as a permanent delegate. They therefore contrived a plot at his arrival worthy of a Hollywood screenplay. They arranged for Satolli to be named the Vatican representative to the Columbian Exposition in Chicago as an official guest of the United States government. O'Connell came as his secretary, and a Treasury cutter met them at quarantine outside New York harbor. They carefully kept Corrigan ignorant of the ship's arrival, so that his absence was construed as a snub.[45]

In November, Satolli presented the archbishops with a series of points on the school question, all supportive of Ireland and all drafted by O'Connell. He then asked the prelates for their opinion on having a permanent apostolic delegate. With the exception of Ireland, all said they would have to consult their suffragans. Satolli was dismayed. "Sooner or later," he wrote Cardinal Mariano Rampolla, the secretary of state, "it will be necessary for the Holy See to establish this delegation on its own impulse and there will not be anything to fear, even from the reluctant archbishops."[46] The archbishops, however, were more than reluctant. After Satolli had left the meeting, they instructed Gibbons to thank Satolli for the manner in which he had conducted his "special mission." Gibbons deputed Corrigan, already at odds with Satolli, to draft a report for Rome on the archbishops' attitude toward an apostolic delegation. "The country is not yet in a position to profit by the establishment [of a delegation]," Corrigan told Gibbons. Gibbons forwarded this report to Rome early in January 1893. But before it arrived, O'Connell, back in Rome, cabled that Satolli was appointed the first apostolic delegate.[47]

Ireland and his "liberal" associates were so intent on undermining Corrigan and the conservatives and on making themselves appear the papal loyalists that they had directly contributed to the increased Romanization of the American hierarchy. Not only did Satolli gradually turn against the liberal program and side with the conservatives, but, as a cardinal back in Rome after 1896, he played an increasing role in the appointment of American bishops.[48] His successors as delegates would gain yet more of a role in the appointment of bishops. Despite this setback, however, the liberals continued their aggressive attempt to integrate the church into American society. Their movement gradually became known as Americanism, claiming Father Isaac Hecker, founder of the Paulists, as its spiritual father, and focusing on the advantage to the church of the American separation of church and state. The movement drew the favorable attention of liberal Catholics in Italy, Germany, and especially France. It also drew a carefully worded but direct condemnation from Leo XIII in *Testem Benevolentiae*, in January 1899.[49]

The Holy See, however, did more than merely address a letter to the American hierarchy; it also acted. Increasingly the *ternae* from the United States were set aside in favor of candidates more acceptable to Rome. The first and most dramatic example is that of William Henry O'Connell, who had succeeded Denis O'Connell as rector of the American College in Rome. In 1901, the diocese of Portland, Maine, was vacant. Though O'Connell, a priest of Boston, was not on either the priests' or bishops' *ternae*, he was chosen bishop. He owed his rise to his friendship with Archbishop Raffaele Merry del Val. Even the old-style American conservatives were appalled. Ella B. Edes, an American convert, who had worked as the stenographer and translator for the prefect of Propaganda and Roman agent for Corrigan and McQuaid, found him "invariably rude, ill-bred, and disobliging." But, she told Corrigan, "I do not suppose he knows any better, being low-born and common, pitch-forked, suddenly, to a position which has turned his head."[50] O'Connell was consecrated by Satolli, assisted by Merry del Val and Archbishop Edmund Stonor, rector of the English College. Edes caustically remarked that his rush to be consecrated had made "people laugh and ask if he were not, possibly, afraid the Powers that Be might change their minds and not permit the mitre to rest on his head, after all."[51]

William O'Connell was now an agent in place in the American hierarchy, but he would not stay long in Portland. In April 1904, the eligible priests of the archdiocese of Boston and the bishops of the province met to draw up *ternae* for a coadjutor to the aging Archbishop John Williams. In first place on both lists was Bishop Matthew Harkins, who also received the overwhelming endorsement of the other metropolitans. "The one frank and avowed motive actuating" the construction of the lists, O'Connell told Merry del Val, then secretary of state to Pius X, "was to keep off the *terna* at all costs any name which stood for Rome, for Roman views and for Roman sympathies."[52] At the same time, O'Connell was promoting a letter-writing campaign to Rome. One correspondent charged that Harkins espoused "the Americanist spirit" and allowed his diocesan newspaper to praise "Higher Criticism" of the Scripture.[53] Nothing more was needed in the Rome of Pius X to exclude Harkins from Boston. In January, 1906, O'Connell was named coadjutor archbishop of Boston to begin the colorful career narrated here by James O'Toole.

In the meantime, in June 1908, Pius X issued the apostolic constitution *Sapienti consilio*. Among its provisions was the transfer of the American church from the Congregation of Propaganda to the Consistorial Congregation.[54] This move, however, reflected not so much the independence of the American church from the missionary congregation, which Ireland and others had desired, as the pope's reorganization of the Roman curia. It did enhance O'Connell's influence over the American church, for the secretary of the congregation was a close friend, Cardinal Gaetano De Lai. If anything, the transfer of the American church to the Consistorial represented increased Roman centralization.

In 1915, the episcopal see of Chicago—long a seedbed of intrigue,

as James Gaffey relates—fell vacant. The eligible priests of the archdiocese drew up a *terna* that named in order Edward M. Dunne, bishop
of Peoria; Peter J. Muldoon, bishop of Rockford; and Edward J.
McGavick, auxiliary bishop of Chicago. The bishops of the province
then convened in what must have been a rancorous meeting. After
eight ballots for first place, four for second, and fifteen for third, they
rejected the priests' list. Their new *terna* listed, in order, John P. Carroll, bishop of Helena, John J. Glennon, archbishop of Saint Louis;
and Thomas F. Lillis, bishop of Kansas City. For the obvious reasons
that both Dunne and Muldoon were present for their deliberations,
the bishops failed to give the reasons, required by the Third Plenary
Council, for setting aside the priests' *terna*.[55] When Archbishop Giovanni Bonzano, the apostolic delegate, circulated the lists to the metropolitans, he brought this irregularity to their attention.[56]

By far the most controversial of the candidates was Muldoon, reputed leader of a faction of Chicago priests and former auxiliary bishop to Archbishop James Quigley—who, according to Dunne, had the
diocese of Rockford established to get Muldoon out of Chicago.[57] The
response of the archbishops was varied. Gibbons, Sebastian Messmer
of Milwaukee, and, surprisingly, O'Connell were favorable to Muldoon.
Cardinal John Farley of New York favored Dunne and found it strange
that the bishops had omitted him, the only Roman-trained bishop
among the six candidates.[58] There was clearly no consensus, as Bonzano told Cardinal De Lai, and he suggested that it might be necessary
to select a candidate who was not on the *ternae*.[59] At this juncture,
however, Bonzano recommended no other candidates.

But there were indeed other candidates. In Chicago, rumors made
the rounds that Dennis J. Dougherty, bishop of Jaro in the Philippines,
would be the new archbishop. In the meantime, Buffalo was also vacant, and the Holy See intended to appoint George Mundelein, then
auxiliary bishop of Brooklyn; however, the British Foreign Office requested that the Holy See not appoint a bishop of German ancestry
to a see on the border between the United States and Canada during
World War I. The Holy See, therefore, appointed Mundelein to Chicago
and Dougherty to Buffalo.

In Chicago, Mundelein opened his administration with a dramatic
note. The day after his installation, he was the guest of honor at a
dinner sponsored by Francis C. Kelley, whose career as director of
the Church Extension Society and later as bishop of Oklahoma is narrated here by James Gaffey. According to the official reports, an an-
archist cook laced the soup with arsenic. The assembled dignitaries
escaped mass assassination only because the soup, originally prepared
for 200 people, had to be diluted because of the arrival of 107 more.
Though several guests collapsed and some were confined to bed for

a week or two, neither Mundelein nor the governor of Illinois was afflicted, as Bonzano informed Cardinal Pietro Gasparri, the secretary of state. This circumstance led Mundelein to remark at the end of the dinner that "while so many strong men were falling to the right and left, the Church and the State remained undaunted, and that was the best omen of all."[60]

Mundelein's remark could well have served as a motto for his administration. He was to develop the church in the Midwest to make it outshine the East. In 1924, he would become the first cardinal west of the Alleghenies. He also admitted that he was instrumental in gaining the appointment of Patrick J. Hayes as archbishop of New York in 1918.[61] While both were elevated to the college of cardinals at the same time, Hayes made little effort to extend his influence outside New York. By contrast, Edward Kantowicz points out in this study, Mundelein was to be a masterful diocesan administrator, who virtually established the model for centralized control. He would also become close friends not only with the politicians of Illinois but also with President Franklin D. Roosevelt. But he owed his rise to power to his friendship with Bonzano.[62]

Soon after taking office, Mundelein attempted to rid himself of Muldoon. The occasion arose from the difficulty in filling a see that had fallen vacant in September 1915, only two months after Quigley's death in Chicago. The diocese was Monterey–Los Angeles, covering a vast territory but relatively insignificant. There were no irremovable rectors in the diocese, so the consultors alone drew up a *terna*, which the bishops of the Province of San Francisco rejected. First on their list was Patrick J. Hayes, auxiliary bishop of New York. Bonzano found the selection "strange," as he told the archbishop of New York, John Farley, especially because "the Diocese of Los Angeles is so far away and is not considered one of first importance."[63] Farley did not find it so strange—he recognized the hand of Archbishop Edward J. Hanna of San Francisco, a former priest of Rochester. But he was emphatic: "It would look most unreasonable to take my only auxiliary *and for Los Angeles!*"[64]

The Holy See now searched for a candidate for the distant see. In March 1916, Gasparri notified Bonzano that the original *terna* had been rejected, and he proposed Bishop Charles W. Currier, who had been bishop of Matanzas, Cuba, for thirteen months before retiring to Baltimore. Currier turned this proposal down, and Bonzano suggested John J. McCort, auxiliary bishop of Philadelphia. In June, McCort was named bishop-elect of Monterey–Los Angeles, only to have Archbishop Edmond F. Prendergast of Philadelphia protest so strenuously that the appointment was rescinded in October.[65] Bonzano now thought of a way of helping Mundelein free himself of Muldoon.

Muldoon had been born in California, Mundelein wrote to Bonzano in December, and would be a good administrator. He thought it essential, however, that the Holy See appoint him rather than ask him, for he would probably decline. The archbishop thought the appointment especially appropriate, because, "considering the fact, likewise, that he was twice a candidate for Chicago, and twice passed over, it might be looked upon as a partial recognition to be promoted to a See much larger than his present See, at a distance."[66] Despite his own protests and the protests of his diocesan consultors, Muldoon was named to Monterey–Los Angeles in April 1917. But he had not ceased his efforts to remain in America's heartland. More priests protested to Rome about his transfer, and he returned the bulls of appointment, much to the chagrin of Bonzano and Mundelein.[67]

As the vacancy in Monterey–Los Angeles reached into its second year, Bonzano was deluged with letters about the poor state of the diocese, especially because of factionalism among the Irish clergy and other abuses. He even received a letter from a thirty-five-year-old priest in Victoria, British Columbia, offering himself as a candidate— he had tended the cathedral in Victoria, had a good baritone voice, and would be kind to the priests.[68] But the Holy See needed more than a good singer for Los Angeles. Late in August, 1917, it turned to John J. Cantwell, vicar general of San Francisco. The only objection of which Bonzano could think was that he was Irish-born, and it was the Irish priests in the South who in his opinion needed correction. But the delegate thought Cantwell could easily overcome this shortcoming with Hanna's guidance. In September, after a two-year interregnum, Monterey–Los Angeles finally got a new bishop.[69] The difficulty of finding a candidate willing to go to Los Angeles between 1915 and 1917 illustrates how rapidly the city was to grow from obscurity to international prominence. Cantwell became the first archbishop of Los Angeles in 1936. Nine years later, he was succeeded by James F. McIntyre, who had begun his ecclesiastical career as chancellor to Cardinal Patrick Hayes, the first candidate for the see in 1915.

In view of such situations as the factionalism in Chicago and the difficulty in finding a candidate for Monterey–Los Angeles, it was understandable that the Holy See chose to name its own candidates to those sees. It now decided to change the procedures for the appointment of American bishops. Although the Congregation of Propaganda had insisted in 1883 that certain priests be allowed to draw up a *terna*, in 1916 the Consistorial Congregation removed that right. Henceforth, each bishop was to submit to his metropolitan a biennial list of one or two priests he thought worthy of being elevated to the episcopate. To arrive at his list, he could confer with his consultors and irremovable rectors, but individually and under a bond of secrecy. The bishops of the province were then to gather, in a convivial manner in order not to draw public attention, discuss the names submitted, determine the most suitable, and send them to the apostolic delegate for forwarding to Rome. This procedure was to enable the Holy See to have a file on suitable episcopal candidates, but the bishops were no longer nominating for a specific see. When a see was actually vacant, the Holy See would seek the hierarchy's opinions on the most likely candidates, either "through the Most Reverend Apostolic Delegate or in some other manner."[70] The apostolic delegate had now canonically received an increasing role in the nomination of American bishops—a role the delegate had already been playing on a less official level.

To the exclusion of priests from submitting names, however, there was one striking exception. On at least the first occasion, Bonzano invited the Dominicans also to submit a list of names drawn up by their provincial council. On January 9, 1917, Raymond Meagher, O.P., sent Bonzano a list of four names, including John T. McNicholas, O.P., then the socius to the master general in Rome.[71] In 1918, McNicholas became the bishop of Duluth. In 1925, he was transferred to Cincinnati.

Bonzano was directly to influence the succession in several key dioceses within a few years. In 1918, the see of Philadelphia fell vacant. The candidates were Philip R. McDevitt, bishop of Harrisburg; John J. McCort, auxiliary bishop of Philadelphia, who had first accepted and then turned down the diocese of Monterey–Los Angeles; and Dougherty. Bonzano made it clear that Dougherty was the best candidate.[72] When Dougherty arrived in Philadelphia, however, he had to wrest control from McCort, and thought the auxiliary bishop should be appointed to Des Moines, a proposal McCort viewed as "undeserved humiliation."[73] McCort was then appointed to Altoona, first as coadjutor and then as ordinary, to get him out of Philadelphia.[74]

While the American bishops were thus becoming more dependent on Roman officials for their appointments, they were also becoming more ethnically diverse. The nineteenth-century German-Irish tension was giving way to new tensions with the Eastern-rite Catholics and the Poles. In 1890, the American bishops had been indignant when Peter Paul Cahensly, in the name of the various branches of the Saint Raphael Societies, recommended to Propaganda that each national group be represented in the hierarchy. They were extremely sensitive to charges of not being American. At the archbishops' meetings in the 1890s, however, one topic took up more space in the minutes than either "Cahenslyism" or Ireland's controversial school plan—the question of Eastern-rite Catholics who were beginning to immigrate to the United States. These new immigrants brought with them a different rite and, more particularly, a married clergy. Ireland had refused to grant faculties to one of their priests—he argued that he had a Polish priest to take care of Eastern Catholics—and fomented an exodus to the Russian Orthodox church. On this issue, he found an ally in Corrigan. Together with archbishops Patrick Feehan of Chicago and Patrick J. Ryan of Philadelphia, in 1894, they drafted a proposal to the Holy See rejecting the appointment of a national vicar general for Eastern-rite Catholics and petitioning that only the Latin rite be recognized in the United States. But, in 1897, Rome requested that each metropolitan, in consultation with his suffragans, appoint as vicar for Eastern Catholics an Eastern-rite priest, who was preferably unmarried.[75]

In 1898, the Holy See asked for an evaluation of the new procedures. Archbishop Patrick Ryan of Philadelphia responded: "I know no good *unmarried* Greek priest. The only one I know is intemperate." He had appointed a married priest as his vicar, but strongly recommended that the Holy See send an official visitor.[76] Ireland found that the regulation had little application in his province, where there had been a small community of perhaps thirty families in Minneapolis, whose "pastor sold himself out for Russian gold"; he said, "Since then these people, or the larger number of them, are under the jurisdiction of the Greek Schismatic Bishop of San Francisco." Those who returned to the Catholic church, he went on, "have united with Polish parishes of the Latin rite and are perfectly satisfied." As far as Ireland was concerned, these people had now conformed to the Latin rite and he recommended that where Oriental Catholics were "scattered in small numbers," they be allowed to "join the Latin rite."[77]

Granted Ireland's strong opposition to Eastern rites, it was ironic that he himself supported what he had earlier accused the Germans of suggesting—the intrusion of a foreign government into the domestic affairs of the American Church. In 1899, after the condemnation of Americanism, Ireland was in Rome, where the Austro-Hungarian ambassador to the Holy See approached him about the plight of the Ruthenians in the United States. The ambassador reported to his government that Ireland wished "to wash himself clean of the reproach of Americanism" and promised to propose the appointment of a vicar general for the Ruthenians at the next archbishops' meeting.[78] There is no record, however, that Ireland ever broached the subject with his fellow archbishops. The next year, Rampolla asked Archbishop Sebastian Martinelli, the apostolic delegate, for his opinion on the Austro-Hungarian Emperor's request that the Holy See appoint a Ruthenian priest to the delegation to deal with Ruthenian affairs. Martinelli opposed this, because it would increase the criticism that the American Church was subject to foreign political influence.[79]

Early in 1902, however, at the request of the emperor, Leo XIII appointed a Ruthenian priest, subject to both the delegation and the local ordinaries, to conduct an official visitation of the Ruthenians. The visitor was Monsignor Andrea Hodobay, who soon ran afoul of the Latin-rite ordinaries and various factions among Eastern Catholic priests, some of whom accused him of clerical misconduct and were threatening to elect their own bishop. In May 1906, Propaganda decided to appoint a bishop and instructed the apostolic delegate, Diomede Falconio, to canvass the Latin-rite bishops for possible candidates. The Austro-Hungarian government also expressed its concern about the Ruthenians and even offered to pay the salary of a bishop to keep him independent of voluntary contributions—a proposition that Cardinal Merry del Val, the secretary of state, firmly rejected.[80]

On March 8, 1908, Cardinal Girolamo Gotti, prefect of Propaganda, announced the appointment of Soter Ortynski, a Basilian monk, as bishop for the Ruthenians. With this appointment, Hodobay was recalled from the United States.[81] Ortynski was to be immediately subject to the Holy See under the apostolic delegate's direction, but he was to receive only delegated authority from the Latin-rite ordinaries in whose dioceses Ruthenian Catholics resided.[82] In 1913, Ortynsky was made the first exarch of Philadelphia, with full jurisdiction over Ruthenians. He alienated many of his subjects, however, because of his strong Ukrainian nationalism and his imposition of clerical celibacy on priests. There was such dissension after his death in 1916 that only in 1924 did the Holy See appoint a successor. Constantine Bohachevsky became exarch of Philadelphia, with jurisdiction over Ukrainians. At the same time, Basil Takach became the bishop of the new exarchy of Pittsburgh for Ruthenians.[83]

Some of the Latin-rite American bishops had opposed the establishment of Eastern-rite dioceses out of fear that other national groups would demand similar treatment. The Poles, in particular, began agitating for more representation in the hierarchy in much the same manner as German-Americans in the 1890s. When Mundelein was appointed to Chicago, he received a request from Cardinal de Lai to consider appointing a Polish auxiliary bishop as Quigley had done with Paul P. Rhode, then the bishop of Green Bay.[84] The Polish question was especially sensitive, because a group of Poles had gone into schism in 1897 to form the Polish National Church. In 1920, a group of Polish-American priests petitioned the Polish government to intervene with the Holy See in their behalf. They accused Mundelein of failing to accede to Polish concerns, called for Rhode to be made an archbishop, and asked for Polish auxiliary bishops in several dioceses. The Polish legation to the Holy See then submitted the petition to Cardinal Gasparri, who, in turn, forwarded it to Gibbons for consideration by the bishops at their annual meeting. The bishops formally protested "against the interference of any foreign government in the ecclesiastical affairs of the United States," and Gibbons then appointed a committee, composed of Mundelein, Dougherty, and Messmer of Milwaukee, to draft the reply to Gasparri's letter. Mundelein's original notes on the letter bristled with sharp comments about the Poles in general and Rhode in particular, but in his actual draft he confined himself to a calm refutation of the charges that the American bishops were not sensitive to the Poles. Messmer's section was most revealing; although he had been one of the German-American leaders in the dispute with Ireland, now he argued that appointing Polish bishops would isolate Poles from other American Catholics and would "preserve a distinct and separate Polish nationality in the United States."[85] Messmer, who was having his own difficulty with Poles in his diocese, was now sounding like the Irish-Americans he had opposed a generation earlier.

The annual meeting of the hierarchy to which the Polish petition was presented was the expression of a new form of American episcopal collegiality. In 1917, the archbishops, who been meeting annually since 1890, established the National Catholic War Council to coordinate Catholic efforts during World War I. On February 20, 1919, when Cardinal Gibbons celebrated the golden jubilee of his episcopacy, the representative of Benedict XV for the occasion was Archbishop Bonaventura Cerretti, secretary of the Congregation of the Extraordinary Affairs of the Church. Cerretti called on the bishops to unite to work for peace, especially in the areas of education and social justice. Gibbons immediately appointed a committee, which proposed the next day that the bishops hold annual meetings and appoint a standing committee to coordinate Catholic activities between meetings. On April 10, Benedict XV approved this organization, which eventually took the name National Catholic Welfare Council.[86]

To a large measure, it was Gibbon's presence that kept tension among the bishops from surfacing, but, on March 24, 1921, he died. It was the end of an era and one that the Holy See did not wish to be repeated. Monsignor John Tracy Ellis's essay on Gibbons focuses on the cardinal's humanity—including the flaw of his vanity. With this evaluation Bonzano would have agreed, as may be understood from his report on Baltimore submitted to De Lai after Gibbons's death. He reminded the cardinal that the bishops in the previous century had requested privileges for Baltimore, but that the Holy See granted only the honor of "prerogative of place." Though Baltimore had historical importance as the nation's first see, he continued, its Catholic population was lower than that of some dioceses. In Gibbons's earlier days he had been an able and eloquent apologist for the church, but in his own diocese he had failed to implement the legislation of the Third Plenary Council, over which he had himself presided. He was too lenient in regard to mixed marriages and, according to many complaints, allowed himself to be dominated by the Sulpicians. Bonzano was convinced that "never should any Archbishop of Baltimore or Cardinal acquire the preponderance that in all affairs, by right or manipulation, Cardinal Gibbons had assumed, not only in the meetings concerning the [Catholic] University but also in those of the archbishops and bishops." When Bonzano asked other prelates why their meetings had accomplished so little, he received the reply: "Ipse dixit: the Cardinal does not want it." The delegate, therefore, strongly recommended that Bishop Michael J. Curley be transferred from Saint Augustine to Baltimore.[87] By personality and temperament, Curley would never attempt to assume any national leadership.

With Gibbons's death, there were then two cardinals left in the American church, O'Connell in Boston and Dougherty, who had received the red hat earlier that year. O'Connell, the senior cardinal, now sought to establish his influence over the entire American hierarchy. In January 1922, Benedict XV died, but neither O'Connell nor Dougherty made it to Rome in time for the conclave that elected Pius XI. As Dougherty was leaving Rome, however, Cardinal De Lai handed him a decree ordering the National Catholic Welfare Council to disband immediately.

The administrative committee of the NCWC, however, immediately mobilized to prevent the condemnation. The committee members were well aware that O'Connell was behind the decree. First, they obtained Gasparri's assurance that the Consistorial's decree would not be published until they could send a representation to Rome. Next, they delegated Bishop Joseph Schrembs of Cleveland and Archbishop Henry Moeller of Cincinnati to present their case in Rome. Finally, they gained the signatures of 90 percent of the American bishops in favor of the organization. In Rome, Schrembs and Moeller found some of the cardinals still fearful of the old specter of Americanism or suspicious of Modernism. Although O'Connell bombarded the apostolic delegate and his Roman friends with a series of letters telling them not to be swayed by a "plebiscite," Gasparri was won over, and he received instructions from Pius XI to tell the Consistorial Congregation that he too favored the continuation of the NCWC. On June 22, the Consistorial issued a new decree allowing the NCWC to continue. On July 4, it published an instruction that recommended, among other things, that the bishops not meet annually, that attendance at the meetings be voluntary, that decisions of the meetings were not to be binding or to be construed as coming from a plenary council, and that the word "Council" be changed to something like "Committee."[88]

O'Connell continued to fulminate against the NCWC. He attempted to prevent the bishops from meeting more than every three years. He demanded that *he* issue the call to the annual meetings and, as senior cardinal, preside over them. He charged the administrative committee with disloyalty to the Holy See in changing the title of the organization from Welfare Council to Welfare Conference. But in making these objections, he was grasping at the last straws of his once-formidable power. He had already lost much of his Roman influence when Benedict XV replaced his friend Merry del Val as secretary of state with Gasparri. In Boston, he had recently survived the scandal of having his nephew and chancellor forcibly dismissed from the priesthood for being secretly married. After 1922, he would continue to preside at many of the annual meetings of the bishops, but he gradually withdrew into his own diocesan concerns. His style of Romanization would never dominate the American hierarchy, because his ideal Rome had ceased to be.[89]

In retrospect, however, regarding the name of the bishops' conference O'Connell had a point. There was confusion over the use of the same term, National Catholic Welfare Conference, to designate both the annual meetings of the hierarchy and the standing departments in Washington, D.C. Apart from the limitations of its name, however, over the next two decades the NCWC of the bishops proved its service to the church. In 1941, after the United States and the Axis had declared war, Archbishop Edward Mooney of Detroit, the chairman of the NCWC's administrative board, issued a statement pledging the support of the hierarchy in the war efforts. Archbishop Francis Beckman of Dubuque threatened to dissent from the statement, and the Vatican also heard that Curley as well was opposed to the declaration of war. Archbishop Amleto Cicognani, the apostolic delegate, was instructed to gain their conformity with Mooney's statement. He won Beckman's silence by referring him to an earlier Vatican pronouncement opposing public disagreement among the bishops and reminding him that there would be dire consequences for acting contrary to the unanimous opinion of the hierarchy.[90] In the exigency of war, the Vatican had thus forced conformity with Mooney's statement. But this was not so much a grant of authority to the NCWC as the enforcing of the Vatican's own policy in regard to the war.

While the NCWC was a practical expression of collegiality, the theological concept itself was lost to the American church. Despite the organization and the annual meetings of the hierarchy, American bishops tended to be individualistic or at most regionalistic. Cardinal Dougherty never tried to exert his influence beyond Philadelphia and pointedly refused to contribute to the maintenance of the NCWC. As I point out in my essay on Cardinal Spellman, the New York prelate acted alone. While the American public regarded him as the most powerful American bishop, archbishops Edward Mooney of Detroit, Samuel Stritch of Chicago, and John T. McNicholas of Cincinnati dominated the NCWC and consciously acted in concert. While they and Spellman would contribute to the reshaping of the hierarchy, they were not alone. In Cleveland, Bishop Edward Hoban, a close friend of Cicognani's, would contribute his share of future American bishops—Cardinal John Dearden of Detroit, Cardinal John Krol of Philadelphia, Archbishop Paul Hallinan of Atlanta, and Archbishop John Whealon of Hartford, to name some of the most prominent. As Vatican II approached, however, collegiality to many American bishops was simply an abstract theological concept. They would learn it belatedly at the council.

When the council introduced the topic of collegiality, few American bishops expressed their theological support. Notable exceptions were Cardinals Albert Meyer of Chicago and Joseph Ritter of Saint Louis. For Spellman, the doctrine was clear that "the authority of the Supreme Pontiff is supreme and full in itself." Therefore, he concluded, "it is not necessary that he share it with others, even if they are bishops whose collaboration in governing the universal Church can be asked for by the Supreme Pontiff himself, but is neither necessary nor essential."[91] He came dangerously close to implying that the authority of bishops was merely delegated. Cardinal James F. McIntyre of Los Angeles feared that, if regional conferences of bishops were given juridical authority, they would infringe on the authority of the local bishop.[92] Ritter wanted conferences to possess juridical authority, because "many times a unanimity of voice and action is required on the part of the national body of bishops in order to attain a common goal." He also thought such conferences would assist in internationalizing the Roman Curia.[93] Meyer proposed that the president of the conference be elected by a secret ballot and serve for a fixed term. He further wanted to protect "the freedom of a bishop to act according to his conscience" and to avoid "a new form of centralization that is too extensive, indeed sometimes hateful."[94] Some of Meyer's observations remain pertinent to discussions about the authority of episcopal conferences in the late 1980s.

The conciliar provision that presidents of episcopal conferences be elected by the bishops occasioned an interesting footnote to the history of the United States episcopate. The Holy See, as we noted above, had formally refused to designate Baltimore as the primatial see of the United States. In 1974, however, Paul VI accepted the resignation of Cardinal Lawrence J. Shehan "from the primatial See of Baltimore."[95] The Holy See could confer the honor on Baltimore now that the title was devoid of its earlier canonical connotations and the role of primate was largely taken over by the conference president.

It was to episcopal conferences, as established by the council, that liturgical renewal was left. Joseph Ratzinger commented at the time that, as a result of the constitution on the liturgy, episcopal conferences were formerly "of a merely deliberative character," but "now that they possess as a right a definite legislative function, they appear as a new element in the ecclesiastical body-politic, and form a link of a quasi-synodal kind between the individual bishops and the pope."[96]

The Americans were little prepared for a change in the liturgy. But, as the council began its discussions, Archbishop Paul Hallinan was appointed to the international commission on the liturgy. He would likewise be influential in having the American bishops undertake the liturgical reforms that would be the one effect of the council that most American Catholic lay people initially noticed. As Thomas Shelley writes, Hallinan was unlike many American bishops who found the council a learning experience.

In accordance with the council's decree on "the pastoral office of bishops," in 1966 the American hierarchy reorganized the NCWC into two distinct but related bodies, the National Conference of Catholic Bishops (NCCB) and the United States Catholic Conference (USCC). The reorganization thus avoided the confusion between the national hierarchy and the standing departments that provided information for the bishops and acted in their behalf on issues of national concern. Over the next two decades, the bishops showed the lessons they had learned at the council. No longer finding themselves on the defensive against an anti-Catholic society, they addressed themselves to issues that would have been off limits to their predecessors. Hallinan and his auxiliary bishop in Atlanta, Joseph Bernardin, took the lead by issuing a pastoral letter to the archdiocese on selective conscientious objection to war—a position adopted by the NCCB in its pastoral in 1968. This was but a beginning of a recognition that patriotism need not be identical with supporting the nation's public policy. In 1983, the bishops challenged American policy on nuclear arms, and, three years later, called for economic reform. Fear of being challenged for being un-American would have made it impossible for earlier bishops to issue such statements.[97]

Comfortable as both Americans and Catholics, the bishops initiated other changes unthinkable to their predecessors. In 1891, the bishops protested against the recommendation of the Saint Raphael Societies that there be ethnic representation in the hierarchy. From the 1890s into the twentieth century, they took the same stand against both the Eastern-rite Catholics and the Poles. They had taken this stand not only because of ethnic tension but also because of the fear of being called foreign. The lack of Italian-American bishops was due to similar reasons and also to the heavy reliance of Italian parishes on religious communities, from whom bishops were not usually chosen.[98] Though there were Italian bishops of American sees in the nineteenth century, they were missionaries. In 1954, Charles Greco, born in Mississippi, became the bishop of Alexandria, Louisiana. In 1954, Spellman had the Italian-born Joseph M. Pernicone named his auxiliary bishop in order that he might mobilize Italian-Americans to influence their relatives in Italy to oppose communism.[99] By the 1970s, however, the American bishops consciously sought ethnic and racial diversity in the hierarchy as the first Hispanic and black bishops took their places in the ranks of the episcopate, to be joined in 1986 by the first native American.

In 1972, the Holy See altered the procedures for selecting bishops. Now the bishops of each province were to continue to meet annually to submit names of priests who would be suitable for the episcopacy. The Holy See also reintroduced the *terna*. The bishops could consult clergy, religious, and laity, but never collectively. Presently, if a see falls vacant, the pro-nuncio (the apostolic delegate before 1984) draws up a *terna*. In preparing the list, he seeks information from the administrator of the diocese (or ordinary, if it is a question of a coadjutor) about the state and needs of the diocese. Not only priests, but also religious and lay people can be consulted both individually and collectively, but not about particular candidates. The pro-nuncio then forwards a list of eight to ten names to the president of the NCCB, with the request that he reduce it to three in order of preference. The pro-nuncio then sends his final list to Rome. If the appointment is that of an auxiliary bishop, then the ordinary submits a *terna* to the pro-nuncio. This new system avoids the dominance of a single person, such as Spellman or Hoban in the past, but retains the major role of the papal delegate. When a priest is actually under consideration for the episcopacy, the pro-nuncio sends out a questionnaire under secrecy. Covering a broad range of qualifications necessary in a bishop, the questionnaire also asks about the candidate's attitude toward clerical celibacy, ordination of women, and sexual ethics.[100]

The two hundred years that separate John Carroll from the present have witnessed to vast changes in the American hierarchy. From one bishop over the thirteen original states and their territories, the church has grown to over 180 dioceses covering a continent. John Carroll, at times an aloof intellectual, gave way to missionary and immigrant bishops, like Benedict Flaget or John England or John Hughes. As the older immigrants, like the Irish, became more assimilated and the country more settled, this type of bishop was replaced by the Americanizers, such as John Ireland and James Gibbons, and their opponents, who upheld perceived Catholic values, such as Michael A. Corrigan. The period from World War I to the late 1950s was one of consolidation—a period for managers like Mundelein, builders like McIntyre, or self-conscious patriots and power brokers like Spellman. With Vatican II, a new type of bishop arose—a pastor rather than merely an administrator, tuned more to the spiritual challenge confronting his people than to their defense against a hostile culture. Paul J. Hallinan, the subject of Thomas Shelley's essay, represents the transition from pre- to postconciliar bishop.

The history of the hierarchy in the United States is but a piece of the history of the universal church—a history that reveals periods of the ebb and flow of papal centralization. Reflecting the story of hierarchies in other nations, the American bishops in almost every generation have experienced tensions with the Holy See. The issues ranged from priests' rights, ethnic disagreements, parochial schools, and episcopal collegiality to the American praise of the separation of church and state. Tension such as arose in these debates need not be detrimental. It can be a sign of growth and vitality, for it can lead to the development of doctrine, as in the case of the influence of the American bishops on the Declaration on Religious Liberty proceeding from Vatican II. If the American church witnessed apostolic visitations of the Archdiocese of Seattle and the Diocese of Richmond in the 1980s, these too had historical precedents in the visitations not only of dioceses but also of the entire American church. The purpose of the study of history is not merely to recount the past, but to discover what is essential and what is accidental. The history of the American bishops shows, if nothing else, that the hierarchy was never a monolith.

PART ONE

The Period of Anglo-French Domination, 1789–1850

John Carroll's small church, composed of old Anglo-Maryland plantation owners and a smaller number of Pennsylvania farmers, rapidly gave way to an ethnically pluralistic series of urban communities. The beginning of immigration and the movement to cities necessitated the establishment of new dioceses. But Carroll's Saint Mary's Seminary in Baltimore had not yet produced a sufficient number of native priests who could become bishops. The American church had to look elsewhere for its bishops. One major source of bishops was the Society of Saint Sulpice, whose French-born priests staffed the seminary. From the Sulpicians were drawn two of the bishops included in this section. Some French bishops, however, were not Sulpicians—for example, the first bishop of Boston, John Lefebvre de Cheverus, who had been imprisoned in France for his opposition to the Civil Constitution of the Clergy and who then went on to missionary work in England and eventually in Maine and Massachusetts. When he was named archbishop of Bordeaux in 1826, a number of Boston's leading citizens protested his transfer back to Europe. In 1836, he became the first cardinal who had served in the United States. By contrast, however, further south there was frequent tension between French bishops and their flocks.

1

The Irish were becoming an increasing force within the American church. Many of these early Irish immigrants belonged to the middle class. They brought with them the experience of a church that was *de facto* separated from the state, for Catholics were still subject to some penal laws in Ireland. They therefore readily adapted to the voluntaryism of the American religious scene and embraced the separation of church and state, but they did not so readily adapt to what they perceived as a monarchical episcopacy. They, like other immigrant groups that followed, purchased land for churches, erected the buildings, incorporated the property—and then demanded the right to appoint pastors. Lay trusteeism had begun.

Carroll had already experienced difficulties with certain aspects of lay trusteeism in New York and Philadelphia. In New York, Irish trustees preferred an Irish Dominican other than the one to whom Carroll—then only the superior of the American mission—had given faculties. In Philadelphia, German Catholics built a church and then attempted to appoint their own pastor. Trustees in both cities threatened to invoke the civil law if Carroll did not accede to their wishes. The emerging lay trustee problem was one of the factors that led the ex-Jesuits in Maryland and Pennsylvania to petition the Holy See to have a bishop. Carroll acknowledged certain rights of the trustees, such as the ownership of property and even a say in choosing a suitable priest, but not in actually hiring or firing a pastor. But the problem grew worse in the nineteenth century.

Trustee conflicts led to schism in New York, Philadelphia, Norfolk, and Charleston. The trustees based their argument on the "Patronato Real," the right of royal patronage enjoyed by Catholic monarchs in Europe. If the pope signed a concordat with a king giving him the right to nominate for church offices, they reasoned, then in a democracy the pope should enter into a concordat with the people, who, after all, had provided for the temporal support of the church. Trustees aired their views in pamphlets sprinkled with references to medieval and modern European ecclesiological theorists. They petitioned Rome and their respective state legislatures. One part of the difficulty with the Irish trustees in the early 1800s was ethnic tension with the French-dominated hierarchy, particularly Archbishop Ambrose Maréchal of Baltimore, but the root of the problem was less ethnic than theological. Europe itself had just gone through the French Revolution. The American trustees were shaped in part by their European heritage and were trying to adapt an old tradition to new circumstances, but, in the process, they were usurping the rights of the ecclesiastical authority.

In 1820, in response to trusteeism, the Holy See established the two dioceses of Richmond and Charleston. Both of the new bishops were Irish. To Richmond came John Kelly, who taught school for a while in Norfolk and after two years retired to Ireland. Richmond was returned to the administration of the archbishop of Baltimore until 1840. To Charleston came John England, who was able to assess the positive as well as the negative aspects of trusteeism. At the First Provincial Council of Baltimore, in 1829, held largely at his insistence, the bishops formally condemned lay trusteeism and rejected the trustees' claim to be heirs to the Patronato Real. Trustee problems would continue to plague bishops well into the nineteenth century, as groups other than the Irish would make the same claims. Unfortunately, the condemnation of lay trusteeism also meant the end of an official lay voice in the church. Later in the century, Pius IX refused to invite any of the monarchs of Europe to Vatican I, and thereby, in a sense, eradicated the last remnant of the Patronato Real; but he had also removed any lay voice in the council.

While the eastern cities of Boston, New York, and Philadelphia were becoming principal Catholic centers, the nation was expanding both by settlement of the interior and by acquisition of new territory. Kentucky had been carved out of territory claimed by Virginia and admitted as the fifteenth state in 1792. Catholics from Maryland moved out to this new frontier to take advantage of the rich farmland. By 1808, Bardstown, Kentucky, was enough of a Catholic center to be named a diocese, at the same time as Boston, New York, and Philadelphia. The first diocese west of the Alleghenies was to be the first of numerous new sees erected on the rapidly advancing frontier. Burgeoning eastern cities and developing frontier hamlets added to the patchwork quilt that was becoming the nation and the American church. But that was not all.

Louisiana introduced a new factor. Settled by the French, ceded to the Spanish, given back to France, it more than doubled the territory of the United States when Napoleon sold it to Thomas Jefferson. Louisiana was a study in contradictions. It already had a diocese, vacant since the death in 1801 of Bishop Luis Ignacio Maria de Peñalver y Cardenas. It was also a frontier, but a European one. It had many of the same problems of trusteeism as the eastern cities, but without the same ethnic dimension. Here, the colorful Père Antoine so influenced the marguilliers or trustees that Bishop DuBourg had to move up the river to Saint Louis. As a reward for Irish support against the trustees, Bishop Anthony Blanc gave them their own parish—perhaps the only Irish national parish in the country. The French population of Louisiana expressed not so much a lack of religion as a brand of anticlericalism, cultivated by the city's remoteness from both Quebec, which exercised jurisdiction over the territory until 1763, and Rome. Well into the twentieth century, New Orleans would depend heavily on French-born clergy.* It was an anomaly in many ways. Though situated in the Protestant South, it was Catholic in culture. Though a melting pot of ethnic groups, its dominant Catholic population was neither Irish nor German as in other immigrant centers. Though it was a diocese subject directly to the Holy See, it also oversaw the extension of Catholic presence into Texas. It set a pattern all its own.

---

*For providing me with this information, I am grateful to Dr. Charles E. Nolan, archivist of the Archdiocese of New Orleans.

CHAPTER
1
An Eighteenth-Century Bishop: John Carroll of Baltimore

James Hennesey, S.J.

John Adams once remarked with undisguised relief that in his hometown of Braintree, Massachusetts, Roman Catholics were "as rare as a comet or an earthquake."[1] Intolerance of "papists" came easily to one born and bred, as Adams was, in Puritan New England. Yet, on February 18, 1776, in a letter to James Warren, the same John Adams perfectly characterized John Carroll (1736–1815)—later to become first archbishop of Baltimore and father of the Catholic hierarchy in the United States—as "a Roman Catholic priest and a Jesuit, a Gentleman of learning and Abilities."[2] Carroll ceased to be a Jesuit with the suppression of the Society of Jesus in 1773, but he never ceased to think of himself as a son of Ignatius Loyola. His learning and abilities made their mark on the infant church that emerged in the United States during the Revolutionary era, and his understanding and Anglo-American style of Catholicism made their mark as well.

John Carroll was the fourth of seven children of Daniel Carroll (1696–1751), an Irish immigrant into the colony of Maryland, and

Note: This is a revised version of an article that appeared in the *Archivum Historiae Pontificiae* 76 (1978):171–204 (reprinted with permission).

5

Eleanor Darnall (c. 1703–1796), daughter of an old Maryland English family closely associated with the lords proprietor, the Baltimores. Educated in 1746–1748 at Father Thomas Poulton's school on the Jesuit estate of Bohemia Manor in northeastern Maryland, young Carroll was then enrolled at the English Jesuit college at Saint Omer in French Flanders, where he remained until he entered the English Jesuit novitiate at nearby Watten in 1753. His cousin, schoolmate, and lifelong friend, Charles Carroll of Carrollton, reported of him in 1750: "I believe Cousin Jack Carroll will make a good scholar, for he is often first."[3] John Carroll's destination in life might have seemed to remain, as with other Maryland-born Jesuits, a teacher in the Flanders colleges. After a usual course of philosophical and theological studies at Liège he was ordained and then made his solemn profession as a Jesuit in 1771. Shortly thereafter he made the "grand tour" of Europe as tutor to the eighteen-year-old heir of the English Lord Stourton. By the fall of 1773 he was prefect of the Marian Sodality at Bruges, but soon after he went to England as chaplain to Lord Arundell. In the spring of 1774 he sailed home to America, where he carried on a pastoral ministry from his mother's home at Rock Creek, Maryland, until his appointment by Pope Pius VI in 1784 as ecclesiastical superior of the mission in the thirteen United States of North America. He was named first bishop of Baltimore in 1789 and archbishop in 1808. In 1776 he had, at the request of the Continental Congress, accompanied an official mission to Canada in the vain hope of attracting the habitants to the rebel cause. The three commissioners with whom he traveled, Benjamin Franklin, Samuel Chase, and his own cousin, Charles Carroll of Carrollton, all became shortly after their return from Canada signers of the Declaration of Independence. John Carroll's older brother, Daniel, was likewise an active patriot, and in 1787 he was a signer of the federal Constitution. The future bishop was, as John Adams suggested, a gentleman of learning and abilities, who moved easily in American society. He was also, as will be seen, well versed in theology and Christian tradition and, as a perceptive observer of the era in which he lived, extraordinarily capable of fitting the one to the other.

THE JESUIT, 1753–1773

John Carroll's Jesuit experience was a significant formative factor in his life. Few documents from this twenty-year period survive, but his partial account of travels in the early 1770s with the Honorable Charles Philip Stourton is informative.[4] They were in Rome in the winter of 1773, and Carroll was ever after haunted by memories of the events of that year which saw the destruction of the religious order to which he belonged. He had kept a close incognito and avoided Jesuit houses, although he did make discreet contacts with English Jesuits in the city. Four letters dated between October 1772 and June 1773 and written to Thomas Ellerker, Jesuit contemporary and theology professor at Liège, detailed intrigues leading up to the suppression of the society in the summer of 1773.[5] A dozen years later, memories had not dimmed as Carroll challenged Franciscan controversialist Arthur O'Leary for his "servile" defense of Pope Clement XIV and declared: "Certainly I saw repeated instances of conduct, which upon the coolest and most unprejudiced consideration appear irreconcilable not only with benevolence, but even with common humanity, and the plainest principles of justice." In a draft he had added: "I had almost said, with the clearest dictates of Religion."[6]

When in 1790 his most frequent correspondent in England and fellow ex-Jesuit, Charles Plowden, was gaining prominence as a literary defender of the papacy, the newly consecrated bishop of Baltimore wrote and warned him:

> You have been used of late to see so much unjust suspicion entertained against the popes, that your zeal to defend the just prerogatives of the holy See makes you justify expressions, which certainly were introduced for the sake of usurpations on the rights of the civil power, or of the Diocesan clergy. Remember the iniquities and oppressions of popes such as Ganganelli, and you will be careful to obey and respect their orders, within the line of their rightful jurisdiction, but not to extend it farther, which sooner or later always does harm.[7]

Five years before this last letter, Carroll had urged Plowden to "disabuse the world of prejudices in his [Clement XIV's] favour, which were first inculcated by the indefatigable industry of an inveterate faction," but at the same time had urged him, "when you treat of that pope's character, to give no way to your imagination; but support all your assertions with such authority, as shall convict the most hardened prejudices."[8] Despite this somewhat tainted plea for historical objectivity, Carroll was as subject to his own prejudices as the next man. But in the matter of papal authority, he always clearly distinguished his difficulties with concrete functional aspects of the papacy from the "just prerogatives" and the "rightful jurisdiction" of the Holy See.

Pope Clement XIV and the papal brief *Dominus ac Redemptor* of July 21, 1773, were not Carroll's only functional problems with the Roman Curia of his day. He shared with many eighteenth-century Jesuits the conviction that the Sacred Congregation for the Propagation of the Faith (or "Propaganda") had played a role in the downfall of the Jesuits, and he was convinced that the influence of this congregation in America was to be resisted at all costs. His arguments were both theological and political. They were also emotional, colored by memories of 1773. Theologically Carroll argued that the American Catholic community formed a church and not a mission, and that only the latter was a proper object of Propaganda's interest. Politically he argued that Propaganda had the image of a foreign political operation ("a Congregation existing in his [the pope's] States") and that as such its interference was unacceptable in the emerging United States. These were not basic positions from which he retreated, but much of the earlier emotion did drain away and even as he sailed over the Atlantic to his episcopal ordination in the summer of 1790 he was able to write to the prefect of Propaganda, Cardinal Lorenzo Antonelli, of his gratitude for "the expectations and good opinion" entertained of him by the congregation and of its "benevolence" toward him.

THE THIRTEEN UNITED STATES OF NORTH AMERICA

General hostility to Roman Catholics was the legacy in English America of two centuries of bitter antipapist feeling both in the mother country and in its colonies. It lingered through the Revolution and was a factor with which Carroll was obliged to cope. The United States also manifested symptoms that would become more and more familiar as increasing numbers of nations emerged from colonial situations. There was considerable determination to create a future that would have as little reference as possible to the Old World of Europe. John Carroll shared the American sense of newness, but combined it with a profound realization of the importance of the historical dimension to an integral understanding of Christianity. His thinking was congenial with that of his friend Benjamin Franklin, of whom he wrote in 1785: "The Doctor wishes his country to be unconnected with Europe in every other way, than that of a communication of all useful knowledge."[9] Carroll added the idea of the pope as head of the church and of the see of Rome as the center of ecclesiastical unity. He was conscious of his own role as a bishop in the worldwide body of bishops. But he distinguished these spiritual connections from anything remotely savoring of a political connotation. He understood, because he shared them, republican ideas prevalent in America. In 1782 he wrote playfully to his royalist British friend Charles Plowden that he was happy that the Emperor Joseph II loved both justice and innovation, "since it is so new a thing for crowned heads to be just, or rather for those who govern under them." He had, he admitted, "contracted the language of a republican."[10]

Carroll's task was to work out the accommodation between American republicanism and monarchial forms inherited from the church's past. In pursuit of that goal his own genuine acceptance of concepts basic to the American religious experience helped: religious pluralism in a state religiously neutral, freedom of conscience and of the exercise of religion for all, sensitivity toward and toleration of religious divergence. This program was not without its problems. Increasing age and coping with local problems challenged Carroll's openness to democratic forms in the church. Early sympathy with his friends of England's Catholic Committee eroded. He was appalled by the French Revolution and by what he saw as a type of ecclesiastical populism emerging in the former German ecclesiastical states of the Rhineland. The emperor's brand of regalism and its Italian version in Tuscany had never appealed to him, and he proved an attentive reader of the constitution issued by Pius VI on August 28, 1794, *Auctorem Fidei*, with its enumeration of the errors of the 1786 Synod of Pistoia. Reprobation in church matters of "furious democracy" began to creep into his correspondence. But withal there was something precious in the American experience that he tried to the end to retain as he worked to evolve an ecclesiological framework that would suit the contrasting demands of the political and the religious communities to which he belonged.

ORGANIZATION OF THE CLERGY, 1782–1784

Carroll had not been happy with his homecoming in 1774 to a church that rapidly became in practice autocephalous, severed from now nonexistent Jesuit superiors in England and Rome, and soon after from the admittedly always loose surveillance of the vicar apostolic of the London District. He served "a very large congregation," often riding twenty-five or thirty miles to attend the sick. Once a month he made a round trip of over one hundred miles to offer mass at another congregation in Virginia. The rest of the clergy—ex-Jesuits all until the Revolution—were supported by revenue from the extensive farms that they had inherited from the Society, but Carroll received no stipend because he had refused to accept the right of the last Jesuit superior, Father John Lewis, to transfer him from place to place. The situation disturbed him, as he wrote to Plowden in 1782:

> The Clergymen here continue to live in the old form: it is the effect of habit, and if they could promise themselves immortality it would be well enough. But I regret, that indolence prevents any form of administration

being adopted which might tend to secure to posterity a succession of Catholic Clergymen, and secure to these a confortable subsistence.

In Carroll's view, the "ignorance, indolence and delusion" of the ex-Jesuits combined with John Lewis's "irresolution" to prevent serious attention to the substantive problems facing the tiny Catholic community.[11] He took the matter in hand himself and in 1782 circulated the draft of a plan for organizing the clergy.[12] It had been nine years since the suppression of the Society of Jesus had severed one set of religious ties for the Maryland and Pennsylvania missionaries and six years since the Declaration of Independence had effectively, if not canonically, severed the Americans' last link with the vicar apostolic of the London District.

The Constitution of the Clergy drawn up in three meetings of priests at Whitemarsh plantation in Maryland during 1783 and 1784 reflected the political climate of the times.[13] It included both financial arrangements and a rule of life for the clergy. Control of the clergy's assets was sharply separated from "spiritual power derived from the Bishop." The latter was left with Lewis, who had become vicar general to Bishop Richard Challoner of the London District when his office as Jesuit mission superior was extinguished by the 1773 suppression. Under the Whitemarsh plan the estates were held in common under the superintendence of a Chapter of Deputies (two from each of three districts into which the mission stations and their priests were divided) which met at least triennially and which elected as its agent a procurator general. Writing to the Luxemburger ex-Jesuit Bernard Diderick, who took exception to decisions made by the Chapter of Deputies, Carroll insisted that it had "the supreme legislative authority in matters of internal government" of the clergy.[14]

While the spiritual superior had no control over the clergy's property, he retained considerable indirect power in the spiritual area. The superior made pastoral appointments and gave faculties, but no priest could be supported from the revenues of a district unless he had been accepted for service there by the district's deputies. Nor was a priest to be "imposed on any District without their consent, expressed by their members of Chapter." Vacancies were filled by the deputies, "application having been first made to the Superior in spiritualibus." It was up to the Chapter of Deputies or to the procurator general to withdraw financial support from a priest stripped of his faculties by the superior. The Whitemarsh Constitution did more than protect the ex-Jesuit property from outside interference. It introduced at the very origins of the American Catholic church a strongly democratic clerical form of church government.

REPUBLICAN IDEAS AND FOREIGN JURISDICTIONS

The Whitemarsh Constitution enabled the clergy to get on with their business, but it was only a beginning. The precarious situation of the little band of Catholics in a hostile environment—they numbered less than 1 percent of the national population—played a part in shaping their attitudes, just as did the fact that they had generally supported the Revolution and after its end were as enthusiastic as any of their compatriots about the new democratic climate of the country. These thoughts, along with his anti-Propaganda bias, were in Carroll's mind as he wrote to Plowden on September 26, 1783. The Englishman had relayed reports from the Anglo-American ex-Jesuits' agent at Rome, Father John Thorpe, about Propaganda's interest in the clergy's American real estate. Carroll commented:

> Your information of the intention of the Propaganda gives me concern no farther, than to hear that men, whose institution was for the service of Religion, should bend their thoughts so much more to the grasping of power, and the commanding of wealth. For they may be assured, that they will never get possession of a sixpence of our property here; and if any of our friends could be weak enough to deliver any real estate into their hands, or attempt to subject it to their authority, our civil government would be called upon to wrest it again out of their dominion. A foreign temporal jurisdiction will never be tolerated here; and even the Spiritual supremacy of the Pope is the only reason why in some of the United States, the full participation of all civil rights is not granted to the R.C. They may therefore send their Agents when they please; they will certainly return empty handed.[15]

The problem of foreign jurisdiction—and the consequent charge of divided loyalty—had plagued English-speaking Catholics since the Reformation, and it early became a staple ingredient in American colonial anti-Catholicism. Carroll did his best to confront it. Writing on July 10, 1784, to praise English controversialist Joseph Berington for his *State and Behaviour of the English Catholics*, Carroll asked him to take up two subjects: the use of Latin in the church's liturgy and "the Extent and Boundaries of the Spiritual Jurisdiction of the Holy See."[16] The latter question soon came to a head in a practical way. Trilateral negotiations during 1783 and 1784—involving the apostolic nuncio at Versailles, France's foreign minister, and the American minister plenipotentiary, Dr. Franklin, but ignoring the American clergy—resulted in Carroll's appointment (June 9, 1784) as "Superior of the Mission in the thirteen United States of North America." The appointment was processed through Propaganda.[17] Carroll was angry at the process, briefly considered refusing the proffered office, and wrote Plowden: "Little do they know the jealousy entertained here of foreign jurisdictions."[18] He repeated the theme in a November 26, 1784, letter to the nuncio at Versailles, Prince Giuseppe Doria-Pamphili, warning him that the notion was unacceptable to Americans that "our faith demands a subjection to His Holiness incompatible with the independence of a sovereign state."[19] Three months later the same caution was relayed to Roman agent John Thorpe. Even though, he said, he knew that his ideas would "sound ungrateful at Rome," he had to express them for the sake of "the permanent interests of religion."[20]

In an official letter as superior to Cardinal Lorenzo Antonelli, prefect of Propaganda, dated February 27, 1785, Carroll explained that the situation in the new republic was delicate, that all foreign jurisdiction was hateful, that American Episcopalians had severed their ties to the bishop of London and were selecting their own bishops, and that arrangements must be made for an eventual choice of a Catholic ecclesiastical superior that would take into account both "the Independence of our country" and "the spiritual jurisdiction of the Holy See." Lest Antonelli take the hint lightly, he added that prominent laymen, and in particular the Catholic members of the Continental Congress and of the state legislatures of Pennsylvania and Maryland, wanted to memorialize the pope directly and had been dissuaded only because he had convinced them that his present letter was a more appropriate avenue of approach. Finally, Carroll told the cardinal, there was the matter of the sixth Article of Confederation, which could possibly be understood to apply to ecclesiastical as well as civil offices.[21]

A NEW PEOPLE, A NEW WORLD

John Carroll was gifted with a remarkable historical consciousness. He knew he lived and was called to exercise authority in a time and place that were new and different. To Plowden on February 27, 1785, he wrote that there had to be from Rome "some appearance of an inclination to leave us that Ecclesiastical liberty, which the temper of the age and of our people requires, as well as the lasting benefit of Religion."[22] Six years later he had not changed his mind. He sensed that a new and far more extensive world was in the making, one that would be no longer merely a colonial appendage of Europe. He had been discussing a possible division of his diocese of Baltimore, then threw the question into a larger context:

> Our distance, tho not so great, if geometrically measured, as S. America, Goa and China, yet in a political light is much greater. S. America, and

the Portugese possessions in Africa and Asia have, thro' their metropolitical countries, an intermediate connexion with Rome; and the missionaries in China are almost all Europeans. But we have no European metropolis, and our Clergy will soon be neither Europeans, nor have European connexions. There will be the danger of a propensity to a schismatical separation from the centre of unity.

Having faced the problem, he was sanguine of the outcome: "But the Founder of the Church sees all these things, and can provide the remedy. After doing what we can we must commit the rest to his providence."[23] These were the terms within which Carroll understood his responsibilities and attempted to define the status of a national church within the Catholic communion. He worried constantly over the inevitable foreign cast that the tie to Rome involved, but "the Pope's Spiritual supremacy" and the See of Saint Peter as "the centre of ecclesiastical unity" remained constants in his theological world. At the same time he was keenly attuned to the republican new world in which he lived and determined that the Catholic church in the United States be structured in ways that compromised neither attachment to its Roman ecclesiastical center nor its American political context.

"MISSION" AND "CHURCH"

Basic to Carroll's approach was a theological understanding of the church that included a clear distinction between two forms of organization of the ecclesial community, the "mission" and the properly organized national "church." Soon after he had received word of his appointment as mission superior, he wrote a letter in late 1784 to the veteran ex-Jesuit from Württemberg and pastor at Philadelphia, Ferdinand Farmer. The faculties he had received were "much too confined for the exigencies of this country," he reported. But what was worse, they were granted by Propaganda, Rome's missionary arm, and this fact he found inappropriate. The faculties were given "during their pleasure only"; no priests were to work in America but such as came with Propaganda's approval, and, when eventually a bishop was named, , he would be a vicar apostolic. To all this Carroll was opposed. He summed it up when he wrote: "They consider us missioners; and our labours as employed in mission."[24] That was not the way Carroll understood matters. A key to his approach can be found in notes he took on his readings in Alexander Natalis, *Selecta Historiae Ecclesiae Capita*, on the way bishops were chosen in the fourth and fifth centuries. One note reads: "The Roman Pontiff will provide with respect to Bishops for nations recently converted to the Faith."[25] Carroll's distinction of "church" and "mission" is rooted here. The United States was not a "nation recently converted." It was a country in which the Roman Catholic community was established and recognized as sharing equal rights and privileges with other Christians. Its Catholic community constituted a proper "church." In Carroll's mind certain organizational facts followed from this: a national church needed bishops, and basic choice of persons for episcopal office should be made in the country itself, not in Rome; a "church" must have its own priests and a home seminary in which to educate them. Carroll argued his way through each of these questions.

VICARS APOSTOLIC AND ORDINARY BISHOPS

Carroll's letter late in 1784 to Farmer expanded on the theme of "church" versus "mission." It was a theme familiar to anyone brought up as he was in the tradition of English Catholicism, where the question of having a "bishop in ordinary" or a "vicar apostolic" as presiding prelate had long been controverted. Underlying the question of the presiding prelate was the more basic question: was England (and now America) a missionary country or one where the church was to be considered as normally established? John Carroll had no doubts. He rejected the idea of a vicar apostolic for the United States ("a refined Roman political contrivance" he called the office) and gave as his reason what he foresaw as the prospective incumbent's "utter dependance, both for his station and for his conduct, on a foreign jurisdiction." Carroll went further. Episcopal appointment in the United States should not come from the pope ("for that would create more jealousy in our government, than even in France, Germany, or Spain"), nor from American civil authorities or legislatures ("which being composed of discordant Religionists [non-Catholics], would be very improper for the business"). The bishop should be chosen by the clergy, as had already been done by American Episcopalians when they had to effect a separation from procedures used in the Church of England.[26]

Carroll used a twofold argument: the church must avoid the appearance of being "foreign," and it had the right to a degree of autonomy. He took up the first point in February 1785 in a letter to his Roman agent, John Thorpe, telling him bluntly that it was intolerable in the United States that the Catholic ecclesiastical superior, whatever his title, should "receive his appointment from a foreign state, and only hold it at the discretion of a foreign tribunal or congregation." Such a situation would ultimately lead to an attack on Catholics' civil rights. "For these reasons," he continued,

Every thinking man among us is convinced, that we must neither request or admit any other foreign interference than such, as being essential to our religion, is implied in the acknowledgement of the Bishop of Rome being, by divine appointment, head of the universal Church; and the See of S. Peter being the centre of ecclesiastical unity.[27]

But Carroll's argument was not merely the negative one of avoiding a foreign tinge in American Catholicism. He was sincerely convinced that the local church had the right to a degree of autonomy, while at the same time it preserved its links with the pope as head and Rome as the focal point of ecclesial unity. He was disappointed, he wrote to Joseph Berington, in the English hierarchy: "Long before I left Europe, I used to be astonished, that the English Bishops did not exert themselves to obtain a more independent Appointment and Jurisdiction. And I am more persuaded now, since the rigour of the penal laws is somewhat abated."[28] In 1789, after the American petition for a bishop in ordinary had been granted, Carroll returned to the theme of rightful autonomy in a letter to Charles Plowden:

> I do not know, on what principles your respectable V.V.A.A. govern themselves, by opposing the appointment of Ordinaries for England. I think, it would remove many plausible objections against the Catholic Religion, give a more decided authority to the Prelates, and introduce an Ecclesiastical government more consonant to other churches and the established discipline.[29]

By the time the American priests made a formal petition to Pope Pius VI for establishment of a diocese in the United States, practical problems were multiplying that provided further ammunition. They now argued that episcopal rank and ordinary authority were necessary for the man who was to preside over what was becoming a fractious church. The official letter of petition, signed by Carroll and two priests, John Ashton and Robert Molyneux, was dated from Baltimore, March 12, 1788.[30] It informed the pontiff that the superior, "a simple priest [having] only delegated authority," had been accused by rebels in the New York City congregation of Saint Peter's of wielding an authority that was "illegal, because it was set up by a foreign tribunal and was dependent on this tribunal both as regards its exercise and its duration." The "same would hold for a bishop who enjoys vicarious and not ordinary powers." Similar arguments were made to Cardinal Antonelli in a letter dated March 18/April 19, 1788. Carroll emphasized that in deciding on procedures to be followed with respect to the United States, Propaganda must

> seriously weigh the spirit and the prejudices which prevail in these States, and . . . so arrange the naming of a bishop, and give him such authority that, while union and due obedience to the Apostolic See is maintained,

in so far as possible, he be freed from the suspicion of any kind of subjection which is not absolutely necessary.[31]

A REGULAR CLERGY

Carroll had strong views on the necessary autonomy of a national church once it had been established and on the role that a bishop played in the church. He also held strong views on the makeup, education, and function of the clergy who staffed such a church, the "regular clergy," as he referred to them. The term in his correspondence does not have its normal canonical reference to clergy belonging to a religious order but designates those in the regular service of the diocese. No national church, Carroll was convinced, could claim the title unless it had its own clergy and had made provision for their continuation. Writing to Plowden on September 18, 1784, he touched on the subject when he criticized Propaganda: "To govern the spiritual concerns of this country, as a mission, is absurd, seeing there is a regular Clergy belonging to it; and with God's assistance there will be in time, a succession of ministry to supply their places as they drop off."[32]

Several months later, in his letter to Farmer about the new prelacy, he amplified his ideas:

> We form not a fluctuating body of labourers in Christ's vineyard, sent hither and removeable at the will of a Superior; but a permanent body of national Clergy, with sufficient powers to form our own system of internal government, and, I think, to chuse our own Superior, and a very just claim to have all necessary Spiritual authority communicated to him, on his being presented as regularly and canonically chosen by us.[33]

A SEMINARY FOR YOUNG CLERGYMEN

Carroll's years as superior, and later as bishop, were plagued by a procession of clerical adventures, "a medley of clerical characters," he called them, wandering priests whose European bishops or religious superiors had been only too happy to release them for service in America. They promised little for the future of the church in the United States. Carroll had shared with Farmer his hope that each year one or two Catholic young men educated in secular colleges in Pennsylvania and Maryland (Farmer was a trustee of the University of Pennsylvania; Carroll of Saint John's and Washington Colleges in Maryland) would take up a religious vocation. He initially saw it as a simple process. After the youths had completed their college education, the business will be to form them to the virtues necessary for their state, and give them a Theological institution: and here will appear the necessity of a Seminary for young Clergymen to the raising of which all our savings, all the contributions of our friends must be directed. In such a seminary, which may be contiguous to one of our own houses, we need have only one elderly Gentleman unfit for hard labour, but of approved virtue, and conduct, to train the young men to the duties of their State, and one other, a man of learning and abilities to teach them Divinity.[34]

In later years a primary purpose in the founding of the academy at Georgetown was "the education of youth and perpetuity of the body of Clergy in this country," as the Chapter of Deputies wrote sharply to the "Gentlemen of the Southern District," the conservative ex-Jesuits in the parishes of southern Maryland who were reluctant to spend money on either bishops or schools.[35] Carroll put it succinctly for Charles Plowden: "our great view, in the establishment of an academy, is to form subjects capable of becoming useful members of the ministry."[36]

There was another dimension to Carroll's thought on clerical education, one that highlights his concern for a truly national aspect in the local church. He was wary of suggestions that American clergymen be trained abroad. Cardinal Antonelli had proposed that two seminarians be despatched from the United States to Propaganda's Urban College in Rome. To Thorpe Carroll wrote on February 17, 1785:

> With respect to sending two youths, I shall inform Propaganda that it would surely be very acceptable to us to have children educated gratis in so religious a seminary; and very acceptable to us all to have a succession of ministers of the altar thus provided for: but, as I suppose they will not receive any into their College, but such as shall afterwards be subject to their government; and it being yet uncertain what effect my representations may produce I shall delay that measure till farther information.[37]

In a subsequent letter to Antonelli Carroll mentioned that arrangements for the students must await finalization of governmental arrangements in the American church. He then obliquely brought up the question of the "Propaganda Oath," warning that the boys' parents must be informed "whether some promise, and of what nature, would be demanded of their sons before they return to their country." For, Carroll concluded, "all possible care must be taken lest the Catholics, both clergy and laity, should seem to depend on some foreign power in matters of such great moment."[38]

Rome was not the only venue for seminary training about which Carroll had hesitations. When an offer came of places at Mainz, he sent his thanks, but claimed that the church in America could not assume the cost of sending candidates to the archiepiscopal seminary.[39] To Cardinal Antonelli, he gave as his reasons for this reluctance, that he would send no seminarians to Germany until he knew more about the theology being taught there. He was suspicious of views on the authority of the laity that he understood were taught in German universities and thought it better that his seminarians not be exposed to them.[40] Eventually Carroll did send a pair of students to Rome, but his principal provision for "a succession of regular clergy" was made by securing the services of French Sulpicians, who opened Saint Mary's Seminary in Baltimore, in 1791.

LORENZO RICCI REDIVIVUS?

A standard charge against Carroll was that in organizing the clergy he favored his ex-Jesuit brethren. It was made by the Meath diocesan priest Patrick Smyth in a pamphlet, *The Present State of the Catholic Missions Conducted by the Ex-Jesuits in North America* (Dublin, 1788) and by the French priest Claude de la Potterie, in *The Resurrection of Laurent Ricci: Or, a True and Exact History of the Jesuits* (Philadelphia, 1789), dedicated to "the new Laurent Ricci in America, the Rev. Fr. John Carroll." (L. Ricci, S.J., 1703-1775, was the general of the Jesuits at the time of their suppression.) Both authors had been among Carroll's "medley of clerical characters," the Irishman serving at Frederick, Maryland, and the Frenchman in Boston, and both were intemperate in the criticisms they leveled at him. At the same time, it was true that Carroll did seek a measure of homogeneity among his clergy, and this desire led him to turn instinctively, when he could, to those who had been trained as he was. He made every effort to attract home to their native land those American ex-Jesuits who had remained abroad after the suppression of 1773, and he was likewise hospitable to others who had been members of the Society of Jesus. When, in 1788, dissidents among the German parishioners in Philadelphia asked for one of the Capuchin Heilbron brothers as their pastor in place of the former Jesuit novice from Bavaria, Lorenz Graessl, Carroll refused and told Plowden that he had made no secret of his reason, "viz:, that as long as there was an exjesuit alive, willing and capable of serving a Congregation, which had been raised by that body of men, he should have preference."[41] He had enlisted Plowden in his program to recruit ex-Jesuits, writing him on June 29, 1785: "I have written in a pressing manner to all, whom I conceive likely to come to our assistance. . . . Encourage all you can meet with, Europeans or Americans, to come amongst us."[42] But he was also a realist, as he confided a year later:

> I shall be under the necessity of calling in other assistants besides those
> who were raised in the Society or under its former members. To preserve
> peace, and uniformity, I wish'd to avoid this in Maryland and Pennsyl-
> vania, and perhaps Virginia. A wider field I knew we could not embrace:
> but if larger supplies do not arrive soon, the great and prevailing con-
> sideration of charity will oblige me to admit labourers, whatever they
> come from, if their faith and morals are sound. I am well aware of the
> inconveniencies and mortification, which must result from this measure.[43]

To the Gentlemen of the Southern District, opposed as they were to
anything that smacked of change, went the warning from Carroll and
the members of the Chapter:

> We can not rationally carry our views so far as to form to ourselves the
> idea of a Society to be established in this Country sufficiently adequate
> to its extent; nor can we put such a clog on people's dispositions, as to
> leave no door for admittance to H. Orders, but thro' that of the Novitiate.
> Religious orders in the church are only auxiliaries to the Ecclesiastical
> Hierarchy established by Christ, and we may hope that as Providence
> has provided for us, so it will provide for those, whom it calls in another
> way.

Later in the same letter, the argument was summarized with the
question: "Was the Society instituted for the good of souls, or must
souls be sacrificed for the good of the Society?"[44] The national church
and its needs were paramount. John Carroll accepted religious and
secular priests from a variety of backgrounds and in that way, whatever his personal preferences, secured a succession of regular clergy.

SELECTION OF BISHOPS

John Carroll's thought on the nature and structure of a national church
can perhaps best be traced in the evolution of his ideas on the selection
of bishops. His approach was clearly non-Erastian, but he was not
averse to cooperation with civil government. He sought a formula
that would maintain both the rights of the Holy See and the autonomy
of the local church. Government interference was never a problem
for Carroll, but Rome was understandably somewhat reluctant about
some of his suggestions. Further, the interference of Rome in American
affairs of European episcopal colleagues, especially among the Irish
bishops, complicated matters to a considerable degree.

CHURCH AND STATE

Carroll opposed participation by civil government in the choice of
bishops, but was not himself loath to use the influence of secular of-

ficials. When in 1788 the question of naming a bishop came to a head, he sought and obtained the intervention of the Spanish minister at New York, Don Diego de Gardoqui, and, through Gardoqui's good offices he secured an unlikely ally for an ex-Jesuit, the Conde de Floridablanca, chief minister of Charles III and the diplomat who in 1773 had orchestrated the final campaign of the Spanish Bourbon court against the Jesuits. Carroll was pleased with what he termed Gardoqui's "thorough penetration into the nature and necessary effects of our Republican governments." He was even more pleased with the minister's concurrence that one of those necessary effects was that the church in the United States should be governed by a bishop chosen by the American clergy and then "approved by the Holy See for the preservation of unity in faith."[45]

Five years earlier, Carroll had been less happy over the Paris negotiations prior to his appointment as superior, since they had been carried on without reference to the American clergy. In this he had shown himself rather more "American" in his indignation at the intermingling of church and state than had the American minister, Benjamin Franklin, whose diary suggests that he enjoyed his brief interlude as ecclesiastical counselor. Carroll was annoyed that "the Court of Rome" dealt with Franklin without "ever deigning to apply for information to the Catholick Clergy in this country." He briefly considered writing to Franklin "about the impropriety of Propaganda intermeddling here" and regretted that his contacts in the Continental Congress were limited, since his brother Daniel's term had just expired and the only other Catholic member, Thomas FitzSimons of Philadelphia, had resigned. Otherwise he would have seen to it that Congress make an even stronger reply than it had made to the Roman request for its views on the choice of a bishop.[46]

Twenty years later, when there was question of a vicar and then a bishop for the newly acquired Louisiana Territory, Bishop Carroll did not hesitate to consult, in person and by letter, Secretary of State James Madison and to list among the qualities required in a candidate that his "attachment to the United States was unequivocal."[47] In the same connection he assured his own nephew, Daniel Brent, a clerk in the State Department, that

> if any clergyman acting there [in New Orleans] under my authority should ever betray dispositions, or countenance measures unfriendly to the Sovereignty of the United States; or if he should ever hold correspondence of a suspicious nature with a foreign nation, he shall be deprived of any commission from me and of the care of souls.[48]

Carroll was committed to the anti-Erastian consequences of the religiously plural society emerging in the United States. At the same time he actively sought ways in which church and state could find their way in coexistence and cooperation.

ROME AND THE CHOICE OF BISHOPS

In the spring of 1790 the fiery Irish ex-Jesuit procurator general of the clergy's estates, John Ashton, angrily attacked provisions of the bull *Ex Hac Apostolicae* (November 6, 1789), by which the diocese of Baltimore had been established. He objected to indications in the bull that future bishops of the see would be chosen in Rome and that the ordinary seemed to be given control of "all ecclesiastical incomes," contrary to the bylaws of the Corporation of the Roman Catholic Clergymen. In reply Carroll explained his own position: he opposed "the popes having the nomination of the Bishop," because of "the certainty I have, that the exercise of such power by the pope would draw on our Religion a heavy imputation from the government under which we live." Having said that, John Carroll entered on a long process, never satisfactorily resolved, of trying to determine a method of choosing bishops for the American church in a way that would be acceptable both to Rome and to Americans.

In his letter to Ashton, the bishop argued further that in the future it would not be possible to have all the clergy share in the election of a bishop, as had been done in his own case. It was for that practical reason, he thought, that the bull had not specified a process. He understood full well the position taken in the document: "The pope, according to the pretensions, which the see of Rome has always supported, says, he will nominate hereafter." But that did not close the question: "But I conceive that the Clergy will have as good right to say, that the election shall be held by members of their own body, and that they never can, with safety, or will admit any Bishop who is not so constituted."

"The time for holding this language," he continued, "will be in a Diocesan Synod of all the Clergy, and not at a meeting of Chapter only." In a final paragraph, the bishop-elect provided another interesting hermeneutical insight. Addressing himself to Ashton's concern about assignment of temporal administration to the new ordinary, he commented:

> As to the investing of the Bishop with the administration etc., I never conceived it as anything more than the expression of those claims which Rome has always kept up, tho universally disregarded; viz; that the pope is the universal administrator, some have even said, Dominus of all ecclesiastical property.

"Rome cannot give," he assured the worried procurator, "what it has never possessed, administration of our estates; and I presume that a Bishop, who should attempt anything under such an authority, would be resisted, and deservedly, as the pope would have been, had he attempted it since the dissolution."[49]

As pointed out earlier in this chapter, Carroll's thought was rooted in the distinction he made between a "mission," the first planting of Catholicism in a region, and an organized local "church" with all the autonomous characteristics suggested above. In such a local church, as he understood the Catholic tradition, selection of bishops was a local matter. The name of the person chosen was notified to the pope for approval, for canonical institution, or, in an older phrase, for acceptance into communion. Since the Second Lateran Council (1139), choice of bishops belonged properly to the canons of the diocese's cathedral chapter, although in point of fact the prerogative had in the so-called Catholic countries frequently been usurped by the state, sometimes in concordatory agreement with Rome. In Carroll's day the pope claimed direct right of episcopal appointment only in the Papal States and in mission countries. It was this latter designation that Carroll resisted for the United States.[50]

PRACTICAL IMPLEMENTATION

Carroll continued to think on ways in which a procedure could be shaped. He considered alternatives. In the spring of 1788 he had written to William O'Brien, O.P., at New York, that "the officiating Clergymen in America" would be the episcopal electors,[51] but to Plowden he wrote that he hoped election would "never be vested in the whole body of officiating clergy; but only certain select persons etc."[52] This last idea was spelled out in a proposal made by participants in the Diocesan Synod held at Baltimore on November 7 and 8, 1791. They recommended that the ten priests who had worked longest in America, together with another five chosen by the bishop, serve as episcopal electors. The Holy See would retain the "right to reject candidates until someone is chosen who meets the full approval of the Pope."[53] Carroll explained to Plowden that the latter provision was made because of his "sollicitude to provide for a close and intimate union with the Holy See."[54]

The electoral committee envisioned in 1791 was never created, although Carroll did not give up the idea. In 1793 he nominated Lorenz Graessl to be his coadjutor with right of succession, informing Cardinal Antonelli that he did so after having sought "the counsel of the older and more worthy workers in this vineyard of the Lord." In the same letter he asked authorization "to organize ten or twelve priests who are in charge of the principal congregations in this diocese into a sort of chapter, an advisory body for the bishop." The dignity would inhere in the major congregations and pass to the successors of these quasi-capitulars. They would elect their own dean and be responsible for spiritual direction of the diocese during an episcopal vacancy. They would act as a substitute for the cathedral chapter more usual in organized dioceses, but not in Baltimore, since it was impractical to have so many priests live in one place.[55]

Events in Europe effectively severed communications between Carroll and Rome. Graessl died of yellow fever before action could be taken on his nomination, and Carroll reported that he was once again consulting the more prudent and experienced priests.[56] Finally he proposed another ex-Jesuit, Leonard Neale, pastor at Philadelphia and onetime missionary in Demerara.[57] It was to be five years before the bulls arrived and he could be consecrated bishop of Gortyna and coadjutor to Carroll.

AN AMERICAN HIERARCHY

The international situation was not the only difficulty troubling the sixty-five-year-old Carroll as he faced the new century. He knew that the episcopal base in the United States had to be broadened to provide adequate care for a growing Catholic community, but a series of challenges to his authority by priests and congregations in several cities had made him cautious. Even before the 1791 synod he had shared with Plowden his fears about division of the diocese. He wanted first, he said, to be sure that "an uniform discipline may be established in all parts of this great continent; and every measure so firmly concerted, that as little danger as possible may remain of a disunion with the Holy See."[58] This concern for Catholic unity nudged him away from positions as bold as the one he had taken with John Ashton in 1790. Writing to the secretary of the Propaganda, Stefano Borgia, on February 14, 1804, he told the prelate that he had rejected requests that he take a hand in church affairs in the newly acquired American Louisiana Territory. He said, "[I had told petitioners] that I had no authority over them, that their episcopal see established by the Apostolic See still functioned, that if it was now vacant no doubt a successor would be named by the Holy Father, and that the person chosen and confirmed would shortly receive notification."[59]

Carroll's correspondence about division of the Diocese of Baltimore was equally mild. In June, 1807, he recommended candidates for dioceses to be erected at Boston, Philadelphia, and Bardstown. He suggested that a fourth new diocese, at New York, be temporarily entrusted to the bishop of Boston, and that he himself be administrator of the Diocese of Louisiana and the two Floridas.[60] There is no available evidence on what, if any, consultative process he used in selecting episcopal candidates. His nominees were named to Boston, Philadelphia, and Bardstown, but Rev. Charles Nerinckx was appointed administrator for Louisiana (he declined) and an Irish Dominican resident in Rome, Richard Luke Concanen, was designated for New York and consecrated by Cardinal di Pietro five months before Carroll, the new metropolitan at Baltimore, learned that he was an archbishop with four suffragan sees. His initial reaction to introduction of the "Irish Connection" was calm. He thanked Archbishop John Troy, O.P., of Dublin, who had been the first to tell him of the diocesan realignment; explained matter-of-factly to Plowden that "His Holiness wished to provide at once for all the places and nominated Fr. Concanen;"[61] and wrote to another English ex-Jesuit that he had "always had a favourable account" of the new bishop.[62]

Concanen in the event never arrived in America. Bishops Michael Egan, O.F.M., Jean Lefebvre de Cheverus, and Benedict-Joseph Flaget, S.S., were ordained to the episcopacy at Baltimore in October 1810, and then met with Carroll and Neale to discuss urgent problems confronting the church. The fourth in a series of resolutions that they adopted reads:

> Nomination of Bishops. In case the Holy See will graciously permit the nomination to vacant Bishopricks to be made in the United States, it is humbly and respectfully suggested to the Supreme Pastor of the Church to allow the nomination for the vacant Dioceses to proceed solely from the Archbishop and Bishops of this Ecclesiastical Province.[63]

Opposition was building to foreign intervention such as had resulted in Bishop Concanen's appointment to New York.

The next crisis arose with the death on July 22, 1814, of Bishop Egan of Philadelphia. Archbishop Carroll circularized the surviving suffragans, together with Anthony Kohlmann, S.J., administrator of New York, and Louis DeBarth, administrator of Philadelphia. He wanted their advice so that they could pick the "one, two or three persons, best esteemed by us and send on their names, character etc. to Rome, with our respective nominations." He also asked their permission to consult in the matter "the most discreet and experienced "clergy of the deceased bishop's diocese. All this Carroll did, although, as he told the bishops, no answer had ever come to their 1810 petition and so "nothing can be done authoritatively in this matter."[64]

All the names produced by this system were those of priests active in the American ministry, as Carroll wrote Bishop Neale,[65] and they were forwarded to Cardinal Lorenzo Litta at Propaganda on November 28, 1814.[66] But not everyone was happy. From Kentucky Bishop Flaget of Bardstown protested the nomination of John Baptist David, S.S., for Philadelphia, and claimed he had not been consulted. Carroll reminded him that he had been asked, had refused to vote, and had opposed nomination of more bishops until a greater supply of priests was available.[67] The system had persistent domestic kinks.

THE IRISH CONNECTION

Carroll had taken Concanen's appointment in stride, but increased Irish activity in American church affairs was altogether another matter. In his letter to Litta Carroll noted that no nomination was included of a bishop for New York since it was the understanding of the American bishops that the pope had already chosen the French Sulpician Ambrose Maréchal for the post.[68] Maréchal was known and respected in the United States, and there was no opposition to his selection, although there had been no initiative for it from the United States. But in fact another Irish Dominican, John Connolly, had been named to the vacant diocese and consecrated at Rome on November 6, 1814. The news reached Carroll in a letter from Archbishop Troy sometime in the early part of 1815. His reply was relatively calm, but news about still a third Irish Dominican episcopabilis (episcopal candidate) did disturb him. This was William Vincent Harold, who had been a priest in Philadelphia from 1808 to 1813 and was now being mentioned as Egan's successor. Carroll tartly inquired of Troy: "Would it not be resented as a very improper interference if we the Bishops in the United States should presume to suggest to the Holy See the persons to be appointed to fill the Vacant Sees of Ireland?"[69]

By June 1815, the archbishop's temper had risen considerably. Writing to Plowden he included Connolly's nomination to New York among his grievances. No one in America knew or had been consulted about Connolly. Carroll worried whether "this may not become a very dangerous precedent, fruitful of mischief by drawing censure on our religion, and false opinion of the servility of our principles." As for Harold, he now knew that Troy was one of his recommenders, along with his coadjutor, Daniel Murray, and the French archbishop of Bordeaux. They were, he complained, interfering "in an affair . . . foreign to their concern, and to which they are . . . incompetent." He asked Plowden to inform the English Bishop John Milner of the situation, if the latter were still at Rome.[70]

Archbishop Carroll learned in midsummer 1815, that letters sent to Rome as long ago as 1810 had never been received by Propaganda. He hastened to update Cardinal Litta on the American bishops' recommendations for Philadelphia and their opposition to Harold. He was not, however, inclined to do battle over New York, accepting Connolly's appointment as a fait accompli.[71] He had in fact come to the end of his course; he died in Baltimore on December 3, 1815, just shy of his eighty-first birthday. To the end he resisted foreign influence in the selection of American bishops, but he never managed to get in place a workable system for local selection, and the letters of his later years suggest an almost routine acceptance of Roman appointments not easily reconciled with theories he had espoused earlier.

JOHN CARROLL AND THE HOLY SEE

John Carroll's ideas and practice in the matter of selecting bishops reveal a great deal about his concept of the status of a national church. But the pope and the Holy See both played a central and integral role in his understanding of Catholicism. Writing to Leonard Neale, who had finally become his coadjutor eight months previously and who served as regional bishop in the southern part of the diocese, Carroll recommended that he subscribe to a new London Catholic magazine where he would find

> an excellent encyclical letter of the present pope to all Patriarchs, Archbishops, Bishops etc. Instead of a sermon to day, I read the first part of it to this congregation and will continue it next Sunday; and advise you to recommend the same to your Br [brother Francis Neale, pastor in Georgetown], and the pastors of other Congregations subordinate to your immediate inspection. For tho the letter is only addressed to the prelates of the Church, yet it contains many points useful to all.[72]

Carroll had his problems with individual popes and their decisions, most strikingly in the case of Clement XIV. In his early years he had his suspicions of "congregations existing in the pope's states," particularly Propaganda. Even his recommendation to Neale of the encyclical *Diu Satis* (May 15, 1800) has about it a note of reserved detachment. Nevertheless for John Carroll the pope's role as head of the church and of the See of Rome as center of ecclesiastical unity was paramount. The church, and the papal position in it, were of divine origin. Other elements had to be seen in that context.

In a letter to the Sulpician Antoine Garnier, who had left the United States for France in 1803, Carroll expressed his apprehensions about the council of the Church in France convoked at Notre Dame in Paris on June 16 of that year by the Emperor Napoleon:

> There is great reason to fear, that the time is approaching and perhaps is actually come, when intrigues, terror, promises, and all means of persuasion have induced the Bishops, uncanonically assembled, to adopt

decrees tending to the fatal effect so dreaded and condemned by S. Cyprian, of constituting a church on a human, instead of a divine foundation: Humanam faciunt ecclesiam.[73]

John Carroll wanted no "human church." He had always been clear on that. The earliest flicker of his later large-scale disenchantment with the English priest and controversialist Joseph Berington occurred in 1786 when he reread Berington's *State and Behaviour of English Catholics* and faulted him for seeming "to import that [the Pope] has no prerogative which has not been surrendered to him by the Community. Is this quite accurate? Is he not jure divino Head of the Community?"[74] In another contemporary letter, this time to Franciscan Arthur O'Leary, he had returned to the theme, suggesting that Berington's seeming failure to ascribe to "the Successor of St. Peter" a supremacy *jure divino* must be due to "a slip of the pen (for I cannot think it anything else)."[75]

Carroll's thought was clearly enunciated in two letters that he wrote to the former Constitutional bishop, Henri Grégoire. Thanking Grégoire on September 9, 1809, for the gift of his *Legitimité du serment civique*, he told him straight out, "I do not approve some of the principles avowed in the pamphlets and proceedings of what is called the constitutional clergy," and then proceeded to explain his basic understanding of Catholic polity:

> It must be evident to every sincere believer in the religion of Jesus Christ, from a view of late and present events, that it will be best preserved in its unity and integrity, by the intimate union and correspondence between its visible head, and the bishops and pastors diffused over the Christian world.

But at the same time he balanced that statement carefully. The letter continues:

> I shall contribute the little support, within my power, to inspire veneration for the independent power of the H[oly] See, and the episcopacy; confining however that jurisdiction within the limits of the divine bestower of it, and beyond which it ought never to have been extended; I mean things purely spiritual.[76]

For John Carroll, pope and bishops belonged together; their power was something that belonged in the spiritual realm, and there only.

Two years later, Grégoire sent the archbishop a copy of his work on religious sects, and expressed the hope that it would help in efforts toward Christian unity. Carroll, on June 4, 1811, wrote his doubts that such a purpose would be achieved by denying or rendering "wholly uncertain" the existence of any center of Catholic unity. He had no doubt that such a center did exist, and where it was to be found: "in the stedfast, public, avowed doctrine, confession and authority of the Successor of S. Peter, united in language and belief with all (I mean morally all) the Bishops of the Catholic world."[77]

Challenges to his own episcopal authority were occasions which Carroll used to effect in spelling out his concept of the pope's role in the church. In 1789, for example, he emphasized to the refractory Capuchin friar John Heilbron that resistance to the bishop was resistance to "the authority established by the H. see."[78] The same message went to the friar's supporters in Philadelphia's Holy Trinity German congregation.[79] Eight years later, when the same group was again in turmoil over the claims of two more recently arrived German clergymen, John Goetz and William Elling, Carroll reminded the parishioners that "the Holy Catholic Apostolic Roman Church" was "the Mother and Mistress of all Churches," that "true obedience" had been promised to, and was owed to, "the Bishop of Rome, Successor of St. Peter, Prince of the Apostles, and Vicar of Jesus Christ," and that the "spiritual supremacy of Christ's Vicar" was

> an essential tenet of our religion . . . the bond of our union, which cements and keeps together, in the profession of the same faith, in the celebration of the same solemn and public worship, and under one uniform government, established by Jesus Christ, and perpetuated by succeeding pastors, so many different nations, so distant from each other, and unconnected in every other respect.[80]

Unity of faith, Carroll was convinced, could not endure "apart from the authority of the Holy See." He dedicated his episcopacy, he told Cardinal Antonelli, to laying

> the most solid and enduring foundation not merely of union with the Holy See but also of conformity, obedience and love. For daily experience teaches me that faith and morals are kept intact if there is a close union with Christ's vicar on earth, and that nearly every lapse in either originates in a diminution of respect for the See of Peter.[81]

These preoccupations remained constant, and in Carroll's mind were not in any way incompatible with his strong advocacy of and concern for the integrity and dignity of individual national churches.

INFALLIBILITY

Intimately involved with Carroll's attitude to the Holy See was his theological understanding of the place and extent of infallibility in the church. His major theological effort was *An Address to the Roman Catholics of the United States of America* (1784), a reply to the pamphlet published by his kinsman and fellow ex-Jesuit Charles Wharton, *Letter to the Roman Catholics of Worcester,* in which Wharton explained why he had left the Roman and joined the Anglican communion. Carroll argued strongly for the church's claim to be endowed with infallibility, and then proceeded to a further point: "He says, that 'all Roman Catholics are bound to admit an infallible authority; yet few of them agree, where or in whom it resides.' " For Carroll the matter was not in doubt:

> In the doctrine which we teach, as belonging to faith in this point, and as an article of communion, there is no variation; and with all his reading and recollection, I will venture to assert, that he cannot cite one catholic divine, who denies infallibility to reside in the body of bishops united and agreeing with their head, the bishop of Rome.

Wharton, he continued, was wrong in suggesting that three specifications of the locus of infallibility—in the pope, in a general council, or "in the pope and council received by the whole church"—were all simply opinions of theologians, "for the last is not a mere opinion of schoolmen, but the constant belief of all catholics; a belief in which there is no variation." He added: "Some divines indeed hold the pope, as Christ's vicar on earth, to be infallible, even without a council; but with this opinion faith has no concern, every one being at liberty to adopt or reject it, as the reasons for or against may affect him."[82]

THE OBJECT OF INFALLIBILITY

Carroll never retreated from the position he took on papal infallibility in his *Address to Roman Catholics.* That doctrine was a respectable theological opinion, no more. But there was another question in which he became involved during his visit to England for episcopal ordination in 1790. He arrived to find English Catholics debating the oath fashioned by the Catholic Committee to accompany what eventually became the Catholic Relief Act of 1791. A provision in the oath required explicit denial of the pope's infallibility. Carroll's host, Thomas Weld of Lulworth Castle, his friends Lords Arundell and Clifford, and the ex-Jesuits and their former pupils generally, were ultramontane defenders of the papal prerogative.[83] Charles Plowden, his own faithful correspondent, had just published *Considerations on the Modern Question of the Fallibility of the Holy See in the Decision of Dogmatical Questions.* But the American bishop-elect also had friends in the Catholic Committee. He met several times—and dined at least once with—the Catholic Committee's secretary, Charles Butler.[84] Lord Petre he encouraged in his efforts at Catholic emancipation, and he predicted that the American example in religious toleration would influence English practice.[85] There was an awkward moment when Lord Arundell asked his advice on the oath. Carroll referred him to his spiritual advisors, but admitted to Archbishop Troy that "the oath in its present form appears to me to be inadmissible; that it implies a renunciation of the pastoral powers of the successor of St. Peter; and that its obvious meaning is different from that which the advocates for the oath fix to it."[86]

Carroll tried to keep a prudent silence, but he did inquire of Plowden why an answer could not be given to the vexing question of the scope claimed for the pope's infallibility. Did it apply to "all orders he issues, or facts, which he asserts" or was it applicable only in doctrinal matters? Confusion on the answer to this question was making the internecine debate among Catholics even more difficult than it would in any case have been. Ex-Jesuit Joseph Reeve, chaplain at Ugbrooke Park to Lord Clifford of Chudleigh, had argued with Carroll that the infallibility disclaimed in the oath was only "infallibility as to facts."[87] But Charles Butler had told Carroll that it made no difference. Non-Catholic Englishmen thought that even an infallibility restricted to doctrine was "a pernicious tenet, and dangerous to civil government."[88]

No further theological precision emerged from Carroll's inquiries, but his experiences during the summer and fall of 1790 in England pointed up some of the conflicts that tore at him as he struggled to elaborate an ecclesiology suited to the era in which he lived. Emotionally he was more in tune with Plowden and friends than he was with the Catholic Committee. But his American experience of life in a land where religious toleration was the norm, if not always the practice, influenced him strongly in the opposite direction. The problems of contemporary English Catholics served him as a laboratory in which to study and clarify his ideas. So, for example, he was put off by extremism like that of the erratic Scottish protégé of Lord Petre, Alexander Geddes, whom he dismissed as a "designing and unsound teacher."[89] He was sympathetic with the desire for greater local voice in selection of bishops, but when it was connected, as in England, with "swallowing down such an oath," he defected to the conservatives.[90] Years later, summing up his thoughts on Charles Butler, he recorded his respect for that lawyer's talents, but said, "His desire to effect the entire destruction of penal and restrictive laws carries him sometimes much too far in his compliance with the views of government."[91] The pope's infallibility was for John Carroll a freely debatable position. The scope of infallibility was something on which he was not clear. But government interference in church matters was unacceptable.

BISHOP OF AN ORDINARY NATIONAL CHURCH

A national church, as John Carroll understood it, was distinguished from a mission by its note of permanence. Writing to Ferdinand Farmer in 1784, he argued that one key factor in that permanence was civil recognition that "our Religion has acquired equal rights and privileges with that of other Christians."[92] Characteristics of a national church included communion with the bishop and church of Rome and recognition of a primacy there that was central to the structure of Catholicism. Ultimate teaching authority, however, and the charism of infallibility resided "in the body of bishops united and agreeing with their head, the bishop of Rome."[93] The bishops dispersed throughout the world had a clear function: "The body of bishops everywhere claim a divine right, in virtue of their ordination, to interpret the decrees of councils and the ordinances of popes."[94] Within the national church, bishops should be locally chosen and then approved by the pope and there should be a clergy belonging to the church as well as an educational system to provide for its continuance. Carroll wrote also on other aspects of local church polity, and in particular on the topics of parish governance and of liturgy.

The first case in which Carroll had to address the question of lay involvement in church governance occurred in New York City, where a distinguished group of laymen had on June 10, 1785, incorporated themselves and begun construction of a church building in Barclay Street. Carroll, as newly appointed superior, laid the cornerstone of the church on November 5. But the trustees were soon embroiled in a battle over which of two Irish Capuchins should be their pastor. The superior addressed the laymen on January 24, 1786, in a letter that firmly asserted his own rights. He refused to accept that the congregation had "a right not only to chuse such parish priest, as is agreeable to them; but of discharging him at pleasure; and that after such election, the Bishop, or other Ecclesiastical Superior cannot hinder him from exercising the usual functions." If ever such principles should become predominant, he continued, "the unity and Catholicity of our Church would be at an end; and it would be formed into distinct and independent Societies, nearly in the same manner, as the Congregational Presbyterians of your neighboring New England States." He also pointed out that technically there could be no question of appointing or dismissing a pastor, since no regular hierarchy had yet been set up in the United States, but he then made a significant statement that reflected his own thinking on the lay role in church governance:

> Whenever parishes are established, no doubt, a proper regard, and such as is suitable to our Governments, will be had to the rights of the Con-

gregation in the mode of election and presentation: and even now I shall ever pay to their wishes every deference consistent with the general welfare of Religion.[95]

It did not quite work out that way. Carroll was acutely sensitive to the spirit, in England as well as in America, of "indocility and independance on all authority," and he soon thought it "fatal" to allow congregational nomination of pastors.[96] In 1805 his thought had achieved a lapidary quality, as can be seen in his statement to James Kernan, secretary of the board of trustees of the congregation at Charleston: "The laity are neither the source of spiritual jurisdiction, nor can stop its course."[97] Nine years later he took for his own the English bishop John Milner's denunciation of "ecclesiastical democracy" and informed the trustees at Saint Mary's, Philadelphia, that "an over-bearing influence of the people, in the appointment of the Pastors" would never be accepted. Catholics, he reminded them, were not Presbyterians.[98]

Carroll's advocacy, as early as 1784, of a vernacular liturgy is well known. On July 10 of that year, in a letter to Joseph Berington, he paired use of Latin in the liturgy with papal power as the two greatest obstacles to reunion of Christian churches, and he thought Latin a barrier to the wider diffusion of Catholicism in North America. He could not help thinking, he wrote, "that the Alteration of this Discipline ought not only to be solicited, but insisted upon, as essential to the Service of God and Benefit of Mankind." He was concerned that, "either for want of Books, or disability to read, the greatest part of our Congregations must be utterly ignorant of the meaning and Sense of the publick Offices of the Church." He understood that it might once have been necessary to resist the "insulting and reproachful Demands of the first Reformers" for change, but that era was gone, and he could attribute present inaction only to "chimerical fears of Innovation, or to Indolence and Inattention in the first Pastors of the national churches, in not joining to sollicit, or indeed ordain this necessary alteration."[99]

Berington injected Carroll's ideas into the struggle in which he was then engaged with Bishop John Douglass of the London District, which brought down on the American's head a storm of protest. But on September 29, 1786, Carroll wrote to him again; he discussed the need for governmental autonomy and then continued, "I remain equally persuaded of the Expediency of using the vulgar Tongue in the public Offices of Religion. But hitherto I am able to do no more than express my Wishes, and inforce on my Brethren my own Sentiments." He added, "Most of them feel the Necessity of such a Change in this Country equally with myself."[100]

By the following year the superior was having second thoughts. He wrote to Franciscan Arthur O'Leary: "Mr. Berington's brilliant imagination attributes to me projects, which far exceed my powers, and in which I should find no cooperation from my Clerical Brethren in America, were I rash enough to attempt their introduction, upon my own authority."[101] His alarm had become all the greater, he wrote Plowden in June, 1787, when he heard from P. J. Coghlan, the English Catholic bookseller, that his name was being bandied about not only in connection with Berington's crusade for a vernacular liturgy but also with agitation for abolition of clerical celibacy.[102] To Coghlan himself he wrote acknowledging his advocacy of the vernacular, but on the expressed condition that such a change was authorized by "the Holy See and first Pastors of the Church." It was not for an individual "Bishop or Ecclesiastical Superior" to act.[103]

CONCLUSION

Carroll's concept of a national church included other projects. He was delighted at publication in 1785 at Philadelphia of a translation of a Bible history done by the English Jesuit Joseph Reeve.[104] He actively encouraged publisher Matthew Carey to bring out his edition of "the Doway Bible, agreeably to the last corrections made in it by the late Bishop Challoner," and he acted as an unpaid salesman for Carey, dunning both clergy and laity for subscriptions.[105] He remained active to the end, and his last years were as troubled as any earlier had been. Only a year before his death he shared with his fellow citizens in the "state of alarm and danger" when British forces bombarded Fort McHenry at Baltimore and Francis Scott Key penned the words that were to become the American national anthem.[106] Before his death he had the consolation of knowing that Pius VII had returned to Rome. In the period 1809–1810 he had carried on a correspondence with the archbishop of Dublin in which they discussed the course to be taken should the pope die a prisoner of Napoleon. Carroll's opinion on the subject reflected once again his general understanding of the episcopal office in the church:

> When it is considered that none remain of the College of Cardinals, or, if any, so few that reasonable exceptions may be taken at any choice of the successor to be made by them only, what other remedy remains but for the Prelates of the Church who are yet able to give a free vote, to interfere and provide for the extraordinary exigency?[107]

John Carroll was a man of his time. It was his lot to live during a pivotal period in history. His Europe was that of Enlightenment; his America was that of Revolution. A man of the eighteenth century, he understood that the nineteenth would be home to a different and expanded world. His church was that which antedated in Catholicism the neo-ultramontane movement. In secular politics he was a Federalist, a conservative, an admirer of George Washington. The "furious democracy" of France's revolution appalled him. He liked the "levelling spirit of the times" no more in civil than in church life. But he did not confuse American and French revolutions, and he believed that the church in the United States should be open to new forms of being and functioning that responded to the new setting in which it found itself. His working out of this in practice was not always easy nor was it always successful. John Carroll's "learning and abilities" were put fully to the test. On balance he met that test. His like has scarcely been known again in the history of American Catholicism.

CHAPTER
2
Louis William DuBourg

Annabelle M. Melville

$\mathcal{O}$f the French clergy who became bishops during the period of Anglo-French domination, 1789–1850, six were refugees from the upheavals of the French Revolution, arriving in the United States during the first six years of John Carroll's episcopacy.[1] All of these émigrés—Jean Dubois, Benoît Joseph Flaget, Jean Baptiste David, Ambroise Maréchal, Louis Guillaume DuBourg, and Jean Cheverus—thus found in Carroll their first exemplar of American episcopal leadership. All except Cheverus of Boston had, before becoming bishops, lived in Baltimore and its environs and were in frequent communication with Carroll. His policies became their precedents, his virtues their episcopal models.

Yet, because they were French and had been shaped as priests in French seminaries, their careers as bishops had something of a hybrid character. Because they possessed distinctly individual personalities, each man in his turn left his own mark on the diocese he headed. Of the six, this was peculiarly true of Louis William Valentine DuBourg, bishop of Louisiana and the Floridas from 1815 to 1826.

DuBourg was born in 1766 of French parents in the French colony of Saint-Domingue.[2] His father, a *Bordelais*, was Pierre DuBourg, Sieur de Rochemont, and his mother was Pierre's second wife, Marguerite Armand de Vogluzan. Because his mother died while he was still an infant, William was sent to Bordeaux to be educated. His early formal training took place at the noted Collège du Guyenne, or Guienne, where many distinguished French statesmen and diplomats were formed. Here DuBourg regularly outdistanced his companions, taking prizes on honors' day each year and receiving his *lauréat* in philosophy when he was only fourteen. In later years he recalled, "At Bordeaux, I undertook a classical course and an extended study of theology, in which I was presented with first honors." With the reluctant consent of his father and the encouragement of the archbishop of Bordeaux, Charles-François d'Aviau du Bois de Sanzay, DuBourg then went up to Paris to enter the Seminary of Saint-Sulpice.

In Paris he was placed with the Community of the Robertins, the house where the most brilliant and promising young ecclesiastics were united to pursue their first seminary studies. On completing his training in the Robertins, DuBourg on October 12, 1786, entered the division of the major seminary for those of nonnoble lineage.[3] In March 1790 he was ordained to the priesthood by Archbishop Antoine-Elea-nore-Léon de Clerc de Juigné.

Although DuBourg did not join the Company of Saint-Sulpice upon ordination, he was encouraged by his Sulpician seminary professors to start a boy's school intended to nurture possible vocations to the priesthood. It was at this school in Issy, now a suburb of Paris, that the future bishop discovered his special gift and love for attracting young minds to learning and good works. The Issy experiment in "Mr. DuBourg's House" was soon cut short by the violence of the 1790s, but it was remembered in the history of the minor seminary movement in France as a pioneering *petit séminaire* of the Old Regime.[4]

The arrest of King Louis XVI on August 10, 1792, and the ensuing search of the Sulpician houses in Issy rang the death knell of DuBourg's experiment. After hastily reporting to Saint-Sulpice in Paris the perilous situation in Issy, DuBourg headed south to Bordeaux to bid adieu to his relatives there. His destination lay farther south in Spain, where clergy and nobility alike were seeking refuge from the rabid hatred culminating in the September Massacres.

As one of the hundreds of nonjuring clergy flooding Spain, DuBourg remained there in exile for two years, chiefly under the protection of Archbishop Francisco Antonio Cardinal de Lorenzano of the Diocese of Toledo. Finding passage for the United States on an American vessel late in 1794, DuBourg sailed from Cadiz and arrived in Baltimore where some of his family from Saint-Domingue had fled the previous year, and where friends from Saint-Sulpice in Paris had been established since 1791.[5]

DuBourg's next eighteen years were spent in Maryland and involved activities that could have marked a lifetime's career for many another man. Certainly for DuBourg they were the years when his dual fame as educator and preacher came to full flower. Under the aegis of Francis Charles Nagot, his former seminary rector, DuBourg joined the Sulpicians soon after his arrival and became an urgent voice in the deliberations of Saint-Sulpice in Baltimore. Having learned fluent Spanish during the two years in Spain, he now learned excellent English with equal rapidity. Before two years had passed Nagot and Bishop Carroll agreed to DuBourg's appointment as head of Georgetown Academy in the District of Columbia, the first Catholic school for young men in the nation. Supported by Carroll and his colleagues among the former Jesuits of Maryland, Georgetown had opened its doors in 1791, the same year as the founding of the Sulpician seminary.

Like the seminary, the academy had languished during its first years, lacking both students and faculty in sufficient numbers. Under DuBourg's leadership new life was injected into the school on the Potomac. Georgetown flourished and its reputation grew. But so did its debts. By the end of 1798 disagreements between Georgetown and DuBourg brought the latter's resignation.[6] After an abortive attempt to start a Sulpician boy's school in Cuba in 1799, DuBourg returned to Baltimore to begin on Sulpician property Saint Mary's College for laymen. This school became his major concern for the next dozen years, and was to demonstrate his considerable talents as a teacher and administrator of Catholic education in the early nineteenth century.

Begun as an academy for French and Spanish boys chiefly from the Caribbean Islands, Saint Mary's was within four years attracting students and faculty from far and near and accepting students both Catholic and Protestant. As one New York parent put it, DuBourg's college ranked "among the first in this country" and was a place where one's son would be "perfectly safe among enlightened Catholics."[7] More important to religion, it was DuBourg's school that financed the first Catholic seminary in the United States during the critical years when its fate hung in the balance.

Yet, again, DuBourg's accomplishments left debts in his wake. For a third time, as at Issy and Georgetown earlier, his projects were abruptly interrupted before his expenditures could prove well advised. In the spring of 1812 Bishop Carroll named DuBourg administrator apostolic for the unwieldy and unruly jurisdiction that Carroll termed "the Church of N. Orleans and the diocese of Louisiana."[8] It was an appointment that culminated three years later on Sunday, September 24, 1815, with DuBourg's consecration in Rome as bishop of Louisiana and the Floridas.

On his departure for New Orleans in October 1812, DuBourg left a remarkable legacy to Catholic education in the eastern United States. In addition to setting Georgetown on the road to expansion and fame and founding Saint Mary's College in Baltimore, thus saving the seminary, he had also given the impetus to the founding of Mount Saint Mary's seminary and college in Emmitsburg, Maryland—a "cradle of bishops" in later years.[9] Last, his prescience brought about an educational work that was the forerunner of the American parochial school; for it was William DuBourg who first sensed the importance Elizabeth Bayley Seton was to have in the history of the church in her native land.

DuBourg had seen Elizabeth Seton first at the altar rail of Saint Peter's of Barclay Street, New York, in November 1806,[10] not long after her conversion from Anglicanism to Roman Catholicism. Three days later, en route to Boston, he was alreading conceiving a plan to bring her to Baltimore to start a school for girls, a plan he broached to Francis A. Matignon and John Cheverus on his arrival.[11] With the approval of these Boston clergy and subsequently that of Bishop Carroll, DuBourg arranged for the opening of a school on Paca Street, Baltimore, with Mrs. Seton at its head. "I remain more and more satisfied," he told her at this juncture, "that, even were you to fail in the attempt you are going to make, it is the will of God you should make it."[12]

When in Baltimore Elizabeth Seton perceived her religious vocation and founded the Sisters of Charity of Saint Joseph, Carroll at Nagot's recommendation appointed DuBourg the community's superior. It was DuBourg who supervised the community's move to Emmitsburg in the summer of 1809. Although DuBourg did not long act as the superior of the Seton foundation, as long as he remained in Baltimore he continued to supervise their temporal affairs. He never thereafter lost a lively interest in their endeavors, and as he left Louisiana in 1826 he confided in one of the sisters surviving Mother Seton that if anything could console him for the barrenness of his efforts as a bishop it was the success of the sisters. "Seven branches already!" he exclaimed. "God be forever blessed."[13] Not long before his own death he expressed a plea for prayers "not only from that sacred vale of St. Joseph, where I fostered the promising infant, yet in the cradle; but also from every quarter where it has extended its gigantic strides."[14]

In the summer of 1812, however, DuBourg's thoughts had been more immediately preoccupied with the difficulties he faced in going to Louisiana. The situation there was a far cry from the stability and order normally prevailing within the diocese of Baltimore. The territory had been formally transferred to the United States on December 20, 1803, but Carroll's jurisdiction over Louisiana remained tentative for some time afterward. Louisiana had known resident Spanish bishops since 1785, but the diocese created only four years after Carroll's own had been vacant since 1801. Until Rome acted to fill the vacancy, Louisiana was left a hotbed of rival claims to power by those on the scene in New Orleans.

One claimant, a Spanish Capuchin named Antonio de Sedella, but familiarly known in the city as Père Antoine, was ensconced in the cathedral parish of Saint Louis with the approval and fervent support of the lay trustees, the *marguilliers*. Although Carroll at Rome's request had named a vicar general for Louisiana in 1806, Sedella and the *marguilliers* resolutely clung to control of the church properties and as resolutely refused to recognize the authority of Carroll's appointee, a virtuous French priest from Upper Louisiana named Jean Olivier. Describing the balance of power in church affairs in New Orleans, Sedella asserted: "My pastoral ministry limits my functions uniquely to the administration of the Sacraments, etc. Everything which belongs to the material and temporal concerns of the Church and its council is within the competence of the *Marguilliers'* administration."[15] Content with this arrangement, the trustees petitioned both Carroll and Rome to make Sedella vicar general. Rome instead, in 1808, empowered Carroll to name an adminstrator apostolic with some episcopal authority.

The problem was to find a man who could make the authority conferred by Rome acceptable to an arrogant laity and an insubordinate clergy. In 1810 Carroll consulted with the new bishops during their stay in Baltimore, and they agreed that DuBourg was suited to the post.[16] At the time, however, he was in bad health, and his college was already shorthanded. It was not until February 1812 that Carroll recommended that since DuBourg was possessed of eminent talents as well as sound faith and morals and was highly commendable for his zeal, he appeared "to those with whom I advised, and to myself, a very fit person to restore order and ecclesiastical discipline, being a priest of firmness and activity, and acquainted with the three languages used there."[17] Both men understood that if and when this nomination reached the pope, who was a prisoner on French soil, DuBourg was being proposed for episcopacy. In the interim he would go to New Orleans as administrator apostolic.[18]

DuBourg arrived in New Orleans on December 2, 1812,[19] to administer a diocese that either remained oblivious to his coming or, worse, greeted him with outright hostility. From the start, his position in Louisiana differed from that of the other first bishops in the United States in three critical ways. He was sent without full power; although proposed for the see in 1812, he was not until 1815 consecrated bishop for this flock which questioned both Carroll's and his appointee's right to act in its ecclesiastical affairs. In the second place, Louisiana presented far greater ethnic complexity than did the original states, where an Anglo-American culture dominated. A third difference lay in the volatile political situation created by adding a vast area to the United States by cession, without either the consent or the conquest of its people, whose loyalties remained in question. After a tumultuous period of territorial government, Louisiana had become a state only six months before DuBourg set sail from Baltimore. It is not surprising that in giving consent to DuBourg's appointment his Sulpician superior in France had commented, "This diocese is more important and more delicate than any of your new dioceses."[20]

The people of Lower Louisiana where DuBourg began his ministry were an uneasy mingling of races, national origins, and tongues. Both Spain and France had explored the region in the sixteenth and seventeenth centuries; both had colonized in the eighteenth, with the French leading in permanent settlements for the first three decades and the Spanish, after 1762, dominating for the last four. By the time the United States assumed control of the territory, the French-speaking inhabitants were by far the largest part of the population, but church records in New Orleans were still kept in the Spanish language until 1828. In addition to these Latin strains there were the blacks, who constituted more than half the population of New Orleans; the Rhineland Germans, living upriver some twenty miles along the "German Coast"; native Americans like the Choctow Indians; and sprinklings of Swiss, Scots, Irish, and English. Naturally, all of these *Louisianais* remained suspicious of the Anglo-Americans recently come into power.[21]

Such ethnic diversity not only exacerbated the transitional difficulties of the successive governments of Louisiana, but it made DuBourg's position almost untenable. Whether French or Spanish, the old order had been based on a union of church and state; the new regime, which insisted upon a separation of civil and religious authority, was not easily assimilated, and in the city of New Orleans it was blatantly rejected. Rebellious priests and trustees time and again invoked notaries, mayors, governors, the state legislature, and even the Congress of the United States in their quarrels with each other and with DuBourg. When sending DuBourg to New Orleans, Bishop Carroll had furnished him with a letter of introduction to Governor William C. C. Claiborne and had urged him to make friends with both Claiborne and General James Wilkinson.[22] On the scene, DuBourg soon came to use local officials for the safe conduct of important messages to hostile clergy.

DuBourg's first thought had been to establish himself in the cathedral parish, but he quickly reconsidered this on perceiving how disagreeable it would prove. Père Antoine's many partisans regarded him as an unwelcome interloper, and even less palatable was the prospect of seeming to condone the scandal given by Sedella's two assistants. One of these, Claudio Thomas, a Dominican friar, had come to New Orleans from Saint-Domingue accompanied by his mulatto concubine-housekeeper and her children, and finding favor with Père Antoine had almost at once become first assistant at the cathedral. The other, Jean Koüne, also lived with his housekeeper, and the children who ate at table with him called him "Papa."

Jean Olivier had tried earlier to pry these assistants from Saint Louis by interdict, only to acknowledge his failure with this comment to Carroll: "These are the men who suit Père Antoine, who has no more faith in religion than they, and whose conduct in his youth was the same as theirs."[23] DuBourg realized that time alone could enable him to remedy evils that had been tolerated for so long. Meanwhile, he chose to live, as his good friend Louis Sibourd had been doing, near the chapel of the Ursulines, where he could celebrate mass in simplicity and decency when not appearing in the cathedral. Since Sedella showed no immediate inclination to flout DuBourg's authority, DuBourg believed his decision a prudent one. As he explained to Carroll:

> To it I owe certainly the external obedience which he professes to my authority, and the liberty which I enjoy of preaching and officiating when I please in the cathedral. . . . I have had two or three occasions of laying injunctions on him with which he has regularly complied. . . . More than this I could hardly expect.[24]

Instead of confronting Père Antoine with any rash show of belligerence, DuBourg applied his energies to establishing catechetical instructions and preaching in English on Sundays, when both Catholics and Protestants seemed to vie in eagerness to attend. He was happy doing what he did well, teaching and preaching, and he went at it with good will. He was not, however, deceived about the complexities attending his position, sizing it up for Carroll:

> It is impossible to convey in words the excess of dissolution and irreligion prevailing here through every class of society. The long silence of the pastors was in reality their great title to the pretended affection which they enjoyed. The people do not like to be disturbed in the possession of their wicked habits. Hence you may imagine that the new Preacher is not at all to their taste.[25]

His first year on the job ended, nevertheless, with a surge of optimism, for the New Orleans *Moniteur* announced from November 23 to December 7 that the Reverend William DuBourg would be preaching on alternating Sundays at the cathedral and convent chapel in the the interests of the New Orleans Society of Charity. If there was anything he enjoyed more than preaching, it was preaching for a charitable cause.

The inevitable showdown with Père Antoine came six months later with a fury even DuBourg could not have anticipated. It erupted in the summer of 1814, when DuBourg tried to remove Sedella's second assistant, Jean Koüne. DuBourg had temporarily left both assistants at Saint Louis Church out of absolute necessity. Until he could find their replacements, Thomas and Koüne were needed, particularly at the season of the epidemics of fever that ravaged the city every summer. When all his efforts to find substitutes failed, he determined to remove at least the more flagrantly dissolute of the priests, explaining to Carroll:

> I at last resolved on suspending him from the ministry of the altar and administering the sacraments in the Church, permitting him to continue in the exercise of all other functions such as visiting the sick, burying the dead & serving as subdeacon, etc.—and vainly admonishing in private, and with the joint advice of MM. Olivier and Sibourd, I sent him by constable a sentence of suspension . . . a copy of which was handed by the same officer to Father Antonio.[26]

To DuBourg's complete dismay, New Orleans rose in protest. The mayor, lawyers of renown, the city's most violent demagogues, even prostitutes rallied to Koüne's defense. They threatened DuBourg with suits for defamation of character, impugned his own morals, and announced that if necessary they would carry Koüne to the altar against any and all opposition. The justice of the peace, worn out from days of taking affidavits in Koüne's favor, begged to confer with DuBourg privately.

Some affidavits tended to clear Koüne of paternity, the justice argued. The priest would hire a room somewhere else for the housekeeper. In the interests of public tranquillity could not DuBourg revoke the sentence? Upon reflection, DuBourg agreed. The affidavits were furnished and Koüne in the presence of the justice of the peace gave his assurance of good faith. The crisis seemed over.

They reckoned without Père Antoine. Koüne's submission to DuBourg sent him into a towering rage. When the *Gazette de la Louisiane* announced that DuBourg would preach at the cathedral in favor of a collection for the poor, crowds gathered near the church door, where the mayor promised that if DuBourg tried to ascend to the pulpit he would be dragged away. Many of the mob came armed with stones. DuBourg told Carroll cryptically, "While the storm lasted in its full fury, I thought it my duty to face it, tho' attended with serious danger. The moment I saw it had subsided, I left town. . . ."[27] For the moment he had been routed.

His days in the schoolrooms of the East Coast had left him totally unprepared for the hot passions and turbulent behavior of this steamy port city. For a few days he thought he might never go back, that he might make his residence in a quiet settlement 150 miles up the Mississippi; but by nature he was a man of enormous activity, and he embarked meanwhile upon a visitation of the churches and clergy remote from the scene of his recent discomfiture. The woeful state of these churches and the infrequency of their rites roused all his customary fervor for building and enlarging and for exhorting laggards to a better life. He returned to New Orleans with renewed zeal.

The events of June had been trials too severe for his weakness, he confessed to Carroll, but now:

> The Almighty in his goodness has uplifted me from the ground and renewed my resolution to sacrifice all views of personal consolation to the interest of this most abandoned portion of his church. . . . He chose to humble me, by showing me my nothingness, in order to convince me that in Him alone must be placed all my dependence.[28]

He hoped he had learned that lesson.

Early in the year John Carroll had said, "Your and our great deficiency is that of needing many more zealous labourers in the Lord's vineyard."[29] At the root of every difficulty Louisiana presented lay the lack of a virtuous and vigorous clergy. The fact was that on the verge of entering his own fiftieth year, DuBourg was the youngest priest in his jurisdiction; only twelve older than he remained to serve a Catholic population of over 60,000. When these old men died, who was to succeed them? DuBourg must find recruits.

After consulting with Olivier and Sibourd, DuBourg decided to go abroad in the spring of 1815. The pope was back in Rome since Napoleon's abdication, and DuBourg would go there first; afterward, he would "ransack all of Catholic Europe." He issued a circular to the clergy of the diocese, asking for their support.[30]

DuBourg's European sojourn, which lasted for two years,[31] gave him advantages not shared by the other French bishops proposed by John Carroll. Until Ambrose Maréchal went to Rome briefly in 1822, DuBourg was the only one of the six who had been there, had been consecrated there, had seen at first hand the workings of the Sacred Congregations, had found a firm friend in the prefect of the Congregation of the Propaganda, had had a pope personally forward his episcopal projects,[32] and had enjoyed having his opinions on the church in America listened to with interest.

It was natural that DuBourg's views on American affairs should interest churchmen in Rome. He was the first of his rank to speak to the issues in person. Further, he was acquainted with the scope of the church in the United States and the Caribbean. As a college president he had traveled the East Coast extensively, and he knew students from both the mainland and the islands. He had assisted in New York City and at Carroll's request had mediated in controversies there; he was regularly in Philadelphia. He had lived in both Cuba and Martinique. His facility with languages, his fine intellect, and his persuasive manner made him an impressive reporter. His reception in Rome encouraged him later as a bishop on the frontier to write frankly and spiritedly of his problems and the solutions he recommended to Rome.

His Roman experiences left DuBourg with an undeviating loyalty to the papacy and personal affection for Pius VII. Through Cardinal Lorenzo Litta DuBourg learned that Propanganda's view of controversies in the mission churches was very guarded; that all sides must be heard, the laity as well as the clergy, the priests as well as the bishops. "It belongs to us," Litta instructed him, "to guard with care that the Church sustain no damage, and it is sometimes necessary to bend ordinary rules to prevent people from apostatizing."[33] It was advice DuBourg would ponder on his return to New Orleans.

As a result of his European travels generally, DuBourg came to develop lasting connections in many places with people to whom he could appeal for support. In Italy he went south to Naples and north to Milan; in France he had success in Montpellier, Bordeaux, Lyon, and Paris; in Flanders under the aegis of the bishop of Gand he quickly collected ten volunteers. In the end the most effective and lasting support for DuBourg's mission came from Lyon, where a widow and her son whom DuBourg had once befriended in Baltimore began a regular collection of funds for Louisiana. This beginning in 1816 was later consolidated with other mission-aid efforts to become the Society for the Propagation of the Faith. In 1816, however, the activity of the Widow Petit and her son Didier Petit, supported by Jean Cholleton, who headed the Sulpician seminary in Lyon, was specifically directed toward DuBourg's diocese.[34]

DuBourg's energetic canvass produced astonishing results. In June 1816 he sent off from Bordeaux thirteen men to await further orders in Kentucky; a year later another thirty accompanied DuBourg to Baltimore; not long after their arrival in Missouri another dozen followed at varying intervals from Italy and France. Among these recruits were priests, seminarians, Christian Brothers, and workingmen. Most important, from the bishop's view, were the two priests intended for founding a seminary.[35] For the education of women DuBourg sought Ursulines in Montpellier and Lyon to augment the New Orleans convent, while from Paris he secured for Upper Louisiana the Religious of the Sacred Heart led by Philippine Duchesne to found the first house of that order in the United States.

It seems unlikely that any other bishop ever led such an army of eager recruits to toil in his vineyards. Certainly in the early nineteenth century no other bishop aroused in western Europe such excited interest in and continuing devotion to the mission church in the United States. Félicité de Lamennais saw in DuBourg a saint whom the Old World reluctantly ceded to the New, a man not soon to be forgotten.[36] Indeed, a decade later in the Chamber of Deputies Denis Frayssinous, bishop of Hermopolis, interrupted a passionate defense of the Society for the Propagation of the Faith to invoke the name of Louisiana and its bishop, that "man of very rare spirit and capacity."[37] The triumphal tour of Bishop Flaget two years after DuBourg's death in 1833 was only a four-year reprise of European fascination with the American frontier introduced by the bishop of Louisiana on the first "begging tour" made by the American hierarchy.

The diocese DuBourg's missioners were to serve was extensive enough to absorb them all. At the time of DuBourg's consecration in Rome in 1815, the Congregation of the Propaganda retained the Spanish name for this jurisdiction: Diocese of Louisiana and the Floridas, a name that comprehended uncertainty regarding both regions, since the American boundaries of these territories were not fixed until after DuBourg reached his diocese in 1818. In addition, the diocese was also understood in Rome to include, for the time being, the Illinois and Mississippi territories on the eastern side of the Mississippi River.[38]

Episcopal visitations of this vast jurisdiction were perforce hazardous and exhausting, up and down rivers in primitive craft experimenting with steam, overland on horseback over rough roads or none at all, through bogs, bayous, and canebrake, enduring weather freezing in the north or steamy in the fetid and fever-breeding coasts of the Gulf of Mexico. DuBourg's years as administrator had made him familiar with the climate of Lower Louisiana; as bishop he would become inured to the icy blasts of Upper Louisiana while making his headquarters in Saint Louis.

DuBourg chose Missouri with Rome's consent and with good reason. During his absence in Europe Sedella and the *marguilliers* had obtained from the state legislature an act of incorporation placing all of the church's temporalities under their control. Sedella had boasted that they would have nothing to do with popes or bishops of the pope's making. Documents from Rome announcing DuBourg's authority were openly ridiculed in noisy cafés. DuBourg justified his decision: "When a general wishes to conquer a country he does not always stop to besiege fortified cities lest this should weaken his army and hamper at every step the progress of the campaign."[39] The vigorous and virtuous young recruits assigned to New Orleans under Louis Sibourd's direction would soon offset the scandals of the old Spanish clergy of that city.

Arriving in Saint Louis, where he was installed on January 5, 1818, Bishop DuBourg, with characteristic impetuosity, immediately set in motion four major projects: a church to replace the "miserable log cabin open to every wind," which had seen no resident pastor for years; a seminary where his Vincentian priests would nurture a native clergy; a convent for Philippine Duchesne and the Sacred Heart nuns; and a school for boys in Saint Louis. His determination succeeded. On March 29, the cornerstone of the new cathedral was laid; by April 22 workmen were summoned to begin the seminary in Perryville; on September 7, DuBourg on horseback conducted the carriage of the Religious of the Sacred Heart to the neat little house in Saint Charles, and on September 14 the bishop was composing the prospectus for the first school for Catholic girls west of the Mississippi River; on November 16 an academy for young gentlemen opened under the direction of four priests and "under the superintendence of the Right Rev. Bishop."[40]

To be sure, these were only the first stages of works whose individual sites, timetables, and degrees of success would subsequently vary. But they were begun, and in a year of inexorable poverty. The bishop consoled himself and all his workers with the words he sent Duchesne at the close of 1818: "Beginnings, above all in a new country, still undeveloped, are always more harsh."[41]

The progress of religion in upper Louisiana by 1820 was such that DuBourg prepared to visit New Orleans and the other parishes along the way. He was less ebullient than usual, uncertain of his reception in Lower Louisiana and even more uncertain about his wisdom in bringing so many worthy workers to his diocese. Already both the saintly men he had intended for his seminary were in their graves— Louis Bighi in New Orleans and Felix De Andreis in Saint Louis. Philippine Duchesne had almost died that October, and one of her co-workers was bedridden for more than a month with a broken leg. As Duchesne was wont to say, it was a country to discourage people.

DuBourg's reception downriver was beyond his rosiest dreams, both in the frontier churches along the way and in New Orleans itself. Bertrand Martial from Bordeaux was successfully running a boy's school in the city, and Louis Moni had so ingratiated himself at the cathedral that Sedella had made him first assistant. DuBourg found Père Antoine and Louis Sibourd together with a crowd of citizens waiting to greet him outside the city. Christmas Eve the church was crowded at his entrance and all the clergy came to meet him at the door. "Tears flowed on everyone's part at the comparison of the past with the present." The Ursulines, overjoyed at the sight of their "most illustrious bishop," voted that, on moving to a larger convent outside the city, they would give DuBourg their old one for an episcopal palace.[42]

In his report to Propaganda on February 24, 1821, DuBourg said that the tone of the whole city permitted him to celebrate publicly a synod where a year before merely to have shown himself would have been extremely dangerous.[43] The Synod of 1821, although unrecognized in the history of the diocese of New Orleans, was the first consultation of the clergy on diocesan discipline and regulations by a bishop west of the Mississippi. It consisted of twenty priests of Lower Louisiana who, during five days of deliberation, unanimously manifested their obedience to their bishop and their zeal for upholding ecclesiastical discipline. They further agreed that on Christmas day a collection would be taken up in Lower Louisiana for the benefit of the Perryville seminary, that the number of feastdays prevailing in Baltimore applied in Louisiana, and that the Spanish custom of eating meat on Saturdays still prevailed. DuBourg left New Orleans with a lighter heart.[44]

His return to Saint Louis dispelled some of this optimism. The Panic of 1819 had left the church with a debt the impoverished congregation could not retire, and the more prosperous trustees made themselves personally responsible for it by means of a mortgage on the church property. Missouri trustees had no desire to name their clergy or nominate their bishop, as had the New Orleans *marguilliers*, but they were determined to get their money and resorted to selling four blocks of the church land. But this still did not suffice, and DuBourg's old enemy, debt, hung like a cloud over his future in Upper Louisiana.

DuBourg meanwhile, like the other American prelates, had concerns beyond his own see. On the issues of common interest to the church in the United States, DuBourg, Flaget, and David—through long friendship, past collaboration in Baltimore, and a coincidence of episcopal interests beyond the Appalachian Mountains—tended to stand together. Maréchal in Baltimore found his strongest ally in Cheverus of Boston. All, however, were equally invited by Rome to give their opinions on American affairs and to recommend men to fill vacant American sees. All on occasion felt free to criticize each other to Rome and interfere in each other's affairs.

Because of DuBourg's anomalous position as the only bishop not a suffragan of the archbishop of Baltimore, the relations between Maréchal and DuBourg were often strained. Maréchal bitterly resented DuBourg's wooing the Belgian Jesuits away from Maryland.[45] DuBourg was outraged by Maréchal's attempt to place the rector of

DuBourg's seminary in charge of the proposed Vicariate of Alabama and Mississippi in 1822,[46] and was further angered when Maréchal succeeded in having the head of DuBourg's school for boys in New Orleans named administrator apostolic of Alabama and Florida.[47]

Like all the other bishops, DuBourg recommended to Rome his own preferences for jurisdictions old and new. The two names he proposed most often for high office were those of Benedict Fenwick, S.J., and Simon Gabriel Bruté, S.S.[48] As for new dioceses, he joined Flaget and David in recommending that Cincinnati and Detroit be cut from the Northwest Territory to relieve Flaget's burdens there. When Maréchal countered with Cincinnati and Saint Louis, Rome created only one new diocese in 1821, in Ohio at Cincinnati. The bishops spent the next four years in abortive proposing and counterproposing new dioceses, accompanied by the game of nominating suitable candidates from any diocese not one's own.

DuBourg perceived the absurdity of so many conflicting views going to Rome. He recalled that in 1817 when he had criticized to Cardinal Litta Rome's handling of vacant sees, Litta had retorted that the Holy See intended to adhere to the advice of the bishops "at least if it is not forced to act otherwise by reason of their disagreement, or silence, or for another urgent reason."[49] The telling phrase was "by reason of their disagreement." Edward Fenwick, S.J., had been consecrated for Cincinnati only after Maréchal came to agree upon a man Flaget, David, and DuBourg had recommended earlier for Ohio.

DuBourg had definite thoughts on the episcopate. He had always relished the words of Saint Cyprian, *Episcopatus est in solidum.* He believed that in all that consolidates religion, and turns to the greatest glory of the common Master, bishops were and ought to be involved in each other's undertakings. "The episcopate is one," he told Maréchal in 1821, "as is the faith. Unhappy the man who isolates himself from the great interest which ought to unite us all in the same cause."[50] It was a subject DuBourg mulled over during long rides about his diocese.

In 1825, on a harrowing visitation of Louisiana's western wilderness, he decided to take the initiative and address the hierarchy and Propaganda on the nomination of American bishops. From Natchitoches on October 4, 1825, he sent out a letter containing his own suggestions, asking for reactions to these suggestions, and announcing that he was sending his letter to Rome. He believed, he wrote, that Rome wished to proceed in these nominations only "upon the joint suffrages of the American Bishops." The difficulty was in carrying out Rome's wish. It certainly had not worked with each bishop privately sending his own nominations. These isolated opinions, DuBourg urged, only perplexed Propaganda, particularly since each candidate could conceivably get only one vote, "the consequence of which must be an indefinite protraction in the appointments, the greatest calamity that can befall our infant churches."

He then made proposals for accelerating the filling of vacant sees. He closed his letter saying:

> Recollecting the word of St. Cyprian, *Episcopatus est in solidum*, which is particularly enforced in the application made to each of us by the Holy See, I have concluded that every member of the Episcopal body is strictly indebted to all of his Brethren for a candid disclosure of all his own views toward the consolidation and advancement of the common interest.[51]

The plan DuBourg favored as practicable was the one John Carroll had used when Bishop Egan of Philadelpia died in 1814. Carroll had sought the recommendations of all the bishops; the candidates were narrowed down to two; everyone had been notified; and then the names were forwarded to Rome. The western bishops agreed that such a polling was advisable, with one set of recommendations sent by the American hierarchy, but it was only after Maréchal's death that the method of nominating American bishops was finally worked out.[52]

As far as Louisiana was concerned, DuBourg was determined that its future should not be endangered by wrangling over his successor. He was in Saint Louis only a year when when he asserted: "The condition of my diocese is such that should I die before having provided for the succession . . . it would inevitably fall back into chaos."[53] He needed a young, strong coadjutor, he insisted, and this need became the leitmotiv of his Roman correspondence for the next four years.[54] In 1823 he finally was granted Joseph Rosati, C.M., who was everything DuBourg desired and proved a splendid successor after 1826.

With his coadjutor Rosati in charge in Upper Louisiana and the old Ursuline convent available for his residence in New Orleans, DuBourg returned there for the rest of his American episcopacy. He remodeled the convent into bishop's quarters and a college for young men, and then turned his energies to his domain. By 1826 all of the twenty parishes of Lower Louisiana except two were served by clergy the bishop had provided.[55] Some were newly created by DuBourg; in others miserable old wooden churches were replaced by larger brick ones. The one thing sadly lacking, from DuBourg's view, was a seminary for the South. In spite of his importunings, the Vincentians could not spare him men for that project until their own ranks were enlarged.

The other religious groups were extending their work. The Jesuits at Florissant in Missouri were educating Indian boys. Madame Duchesne's women had three houses, and she herself was impatient to begin educating Indian girls. A little band of Sisters of Loretto, whom DuBourg had drawn from Kentucky, were working wonders near the Barrens. Rosati was sending missionaries to the Creole Catholics and Indians in Arkansas. It should have been a time for a bishop to rest on his laurels, but such was not DuBourg's destiny.

Once again a hue and cry was raised against him, and again his episcopal authority was challenged. The personal attack came from the *marguilliers*, who charged the bishop with driving the Ursulines out of the city in order to seize their convent; his authority was further flouted by a church on the "German Coast" which, during DuBourg's absence on an episcopal visitation, had installed an immigrant Spaniard as pastor and refused to give him up. The calumnies in the press surpassed those of ten years before; the disturbances were even more widespread. As one of DuBourg's priests told Propaganda: "In this city, this sewer of all vice and refuse of all that is worst on earth, the prejudice against him is so strong that in spite of all his sacrifices and all his exalted ability, he could not have effected any good here. . . . You cannot imagine all the abominations which fill the newspapers."[56]

To the bishop it was clear that he was the stumbling block. Even the name DuBourg was anathema. The good he wished to accomplish would always be frustrated by the opposition he unwittingly roused. To Pope Leo XII he wrote: "I see that the hatred which, right or wrong, from the very beginning of my administration, inspired the various classes of our population against me, will never die out, and that, whatever I do, the progress of religion will be thwarted." His coadjutor, on the other hand, was "most welcome to all the clergy and . . . not hated by any of the laymen; by him the Church will certainly be well provided."[57] More than the vilification of himself, it was the disdain for the episcopacy that wounded most deeply. He asked Rome to accept his resignation. On July 3, 1826, the pope consented. On August 13, 1826, King Charles X of France signed an ordinance naming Louis-Guillaume DuBourg to the Diocese of Montauban.[58]

DuBourg's last seven years were spent in France as bishop of Montauban and archbishop of Besançon. Yet to the end of his life his love for his first diocese persisted. On his death his body was interred in the *Caveau des Archevêques* in the Cathédral de Saint-Jean in Besançon, but his heart was sent at his request to New Orleans, the city that had twice rejected him, where it reposes in the mortuary chapel of the Ursulines, who remained his friends to the end.

Although DuBourg died virtually penniless, he left a remarkable legacy to the church in the United States. He gave tremendous impetus to Catholic education both east and west of the Mississippi—schools for men and women in Maryland, and in Missouri Saint Mary's Seminary for priests at the Barrens, Saint Regis Seminary for Indian boys in Florissant, and the university and library in Saint Louis. In both Upper and Lower Louisiana the Religious of the Sacred Heart educated young women. The infant Catholic institutions and parishes beyond the Mississippi were made possible because of his European recruits.

DuBourg possessed a gift for selecting the right people for his purposes and relied on them to succeed on their own. Elizabeth Seton, Joseph Rosati, Philippine Duchesne, Antoine Blanc, Eugénie Audé, Charles Van Quickenborne—all were spurred by his optimism and ebullience to efforts beyond their imaginings. Even the volunteer who deceived DuBourg and disgraced himself in Rome, Angelo Inglesi, benefited the church. In 1822 he sent Louisiana six valuable recruits, among them a future bishop of New Orleans,[59] and that same year in Lyon it was Inglesi's eloquence that produced the merger of three separate plans into the Society for the Propagation of the Faith, the society that forthwith sent two-thirds of its money to Louisiana and Kentucky.[60]

Those who worked with DuBourg over the months and years knew his spiritual resources, his love for the Society of Saint Sulpice, his resilience in the face of repeated setbacks, his insistence on working ever harder—instead of grieving hopelessly—when circumstances or his own nature brought defeat, and above all, his confidence in God. Amid the pervading poverty of his episcopacy he refused to be cast down by debt. When new recruits appeared from Europe he would say: "I wished prudently to have funds before looking for men, but here the men are, come before the funds. It's God's way of disconcerting the plans of our poor human prudence; may His will be done!" God had sent them; He would not let them starve.[61]

Perhaps Louis William DuBourg still has something to say to bishops in the United States: in his willingness to "ransack" other continents for workers needed in American parishes, in his advocacy of Saint Cyprian's *Episcopatus est in solidum*, and in his fealty to the papacy as the friend—not the antagonist—of the church in the United States. In his own time he proved to be, as John Carroll had predicted in his last word on the subject, "the man best suited for the episcopal see in Louisiana."[62]

CHAPTER
3
Benedict Joseph Flaget: First Bishop of the West

Clyde F. Crews

*B*enedict Joseph Flaget (1763–1850), exile from the French Revolution, arrived on American shores as a young priest only twenty-eight years of age. The United States that he entered in 1792 was in its own youth, with George Washington still in his first term of office as president. In a very real sense, the young cleric and the new nation matured together. By the time of his death as bishop of Louisville at age eighty-six, Flaget had served as major actor in the drama by which Catholicism became a naturalized corporate citizen on the American scene. As Herman Schauinger was to phrase it: "Under [Flaget's] leadership, Catholicism had become respectable in the Western democracy."[1]

As first bishop of the West, at Bardstown, Kentucky, this French prelate not only would set in place a climate of devotion and discipline on the frontier but he would also initiate major structures of ecclesial life, both for his own initially immense diocese and for Catholicism in the Middle West and Upper South. He left behind him a litany of churches and institutions that have shaped theologies, spiritualities, and lives. "It is a litany," John Tracy Ellis has written of the early Kentucky experience, "that arouses in the minds and hearts of informed American Catholics thousands of miles removed, a glow of grateful remembrances."[2]

Flaget's lifework, the forming of a Catholic people in a wilderness largely unacquainted with the ancient faith, was by turns for him a torture and a consolation. One colleague had called the man "the poorest bishop in the Christian world."[3] Flaget himself spoke of the episcopacy as a life full of thorns and once lamented, "The weight of the miter is crushing me."[4] It is not by accident that his spirituality was deeply associated in his own mind with the reality of the cross. He reminded a fellow missionary on one occasion that they were both serving a "crucified God" and referred to himself at times in his work as meeting "croix sur la croix"—cross upon cross.[5] Yet, professional and personal satisfactions were also aplenty in this long life, as his diaries and letters demonstrate.

To this day, the person of Benedict Flaget is held in the greatest reverence in Kentucky, where his status is perhaps best described as that of an uncanonized saint. His burial place, beneath the altar of the Louisville cathedral, remains a place of occasional pilgrimage, and several institutions in the archdiocese today still carry the revered name: a hospital, a spirituality center—even a boy scout trail. The bishop's most recent French biographer has compared the man to the great Jesuit missionary saint Francis Xavier.[6]

In order to assess the life, ministry, and career of this landmark figure within early nineteenth century American Catholicism, I will concentrate on five areas: (1) the frontier church; (2) the Flaget personality; (3) priorities and accomplishments; (4) difficulties and manner of administration; and (5) the impact of his career.

THE CHURCH ON THE KENTUCKY FRONTIER

Just as Kentucky's star was the first western one to appear in the American flag when it entered the Union in 1792, so the diocese of Bardstown was to be the first western area of ecclesial jurisdiction for American Catholicism. The primal see had been established at Baltimore, in 1789, and another see was established at New Orleans in 1793. When Baltimore was named a metropolitan see and the suffragan dioceses of New York, Philadelphia, Boston, and Bardstown were added in 1808, the Kentucky town thereby became the center of the first inland diocese of the nation.[7]

When the diocese was constituted, the area of central Kentucky had already been the scene of twenty-five years of Catholic life and development. Of this transplant from the Maryland Catholic community historian John Boles has written:

> Of all the stories of the religious groups that helped tame frontier Kentucky, that of the Catholic settlers and priests is perhaps the most un-

expected and certainly the most remarkable. As Baltimore was the mother of the Catholic Church in America, so was Bardstown, Kentucky, the mother of the Catholic Church west of the Appalachians.[8]

The success of these settlements in what Alistair Cooke has called "the first American West" was all the more notable in that of all the faiths to arrive in the wilderness in the late eighteenth century, Catholicism would have seemed least likely to endure.[9]

The frontier suggested vast open spaces, individualism, and adaptability. Catholicism, at least in the popular mind, was more properly thought to be defined in terms of urbanity, authoritarianism, and disciplined tradition. Yet, by some surprising chemistry, Catholicism proved to be resilient, even flourishing, on the frontier. The ancient faith would help to bring order, education, and classical and humane values to the West, even as Catholicism itself was being subtly shaped by the immense forces of the new nation.[10]

Individual Catholics had entered Kentucky—a part of Virginia until 1792—as early as 1775. But it was to be a decade later, while Americans still chafed under the Articles of Confederation and Kentucky agitated Virginia for its own independence, that the first "colony" or grouping of Maryland settlers arrived in the vicinity of Bardstown.

These first families came from a Maryland-British tradition that combined reverence for the clergy with a strong streak of lay initiative, as well as religious tolerance and democratic pluralism. When much of the early ecclesiastical leadership of Kentucky turned out to be French and more rigorously clerical and disciplined in mentality, the stage was set for many of the strains that marked Kentucky's early Catholic history. Meanwhile, the very earliest Catholic parishes were formed along the creekways of the inner part of the state by the laity themselves. They petitioned Bishop John Carroll for a cleric in their midst, and until one appeared they sustained their religious life by a faithfulness to their bibles, their prayerbooks, and their own inner resources.[11]

The first priest who would come to the new state and remain for a long duration was Stephen Badin (1768–1853), the first priest ordained in the United States. A rigorist in moral issues, like his later companion Charles Nerinckx (1761–1824), Badin would set up a network of mass-stations in private homes which he would visit on a regular weekly basis. He would also, from his home at "Priestland" (now the Motherhouse grounds of the Sisters of Loretto), administrate Catholic affairs as Carroll's vicar general.

Disputes were common fare in that first quarter-century between initial settlement and establishment of the diocese. The laity found their teeth set on edge by the severity of moral tone of the French clerics, especially in such areas as their prohibition of dancing and their sometimes harsh confessional penances. When the Dominican Fathers arrived in the area in 1805, marking out their first American foundation, they were immediately perceived as possessed of a more moderate, British style of religious praxis.[12]

Tensions would also occasionally run high over control of finances, the holding of title deeds to parishes, and the political disposition of a people who were a democratic counterpoint to Badin's federalist tendencies. In the closing days of Kentucky's status as an outpost of the Baltimore church, a ferocious argument had broken out between Badin and several parishioners over his manner of administration. Several prominent families had been busy with letters and petitions to Baltimore; a leader in this angry group was the revered and highly literate Grace Newton Simpson, for whom Badin reserved the epithet "Amazon." Simpson in particular had made appeal to Carroll to spare Kentucky from having the likes of a Badin as its first bishop. When Flaget did, in fact, make his journey west, it was without the financial assistance of his congregations.[13] When the new prelate entered his diocese in the summer of 1811, he found a people somewhat pacified and less agitated than they had sometime been; but he was not entering an area that had known only amity, piety, and unclouded priest-laity relationships.

THE FLAGET PERSONALITY: A TROUBLED HOLINESS

Benedict Joseph Flaget had been a child born to woe, having entered the world November 7, 1763, in the Auvergne region of France. His father had died shortly before his birth, and his mother died about two years after. The orphan lad was raised by an aunt for whom he always cherished tender feelings, and in whose home he maintained, both as a lad and as an old man, that he had seen a vision of his deceased mother. The young boy had two stepsisters by his father's first marriage, as well as two brothers, one of whom would become a wealthy notary and the other a priest like himself.[14]

At about the age of seventeen Flaget became a university student at Clermont, and in the week of his twentieth birthday he entered the seminary to study for the priesthood as a Sulpician priest. After ordination in 1788, he took up teaching duties in dogmatic theology at Sulpician seminaries in Nantes and Angers. He would follow with great interest the writing and intellectual careers of such French intellectuals as De Maistre, Chateaubriand, and Lamennais, even in later years, when he was much concerned with duties that kept him from the academic life.[15]

With the outbreak of the darker side of the French Revolution, the young cleric repaired to his family home for safety and soon determined on service in the American missions as the best manner for carrying out a ministry not afforded to him in his native land. Accordingly, he sailed from Bordeaux in January 1792. His traveling companions on this voyage included John Baptist David and Stephen Badin, both of whom were destined to be colleagues in later years in Kentucky. The group sailed into Philadelphia March 26, 1792, and reached Baltimore three days later.

Flaget was first sent by Bishop Carroll to the mission of Vincennes in Indiana, returning east in 1795 to teach French and geography at Georgetown in Washington. Next he moved on to Havana in 1798, where he served for three years as teacher and tutor. He returned to teach at Saint Mary's Seminary in Baltimore in 1801, and there he would remain, through his own late thirties and early forties, until word of his appointment as bishop arrived in 1808. By the papal brief *Ex Debito Pastoralis* of April 8, 1808, the diocese of Bardstown was established, along with the three other sees of the Northeast. Then began an elaborate attempt by the forty-five-year-old Flaget to turn aside from his appointment as Kentucky's first bishop. He even repaired to Paris to speak to his Sulpician superior James Andrew Embry on the subject. There he was told that he should already be in his new diocese and was given needles and a cookbook as a traveling gift.

Bishop-elect Flaget departed the port of Bordeaux once again April 10, 1810. And once more he sailed with companions destined to have a part in the history of Catholicism in the Ohio Valley: Simon Bruté (1779–1839), who would become first bishop of Vincennes, and Guy Chabrat (1787–1868), who would serve as Flaget's own coadjutor in afteryears. Flaget was consecrated at Saint Patrick's Church, Fells Point, Baltimore, on November 4, 1810. Friends in Baltimore at last having raised travel funds, the new prelate set out for Pittsburgh in the spring, and from there began the descent of the Ohio River on May 11, 1811. This time Flaget was accompanied by David, three seminarians, and a French Canadian priest. Even on board the flatboat, seminary exercises and lessons were begun by David, so that it could truly be said that the first seminary of the West, Saint Thomas of Kentucky, had its beginning on the great inland waterway that is the Ohio River.

The party arrived at Louisville June 4. At the city wharf, Nerinckx met the group and escorted them to Bardstown where they arrived with some degree of state and were met with a significant outpouring of devotion. Flaget took up residence at Priestland, also by this time called Saint Stephen's, holding there the first diocesan clerical conference February 20, 1812.[16] In the summer of 1812, he moved south of Bardstown to Saint Thomas Farm, the second cradle of Kentucky Catholicism. Here the new bishop would remain until 1819, when Saint Joseph's Cathedral and his new residence were completed in the city of Bardstown proper.

The new diocese, of course, was vast, including all of Kentucky and Tennessee. Additionally, the Northwest Territory was under Flaget's jurisdiction, so that such later major centers as Chicago, Detroit, Indianapolis, and Cincinnati all looked to Flaget as their spiritual leader. At the time of the prelate's arrival, he had in Kentucky six functioning priests: Badin, Nerinckx, and four Dominicans. In his other territories, he could count only three more clerics. By the prelate's own estimation, there were by 1810 some 16,000 Catholics in Kentucky and ten established churches.[17]

The demographics and personnel figures made it clear that Flaget would have to become a deeply involved pastoral bishop. From his diaries that remain, it becomes very clear that the greatest amount of the new prelate's time was spent in riding horseback in ministry to his people. During a typical month from this period, January 1814, entries from Flaget's own hand speak tellingly of his work:

Jan. 1 After hearing confessions all morning, I celebrated Mass at Holy Cross until 3:00 p.m.

Jan. 2 I went to St. Charles. Confessions, Mass, sermons until 2:00 p.m.

Jan. 6 Discontented, sad, troubled.

Jan. 8 Visited a sick drunkard. I made him ask pardon publicly.

Jan. 10 Assembled the people of St. Charles to discuss the priest's establishment. Great difficulties to overcome.

Jan. 16 At Loretto, preached. Confessions until noon. Few persons. Feeble hope of success in affairs of the Church. Great confidence in God.

Jan. 18 At the seminary. Correspondence. Theology. The seminarians seem more poised and happy. May it be given me to see them as fervent as angels.

Jan. 20 Left for St. Stephen. Mr. Badin informed me of the news of the defeat of Bonaparte.

Jan. 26 Mr. Hirt's negress died without the sacraments. Could be my fault. Pardon me, Lord. My heart is broken with doubts.

Jan. 30 Confessions from 7 a.m. until noon. Mass. Instructions until 2:30. Dinner at 3:30. Confessions until 8:00. The day is full as to time,

but has the work been well done? Vanity, impatience, careless-
ness—have these not carried [off] the greater part of the merit?
I tremble that even my good deeds will turn to my confusion.[18]

On the frontier, often a place of isolation and desperate loneliness,
the sacrament of confession represented a specially intimate and intense moment of religious experience for Catholic sensibility. Flaget
and his clerical companions responded by a generous donation of their
time and energies to the administration of the sacrament. Nor were
the ministrations confined within the Bardstown area. As an alert
missionary, the Bardstown bishop journeyed throughout the vast territories of his responsibility. In the spring of 1814, for example, he
went to visit at Vincennes, and then into Illinois and Missouri. This
journey of nearly one thousand miles consumed six months. In 1817
he traveled to Saint Louis to help prepare the city for the installation
of its bishop, William DuBourg. The spring of 1818 found Flaget
trekking through the northern missions of Michigan and into Canada,
a missionary journey that was over a year in length. The first visitation
of Tennessee occurred in 1821.[19]

Of the many facets of the fascinating man Flaget that are revealed
in the self-accounting of his journeys, two in particular are worthy
of special remark: (1) a nature-mysticism worthy of the spirit of Francis of Assisi, and (2) a selflessness in ministrations, even and especially
when his own life was in peril. It comes as no particular surprise to
learn that some of Flaget's most constant spiritual reading was in
Butler's *Lives of the Saints*.[20]

On June 24, 1818, the first bishop of the West stood gazing at Ni-
agara Falls. "These falls," he wrote, "present the most grand and sub-
lime spectacle which a mortal can contemplate on earth." This sentiment about natural beauty came from a man who grew up,
incidentally, in the land of some of the most magnificent of cathedrals
and monasteries. Having gazed at the flow of waters, his mind at
once turned to an imagery of the torrents of divine grace longing to
flow forth on the planet earth.[21] On the same voyage to the north,
Flaget stood again in awe, this time at the Saint Lawrence River, and
recorded these words: "O God how good and admirable are thy works!
Grant that they may be for me a book in which I may read thy goodness."[22] One late fall morning in 1821, he had risen early for a walk.
There, as he related in a letter to his brother, he was struck by "the
grand spectacle which nature presents when the sun first begins to
illumine and embellish it with his rays." But not content with sky
gazing, the bishop was fascinated with a mother hen who came by,
solicitously caring for her chicks. Studying in some detail the activity
of the mother, his thoughts turned to God's similar care for the human
family.[23]

Flaget's personal care for his own "family" was as wide as it was intense. Especially during the visitations of the cholera, that deadly scourge of the frontier, Flaget was found in the forefront of those who went into places of contagion to bring not only spiritual solace but practical nursing skills as well. When the bishop learned that one of his young priests, Philip Hosten, first resident priest at Louisville, had been attacked by the disease in the autumn of 1821, he went at once to his side. There he nursed the young man for eight days. "He gave up his beautiful soul in my arms, and I closed his eyes," Flaget would relate. "He died leaving all his wealth—some poor clothes and forty cents." The bishop attempted to preach at the young man's funeral but was overcome by weeping.[24] Again in 1833 the cholera struck the West. Flaget was now nearing seventy; but when informed that a Protestant family near Bardstown had been gravely afflicted, and that neighbors feared to enter the property, he went at once to care for the family, along with sisters from Nazareth and Loretto. When he arrived, he found one servant, whom he knelt to comfort, lying on the floor between two corpses. Later that same year, the bishop himself contracted the malady and nearly died.[25]

Death was not particularly fearsome to Flaget. When he learned of the demise of two of his seminarians, Flaget had expressed his sense of sorrow and loss. And yet, he added tersely: "It excites my envy more than my grief."[26] This man who was remembered for "tenderness of expression" and an "air of goodness,"[27] discovered in his own heart an ongoing oscillation between hope and desolation. "My God," he once wrote, "how virtue is becoming rare."[28] Late in his life he had written to Archbishop Eccleston at Baltimore, "My heart is in desolation and my head is absolutely empty."[29] Nor was this just the sentiment of an older man pained by many personal ills, though these were his lot also. The words "ma nullité"—my nothingness—are to be found often throughout the diaries. As early as 1811 he had written to his good friend Bruté:

> As for me, when I examine my conscience, I see only weakness and misery . . . my head is in a veritable whirl, or rather in unintelligible chaos. . . . The details of administration dry up my heart. I often speak of God. I try to inspire all who come to me with love of Him, but I speak coldly because I love only feebly.[30]

Flaget was sustained in the midst of his inner torments by an unswerving spiritual purpose: "God is very good. I desire to love God and make him loved."[31] This true north point on his own spiritual compass was nurtured by traditional prayers and pieties, as well as by the sacramental life. And yet, it was not prayer alone that buoyed up the spirits and energies of Benedict Joseph Flaget. He had two

other wells from which he learned to draw steadily: one was the times
of rest and quiet he could take for himself, usually at the seminary
of Saint Thomas. The other was a myriad of friendships, encompassing
the great, like George Rogers Clark and Henry Clay, as well as more
ordinary people, clerical and lay, male and female, Catholic and Protestant. Especially in his friendships with such intimates as David and
Bruté, there were to be found tender regard and kindly sensibility.
Flaget kept a special affection for his many Protestant friends, re-
membering his "separated brethren" at Bardstown in a special way
in the very pastoral he wrote to explain the move of the see city to
Louisville.[32] Perhaps nothing so reveals the prelate's sense of life's
vitality and its people as his account of a trip he made downriver in
the winter of 1817. Along with Bishop DuBourg, he boarded the *Piqua*
at the Louisville wharf on December 18 of that year. This was his
description:

> [The boat held] a band of 7 or 8 comedians, a family of 7 or 8 Jews, and
> a company of clergymen, comprised of a tonsured cleric, a priest and
> two bishops; besides others, both white and black. Thus more than 30
> persons are lodged in a cabin 20 ft. x 12 which is again divided into two
> parts. This boat comprises the old and new testament. It might serve
> successively for a synagogue, a cathedral, a theatre, a hospital; a parlor,
> a dining room and a sleeping apartment. It is, in fact, a veritable Noah's
> Ark in which there are both clean and unclean animals . . . and . . . peace
> and harmony reign here.[33]

The last of Flaget's major trips was that undertaken to Europe
from 1835 to 1839. He had not anticipated nearly so long an absence
from Kentucky, but he was urged by Pope Gregory XVI to undertake
a tour of over thirty French dioceses to report on the American missions. It was during this soujourn that several reports were made of
miracles taking place through the prelate's intercessions. Even without these reported phenomena, the name and work of Flaget had
spread sufficiently throughout France that he was an object of celeb-
rity and attention. It was during these travels as well that he had
dined with Prince Metternich and had reported on a moving visit in
Rome to Gregory XVI. On the occasion of the papal audience, Flaget
had offered the pontiff a pinch of snuff and had asked for a pinch in
turn from the papal snuffbox "as a signal favor that I would publish
everywhere I go."[34]

One topic for discussion with Pope Gregory had been the possibility
of moving the diocesan center from Bardstown to Louisville. Once
this proposal had also received the approval of the American bishops,
the move was authorized in 1841, signaling not only the growth of
the city on the river, but also the fact that the Catholic population
was increasingly immigrant German and Irish in Louisville and not

any longer predominantly the old Anglo stock that had come from Maryland. During the 1840s at Louisville, it was coadjutor Bishop Guy Chabrat who increasingly managed affairs, much to the regret of the local clergy.[35]

When Chabrat retired to France for reasons of poor eyesight in 1846, the ailing and aging Flaget again was in full charge until the naming of Martin John Spalding, a native son, as coadjutor in 1848. In 1849, Flaget appeared in public for the last time in order to bless the cornerstone laying of Louisville's new Cathedral of the Assumption on Fifth Street. On February 11, 1850, the grand old gentleman of the American hierarchy died in his room at the cathedral rectory in Louisville. It was, as Catholic historian Robert Trisco has observed, the end of an era in American Catholicism.[36] The new bishop of Louisville, Martin John Spalding, declared the new cathedral still rising to be a monument to his sainted predecessor. Within two years of the old prelate's decease, Spalding had published a lengthy and well-researched life of Flaget; he also caused the remains of the first bishop of the West to be moved from a temporary resting place at the Convent of the Good Shepherd and reinterred in the crypt of the Louisville cathedral.

PRIORITIES AND PROGRESS

No sooner had he arrived on the Kentucky scene as bishop than Flaget established three priorities for his episcopate, namely, the establishment of a cathedral, a seminary, and a community of religious women in educational and charitable service. In contemporary parlance, these same priorities might be translated as those of worship, education, and social service.[37] By 1820, all the original Flaget hopes had been realized. First he had established, under David's steady leadership, Saint Thomas Seminary as a kind of clerical energy source for generations to come, both for Kentucky and for the nation. Over a dozen bishops came forth from the student body of this old seminary, and this in the same era when Kentucky was "exporting" its clerical force as bishops across the country, including such men as Edward Fenwick, O.P. (Cincinnati), Pius Miles, O.P. (Nashville), Ignatius Reynolds (Charleston), John McGill (Richmond), Francis Kenrick (Philadelphia), and Martin John Spalding (Baltimore).[38]

With Flaget's encouragement, two of his priests worked effectively to help the hardy, pious women of Kentucky establish two of the first sisterhoods in America: The Sisters of Loretto and the Sisters of Charity of Nazareth, both communities gathered in 1812. Ten years later the first Dominican foundation of sisters in the United States was begun at Saint Rose in Washington County, making for three mother-houses in Kentucky's "Holy Land," that fertile soil for spirituality within a fifty-mile radius of Bardstown. By the later nineteenth century, these motherhouses would be sending hundreds of their sisters across the nation, from the Southwest to the Northeast, to exercise their considerable talents. The prelate's remaining priority, a fitting center for worship, was realized with the dedication of Saint Joseph's Cathedral at Bardstown on August 8, 1819.

The fervor for the establishment of religious institutions seemed to know practically no check in the first quarter-century of the diocese's history. This was not only an amazing feat in an area so recently a mere outpost of civilization, but also a profoundly Catholic way of spreading the Gospel through institutional structures. Sometimes the red hot intensity of foundations did not reflect careful planning or analysis of resources. When Flaget arrived in his diocese, the Dominicans had already begun the College of Saint Thomas near Springfield (which would boast Jefferson Davis as an early student). By 1821, two more colleges were founded, that of Saint Joseph in Bardstown and that of Saint Mary's near Lebanon; none of these was more than twenty-five miles away from the other; none would survive ultimately, although Saint Mary's remained in existence as a seminary until 1976.[39]

When Bishop Flaget met with Pope Gregory in 1836, he presented to the pontiff, in effect, an account of his stewardship of twenty-five years in his diocese. The chart of accomplishment provided the following details for the years 1811–1836:[40] the number of Catholics had doubled; the clerical force had grown from six to thirty-six; thirty-three churches stood where ten had been before; and 260 sisters were in service, whereas there had been none at the beginning. Also to be noted was the foundation in 1836 of a weekly newspaper, *The Catholic Advocate*. Additionally, between the presentation of this accounting and his death, Bishop Flaget would welcome into his diocese two other religious houses of European origin: the Good Shepherd Sisters, who came to Louisville to establish a protective institution in 1843, and the Trappist monks, who established the Abbey of Gethsemani in 1848. The latter, the oldest continuous abbey in the United States, remains to this day one of the great monastic centers in the Americas.

One of the last of Flaget's accomplishments was also one of the most sensitive: that of moving the seat of the diocese from Bardstown to Louisville in 1841. The old bishop insisted to his aggrieved flock in Bardstown that he certainly was not making the change out of any thought of personal comfort or satisfaction. He lived in happy proximity there to many great spiritual centers, and there his own personal roots had been planted. Still, he maintained, just as the infant church had moved from the Holy Land to Rome for the greater good, so must the Kentucky church move its center of administration from Bardstown to Louisville. In a personnel move that had the touch of public relations about it, Flaget moved his finest preacher, the Roman-educated Father Martin John Spalding, to Bardstown in partial compensation for its loss of prestige.[41]

DIFFICULTIES AND MANNER OF ADMINISTRATION

In forty years of administration, it should not be thought surprising that the cross of conflict should at times overshadow the spiritual landscape of Kentucky. Perhaps the notable fact is that in such an era of burgeoning growth and creative personalities, so much harmony would, in fact, be possible. Some troubles were singular or infrequent in occurrence, such as the cholera epidemics, the occasional fire at a Catholic institution, or the unusual spectacle of Bardstown folk flocking in 1812 to the home of little girls suspected of demonic possession.[42] Additionally, despite a generally tolerant attitude between Catholics and Protestants in Kentucky, occasional flare-ups of anti-Catholic feeling, sometimes aroused by the orations of an angry preacher, had to be confronted.

The greater conflicts of Bishop Flaget, though, clustered around two areas in particular: those with the laity of his own flock and those with the priests of his own service. Difficulties with the laity were largely an affair of the earlier days of the diocese. At times, congregations would balk at particular financial arrangements for the support of the clergy. Such problems arose, for example, at both Saint Charles and Saint Rose. A stern Flaget, dressed in full pontificals and with staff in hand stood at the altars of the respective churches and threatened with excommunication any who persisted in public opposition to his authority. The warning was apparently availing.[43] The people had learned that for all his affability, their bishop could be steely in pursuit of his policies. He was known to be strict in granting dispensations for mixed marriages, for example. Nor was he shy in assigning public penances for what he considered grave moral affronts such as "scandalous marriages" or public drunkenness.[44]

At times, the difficulties between prelate and people were severe enough to require extensive negotiation. At Detroit in 1817, for example, the parish was woefully divided, even to the point of schism. Flaget had imposed an interdict, and when he visited the flock he finally received three promises of support from the people, even as he made three promises to them.[45] Also in 1817, closer to home—in the persistently troublesome Scott County (Kentucky) settlement—Flaget had spent two weeks examining all aspects of the dispute that centered on the division of two prominent families of the parish. Taking a chance remark by one party to the dispute that it would have been better for all concerned if the offending documents had long since burned up, Flaget seized on the idea and arranged for the documents to be burned after a Mass of reconciliation.[46]

The more perplexing and less tractable of Flaget's conflicts was with his clergy, especially with those two great pioneer figures Badin and Nerinckx. Although Flaget struggled mightily to keep his affairs with these gentlemen friendly, the strain at times reached the breaking point. With Badin, the quarrel was concerned with title to church lands that the priest had held since coming to Kentucky. The dispute was finally placed before Bishop Carroll in Baltimore, and an agreement was reached in 1812. Yet inexplicably, Badin was found not only to have cleverly deeded only half the land to his bishop after the settlement; he also boasted around Kentucky about his clever ruse. Flaget considered excommunicating his French compatriot but, fearing grave scandal, decided against such a drastic move. The friction between the two was ultimately resolved only when Badin left the diocese in 1819.[47] One of the disputes with Nerinckx concerned the rule for the Sisters of Loretto, which Flaget found too severe. Once again, it was a departure from Kentucky, this time Nerinckx's in 1824, that brought a semblance of peace again to Flaget's life.[48]

At other clerical levels, too, Flaget often found himself locked in dispute. He quarreled with his fellow Sulpicians over the status of his seminary in relation to their official family of schools. They were reluctant to have this comparatively modest "shoe-string" operation of the early days accorded full title of a Sulpician house (for a time, after all, David alone was the seminary staff).[49] There were also attempts to have David return to the East Coast, and even to have him named bishop of Philadelphia. Flaget struck back each time like a lioness whose cub was threatened. Each time, the snarl was effective, and David remained where he also wished to be, in Kentucky.[50]

All of these troubles, though, were as sideshows compared to the great resignation crisis of 1832, which threw clergy and laity alike into an uproar against Bishop Flaget. The story and the motivations of some of the players are murky, but the outline of the affair can be told succinctly enough. After Kenrick had been taken from Flaget's quiver of leading clergy to be bishop of Philadelphia, Flaget had gone into one of his depressions. Nearing seventy, he considered himself old and wearing down. Without consulting his associates, the bishop now wrote to Rome offering his resignation, asking for the right to allow his favored Guy Chabrat to assist in confirmations. Since David, his coadjutor, was even older than Flaget himself, the bishop of Bardstown may have wished Rome to take his request as a hint that Chabrat be appointed as coadjutor bishop and David be allowed to remain in place in a quiet retirement. In a letter to Kenrick, Flaget had tipped his hand with the blunt assertion, "I did not think they would accept my resignation."[51] But by apostolic brief of August 25, 1832, Rome did accept Flaget's resignation and appointed David as bishop, with Chabrat as coadjutor. If the entire process was Flaget's ploy to get Chabrat named as his successor, it hadn't worked.

When the news of Rome's action reached Kentucky in December 1832, the results were explosive. David had no desire whatsoever to become bishop. Laity and clerics alike were upset with the secretive process. Flaget chalked this reaction up to their being "good republicans," while confiding, again to Kenrick, "I have found the means of displeasing everybody."[52] Now began a round of visitations to the churches, and consultations in deadly earnest. Flaget appealed to Rome on January 1, 1833, asking to be reinstated, with David sending a supporting letter. Rome now accepted the reinstatement, but was silent about Chabrat. Flaget wrote again, saying bluntly that he could not continue in office without having Chabrat as bishop.

One significant problem, though, remained. Chabrat was not well liked on the Kentucky scene. Historian Ben Webb, who generally spoke with the greatest reverence of clerical figures, noted that Chabrat was "dumpy" in appearance, and, on balance, called Flaget's nomination of him a "blunder."[53] A group of women in the Louisville congregation were resistant, asking, "Must we have another Frenchman for a bishop?" Meanwhile, at Saint Joseph's College, the clerical opposition gathered, led by such bright ornaments of the diocese as Martin John Spalding, Ignatius Reynolds, and Elisha Durbin, the "apostle of western Kentucky." Flaget became testier than ever, writing to Bishop Rosati:

> My God. What a misfortune for Mr. Chabrat that the first Bishop of Bardstown was such a handsome boy and so well mannered. The ladies of Bardstown and some of the clergy would never forgive Mr. Chabrat for not being able to make a beautiful curtsy . . . I am ashamed of them.[54]

Chabrat was consecrated bishop at the Bardstown cathedral on July 20, 1834. This might seem to have settled affairs, but instead, it only drove more tender spots to the surface. The group of aggrieved clerics now wrote to Rome saying that they accepted reluctantly the decision of the Holy See with regard to Chabrat. But they had amassed in the meantime certain complaints against Bishop Flaget: arbitrary reassignment of priests, failure to make frequent pastoral visits, and failure to pay the aggrieved clerics sufficiently. There was in truth discontent under the surface of the diocesan Eden in the West, but Rome was not about to act so late in Flaget's career.[55]

It was shortly after this ecclesiastical rhubarb ended that Flaget slipped away for his visit to Europe. Following that instinct of his nature that caused him to make some of his decisions "close to the vest," Flaget had told only two or three close associates about his intended voyage, and off he went, leaving the unpopular Chabrat in charge for four years. When Flaget returned to his people, it was as an old man, waiting for death. Pressed by friends to remain in his native land, he had responded that the first bishop of Kentucky must "die among his people," and he had gone home to do so.[56] The local Catholic press had been reporting the prelate's successful tour of Europe, as well as the reputed miracles, and the old bishop was feted warmly on his return to Bardstown on October 7, 1839.[57]

Flaget was a man evidently of both kindliness and complexity. He could be by turns confrontational and evasive when major crisis loomed. He did not possess the fiery temperament and mode of action of such a man as Archbishop John Hughes, his contemporary in New York, nor the experimental inventiveness of a John England at Charleston. He afforded considerable scope for action for the many creative people around him, such as Catherine Spalding, leader of the Sisters of Charity, or his academic clerical leaders such as Martin John Spalding, George Elder, or William Byrne. Compared to a later martinet of a bishop such as Louisville's William George McCloskey (1823–1909), Flaget left the religious communities under his charge almost a total autonomy. One of his great talents was to gather around him in the diocese talented people whom he encouraged, edified, and allowed to do their work as they saw it, without hindrance.

He revealed yet another Catholic instinct in his perception that hierarchical leadership was vital to the church. Accordingly, he labored to divide the vast diocese that he originally found into new sees with sterling leaders, many of whom he recommended for their placement. At home, too, he worked steadily for a uniformity of clerical discipline, believing that the way to foster a holy people was to nurture a holy group of priests. He had called for a clergy conference as early as February, 1812, and by a decree of September, 1822, had ordered an annual retreat and conference for all his clergy.[58] Flaget could not exactly be said to have run a tight ship; but as an ecclesial admiral of an inland sea (if the pun be allowed), he did insist that his crew be hardy and disciplined, and ready for any storm that might break.

FLAGET'S IMPACT ON THE CHURCH

Like many pioneers in the American Catholic church, the first epis-copal leader of the West was possessed of earnestness of cause, a deep and balanced piety, and flexibility in dealing with the many-layered complexity that is the human animal. If, instead of Flaget, the first clerical leader of Kentucky had been an authoritarian, a cynic, a slacker, or a mere seeker after worldly comfort, the results would have been strikingly different. The subsequent history of Catholicism in the Upper South, the Middle West, indeed in America would have been decidedly different, not to say diminished and downright inferior. Especially in the first quarter-century of the life of the diocese of Bardstown, the man, the place, and the moment met, providentially, in a felicitous and effective way.

Benedict Joseph Flaget, minor failings and all, left a powerful im-pact on Catholicism in his own diocese and his region of the United States. He had been, in his own person, a study of the interplay of the working of grace, self-discipline, piety, hard work, structure bal-anced by freedom, and tradition balanced by an openness to new con-ditions and situations. He had called forth institutions that would invite others to develop those subtle blendings within themselves; they would export their expertise and sensibilities across the nation. He had helped to draw the maps and leadership lines of many of the subsequently major dioceses of the North American continent.[59] He had done all of these things with a maximum of effective result and with a minimum of rancor and debilitating ill will.

In the spring of 1835, just after one of the greatest times of personal trial for one so sensitive and affected by the feelings of others, Flaget had written to one of his newly ordained priests words of spiritual advice. Unwittingly, perhaps, he offered therein a succinct exempli-fication of his own inner life and the convictions that underrode his many decisions and labors. An excerpt of this letter's contents might well stand as interpretive key and conclusion to a study of the rightly revered Flaget:

> My dear Mr. Chambige . . . dear Francis, to find some solace in your labors and the pains inseparable from them, recall that it is not every two or three months that we must take up the cross and carry it, but indeed every day of our lives, and that it is not so much to suffer for ourselves, as is only just, but to suffer with Jesus Christ and as Jesus Christ. . . . Without a firm conviction touching this eternal truth, I would have fallen into despair myself. Courage, then; drink without fear the chalices pre-sented by Divine Providence. They will be at times bitter, even disgusting; but once swallowed, your heart will experience an inexpressible sweetness that will be a foretaste of eternal delights.[60]

CHAPTER
4
John England: Missionary to America, Then and Now

Peter Clarke

*J*ohn England (1786–1842) was bishop of Charleston, South Carolina, from 1820 until his death on April 11, 1842. Without question, during those years he was the most prominent member of the American hierarchy.[1] England founded the first Catholic newspaper in the United States, *The United States Catholic Miscellany.*[2] He addressed the United States Congress for two hours.[3] He founded the Sisters of Charity of Our Lady of Mercy who continue to serve the church in South Carolina.[4] He is called the "Father of the Baltimore Councils." He was the first U.S. prelate to be given a diplomatic mission by the Holy See.[5] During that mission to Haiti, England became the first U.S. bishop, and probably the first Catholic bishop in modern times, to ordain a black man to the priesthood.[6]

John England published the first missal for the laity[7] in the United States and published separately the *Laity's Directory for 1822,*[8] which provided a calendar for masses to be celebrated each day and information about the feasts and the seasons of the church year. This *Laity's Directory* contains what might be called the first history of the Catholic church in the United States.

But John England's unique contribution to the church in the United States was his written *Constitution* for the Diocese of Charleston and the annual conventions called for by that constitution.[9] These annual conventions of clergy and laity governed the diocese for twenty years. England's *Constitution* is a statement of faith in the tradition of the Catholic church and in its adaptability to a new age. This document is not the whole of England's style of leadership, as we shall see, but it was the foundation and the structure that allowed his vision of a consultative and collaborative church to bring about the cooperation of the people, priests, and bishop in the ministry of the church. But before looking at his style of leadership it would be good to see the life in Ireland that shaped the priesthood of the first bishop of Charleston.

John England was born in Cork, Ireland, on September 23, 1786, to Thomas and Honora Lordan England and was baptized on September 25 in Saint Finbar's Chapel. He would return to Saint Finbar's for his consecration as bishop of Charleston on September 21, 1820. England first studied law, but after two years he entered Saint Patrick's College, Carlow, where he studied for the priesthood. At the age of twenty-two he was ordained to the priesthood on October 11, 1808, in the new Saint Mary's Cathedral, Cork, by Bishop Francis Moylan. England was appointed to the cathedral and remained there until 1817, when he was appointed pastor in Bandon, a large city outside of Cork. It was in Bandon that John England was notified of his appointment as bishop of Charleston.

While he was at the Cork cathedral, England was involved in many other affairs of the church. He was chaplain of the North Presentation Convent, where at times he was seen helping in the construction of an addition to the convent building. He founded a monthly magazine called *The Religious Repertory* and was managing editor of the *Cork Mercantile Chronicle*. It was in this newspaper and in *The Religious Repertory* that he gave leadership to the voices who opposed the granting of a veto to the English monarch over the appointment of Irish bishops.[10]

The young priest was also the chaplain of the Cork jail and often heard the last confession of prisoners who were being sent to Australia, which was used as a penal colony. Several of these persons wrote to John England to tell him of the sore need they had for a Catholic priest and Catholic worship, for at that time no priests were allowed in Australia; in response, England wrote an open letter to the British government and to the Irish bishops pleading that the bishops appoint and the government permit Catholic priests to be sent to minister to these Catholic prisoners so far from home. Within days the matter was brought up in the House of Commons and priests were sent to Australia. By reason of these events, England is considered to be one of the founders of the church in Australia.[11]

England had offered himself for the work of the church in Australia. In January 1817, he wrote to the Congregation for the Propagation of the Faith and volunteered for the church in the United States. Later that year he was named pastor at Bandon in his native diocese. At Bandon, John England was planning a biography of Father Arthur O'Leary, the irenic Franciscan who wrote about toleration and freedom of religion. England's study of the writings of Father O'Leary enriched his own development of a theology of separation of church and state and freedom of religion. However, eventually he left his research with his brother, Thomas, a priest serving as his curate at Bandon, who completed the biography of O'Leary.[12]

In August 1820, the newly appointed bishop of Charleston, still at Bandon, accompanied a man to his execution and was told of a large number of stolen weapons that were in the town. England informed the government of this situation and guaranteed that the arms would be surrendered if the persons harboring them were given amnesty should they be later implicated. In response he was told by authorities that the persons should first present themselves and then they would be given amnesty. England replied that there was little likelihood that these persons, whose identities were concealed, would make their guilt public in this way. As for himself, England would not reveal the names, because in obtaining the information, he undertook "a most solemn obligation, which I do not intend to violate"—his promise to the man who had been executed. England added: "I have acted, to the best of my judgment, for the public welfare and the peace of the country. The advice that I have given has been dictated by an honest motive."[13]

The new bishop of Charleston was a man of courage, involved in the questions of the day and in the problems of the people he served. He was pastor and rector of a seminary; he was editor and journalist; and he was a missionary. He experienced the union of church and state in Ireland where the established church was not his own, and he experienced some of the advantages of separation of church and state where the Catholic church in Ireland was allowed to exist when not being persecuted.

England was also a man of integrity, whose words and actions were "dictated by an honest motive." There is much to tell; but it must suffice merely to outline his style of leadership in Charleston and in the United States.

The new diocese of Charleston embraced North Carolina, South Carolina, and Georgia, the area that now includes the dioceses of

Charleston, South Carolina; Raleigh and Charlotte, North Carolina; and Savannah and Atlanta, Georgia, the latter being the metropolitan see. In England's day there were few Catholics. About one-half of the approximately two million people in his three-state diocese were slaves. England estimated the number of Catholics at 11,000, of whom 1,000 were estimated to be slaves.[14] There were two Catholic congregations in Georgia and none in North Carolina. Saint Mary's in Charleston was the only Catholic congregation in South Carolina but did not become the cathedral because of control by the trustees. England built a new wooden church for his cathedral in Charleston.

The *Constitution* written by John England for the Diocese of Charleston is the heart of his style of episcopal leadership. Yet it did not exist by itself. It grew out of an understanding of the need for a visible church, collaborating in a visible way. This church would have a visible unity within itself and with the Catholic churches around the world. It would seek to be self-sufficient in regard to resources and ministers and to develop an indigenous clergy. Both ministry and decision-making would be guided by a spirit of cooperation, communication, consultation, and subsidiarity. The importance of the local congregation would be stressed. These qualities of the church that England was building were given life by his own qualities of openness and honesty and by his imagination and his missionary spirit. He brought to the task his reflective nature, his pastoral energy, and his strong faith. Elsewhere I have described these qualities.[15] Here I will describe the steps that England followed in building this church. He embodied the scattered church members; he provided them with the tools that enabled them to do the work of the church; and he empowered them to accomplish the work. It is through the *Constitution* that he gave the members and the local congregations voice and vote in the direction of the building of the church. This three-tiered work of embodying, enabling, and empowering would continue simultaneously throughout England's episcopate, but we will now look at these facets of England's style as steps in a consecutive process.

The bishop immediately set about the task of embodying his scattered members. England was just two weeks in Charleston when he set sail down the coast for Savannah, traveled by carriage to Augusta, and proceeded over to Columbia and back to Charleston, a journey of six weeks. In the summer he would go 700 miles through North Carolina. England describes this journey in a diary. In this first missionary journey, England formed eleven congregations. In each place where there was no resident priest, he commissioned lay persons to meet every Sunday and to lead the prayer. He formed catechism classes for the young and for others who were interested in the church. In Plymouth, North Carolina, where he found only two Catholics,

England celebrated mass "to a very numerous audience and recommended the formation of a branch of the Catholic Book Society."[16] The bishop used these societies not only for the instruction of Catholics but also for the gathering of persons interested in the church. He commissioned the two Catholics to meet for prayers in the hope that their regular meeting might be the beginning of a new congregation.

This embodying of scattered members would be a lifelong emphasis of England's ministry. In 1829 he said to the North Carolina Convention, "Next to securing the existence of a ministry, the embodying of our members should demand our care."[17] This embodying of members was one of the purposes of his and the priests' journeys, but it was also the task of the local congregation. England wrote to a friend that he wanted to organize

> Catholics into congregations, so that even when there is no clergyman that they may assemble together on the Lord's day and have appropriate prayers read by some person whom I shall authorize for that purpose, & have instruction by means of proper books which shall be read & and the Catechism be taught to the ignorant. . . . and some progress will be made toward the establishment of religion.[18]

These scattered congregations would be brought together into a visible unity in the annual conventions. England stressed the benefits of the conventions. He told the 1827 Georgia Convention:

> To bring together in affection and charity, the clergy and the principal laity of the state at specified periods, so as to make them feel that they were one body so as to afford them an opportunity of kind intercourse, and bind them together by a more firm league of confidence was thought to be highly useful; their union for a common purpose creates confidence, enkindles zeal, and animates exertion.[19]

The annual conventions were not just meetings concerned about the business of the diocese but were part of the embodying of the members and congregations into the wider church and the making visible the unity of the diocesan church.

England saw, too, the need for the Catholic church in the United States to display a visible unity and for its bishops to gather in a provincial council. From 1789 until 1808, the United States was one diocese. In that year John Carroll was named archbishop, and the dioceses of Boston, New York, Philadelphia, and Bardstown were established. In 1810, Carroll convened the first meeting of the U.S. bishops, which decided that a provincial council would be held in 1812. Unfortunately it was not held until 1829.

Although the bishops had decided on meeting, and regular provincial meetings were called for by church law, it would fall to John England to be the one voice calling for these regular meetings. England wrote on March 1, 1821, to Archbishop Maréchal of Baltimore asking that the bishops be assembled "for the purpose of having established some uniform system of discipline for our Churches, and of having common counsel and advice upon a variety of important topics."[20] Even after the bishops met in 1829 and agreed to meetings every three years, a second meeting was delayed. Finally England went to Rome and Rome practically insisted on the bishops' coming together. England is rightly seen as the "Father of the Provincial Councils" and the one responsible for the beginnings of the collaborative efforts that have resulted in the present bishops' conference.

England saw the collaborative work of a provincial council as a means of binding the American church more closely to the Holy See. In a report to Rome, England pointed out that this closer union with Rome would be one of the effects "of encouraging frequent convocation of councils, whose acts and decrees must in every instance, be submitted to the approbation of the Holy See before promulgation."[21]

In November 1829, after the First Provincial Council, England joyfully reported to the South Carolina Convention:

> It is for us, beloved brethren, a source of great consolation to behold in our day, our provincial church assuming its proper form, and growing into a state of harmonious and extensive organization. Let the example not be lost upon ourselves. We are no longer a number of jealous, scattered, contentious, and badly agreeing congregations, with no point of union but a common faith. No; we are half a million of souls knit into one provincial church, having charity for those who differ from us, and affection for each other. Our efforts are not those of individuals, nor of disjointed societies; we are members of a body in which there exists one vivifying spirit, and which has but one rule of common action. When one member suffers, all sympathize; when one is invigorated all rejoice.[22]

England brought the people and the diocese together and gave them the materials and organizations that were needed to become and to act as the body of Christ. Some of these materials incorporated the sense of a national unity. His reports to Mission Aid societies and to Rome linked the diocese and the church in the United States to the nations of Europe and to the Holy See.

The four things that England almost immediately made available to the Catholics of his new diocese were the catechism, the *Missal for the Laity*, *The Laity's Directory*, and *The United States Catholic Miscellany*.

The bishop noted in his diary in April 1821: "On the last week of Lent was published a Catechism, which I had much labor in compiling from various others, and adding several parts which I considered necessary to be dwelt upon under the peculiar circumstances of my Diocess."[23] In addition to this 1821 catechism, he also published a catechism for children and unlearned persons in 1830. The answers to the catechism questions were often words of Scripture or a reference to a verse of the Bible. England commissioned persons to teach and provided them with the means to conduct their classes. England was proud of his catechism and often quoted from it. In 1835, he sent the catechism to Judge William Gaston and suggested several portions that might be helpful to the judge as he prepared a plea for toleration that he would make at the North Carolina Constitutional Convention.[24]

By October 1821, England had sent the *Missal for the Laity* off to the printers. This was not a new translation but a copy of a missal available in Ireland and England for several decades. For this missal England prepared a one-hundred-page "Explanation of the Mass," which was reprinted several times. In 1822, the same year as the *Missal for the Laity* was printed, England published the *Laity's Directory for 1822*. This little book had a calendar for the masses to be said on each day of the year. Included in the *Laity's Directory* are thirty-five pages of instructions on the seasons and the feasts of the church year. England devotes several pages to the establishment of the hierarchy in the United States and then describes the individual dioceses along with their educational institutions. This directory contains the earliest published record of the U.S. Catholic church. Here England gave to the young church in America a picture of itself, where it had come from, and where its dioceses and educational institutions were located. The missal and the *Laity's Directory* enabled all to follow the liturgical prayer of the church. England's catechism was designed for use by the people of his diocese, but the missal and the directory were available to Catholics everywhere.

England may be best known for having founded the first Catholic newspaper in the United States, the *United States Catholic Miscellany*, a national journal. The *Miscellany* united the congregations with one another and with the Catholic church around the world. It emphasized England's vision of uniting the Catholics of the country beyond the borders of their local communities and dioceses.

On the masthead of every issue of the *Miscellany* were the words from the First Amendment of the U.S. Constitution: "Congress shall make no law respecting the establishment of religion, or prohibiting the free exercise thereof." England was probably the first churchman to put the words "United States" and "Catholic" together. Indeed, he insisted that they belonged together. The Catholic church, he maintained, was at home in America and had a right to be there. The *Miscellany* brought that message to every subscriber week after week.

John England also nourished organizations to bring people together and to accomplish the work of the diocese. He founded a seminary for the training of priests, established the Sisters of Charity of

Our Lady of Mercy, the Ursuline convent and school, the Charleston Book Society, the missionary Society of Saint John the Baptist, the Brotherhood of San Marino, and Saint Joseph's Mutual Benefit Society.

In January 1822, England opened the Philosophical and Classical Seminary, in Charleston where theological students would contribute to their own support by teaching other students. In 1825 it became the Seminary of Saint John the Baptist, a combined college and theologate. Sixty priests were educated at this Charleston seminary. Four of these were bishops: Andrew Byrne of Little Rock, John Barry of Savannah, Patrick N. Lynch of Charleston, and John Moore of Saint Augustine. James A. Corcoran and Augustine F. Hewit were also priests from the Charleston Seminary who, along with Patrick Lynch, were chosen by Bishop Reynolds to edit the collected writings of England.[25,26]

In 1829, England founded the Sisters of Charity of Our Lady of Mercy when, as he wrote three years later in a report to the cardinal prefect of Propaganda, "three young women asked my permission to take religious vows." The report continues: "I encouraged them to form a congregation to instruct the black girls, as also the poor white girls; and moreover to take care of the sick and to practice other works of charity. . . . Others soon joined them; they are now ten in the community, and give promise of being useful beyond my expectations."[27] In 1986, the Sisters of Charity of Our Lady of Mercy celebrated the bicentennial of the birth of John England. In 1834, England visited Ireland and brought some Ursuline Sisters to Charleston to establish a convent and a school. On this same journey, five ladies came from Ireland to join the Sisters of Charity of Our Lady of Mercy.[28]

The Charleston Book Society provided books to Catholics and other interested persons. It brought Catholics and their neighbors together and was a means of enriching both in the knowledge of the Catholic church. England proudly printed the constitution for the society in the *Laity's Directory*. He wrote:

> There are yet no Catholic schools in any part of the newly created Diocese: but great exertions are making to diffuse a correct knowledge of the Catholic church throughout the different states, by the establishment of societies, which have for their object the dissemination of books of piety and instruction.[29]

In 1837 the bishops of the Third Provincial Council formed themselves into "a society for the production and dissemination of books useful to the cause of truth and virtue."

The Society of Saint John the Baptist was founded, England said, "to aid in erecting and supporting an ecclesiastical seminary, and in sustaining a few missionaries to visit the neglected Catholics who are scattered many miles through the two Carolinas and Georgia."[30] The members would gather weekly for prayer, and contributions were to be given weekly. When the Society for the Propagation of the Faith suggested that the diocese form a branch of that society, the bishop suggested to the 1840 diocesan convention that it consider, as a recommendation to the Society of Saint John the Baptist, "whether it would not, if a union with the council in Lyons should be judged expedient, be more advisable to have the existing society become a branch thereof, than to form a new one."[31]

The Brotherhood of San Marino was "the first society of workingmen in the United States to be established under Catholic auspices," according to Peter Guilday. Guilday reports: "Bishop England was President. All the officers were Catholics, but it was not necessary to be a member of the Catholic Church to join the Society."[32] The brotherhood grew out of discussions at meetings of the Society of Saint John the Baptist. These discussions in part concerned the outbreak of a disease called "Strangers Fever," probably a form of malaria, afflicting newcomers and the poor. The brotherhood was formed to take care of the health of its members and care for the property and children of members who died. Each was to take an interest in his brother and lead him along paths of virtue. At times of epidemic, the brotherhood rented houses and operated a hospital with the Sisters of Our Lady of Mercy. The brotherhood even had its own savings bank. It speaks well of the atmosphere of the diocese that the Mission Aid Society gave birth to a brotherhood of workingmen, and the Sisters of Our Lady of Mercy assisted that brotherhood in the establishment of a hospital.

Saint Joseph's Mutual Benefit Society was organized on September 15, 1841, for the purpose of promoting the spiritual and temporal happiness of the members. They joined in prayer at their meetings and made monthly contributions. A weekly cash benefit was paid to members who were sick, and an allowance for funeral expenses was paid when a member died.[33]

England traveled to Europe four times in the last decade of his life to report on the work of the church in his diocese and in the United States. He visited and sent reports to Rome, to the Leopoldine Society in Vienna, and to the Society for the Propagation of the Faith in Lyons. In Ireland he spoke time and again about the needs of the church in the United States. He asked the bishops for priests and proposed a mission seminary for the education of priests for mission areas. He published a pamphlet in Dublin on the history of the church in his diocese. England is credited with stirring a zeal for the missions among the Catholic people of Ireland at a time when they themselves were still only rebuilding a church recovering from centuries of penal laws. He may have inspired the founding of All Hallows Missionary College in Dublin.[34] England believed that he had a right to ask the older churches of Europe for assistance and that he had a duty to account for the funds that organizations sent to the United States.

While in Rome, England reported to the Holy Father on the need for Catholic missionaries among American Indians who were being transferred to reservations and also on the need for Catholic missionaries to go to Liberia, where former slaves from the United States were beginning a new homeland. The matter was referred to the U.S. bishops, who asked the Society of Jesus to assume these two responsibilities. The Jesuits accepted the mission among the American Indians.

On June 19, 1841, the Congregation for the Propagation of the Faith asked Bishop Francis P. Kenrick of Philadelphia, Coadjutor Bishop John Hughes of New York, and Bishop John England to send some missionaries to Liberia. On December 21, 1841, two priests, John Kelly of Albany and Edward Barron of Philadelphia, and one layman, Dennis Pindar of Baltimore, sailed for West Africa. England had initiated the first foreign mission effort of American Catholics, and that mission was the beginning of the Catholic church in sub-Saharan Africa in modern times.[35]

John England not only gathered the Catholic church in America and gave it the means to achieve its mission, but he also empowered its bishops to meet and to consult, to decide and to collaborate in the mission of the church. To the bishops of the United States, he insisted repeatedly on the importance of coming together. The tradition and the law of the church provided for provincial councils. These councils gave to the bishops the power to resolve local difficulties and to cooperate in common projects. England took an active role in the work of the councils and is seen as the writer of all the pastoral letters of the first four provincial councils.

The *Constitution*, which England prepared for his diocese, "empowered the laity to cooperate and not dominate."[36] In a report on church support England speaks thus of church government to the Holy See:

> This is a subject which has been my study during 26 years, and is not confined to any single country. . . . I have during the last eleven years had the trial of a system which, after much examination, I adopted; and so far it appears to please the people and has secured the freedom of the clergy.[37]

The First Provincial Council refused to adopt the *Constitution* as a model for all the dioceses but allowed it to continue in Charleston. It had already been examined twice at the Congregation for the Propagation for the Faith. When an effort was made during the congregation's review of the provincial council to have England again defend the *Constitution*, Cardinal Pietro Caprano, the presenting cardinal for the council decrees, said that England had explained the *constitution*, that there were sufficient safeguards, and that, in short, "it is certain that things are proceeding with complete tranquility in that diocese."[38]

In a letter on June 24, 1824, to the Congregation for the Propagation of the Faith, England wrote, "The *Constitution* is now in force in the Diocese of Charleston and is accepted by all . . . it is now the standard for Catholics, and all our affairs in consequence thereof are progressing peacefully."[39] Thirteen years later, at the 1837 South Carolina Convention, England expressed his satisfaction with the *Constitution:*

> By its provisions the limits of our several powers and duties are accurately defined; it has prevented discord, it has banished jealousy, it has secured peace, it has produced efforts of cooperation, and established mutual confidence and affection between our several churches, as well as between the pastors and their flocks, and between the bishop and the churches and by confirming the rights of all, it has insured the support of all.[40]

The *Constitution* has seven articles:[41] doctrine, government of the diocese, property, membership, local congregations or district churches, the conventions, and the amendment of the constitution. Articles one and two spell out the teachings of the church. The article on property speaks of the necessity of supporting the church and vests the ownership of property in the general trustees of the diocese, consisting of the bishop as president, the vicar as vice president, three clergymen chosen by the clergy at the annual convention, and six laymen chosen by the house of lay delegates at the annual convention. The treasurer was appointed by both houses voting together. Membership was limited to men twenty-one years of age and older who were baptized members of the church in good standing, were residents, and had given their assent to the *Constitution*.

The *Constitution* could be amended in any area, always in accordance with the teaching of the church, by a majority of both houses at two annual conventions and with the approval of two-thirds of the vestries and of the bishop. The only amendment made during the twenty years during which the *Constitution* guided the diocese was a change from state conventions to a single convention for the whole diocese; the first convention for the whole diocese was held in 1839.

The fifth articles deals with "district churches," or the local congregations. The power to create a district church belonged to the bishop. When creating a new district, he would give public notice for a meeting of the members of the new congregation. The bishop would preside at this meeting. The congregation would settle on the number of members for the vestry and decide whether any special regulations were needed. The members would

> proceed to elect by ballot so many discreet, well conducted men having a regard for religion, and if possible, persons who are in the habit of receiving the sacrament of the Holy Eucharist; and those laymen together with the clergyman or clergymen of that district shall be the Vestry of the same.[42]

The vestry had the responsibility of the temporalities of the congregation and it was their duty

> to exert themselves to procure for the Bishop and the clergymen of their own district decent and comfortable support; to have the Church and other buildings to be kept in good order and repair . . . to provide and keep in good order a burial ground for the interment of members in the communion of the church . . . and to see that the church property entrusted to their care be well preserved and improved and faithfully administered.[43]

The vestry chose the organist, clerk, sexton and other lay officers or servants of the church. The vestry appointed the wardens and the secretary and the treasurer. The local clergyman was the president of the vestry and his assent was required for an act of the vestry. However, in the making of contracts or agreements to carry out a matter directed by the vestry, the clergyman had no negative power.

The *Constitution*

> strongly recommended that all things be done in peace harmony and good will: and in any cases of importance, or where the feelings of opposed parties appear to be deeply interested, it would be better that an adjournment should take place, to afford time for calmness and reflection, than that a hasty decision should be made, and jealousy and ill will be excited.[44]

The *Constitution* even calls for a meeting of the vestry, without the clergyman, if the vestry is "displeased with the conduct or the proceedings of the clergyman." It calls for the vestry to assemble on the written request of two vestrymen, to maintain complete confidentiality, and to accept the decision of the bishop "unless they shall see cause for making their appeal to a superior ecclesiastical tribunal."[45] The vestry served one year and was elected each January.

The members of each local congregation also elected delegates to the annual conventions of the church. The churches were ranked according to their Catholic population and could send one, two, or four delegates according to their size. The requirements for delegates were the same as for members of the vestry.

Each person elected to the vestry and each person chosen to be a delegate to the convention was required to make a declaration, which was printed along with the *Constitution*. He promised to observe the doctrines and discipline of the church and to work in his office "for the benefit of religion, the welfare of the Church and the promotion of virtue." The delegate made this affirmation: "I will diligently consult how those great objects may be furthered, and that in all my expressions of official opinion and votes I will endeavour to further the same." He also agreed "to honestly and conscientiously concur for the promotion of religion" in appointments, the collection and expenditures of money, and the examination of accounts; he said, "[I will do all] honestly and diligently to the best of my ability and knowledge, for the welfare and credit of the Church and the honor and glory of Almighty God."[46]

The bishop encouraged the local vestries in their responsibilities to the local congregations. In a letter of June 10, 1826, to the vestry at Newbern, North Carolina—a congregation founded in 1821 and still without a clergyman—England wrote that he had been "led to believe that occasional differences subsist between yourselves to the serious evil of religion and the scandal of your neighbours." He told them, "Nothing was more calculated to grieve me" and added, "To me it would be matter of little moment who was more in fault than another, because there should be no fault of that kind permitted to exist." He told them of ten students in the seminary and hoped to send them a priest after the first of the year. He encouraged them: "You have borne much,—wait now but a little, pray to God for his aid to you and to me, hold together in union and affection, meet in your little church for prayers, and write to me occasionally."[47]

Twenty-eight church conventions were held in the diocese of Charleston from November 1823 to November 1840. These were state conventions until 1839, when they became diocesan conventions. There were twenty-six state conventions—fifteen in South Carolina, nine in Georgia, and two in North Carolina. Two diocesan conventions were held in Charleston in 1839 and 1840. The addresses of Bishop England to twenty-six of these conventions are in the collections of his writings. A third general convention was planned in November 1841. England was delayed in Philadelphia and Baltimore with sickness and with preaching and raising money for the three missionaries going to Liberia. When he returned to Charleston, he was sick, and he never recovered his health.

The occasions for these convention addresses of Bishop England were quite formal and solemn. The first general convention of the diocese lasted seven days. Guilday tells us that there were sixteen priests representing the Georgia districts of Augusta, Savannah, Locust Grove, Columbus, and the mission camps among the railroad builders of that State; the Districts of Charleston, Sumter and Columbia, in South Carolina; and those of Raleigh, Beaufort, Fayetteville, Washington and Newbern, North Carolina. Thirty laymen from as many cities of the three States were present. . . . Saturday was spent in becoming acquainted with one another. . . . On Sunday morning all were present in the Cathedral for the Solemn Pontifical Mass.[48]

After mass the declaration for those entering office was read and all the delegates signed the declaration, which was then presented to the bishop. After receiving their declaration, the bishop addressed the delegates. In the second general convention there were almost twice as many delegates from the three states. The state conventions were smaller but all were opened in the same formal manner with the celebration of mass and the signing of the declaration by all the delegates.

The convention consisted of three "portions which hold their sessions separately"[49]—the bishop, the clergy, and the lay delegates. The bishop or his vicar was the judge of the qualifications of the clergy. The senior clergyman in dignity or in ordination was the president of the house of clergy. The house of lay delegates was the judge of the qualifications of lay delegates and elected its own president. Each house met separately. For an act to be an act of the convention it needed a majority of each of the houses and the approval of the bishop. In elections to offices and positions of trust, a majority of the members of both houses voting together was needed.

The convention had no power in the areas of the doctrine and discipline of the church, in the administration of the sacraments and the ceremonies of the church, nor in matters of spiritual jurisdiction, ecclesiastical appointments, ordinations, and the superintendence of the clergy.

The *Constitution* described the place of the convention in the government of the diocese:

> The Convention is not to be considered as a portion of the ecclesiastical government of the Church; but the two houses are to be considered rather as a body of sage, prudent and religious counsellors to aid the proper ecclesiastical governor of the church in the discharge of his duty, by their advice and exertions in obtaining and applying the necessary pecuniary means to those purposes which will be most beneficial, and in superintending the several persons who have charge thereof; to see that the money be honestly and beneficially expended.[50]

The *Constitution* then set forth the powers of the convention:

1. To dispose of the general fund of the Church in the way that it may deem most advantageous.

2. To examine into, and to controul the expenditures made by its own order or that of a former Convention.

3. To examine into, regulate and controul, with the exception of their spiritual concerns, all establishments of its own creation; or which being otherwise created may be regularly subject to its control.

4. To appoint the lay officers and servants of such establishments.

5. The house of clergy have power to examine into the ecclesiastical concerns of such establishments, and to make their private report thereon to the Bishop or Vicar, together with their opinion and advice. . . . [51]

The *Constitution* encouraged the members of the convention to go beyond the letter of these powers if there was reason:

In those cases where the Convention has no authority to act, should either house feel itself called upon by any peculiar circumstances to submit advice, or to present a request to the Bishop, he will bestow upon the same the best consideration at the earliest opportunity; and as far as his conscientious obligations will permit, and the welfare of the church will allow, and the honor and glory of Almighty God, in his judgment require, he will endeavour to follow such advice or to agree to such request. [52]

England reported on the finances of the diocese, on his travels, and on the needs and the problems he found in the diocese. Indeed, his talks to the conventions are a rich story of the church in the Carolinas and Georgia for those years between 1820 and 1842. Before going to the First Provincial Council in 1829, England invited the priests and laity in the Georgia convention to approach him directly: "Should you have any topics to urge, or any suggestions to make respecting the concerns of the synod, I shall be most ready to receive them and to procure for them a due and deliberate examination." [53] The following year he reported on the provincial council and urged them to "read again attentively, the letters of the prelates to the clergy and laity." [54] In 1831, the bishop told the convention about Rome's approval of the provincial council decrees and of his need for the convention's assistance in carrying out the canons on "the education of the rising generation":

I know not that I have ever been placed in a station which created in me a stronger conviction of the necessity of calling upon you, that we may take counsel for the purpose of devising some mode by which this great duty might be discharged upon a better system than has hitherto been pursued among us. Should you not perceive that we are prepared to attend to it at present . . . I trust that we may ere long be able to enter into the spirit and practice to which the 34th and 35th canons of our provincial council are directed. [55]

Charleston was the first diocese to have a synod in accordance with the decrees of the First Provincial Council. [56] Time and time again,

England would add an invitation to the delegates in these or similar words: "Should you feel that other objects besides what I have pointed out claim your attention, I shall be ready to furnish you with any information which I possess, and to give to you my opinions upon your requisition."[57]

England saw the convention as the great means to achieve the threefold task to embody, enable, and empower:

> According to the principles of that Constitution upon which we have agreed, one of the great objects of the present convention is to consult together how the scattered portion of our flock in this state might be able to cooperate for their mutual benefit, and by what prudent means they might insure to themselves the certain aids of religion, and transmit them to their descendants.[58]

The legacy of John England lives most concretely today in the Sisters of Charity of Our Lady of Mercy, Bishop England's sisters, who begin each day with a prayer composed by England and who continue the work that he and they began so long ago in the diocese of Charleston. Some of his legacy may be missed because his work was so successful. Hardly anybody notices today that England was one of the forces in ending dueling in the state of South Carolina.[59] The Society of Jesus continues to work among native American people. The Holy Ghost Fathers continue the mission begun in Liberia in 1842. Both of these mission efforts were initiated by John England. He is credited, too, along with one or two other missionaries, with arousing the great missionary spirit in Ireland in the last century. While still in Ireland, his work to bring priests to Australia began the establishment of the church in that part of the world.

The Catholic church in the United States has been touched by his spirit. He was the first Catholic to develop and articulate a theology of separation of church and state and of freedom of religion. His appreciation of the goodness of both of these ideas had so entered the Catholic church in the United States that they are accepted by the universal church. When John F. Kennedy defended the right of a Catholic to be a candidate for president of the United States, several Catholic theologians helped him formulate his position. The words they used reflected the ideas of John England's Address to the Congress in 1826.[60] England brought organization and a bond of common purpose to the church in the United States that has remained from the First Provincial Council to the present day. The *United States Catholic Miscellany* has grown into a large and varied Catholic press in this country.

The *Missal for the Laity* was published in 1822 and reprinted in

1843, with further editions in 1861, 1865, and 1867. The lengthy "Explanation of the Mass" that introduced the first *Missal* was ordered printed in the *Ceremonial for Use of the Catholic Churches in the USA* and so guided the clergy for a number of years in their understanding of the mass. It appeared again in 1870 in an edition of the popular *Garden of the Soul* by Richard Challoner. This *Missal* of John England printed over a period of forty-five years and the earlier English missals in England and Ireland are a missing chapter in studies of liturgical piety.

The published writings of John England have influenced the Catholic church in the United States since England wrote his first pastoral letter in 1821. Most of his writings appeared in the *Miscellany* and some were published in pamphlet or book during his life. Interest in England's thought is unique in the history of the American church. England's writings were collected and published in five volumes by his successor, Ignatius Reynolds, in 1849. In 1884, a two-volume edition of selected writings was prepared and published by Hugh P. McElrone. New editions of McElrone's volumes appeared in 1894 and 1900. In 1908 Sebastian Messmer, archbishop of Milwaukee, published a new complete edition of England's *Works* in seven volumes. In consideration of the fact that England's writings were printed over and over again for sixty-six years after his death, it is hard to measure, and not easy to overstate, his influence. His writings remain a storehouse for the development of an American Catholic theology.

But it is the *Constitution* that is at the heart of his legacy. The *Constitution* may be compared to the U.S. Constitution, but its more sure roots are the constitutions of the many religious orders and congregations. It is often said that the Catholic church is not a democracy. England would agree, but he was just as sure that it was not a monarchy. England saw that the *Constitution* allowed the church to function like a body. Today England would see that his method was a truly sacramental expression of church.

Sidney E. Ahlstrom called John England "one of the greatest prelates ever to grace the church in America".[61] Ahlstrom may be right.

PART TWO

The Immigrant Church, 1850–1910

Immigration and ethnic pluralism were already characteristics of the American church before Carroll's death. By 1850, the Catholic church was the largest single denomination in the United States, but its growth was due almost entirely to immigration. From 1820 to 1850, the Catholic population in the United States grew from 195,000 out of 7,866,797 white Americans to 1,606,000 out of 26,900,000. This rapid increase in Catholic numbers evoked the response of anti-Catholic nativism. In the summer of 1834, an Ursuline convent was burned in Charlestown, Massachusetts. A minority report of the state legislature argued that the Ursulines had no right to sue for damages since they recognized "the supremacy of a foreign potentate or power." At their council in 1837, the bishops issued a pastoral letter on the respective rights and obligations that Catholics, as citizens, had toward church and state.

The 1840s witnessed more anti-Catholic demonstrations. In Philadelphia, Bishop Francis P. Kenrick had secured from the public school board the permission for Catholic children to read their own Bible, that is, the Douay version. In May 1844, rioters burned two Catholic churches, and several people were killed. To restore calm, Kenrick ordered his churches temporarily closed. The July heat led to new outbreaks of riots that left thirteen dead and fifty wounded. When Catholics later tried to sue for damages, the opposition argued that this issue had arisen from their trying to remove the Bible from the schools altogether.

After the May riots, the nativists tried to move their show from Philadelphia to New York, where they planned a rally in Central Park. There, they encountered an Irish-born bishop of a different stripe. Ordained for Philadelphia, John Hughes became coadjutor to Bishop John Dubois of New York in 1837 and became bishop in 1842. He blamed Kenrick for not having defended his churches. "If a single Catholic Church were burned in New York," he declared, "the city would become a second Moscow [i.e., general devastation]." Denied the right to sue for any possible damages, he placed over a thousand armed men around each church. There were no riots in New York.

Hughes typified the immigrant Irish bishop of the Northeast. A militant defender of immigrants' rights, he resisted efforts to move them to farmland in the Midwest where they might not have priests. For him, the immigrant was to be urbanized and Americanized, and this meant, in part, to become patriotic. However, this social situation introduced into American Catholicism a false notion that the separation of church and state meant a divorce between religion and public policy. On the eve of the Civil War, the bishops remained aloof from the slavery question and issued careful directives that priests were not to address political issues. Catholics were to be law-abiding and to show their patriotism by serving in the nation's wars, as they did with distinction in the Civil War.

In the postwar years, Catholics were accorded a certain degree of acceptance. Immigration continued to swell their ranks, but the principal objects of anti-Catholicism were more usually the bishops. New tensions developed. The American church was a kaleidoscope of nationalities, and the hierarchy reflected this heterogeneity. The Anglo-French domination had given way to the Irish, with German-Americans making strides especially in Saint Louis, Cincinnati, and the dioceses of Wisconsin. The church and its diocesan structure had now spanned the continent. Sometimes with this expansion a new ethnic group peacefully replaced an older one, as was the case with San Francisco, which was erected as an archdiocese in 1853. Its first archbishop, the Spanish-born Joseph Sadoc Alemany, requested a coadjutor in 1883. The names he submitted were John Lancaster Spalding and Francis Silas Chatard, both American-born, and Patrick J. Riordan, Canadian-born, who received the appointment. The older Spanish Catholic population had given way to an English-speaking people, especially the Irish.

But California was still far from the center of power—and conflict. The principal immigrant antagonists were the Germans and the Irish, but they set a pattern for later conflict between the Irish and Germans on the one hand and the Poles and Italians on the other. The issue was how American the Catholic church could become. Language became one criterion, and here the Irish had an advantage. John Ireland used it as one of his tools in his program of Americanization. But German-Americans had a difficulty. Many of them were skilled farmers who had moved to the rural Midwest. They had retained their language, and it was an important means of preserving the faith of their children. Conflict was inevitable.

Not all the Irish-American bishops were cut from the same cloth. In Saint Louis, Peter Richard Kenrick was named coadjutor to Bishop Joseph Rosati in 1841, succeeded to the see in 1843, became first archbishop in 1847, and remained until he was forced to retire in 1895. He and his brother, Francis P., bishop of Philadelphia and later archbishop of Baltimore—they wrote to each other in Latin in formal style, as befitted two prelates—belonged to a different generation. Peter Kenrick spoke German and had appointed a German vicar general long before there was any demand for such an office, though he did alienate German-Americans in the 1880s by declaring that only the English-speaking churches or quasi parishes enjoyed full parochial rights. An enigmatic man, he had presided over his province, which extended from the border of Canada to New Mexico, until the new provinces of Santa Fe and Milwaukee were erected in 1875. Milwaukee became the principal German center with its succession of archbishops John M. Henni, Michael J. Heiss, and Frederick Katzer. A new generation of Irish-Americans now arose who would foment controversy. John Ireland, who had his own province of Saint Paul created out of Milwaukee to free himself from German influence, was the leader of the Americanizers, almost all of whom, except Cardinal James Gibbons, were Irish-born. The Germans and second-generation Irish like Michael J. Corrigan opposed him.

The Holy See was deeply concerned about this ethnic division. When Archbishop Francesco Satolli was appointed the first apostolic delegate to the American hierarchy, he received instructions to work for the political and social homogeneity of the immigrants within the nation. One way of doing this, of course, was to reduce ethnic identity and tension by increasing Roman loyalty. The process of Romanization of the American church had already begun, but it gained headway with the condemnation of Americanism in 1899. Both Frederick Katzer and Michael A. Corrigan, allied in opposition to John Ireland, now found the pope exercising his infallible office, not only in solemn definitions of faith, but also in the apostolic letter *Testem Benevolentiae*. Their theological mind-set would be a characteristic of the twentieth-century American church.

The studies that follow focus mainly on bishops who gained prominence after the Civil War. Most were of Irish birth or Irish descent. Only Martin J. Spalding could claim a heritage that went back to colonial Maryland. The chapters reflect an immigrant church in transition. John Purcell's theology of papal infallibility at Vatican I stood in sharp contrast with that of Corrigan and Katzer at the end of the century. Ireland and Gibbons were the dominant or at least the most controversial figures at the turn of the century, and, for them, making the church acceptable in the United States was more important than theological nuances. Riordan, sympathetic with Ireland on many things, was more concerned with the development of his own diocese than in national, much less international, affairs.

CHAPTER
5
John Baptist Purcell:
First Archbishop
of Cincinnati

M. Edmund Hussey

$\mathscr{A}$t the beginning of the nineteenth century, Edmund and Joanna
Keefe Purcell lived in a small stone house on Bridge Street in the
beautiful town of Mallow, just seventeen miles north of the Irish port
city of Cork. Edmund was a nailmaker, the only one in County Cork
according to one report. He and Joanna were already the parents of
two daughters, Catherine and Margaret, when on the morning of February 26, 1800, a son was born to them whom they named John Baptist. Eight years later, on March 31, 1808, another son, Edward, was
born, who would later become his elder brother's principal agent and
close associate throughout John's brilliant and useful, but ultimately
heart-breaking, career as archbishop of Cincinnati.[1]

When he was eighteen years of age, John Baptist Purcell emigrated
to the United States. The slender, sandy-haired young man arrived
in Baltimore in the summer of 1818 with little more to his name than
a Latin baptismal certificate.[2] He often said in later years that his
primary purpose in coming to America had been to obtain an education and to study for ordination to the priesthood.[3] He first decided
to strengthen his resources by acquiring a teacher's certificate. Ac-

cordingly he presented himself to the faculty of Asbury Methodist College in Maryland and on September 25, 1818, received a document testifying that he was well acquainted with Greek, Latin, and arithmetic and recommending him for a teaching position.[4]

For the next fifteen years, John was a student and a teacher. He first tutored in the home of a Doctor Wilson in Queen Anne County on the eastern shore of Maryland. During the summer of 1820 he entered Mount Saint Mary's Seminary in Emmitsburg, where he began his own studies for the priesthood while also teaching Latin, arithmetic, and perhaps other subjects to the younger pupils. In February of 1824, he left Emmitsburg to enroll in the Sulpician Seminary at Paris for the completion of his theological studies. Finally on Saturday, May 20, 1826, he was ordained to the priesthood by the archbishop of Paris in the Cathedral of Notre Dame.

After his ordination, John returned to Emmitsburg, where he remained for six years, first as a professor of theology and then as the president of the financially straitened and struggling seminary.[5] He was completing his third year as president when news arrived from Ohio that Edward Dominic Fenwick, the first bishop of Cincinnati, had died of cholera on September 27, 1832. Father Frederic Résé, a German-speaking Swiss priest who had served as Bishop Fenwick's vicar general in Cincinnati, was appointed administrator of the vacant diocese.[6] The diplomatic maneuvers and behind-the-scenes negotiations began the process of choosing a new bishop for the orphaned church. Individual bishops at that time customarily submitted to Rome a list of three nominees, known as a *terna*. Francis P. Kenrick, the coadjutor bishop of Philadelphia, put Purcell's name into consideration by proposing a *terna* which included Peter Kenny, S.J., of Georgetown College, John Baptist Purcell of Emmitsburg, and Frederic Résé of Cincinnati.[7] Bishop Joseph Rosati of Saint Louis and Bishop Benedict Flaget of Bardstown added John Hughes of Philadelphia to the list of nominees.[8]

On February 25, 1833, Pope Gregory XVI presided at a meeting of the *Congregatio de Propaganda Fide* at the Vatican. Bishop John England of Charleston, who was in Rome at the time, also attended the meeting and later that same day dashed off a letter to Purcell informing him that Résé had been appointed bishop of the newly established Diocese of Detroit and that Purcell was the final choice of the three candidates (Kenny, Purcell, and Hughes) who had been considered for Cincinnati.[9] On August 2, the thirty-three-year-old president of Mount Saint Mary Seminary finally received the official notification of his appointment. The ceremony of his episcopal consecration took place in the cathedral of Baltimore on Sunday, October 13, with Archbishop Whitfield officiating.

After winding up his affairs in Maryland, Purcell arrived in Cincinnati aboard the steamboat *Emigrant* on Thursday, November 14, at 10:00 A.M. He was welcomed at the home of a Mr. Santiago across the street from Saint Peter's Cathedral, where he vested in his episcopal robes. A group of priests then accompanied him to the cathedral; there he was met by Bishop Flaget, who formally escorted him to his official chair according to the ritual prescribed for the occasion.[10]

The Catholic church in Ohio was at that time a young but rapidly growing church. In 1816, just seventeen years before Purcell's arrival, Bishop Flaget had assigned Edward Dominic Fenwick, a Dominican, to be the first full-time priest in Ohio. Three years later Fenwick was joined on the Ohio mission by his nephew, Nicholas Dominic Young, who had just been ordained a Dominican priest. These two missioners made their headquarters at Somerset in the southeastern section of the state, but they actually spent most of their time on horseback and were known as itinerant preachers.[11]

Meanwhile the few Catholic families of Cincinnati were working to establish a congregation in their city. In 1819, these families legally incorporated themselves as the "Congregation of the Roman Catholick Church at Cincinnati to be known as Christ Church." They built a small frame church in which mass was celebrated for the first time on Easter Sunday of that year.[12]

Toward the end of that same year, Bishop Flaget of Bardstown, whose jurisdiction included the state of Ohio, sent a report to the *Congregatio de Propaganda Fide* in Rome, recommending that Ohio be made a separate diocese. He wrote: "The State of Ohio may contain from 250 to 300 Catholic families, scattered here and there. Two Dominicans officiate in that country. . . . Monsignor DuBourg and myself are convinced that a bishop there would do a great deal of good."[13] Rome accepted Flaget's recommendation, and on June 19, 1821, documents were signed in Rome establishing the Diocese of Cincinnati, which was to include the entire state of Ohio, and appointing Edward Fenwick its first bishop.

During the eleven years of Bishop Fenwick's tenure, the state of Ohio experienced a rapid growth in population, and the Catholic church shared in that growth. Shortly before his death, Fenwick wrote a description of his diocese to a friend in England, which is a clear and concise summary of his legacy to his successor:

> My diocese in Ohio and Michigan is flourishing. It contains twenty-four priests, twenty-two churches and several more congregations without churches, whereas fourteen years ago there was not a church and I was the only missionary in the State of Ohio. Our college in Cincinnati is in complete operation, excepting the philosophical department for which the apparatus long expected is not yet arrived. Our seminary, which is

united to the college and cathedral, contains thirteen seminarians preparing for Holy Orders. We have a private press and a weekly paper
entitled The *Catholic Telegraph* of Cincinnati.[14]

Purcell would be the bishop and later archbishop of Cincinnati
for half a century, from 1833 to 1883, and would preside over the
transformation of this scattered missionary diocese into a vigorous,
well-developed, and influential archdiocese. The number of priests
and religious would increase dramatically. Churches, schools, orphanages, hospitals, and other institutions would multiply with
breathless speed.

The young bishop of Cincinnati had every reason to be pleased
with the legacy that his predecessor had bequeathed to him. But Purcell had come from Maryland and his point of reference was the well-
established Archdiocese of Baltimore—Cincinnati could only suffer
by comparison. He saw debts, unfinished work, primitive maintenance, and inconveniences, but the Catholics of Cincinnati saw these
manifestations as improvements, progress, and signs of future growth.
In a journal that he kept for the first months of his episcopate, he
recorded some ungracious and exaggerated criticisms of his legacy.[15]
A year after his arrival in Cincinnati, he confided to Bishop England:
"I found myself badly disappointed on arriving here."[16]

But Purcell was by temperament an ebullient optimist with an
enormous amount of energy and a great fund of resourceful prag-
matism. He quickly put aside his initial hypercriticism and threw
himself into his work with enthusiasm and determination. In his first
five months in Cincinnati he resolved some legal complications in
settling Fenwick's estate, wrote a number of articles for the *Catholic
Telegraph*, taught some theology classes to the seminarians, wrote two
pastoral letters to the clergy and the people of the diocese, purchased
a lot for a church for the German Catholics of the city, and blessed
the cornerstone for the new church building.[17]

In April Purcell was ready to visit the rest of his diocese. He left
Cincinnati on April 21 for a three-month tour of the state, traveling
by river steamer, canal boat, stagecoach, and horseback. He celebrated
masses, heard confessions, administered confirmation, dedicated
churches, and preached countless sermons. Along the way, he mailed
back to the *Catholic Telegraph* detailed accounts of his travels, which
are now an excellent resource for the early history of the Catholic
church in Ohio. This was the first of many such tours which not only
enabled him to know and appreciate his diocese but also made his
own dynamic and gracious personality familiar throughout the state.
He cultivated many small groups of Catholic families that subsequently grew into strong congregations. He also devoted considerable

energy to non-Catholics, who were the overwhelming majority of the citizens of Ohio, addressing them in courthouses, in schools, and even in their own churches. His engaging manner and pleasant wit made him a popular figure.

Although he was conciliatory and cordial to non-Catholics, Purcell was never one to retreat from a challenge. At the 1836 meeting of the Western Literary Institute in Cincinnati (more popularly called the College of Teachers), Alexander Campbell, a well-known controversialist and the founder of the Disciples of Christ, offered a challenge that the bishop accepted. Both Purcell and Campbell had addressed the institute at its fall meeting and later began to dispute about the merits of the Reformation.[18]

Campbell, always eager for a debate and sensing a great opportunity, announced that he was prepared to demonstrate seven propositions against the Catholic church and challenged Purcell to debate them in the following January. Purcell was also an avid debater and likewise sensed a splendid opportunity to present the Catholic church favorably to non-Catholics. He, therefore, quickly accepted the challenge.[19]

The debate was well publicized in advance and was quite a spectacle. Visitors from out of town filled Cincinnati's hotels. The discussions were held in the Baptist church on Sycamore Street, and the audience was so large that there was some fear for the safety of the building. Stenographers recorded all the speeches, which were then published within a month by a local printer.[20]

The debate began on the auspicious date of Friday, the thirteenth of January, 1837, and continued for seven days, excluding a Sunday. There were two sessions each day, a three-hour session in the morning and a two-hour session in the afternoon. One proposition was debated each day, with Campbell opening each discussion and Purcell responding. Although both speakers used a rather strong and polemic style of oratory rather than the more careful language of scholarship, yet the debate was conducted on a high level and gave evidence of the impressive biblical and historical knowledge of both men. The printed record shows that Purcell had the lighter touch and evoked more laughter and applause than the somewhat dour Campbell. Purcell was self-confident, witty, and skilled in the oratorical tricks that delight audiences. On the fifth day of the debate, Campbell mournfully complained that his "learned and ingenious respondent" certainly knew "the power of a laugh, an anecdote, a sigh, a compliment, a picture," and he somewhat solemnly insisted that he was treating the debate "as a grave, serious scriptural and rational discussion."[21]

The climax of the debate was the seventh proposition, which claimed that the Catholic church is essentially anti-American. In countering this proposition, Purcell minimized the claims that were often made for papal prerogatives, especially papal infallibility and the papal power to depose kings. When Campbell charged that the deposing power is part of Catholic doctrine, Purcell categorically denied his accusation and showed that this claim was not made for nearly a thousand years and therefore could not belong to the original deposit of faith. The bishop further declared that he would never defend any papal use of this deposing power.[22]

Campbell also repeatedly charged that Catholics believe the pope to be infallible, and each time Purcell denied that infallibility was a Catholic dogma (which was, of course, quite accurate, since the dogma had not yet been defined). The bishop's clearest statement on this issue (which will be important for understanding his later opposition to the definition of infallibility) came on the very first day of the debate:

> Appeals were lodged before the Bishop of Rome, though he was not believed to be infallible. Neither is he now. No enlightened Catholic holds the pope's infallibility to be an article of faith. I do not; and none of my brethren, that I know of, do. The Catholic believes the pope, as a man, to be as liable to error as almost any other man in the universe. Man is man, and no man is infallible, either in doctrine or in morals.[23]

Purcell, as the respondent, had the last word in the debate. With a masterful sense of oratory, he ended by reading George Washington's 1790 "Letter to the Roman Catholics in the United States of America," in which the first president extended his best wishes to the Catholics, "the faithful subjects of our government."[24]

The Cincinnati *Gazette* gave extensive coverage to the debate, and its editor, the brilliant lawyer and journalist Charles Hammond, awarded the honors to Purcell:

> They [the Cincinnati Protestants] heard the Bishop's expositions of the points of exception, and they learned that they had believed much that was disputed and had condemned much that was capable of plausible explanation. They ascertained that Mr. Campbell was often at fault in his arguments. . . . Thus did they come to understand that there was a fair side as well as a foul one for Catholicism, and herein have the Catholics *gained* in something while they have *suffered* in nothing.[25]

Not everyone agreed with the editor of the *Gazette*, of course. The debate received national publicity, with the Catholic press unanimously awarding the victory to Purcell and the Protestant press, although naturally less united, generally supporting Campbell's claim to victory. But even many Catholics had some misgivings about the value of such contests. Bishop England tactfully hinted at these misgivings to Purcell:

> I have read with deep interest the book of your controversy which you were good enough to send me. You had a formidable antagonist and you were in a bad position and got out of it better than I could have imagined. I would not, for anything that I could say, be so placed.[26]

Nevertheless the Purcell–Campbell debate did establish the young bishop of Cincinnati as the leading Catholic spokesman of the Midwest. His eloquence, his conciliatory manner, and his strong devotion to American liberties gained him many Protestant as well as Catholic admirers.

In the 1830s and 1840s Cincinnati became a mecca for the farmers and skilled artisans of Germany.[27] Their native cities and states were experiencing severe economic reversals, and Cincinnati, a growing city on a major river near much fertile land, was experiencing great economic expansion. The new opportunities of the "Queen City of the West" attracted German immigrants in large numbers. By 1840, native Germans in Cincinnati numbered 14,163, or 31 percent, of the city's 46,382 population.[28] It was estimated that three-fourths of these Germans were Catholics.[29]

The continuing immigration of Germans made Cincinnati virtually a German city. "For many years Cincinnati did not even try to assimilate its German immigrants; instead they assimilated Cincinnati."[30] This influx of Germans peaked in 1890, seven years after Purcell's death, when the Germans numbered 57.4 percent of Cincinnati's total population.[31]

Shortly after his arrival in Cincinnati in 1833, Bishop Purcell recognized the need of a second parish in the city, for the use of Germans.[32] There was a special mass for them at the cathedral each Sunday, but that arrangement was no longer adequate for their increasing numbers.

Establishing a pattern that he would follow throughout his fifty-year tenure as bishop and archbishop, Purcell agreed to allow the Germans to manage their own affairs as much as possible. Accordingly the German Catholics held a series of meetings to make the necessary decisions about their new parish, and they chose a board of twelve trustees who would manage the parish. Work on the building proceeded so quickly that the first German Catholic church west of the Allegheny Mountains was dedicated on October 5, 1834, less than a year after Purcell arrived in Cincinnati.[33] By the time the Civil War broke out, there were ten German Catholic parishes in the city and only four English-speaking parishes (which were predominately Irish). Many additional German parishes had also been established throughout the state, especially in rural areas where German farmers had settled.

The German Catholics were an independent lot. They wished to be actively involved in the ongoing administration of their parishes through their own elected trustees. In other dioceses throughout the United States, parish trustees had been the occasion of serious conflicts, and many bishops had overreacted to these tensions by completely excluding parishioners from all decision-making. Purcell certainly recognized the risks of the trustee system. But he also understood the German need for independence and self-determination. Accordingly in 1850 he gave official recognition to the self-government system that the German Catholics had developed, and he sought only to minimize the risks of conflict inherent in the system.[34]

Each German parish was to have six elected wardens, at least thirty years of age, of exemplary character, active in the practice of their faith and listed on the membership roster of the parish. Their responsibilities concerned the temporal affairs of the parish but did not extend to the areas of worship and doctrine. They were to provide funds to meet the debts of the parish, establish the amount of the pew rent, ensure that the buildings remained in good repair, and deposit surplus funds "in some safe public institution." Large and unusual expenditures were to be submitted to the congregation at a public meeting.[35]

This system of wardens apparently served the German parishes quite well, and there is no evidence that Archbishop Purcell ever had to intervene in any disputes. In a circular letter to the clergy in 1864, Purcell expressed his satisfaction with the wardens but showed no inclination to extend this system to the Irish parishes.[36]

Purcell also recognized the special identity of the German Catholics in his diocese by appointing a German vicar general as well as an "English" (or, more accurately, an Irish) vicar general to assist him in the administration of the diocese. Father John Martin Henni, the pastor of Holy Trinity Church in Cincinnati, served as the first German vicar general from 1838 until 1844, when he became the first bishop of Milwaukee. He was succeeded by Father Joseph Ferneding, pastor of Saint Paul Parish in Cincinnati's "Over the Rhine" district. After Ferneding's death in 1872, Purcell appointed the superior of the Franciscan Fathers, Otto Jair, as his German vicar general, thus recognizing the importance of the Franciscans to the German Catholics of Cincinnati as well as Jair's personal leadership in the German Catholic community.

An important reason why Purcell had a good rapport with the German Catholics of Cincinnati was that he genuinely admired them and made every effort to make them feel welcome in the diocese. He realized that they were a great source of strength for the diocese and took every opportunity to tell them so. In turn, they liked Purcell and were grateful for his courtesies toward them. They presented him with a gold cross and chain when he was elevated to the rank of archbishop in 1850 and organized a grand celebration to honor the twenty-fifth anniversary of his consecration as a bishop in 1858.[37]

The German complexion of Cincinnati was no handicap to its Irish archbishop primarily because he recognized their need to have an effective voice in the management of their own affairs and in the settlement of their own disputes. He was also gracious enough to speak well of their many dedicated priests and to praise their awe-inspiring institutions: their beautiful churches, their large and ably managed schools, their well-groomed cemeteries, and their attractive orphanage. In turn, they were devoted to him and supported him loyally.[38]

The Civil War temporarily slowed immigration into the United States and so gave Archbishop Purcell a brief respite from one set of problems. Yet it only put other pressures on him, especially concerning the position he should take on the issue of slavery. Cincinnati was on the Mason-Dixon Line, the symbolic border between the North and the South, and it had long prided itself on being the "Gateway to the South." Its economic vitality depended heavily on trade with the southern states. And Purcell's own Irish Catholic flock, largely laborers, shuddered at any talk about the emancipation of the slaves because they feared that freed Negroes would emigrate from the South to the North and squeeze them out of the job markets.

Certainly no American Catholic bishop was an advocate for the institution of slavery, and most of them, when put on the spot, declared that they hoped for the eventual and gradual emancipation of the slaves in the United States. Yet they carefully avoided any involvement in the pre–Civil War abolitionist movements. There were at least four reasons for their reluctance to support abolitionism. First, many of those who shouted, "No slavery" were the same who also shouted, "No popery." The Catholic bishops could hardly have had a comfortable alliance with such rabid anti-Catholics. Secondly, the immigrant members of their own church felt that freed slaves would be ruinous competition for them in the labor pools. Thirdly, the bishops feared that abolition might become as divisive an issue for their already diverse immigrant church as it had been for the Protestant churches. And fourthly, the bishops were well aware of the importance of the separation of church and state in this country and therefore carefully refrained from public involvement in political affairs.

Slavery was certainly a political and an economic issue. But Purcell also recognized that it was a moral issue of great importance as well. He struggled to avoid personal involvement in slavery as a political issue but in the end realized that he could not avoid it as a moral issue.[39]

As early as 1838, Purcell had publicly acknowledged the inconsistency between the American principle that all persons are born free and the existence of slavery in this country. In a speech in his native town of Mallow in Ireland during that year, he clearly condemned slavery in principle. But he reminded his Irish audience that slavery had been introduced into America by the English, and that it had become deeply established in the economic and political fabric of the country. He then pointed out that prudence sometimes prevents a government from introducing political improvements quickly and without careful preparation.[40] This is his only known statement on the subject of slavery prior to the eve of the Civil War.

After Fort Sumter was fired upon in April of 1861, a large Union flag was unfurled atop the lofty spire of Saint Peter-in-Chains Cathedral in Cincinnati with advance publicity and with great fanfare.[41] This dramatic gesture, however, was a pro-Union rather than an antislavery stand.

In 1862 Archbishop Purcell spent four months travelling in Europe to recruit personnel and to raise funds for his archdiocese. After his return to Cincinnati, arrangements were made for him to present a public lecture at Pike's Opera House, entitled "Impressions of Europe." In his talk the archbishop described European impressions of the American Civil War more than his own impressions of Europe. He then went on to speak about slavery itself. He charged that the South had kept millions of persons in bondage, curtailing their natural rights to marriage and family life and forbidding them to be educated. He declared that the North could have won the war within three months if it had only proclaimed the emancipation of the slaves and had armed them against their former owners. Even now, he went on, the South could convert their strongest abolitionist foes into friends if it would only pledge to abolish slavery "after a given period, say fifty, seventy or a hundred years."[42]

The speech was a great sensation and its antislavery tone drew hostile criticism. The *Catholic Mirror* of Philadelphia scolded the archbishop for "demanding" that the South free its slaves and attacked him for abandoning the pulpit and climbing the political rostrum.[43] Although Purcell had suggested that a gradual emancipation of the slaves might be acceptable, yet he had made a bold step beyond a narrowly pro-Union position.

Less than a month later, President Lincoln issued his Emancipation Proclamation, providing that on the following January 1 all slaves would be declared free in those states still in rebellion. The Peace Democrats of Ohio decided to make the fall elections a referendum on the issue of emancipation. The Cincinnati *Enquirer* trumpeted a campaign slogan playing on the fears of the immigrant workers that freed slaves would move north and displace them: "The Constitution as it is, the Union as it was and the Negroes where they are."[44] The Democrats swept the state in the November elections, which were a disaster for the Union party and for Lincoln.

In accord with the Emancipation Proclamation, on January 1, 1863, the Lincoln administration considered the slaves in eight Confederate states to be free. The proclamation did not apply to the four Border states which had not seceded nor to the Confederate states already occupied by the Union troops, since they were no longer considered in rebellion. Slavery, therefore, continued to be a legal institution for another two years, until the adoption of the Thirteenth Amendment in 1865.

Neither the archbishop nor his newspaper, the *Catholic Telegraph*, took an immediate position on these developments. But on April 8, 1863, an eloquent editorial appeared in the *Catholic Telegraph* declaring that slavery was finally ended in the United States:

> The first cannon at Sumter sounded its knell. It would be much easier to take Richmond or open the Mississippi than to restore slavery in the United States. The thing is gone forever. . . . Whether we like it or not, slavery is extinguished in the United States and all that we have to do is decide how we shall accommodate ourselves to coming events.

The *Catholic Telegraph* was edited by Father Edward Purcell, the brother, trusted adviser, and vicar general of the archbishop. Whether the archbishop or his brother actually wrote the editorial is a matter of dispute. But the secular as well as the Catholic press identified the views of the *Catholic Telegraph* with those of the archbishop. Enemies condemned both in the same breath and friends praised them both together.

Once having embarked on its abolitionist course, the *Catholic Telegraph* continued to press on with zest and to devote significant editorial space to the topic. However, the fears of the white workers also remained a concern for the paper. The *Catholic Telegraph* assumed that the Negroes would remain in the South but realized that the details of this question could be considered only after they were totally free. The ultimate resolution of the problem was the hands of Divine Providence.[45]

Throughout the war the paper had betrayed two somewhat inconsistent editorial tendencies, one stressing the interests of the white workers and the other upholding Negro rights against white prejudice. The first tendency dominated during the early days of the war and the second gradually became more prominent during its later years. A bold statement of the second tendency came on May 25, 1864, in a condemnation of anti-Negro riots: "Those colored men have a right to life and liberty as much as the white men, and those who oppress them without reason and only to gratify an insatiable and disgraceful prejudice, are the enemies of order and religion."

In this period of intense controversy, when feelings ran high, neither the archbishop nor his paper always maintained an even and consistent tone. As the struggle unfolded and revealed to him its implications, Purcell's attitude developed gradually but surely from a theoretical condemnation of slavery through a patriotic but narrow defense of the Union to a bold and frequently unpopular condemnation of the concrete system of slavery in the United States and to a clear although at times strained defense of complete equality for the black people of America. No other bishop took such a strong stand for abolition during the war and no other Catholic paper (except the privately published *Brownson's Quarterly Review*) openly supported emancipation to the extent that the *Catholic Telegraph* did.

The last of Archbishop Purcell's many trips to Europe was in 1869 to attend the First Council of the Vatican. Pope Pius IX had summoned this council because "the Catholic Church . . . and the supreme authority of this Holy See are by the bitterest enemies of God and man assailed and trampled down."[46] The lengthening shadow cast over the Papal States by the Italian risorgimento had prompted the beleaguered pope to seek a vote of confidence for the papal office in the church. He feared that the loss of papal temporal power might endanger the papacy itself. It soon became apparent that the pope hoped that this vote of confidence would take the form of the definition of papal infallibility.

Archbishop Purcell did not consider the impending loss of the Papal States in such catastrophic terms. In fact, in an 1868 letter to Archbishop Spalding of Baltimore, he denounced the idea that the dissolution of the pope's temporal power would bring about the dissolution of the church. To say that the pope needs a royal supremacy in order to have a spiritual supremacy is to reduce his spiritual supremacy to an absurdity. He recalled that in the early centuries of the church popes had had a primacy without any temporal power.[47]

Purcell had also long been uncomfortable with any tendency to see the infallibility of the church located exclusively in the person of the pope.[48] As earlier recounted, in 1832 he had clearly told Alexander Campbell (and anyone else who was listening), "The Catholic believes the pope, as a man, to be as liable to error as almost any other man in the universe. Man is man, and no man is infallible, either in doctrine or in morals."[49] He was equally reluctant to see the infallibility of the church located exclusively in the Bible or in any other single place or single group of persons. Rather he emphasized the whole church as the rule of faith: "We have a . . . pearl of great value, a diamond with which we cut the brittle glass of mere human creeds in pieces, and with which we solve every difficulty. It is this: I believe in the Holy Catholic Church."[50]

As a matter of course, therefore, Purcell allied himself with the Inopportunists throughout the council. During the council's first weeks he tried to keep the very question of papal infallibility off the official agenda. A petition initiated by Archbishop Kenrick of Saint Louis and drafted by Purcell himself was sent to the pope and to the presidents of the council on January 15, 1870. Twenty American bishops and seven other English-speaking bishops signed this petition, which argued that a debate on the question would be divisive, that a definition of papal infallibility would alienate non-Catholics, and that interminable arguments would arise about which specific teachings would or would not be considered infallible.[51]

In March a rumor swept through Rome that the dogma would be passed by acclamation and without any debate or discussion. On March 15, Archbishop Kenrick and Archbishop Purcell, joined by Bishop Edward Fitzgerald of Little Rock and Bishop David Moriarty of Kerry in Ireland, sent a formal notice to the council presidents that, if such a maneuver were attempted, they would leave Rome at once and make public their reason for doing so.[52]

On May 31, Purcell addressed the council assembly to explain his conviction that a definition of papal infallibility would be unwise and inopportune. He cited the already-current disputes about when the pope actually does speak *ex cathedra* and, therefore, infallibly according to the proposed dogma. He then referred to a number of instances in which previous popes had taught heretical doctrines. Next he reminded the bishops that many popes had claimed supreme temporal power throughout the world, including the power to depose monarchs, and insisted that this power must be repudiated lest it be considered infallible doctrine. And he finally offered a rather lengthy affirmation of infallibility as exercised in various ways by the bishops of the church and by the pope in union with the church.[53]

By the end of June, the eventual vote for papal infallibility was a foregone conclusion. Many of the Inopportunists preferred not to cast a public vote against the dogma and asked to be excused from the remaining sessions. Purcell, using illness as his plea, obtained permission to leave the council at the beginning of July.

He arrived at New York aboard the steamer *Saint Laurent* on August 10 and went to Sweeney's Hotel, where a reporter from the New York *Herald* interviewed him that evening. The reporter said that the archbishop had declared himself an anti-infallibilist and had labeled Archbishop Manning of Westminster, a convert from the Anglican church who was a strong advocate of the definition, a fanatic whom the Anglicans were glad to get rid of because of the disturbing influence he had been in their councils. The reporter further quoted Purcell as saying that the dogma could not be officially promulgated until all of the bishops signed it and as predicting that the American Church would never accept the dogma.[54]

Even allowing for some inaccuracy and exaggeration on the part of the reporter, Purcell had some explaining to do. At least two bishops, Patrick Lynch of Charleston and Sylvester Rosecrans of Columbus, immediately wrote nervous letters to Purcell, betraying their anxiety that he might continue to make unwise statements. Lynch tried to impress on him the great caution that is needed when talking to the press.[55]

Shortly after his return to Cincinnati, Purcell hoped to calm the troubled waters with an address at Mozart Hall. In his speech to a large crowd on Sunday evening, August 21, the archbishop defended his opposition to infallibility by rehearsing all of the arguments he had made against the dogma during the council. But, far from settling the issue, this unfortunate and ill-advised tactic left him unable to give a very convincing rationale for now accepting a dogma which he could so easily refute. The Cincinnati *Daily Gazette* remarked that his explanations "smacked of a politician consenting to a platform which he did not fully support."[56]

Purcell's participation in the First Council of the Vatican did involve him in a painful dilemma. He could not vote for papal infallibility because it seemed to him to be in conflict with the true nature of the church, with the pastoral needs of the church in the United States, and with a documented history of papal theological and doctrinal errors. Yet, as an archbishop, he could no longer oppose it once it had been officially declared a dogma of the church.

Because of his own deep loyalty to the church, Purcell sent the pope his own acceptance of the council's decision.[57] But he seems to have remained intellectually unconvinced. About a week after his address at Mozart Hall, he received a letter from a Richard E. Randolph of Topeka, Kansas, who had read the newspaper accounts of the archbishop's lecture. Mr. Randolph told Purcell that he had written to Bishop Hughes thirty-four years earlier, asking him whether the Catholic church believed the pope to be infallible. Hughes replied that the church has never taught or held that the pope is infallible but does believe that the church itself is infallible. Hughes illustrated his point by saying that all Americans believe that the United States is independent. Yet that independence does not reside in the president or in the Congress or in the Supreme Court alone, but rather in all of them combined. On the back of this letter Purcell wrote, in a more careful than usual penmanship: "I subscribe to these views with a perfect assent. J.B.P."[58]

When Purcell returned from the First Council of the Vatican, he was already seventy years old. He had been a young man of thirty-three when he had come to Cincinnati. As the bishop and later the archbishop of Cincinnati, he had helped his small diocese develop into a large and distinguished archdiocese. He had showed himself to be a skillful and eloquent defender of his faith in many public debates. He was the Irish bishop of a largely German city and had functioned so capably in that role that the Catholic church in Cincinnati was virtually free from ethnic tensions. He spoke for the abolition of slavery even before President Lincoln issued the Emancipation Proclamation and then later defended the proclamation vigorously. At the Vatican Council he ably, though unavailingly, argued against the opportuneness of defining papal infallibility. In the years following the council, the archbishop was referred to as the "Patriarch of the West" and was considered the dean of the American bishops by reason of his seniority in the hierarchy.

But in 1878 an enormous and disastrous financial failure disgraced and bewildered the aged archbishop and entangled his archdiocese in massive litigation. Overnight the important and influential archbishop became an embarrassment to his own flock and also to the Catholic church throughout the country.[59]

The archbishop's younger brother and vicar general, Father Edward Purcell, also served as the treasurer of the archdiocese with complete power to act for the archbishop in all financial matters. Over forty years earlier, in the aftermath of financial panics in 1837, persons who were uneasy with the shaky conditions of the banks began to place their small savings in Edward's hands for safekeeping. Within a few years, as the word spread that the bishop's priest-brother would accept these deposits and even pay interest on them, the money flowed in from all sides. Soon Edward had a private banking business of enormous proportions. The very incomplete records available to the courts after the crash in 1878 showed that over $13,000,000.00 in deposits were received by Edward between 1847 and 1877. Because he weathered the frequent financial panics of that era, his reputation as a financial genius grew, and he was even credited with having saved other banks.

But, in fact, Edward was not even a careful accountant, and his bank was only a proverbial house of cards. The long overdue day of reckoning came on the last day of October 1878, when the Cincinnati banking house of Hemann and Company failed for about $386,000. A false rumor started that Father Purcell had been Hemann's backer and had lost heavily by the failure. The general uneasiness and the widespread rumors created a real panic, and crowds began to clamor for their money at the cathedral rectory where Father Edward resided. But there was not enough money to meet their demands.

> On the Sunday before Christmas John Baptist Purcell bowed his head on the pulpit edge in the cathedral and told his anguished people that it was all true: There was no more money in his coffers, no more money to pay his trusting flock. The excitement in the city, the grief, the alternating fury, pity, despair, was indescribable, following upon the long financial strain of the country and following upon so complete a trust.[60]

At first the priests of the archdiocese and some wealthy laymen tried to help the situation by voluntary contributions, but these gave only a few days' grace. A complete inventory of all the claims and all the assets of the Purcell bank was finally filed in the probate court on May 23, 1879, and printed in the Cincinnati *Commercial* the next day. The magnitude of the disaster was now a matter both of public record and of public knowledge. Claims amounting to $3,697,651.49 had been presented by 3,485 creditors. Assets, which included many doubtful and worthless notes and some properties over which many lawsuits would be fought, were estimated at only $1,181,569.47.

Attorneys for the creditors instituted legal proceedings for the sale of over two hundred churches, convents, and schools of the archdiocese in order to satisfy the claims of the creditors. These proceedings, in turn, caused the threatened churches and institutions to employ their own legal counsel for their own defense. A three-judge panel heard the lengthy arguments and then took a year and a half to study the case before rendering a decision. They decreed that the archbishop did not own the churches and institutions of the archdiocese as his own personal property but merely held them in trust for the various congregations. Therefore none of these properties could be sold to pay off the claims of the creditors unless it could be shown that the parishes had borrowed money from the Purcell Bank to buy their property or to build their buildings and had not repaid that money. Appeals to higher courts and hearings to determine the validity of claims and the exact liability of various archdiocesan institutions took twenty years. The final accounts in the legal proceedings were not filed until May 11, 1905, and the creditors were able to recover only 7⅛ percent of their deposits.

The feeling of betrayal caused by the failure was summed up in a petition that the creditors sent to Pope Leo XIII:

> The creditors trusted implicitly in the Archbishop and his brother, . . . being assured, whenever inquiry was made, that the diocese was responsible for the payment. It had been generally known to the clergy of

the diocese during the past forty years that the bishop was the depository of the savings of a large class of the Catholic people . . . and no steps were ever taken to prevent it or put a stop to it. But now that the Archbishop is unable to make payment of the moneys so deposited, . . . they are informed by the priests that they must look to the Archbishop and his brother individually, that the diocese is in no way responsible to them, and that they have no claim on the church property of the diocese.[61]

Archbishop Purcell submitted his resignation to Pope Leo XIII immediately after the financial failure became public. The pope permitted Purcell to retain the title of archbishop of Cincinnati and appointed William Henry Elder, the bishop of Natchez, to be Purcell's coadjutor bishop with full powers to administer the archdiocese and with the right of succession to the title and office of archbishop of Cincinnati upon Purcell's death.

The aged archbishop then retired to the Ursuline Convent in Saint Martin, Ohio, about forty-five miles east of Cincinnati, where he lived the final sad years of his life. On October 31, 1880, he suffered the first of four strokes that would afflict him. His brother, Edward, who had also gone to live at the Ursuline Convent, died suddenly on January 21, 1881, within a few hours after he had suffered a stroke. His testimony had not yet been received by the courts, and so the only one who might have been able to give the complete details of the banking enterprise was removed from the scene. The broken archbishop lingered on for another two and a half years. He died on July 4, 1883, and his earthly remains were laid to rest in the rural convent cemetery.

CHAPTER
6
Martin John Spalding

Thomas W. Spalding

$\mathcal{E}$ven as a Roman student, Martin Spalding was given to apodictic pronouncements. "To speak frankly," he wrote his brother, "I do not relish the observation that you made in your last letter, viz. that the body of American Bishops had not wisdom enough to understand the extended & useful plans of Dr. Eng[land]." He found this "disparaging." He had, moreover, reservations about the doctor's "liberal systems."[1] The first American-born student of the Urban College of the Propaganda to become a bishop learned faster than most. At the college he won the coveted gold medal for scholarship. In 1834, just before ordination, he also won a doctorate by defending 256 theses in a cool display of erudition that impressed even the learned Dr. England.[2] He won, in fact, almost every prize he set out to capture. He was a fierce competitor.

Born in 1810 into a Kentucky family whose migration from Maryland a generation earlier had paid off materially, Martin had come under the influence of a French bishop, a Belgian pastor, and an Irish teacher before he entered the seminary at Bardstown. There he had also fallen under the tutelage of another Frenchman and an Irishman.[3] Benedict Flaget, Charles Nerinckx, William Byrne, John Baptist David, and Francis Patrick Kenrick had each contributed in different ways to the well-rounded personality of this gifted Kentuckian, but none had tempered an assertive Americanism born of the frontier. Neither did his Roman education accomplish this end.

The literary and administrative talents Spalding evidenced as a priest paved his way to the episcopacy.[4] The former brought national acclaim, at least in Catholic circles. While president of Saint Joseph's College, pastor in Lexington and Bardstown, and vicar general of the diocese of Louisville, he published, during some nine years once a month or more, essays and reviews for Catholic serials, a history of the Kentucky missions, the first volume of a history of the Reformation, and an apologetical work. As bishop of Louisville, he produced more essays, a biography of his predecessor, another apologetical work, and the second volume of the history of the Reformation; and he edited a book of retreat conferences. He was also in great demand, both as priest and bishop, for his lectures, charity sermons, and addresses for special occasions. An ambitious speaking tour in 1860 included the Tremont Temple in Boston, the Cooper Institute in New York, and the Smithsonian Institution in Washington. While not as prolific as Orestes Brownson, a writer and lecturer by profession, Spalding was probably the most influential American Catholic apologist at mid-century.[5]

Essentially a response to the recurrent assaults upon popery that began about the time of his return from Rome, his apologetical writings were peculiarly American, for the most part original in the arguments he employed as well as the rhetoric with which he clothed them. As a native American, he was eager to have Catholicism understood by his fellow countrymen. As a writer and speaker, however, his greatest achievement was the set of the attitudes he instilled in the immigrant church, particularly the sense of self-esteem so badly needed by the beleaguered newcomers. No one, Brownson himself would admit in 1874, "contributed more than he to the marked change in regard to manliness and courage that has come over the Catholic population of this country within the last thirty or forty years."[6]

As an administrator, Spalding was both lawgiver and institution builder, providing laws that set limits, as well as institutions that sheltered and at the same time insulated the Catholic immigrant against a hostile environment. Though old-stock in birth and breeding and associated with relatively few foreign-born for the first decade of his priesthood, he came increasingly to identify with the immigrant church after his call to Louisville in 1844 as vicar general. By the mid-1850s, his immigrant charges were his principal concern.[7]

Spalding was not the first choice of the feeble patriarch of the West for a coadjutor, but Flaget's first act after the ceremony of episcopal ordination in 1848 was the total surrender of power to him. Immediately the new bishop made a visitation of the most neglected part of the diocese, noting precisely the needs of each congregation, prescribing remedies and reforms. He charged trustees with the restoration and maintenance of churches and cemeteries and the rectification of property titles. He set pastors' salaries and determined an equitable manner of raising them. He appointed catechists where there were none. At Saint Thomas Seminary he conducted a retreat and a conference for the clergy. Back in Louisville, he ended the year with a burst of activity that included a retreat at the cathedral, a series of winter lectures, the opening of a German church, and a charity sermon to help defray the cost of a new penitent asylum and convent for the Sisters of the Good Shepherd. Early the next year he laid plans for a new cathedral.[8] And so it went for the rest of his life. The pace never slackened.

Five months after the death of Flaget, Spalding held the First Diocesan Synod, the first of three he conducted as bishop of Louisville (1850, 1858, and 1862). More important was the role he played at the First Plenary Council of Baltimore in 1852 and the First, Second, and Third Provincial Councils of Cincinnati in 1855, 1858, and 1861. In Baltimore he was earmarked as one of the "two or three" prelates best qualified to "expedite proceedings," to spark the deliberations on such important topics as the administration of property, diocesan organization, Catholic publications, parochial schools, and secret societies, and to perform such dignified drudge work as revising catechisms and ceremonials. In Cincinnati he submitted the bulk of the agenda for all three councils, acted as promoter, and composed the pastorals, "among the most notable documents of this kind," says Peter Guilday, "ever issued by our prelates."[9] As a legislator Spalding had an impact on the antebellum church second only to that of his efforts as an apologist. Baltimore would offer an even better setting to play the role of Solon.

Baltimore would also open greater opportunities for institution-building, but Louisville afforded an excellent proving ground. There his most satisfying achievement was the creation of a parochial school system. After a begging tour of Europe in 1852–1853, during which he persuaded the Xaverian Brothers to come to staff the boys' schools, he boasted to his friend Archbishop Francis Kenrick: "I intend to open several additional parochial schools & 'to run opposition' to those of the city."[10] Already available for the girls' schools were sisterhoods of Kentucky foundation, and in 1858 Ursuline Sisters came from Bavaria to teach the German girls.[11] His dedication to Catholic education found expression in his writings. Nationally he bowed only to Archbishop John Hughes of New York as a greater champion of the Catholic school.

Akin to the institutions he created were the organizations he promoted that served also to center the lives of his immigrant charges upon their church. These included sodalities, confraternities, temperance and benevolent (mutual aid) societies, literary associations, and charitable organizations. He himself established the societies of the Propagation of the Faith, the Holy Childhood, Saint Vincent de Paul (his favorite), and the Confraternity of Saint Peter.

Spalding's leadership in Louisville was severely tested by the rise of the political organization popularly known as the Know-Nothings. He refused to consider such earlier excesses of nativism as the Philadelphia riots of 1844 as anything but a "foul stain" on the "noble escutcheon" of his native land.[12] At that time Spalding related well to such civic leaders as George Prentice, publisher of the prestigious Whig *Journal*, a newspaper of Louisville; with the collapse of the Whig party, however, Prentice converted his paper into a shrill organ of the American, or Know-Nothing, party, and his incendiary editorials were in large part responsible in 1855 for the murders and mayhem of an election day in Louisville called "Bloody Monday." Spalding pleaded with his fellow citizens: "We are to remain on earth but a few years; let us not add to the necessary ills of life those more awful ones of civil feuds and bloody strife."[13] After Bloody Monday he was never without fear of a violent recrudescence of nativism.

Bloody Monday, moreover, transformed him from a Whig into a Democrat, the political affiliation of most of his immigrant charges. But the Democrats themselves split on the eve of a more violent conflict. Spalding stood by Stephen A. Douglas in the presidential race of 1860, while many of his numerous cousins supported John C. Breckinridge of Kentucky, the choice of the South. To enlighten his Roman superiors on the causes of the conflict that followed, Spalding sent in 1863 a "Dissertation on the American Civil War," which was published anonymously in the *Osservatore Romano*. Lincoln, he claimed, had converted the war from one to preserve the union to one of violent emancipation, confiscation, and destruction. With but one or two exceptions, "among whom is my Metropolitan [Archbishop John Baptist Purcell]," the church had pursued a policy of nonintervention in politics, the one he himself advocated strongly.[14] Despite his anti-Lincoln bias, Spalding endeavored to steer a neutral course and cope as best he could with the ravages visited upon Catholic institutions in Kentucky by regular troops and guerrillas alike.

On July 8, 1863, four days after Lee's defeat at Gettysburg, Spalding recorded the death of Archbishop Kenrick of Baltimore ("the greatest, the best, & the most learned of our prelates") in his journal. "I feel like an orphan—he was my father in Christ," he wrote.[15] Now there was no one in the American hierarchy whom Martin Spalding was ready to recognize as his superior in ability or intelligence. In an obvious attempt to win the premier see, he bombarded Rome with missives designed to draw attention to himself, just as he had done when he knew that Flaget was seeking his third coadjutor. Though there was no clear consensus among the American bishops concerning Kenrick's successor, the Congregation of the Propaganda, with whom the choice resided, had no difficulty in settling upon its illustrious alumnus.[16]

On July 31, 1864, Spalding was installed as seventh archbishop of Baltimore in one of its most troubled periods. Though the federal capital was within his jurisdiction, he made no effort to cultivate the close acquaintance of national leaders. His only letter to the president was to seek a pardon for Bishop Patrick N. Lynch of Charleston, who had gone to Rome as a representative of the Confederacy.[17] For most of the problems arising from the war, he worked through Michael O'Connor, former bishop of Pittsburgh but now a Jesuit. Spalding deemed politicians in general "a mean set" and had as little to do with them as possible.

Fearing a fresh outburst of nativism, he refused to intervene in the execution of the unfortunate Mary Surratt, convicted of complicity in the assassination of Lincoln, and imposed silence upon a priest loud in her defense. He did, however, order a special collection for the suffering poor of the South and tried, unsuccessfully, to induce the bishops of wealthier dioceses to do the same.[18] Maryland remained under the control of a Republican government until 1867, when the Democrats returned to power, to the great joy of almost every Catholic in the archdiocese.

At the conclusion of the war, Spalding made a visitation of the entire archdiocese in order to take stock. Its 150,000 Catholics were double those of Louisville, but below a number of other eastern dioceses. The oldest was still the most richly endowed in religious orders and institutions, but Spalding perceived a variety of needs. Many congregations he praised, but one he told bluntly that he had never seen "a more miserable apology for a church" and another that he would remove the pastor if he were not better supported.[19]

In the course of the visitation Spalding arranged for the construction of some twenty churches and the renovation of others. In his seven and a half years in Baltimore, he would create twenty-four new parishes or missions, including the second parish for Germans and the first for blacks in the District of Columbia, as well as the fifth parish for Germans and the first for Bohemians in his see city. At the start he decided that a new city parish would begin with a temporary chapel that would become a school when the congregation was large enough to build a suitable church. Many older parishes built new and larger churches. Many, at the archbishop's prompting, built schools.

Spalding's greatest efforts at institution-building and the ones in which he was most directly involved were designed for the poor. From Louisville he brought Sisters of the Good Shepherd in 1864 to open a penitent asylum for girls. As soon as the war was over, he persuaded the Xaverian Brothers to come to Baltimore to take control of a combination reformatory, orphanage, and trade school. Saint Mary's Industrial School opened in 1866 and, with the Catholic Protectory in New York, served as a model for similar institutions in other dioceses.[20] For orphan girls over fourteen he persuaded the Sisters of Charity to open Saint Joseph's Industrial School in Baltimore in 1865 and Saint Rose's Industrial School in Washington in 1869. In 1869 he also induced the Little Sisters of the Poor to come to Baltimore to open a home for the aged.

Under Spalding the number of religious orders in the archdiocese almost doubled. Besides the Good Shepherd Sisters, Xaverian Brothers, and Little Sisters of the Poor, he invited the Passionists to found a monastery, the Carmelites to replace the Redemptorists in Cumberland, the Religious of the Sacred Heart to establish an exclusive school for young ladies in southern Maryland, and the Mill Hill Fathers to serve the blacks of Baltimore. The Redemptorists invited the Franciscan Sisters to begin a hospital for the Germans. The Redemptorist, Dominican, and Carmelite fathers invited the Brothers of Mary, the Dominican Sisters, and the Ursuline Sisters to join the several communities already teaching in the parochial schools. Spalding had an excellent rapport with both priests and religious.[21]

Spalding's promotion of societies of many sorts was also directed mostly toward the immigrant poor. The parishes of Baltimore he encouraged to emulate the three in Washington that already had conferences of the Saint Vincent de Paul Society. Seven responded in Baltimore and five more in the District of Columbia.[22] When in 1869 he approved the constitution of a union of the benevolent or beneficial societies of Baltimore formed in 1865, he recommended two objects of special charity: Irish immigrants newly arrived and the children of Irish parents in the public schools or otherwise in danger of going astray.[23] The German societies did well in taking care of their own and needed little encouragement.

Even more than the immigrants, perhaps, the blacks were an object of genuine concern for Spalding. His second synod decreed special parish missions for them. He encouraged a black sisterhood founded in Baltimore, the Oblates of Providence, to extend their usefulness to other dioceses, to incorporate, and to rebuild. In 1870 he invited all the societies of the city to attend the laying of the cornerstone for their new complex, a motherhouse, academy, poor school, and orphanage. "There are no parties in heaven," he told the assembly. "I want all my children—Irish, German, American, African—I want them all to go to heaven." In 1871 he invited the Mill Hill Fathers, later called the Josephites, to take over the black parish of Saint Francis

Xavier in Baltimore and make it their headquarters for extending their usefulness throughout the South.[24]

In other important ways Spalding served the needs of his urban flock. More than any of his predecessors, he encouraged a public display of faith and solidarity. Hardly a cornerstone was laid in the Baltimore or Washington that was not preceded by a parade of banners and bands. That of Saint Martin's, a new parish named for himself and for which he waived the requirement of a temporary chapel first, was the most spectacular. Ten bands could be counted in the two-mile line of march that began in the eastern part of Baltimore and ended near its western border. The Young Catholic's Friend Society and the beneficial societies of the six largest English-speaking parishes of the city formed the honor guard for the ten carriages that bore forty clergymen and the most reverend archbishop. Three nations, he told a throng of at least 35,000, could claim Saint Martin, who was born in Germany, educated in France, and related to Saint Patrick.[25] None doubted this little lesson in history.

The oldest archdiocese had a large rural Catholic population, especially in the southern counties, the "Cradle of Catholicity," which required occasional prodding. The settled patterns of two centuries, however, served needs that were minimal. To a great extent the same was true of the mining and farming communities in the west. The first archdiocese had also the oldest and largest number of families of wealth and social standing. Initially, these Catholic aristocrats welcomed Spalding as one of their own, but they were soon discomfited by his disarming familiarity and democratic ways and proved less tractable than Kentucky Catholics to his efforts to bend their social habits. Spalding preached often against the current fashionable dances, theatergoing, and immodest dress.[26] For the most part, however, the Catholic elite supported him in his projects, many contributing generously to them. In 1868, for example, they pledged almost $22,000, including three full burses of $5,000 each, as part of an endowment for the American College in Rome.[27]

The plan that Spalding presented the American bishops to save the American College from financial collapse was but one of many instances of the leadership he chose to exert over the American church as a whole.[28] Although the "prerogative of place" accorded Baltimore in 1858 bestowed little more than ceremonial precedence, the premier see had from the beginning enjoyed quasi-primatial status. Most of Spalding's predecessors in Baltimore, however, had remained in the shadow of the dynamic John England or aggressive John Hughes. Spalding had no England and no Hughes to contest his exercise of power.

As archbishop of Baltimore his writing assumed a heightened importance. He was not long in his new see when he felt compelled to take up his pen again. Though his commentary on the *Syllabus of Errors* in 1865 took the form of a pastoral letter, it was obvious that he was writing as the spokesman of American Catholics. The reprobation in the *Syllabus* of freedom of speech and worship, of separation of church and state, of progress and modern civilization, he proclaimed with assurance, was directed against European radicals and infidels and certainly not the provisions of "our noble Constitution."[29] In private he was not so sure. He wrote to three of the highest officials of the Roman curia begging a statement to the effect that the condemnations of the *Syllabus* did not comprehend American principles and arrangements. It was a vain effort.[30]

In no undertaking was Spalding's exercise of leadership more apparent than in the Second Plenary Council of Baltimore. As soon as the war was over, and in the face of an initial coolness on the part of his episcopal friends, he pushed for its convocation. He envisioned nothing less than a comprehensive code for the American church, coordinating all previous legislation and enacting whatever else was needed. The *schema quaestionum* he sent the bishops encompassed the needs of the Church as he saw them. Should there be, he asked among other things, an official English version of the Bible, a uniform catechism, an industrial school in every diocese, a Catholic university, cathedral chapters, Catholic tract societies, and libraries like those of the Protestants? Should married convert ministers be admitted to minor orders? Should labor unions fall under the ban of secret societies?[31]

As for the emancipated blacks, he wrote his friend Archbishop John McCloskey of New York:

> I think it is precisely the most *urgent* duty of all to discuss the future status of the *negro*. Four millions of these unfortunates are thrown upon our Charity, & they silently but eloquently appeal to us for help. It is a golden opportunity for reaping a harvest of souls, which neglected may not return.[32]

Spalding parceled out the work among the four closest archbishops and with the help of a committee of theologians refashioned their uneven contributions into a tentative code of 566 decrees he called the *libellus*. This he handed the forty-seven prelates and hundred or more other council participants who assembled in Baltimore in October, 1866.

On the fifth day of debate and without warning, Archbishop Peter Richard Kenrick of Saint Louis, who till then had been Spalding's most enthusiastic collaborator among the archbishops, moved that the *libellus* be discarded and the council start afresh. When the motion was defeated, Kenrick entered a formal protest against the proceedings. Kenrick's opposition, however, was only partially responsible for the council fathers' failure to act on several matters deemed by Spalding of utmost importance: a uniform catechism, a Catholic university, and concerted action in behalf of the blacks.[33]

Fearing that Kenrick's opposition would block Roman approval of the work of the council, Spalding wrote a friend from his days as a Roman student, Cardinal Paul Cullen, that he could safely tell the cardinal prefect of the Propaganda "that with perhaps one exception [Kenrick], there is not in the entire American Episcopate, a single element or vestige of *Gallicanism*--Thank God! We are Roman to the heart."[34] In its emasculated form, the body of laws emanating from the Second Plenary Council (534 decrees) was approved with but few emendations in Rome.

None of the provincial or plenary councils of Baltimore conducted before or after Spalding's episcopacy was so much the work of one man. No other archbishop had had the imagination, energy, or boldness to break the pattern of piecemeal legislation that had obtained at earlier councils. In 1868 in the second of the two diocesan synods he held in Baltimore—the first was held at the conclusion of the visitation of 1865—he effected for the archdiocese what he had accomplished for the church at large, a comprehensive code in which the statutes of all previous synods were systematized and integrated with fresh enactments. This code would serve as the basis for future synods.

On one important problem the council had moved as Spalding wished, that of labor unions. In the postwar years the sudden acceleration of the labor movement had made a number of bishops fretful. "Secret political, oath bound societies and trade unions are becoming fearfully multiplied," wrote Archbishop Purcell soon after Spalding's transfer to Baltimore. "We shall have a herculean task to encounter in the endeavor to keep Catholics from combining with them."[35] Spalding did not share this apprehension with regard to labor unions. In the *libellus* he had inserted a decree that exempted them from the blanket proscription of secret societies decreed by Rome. A majority of the bishops voted to let it stand.[36]

In response to the uneasy questions of Canadian bishops about labor unions, Rome sought Spalding's opinion. "In all commercial countries," he replied, "especially Protestant ones, *capital* (money) is the *despotic ruler*, and the worker is its slave. This being the case, I say, leave the poor workers alone—there being little danger that they can do injustice to the tyrannical employer." This was the reasoning, he insisted, behind the decree concerning labor unions.[37] In staying the hands of its critics among the hierarchy at a crucial phase in its development, Spalding rendered a service to the American labor movement as great as that of Cardinal James Gibbons in a more publicized defense of the workingman.[38]

Spalding's views were highly valued by the Congregation of the Propaganda and other bodies in Rome. In 1869 the cardinal prefect, Alessandro Barnabò, citing the "prudence and skill" with which he had handled the "diverse, difficult, and delicate affairs that have at various times been entrusted to him," asked that he investigate conditions in the Diocese of Chicago, the source of mounting complaints against its bishop, James Duggan.[39] Initially Spalding was sympathetic to the Roman alumni who were the bishop's principal critics. When, however, he himself was portrayed as sympathetic to the "anti-absolutist" party by a group of New York priests, including the social-minded Edward McGlynn, a fact brought to his attention by Archbishop McCloskey of New York, Spalding set himself against a movement on priests' rights.[40] In Chicago, therefore, despite the fact that Duggan had been judged insane, he found the opponents of the bishop the principal cause of the "scandalous tumults."[41] Moreover, he refused to intervene in a controversy between priests and bishop in Cleveland. The leader of the priests, Eugene O'Callaghan, was the notorious flayer of bishops who wrote under the pen name "Jus." Spalding and McCloskey had never discovered the identity of Jus but they thought he was a New York priest.

In Louisville it was another matter. There Spalding took the side of the priests, who wished Rome to investigate the administration of Bishop William George McCloskey. When McCloskey refused to honor Spalding's request to use the legacy of his brother to build an industrial school there, Spalding was even more disposed to credit "the continual wail of grief" that came from his former see. At Spalding's prompting, an investigation was finally conducted in 1871 but, to Spalding's chagrin, by Archbishop Purcell, the metropolitan and friend of McCloskey. The whitewashing that resulted was one of the few defeats that Spalding suffered.[42]

It was inevitable that in an energetic exercise of leadership Spalding antagonized some. Before Vatican Council I, however, he had managed to maintain cordial relations with every member of the hierarchy but Peter Richard Kenrick. Spalding's friendship with Purcell was of longest standing, but it was a brittle one. The relationship between Kenrick and Purcell, on the other hand, was glacial before the ecumenical council that would provide the most serious challenge to Spalding's assumption of leadership.

The archbishop of Baltimore was, perhaps, the only American bishop who went to Rome in 1869 with any appreciation of what lay ahead. This was due in part to his reading habits. He was probably the best informed of the American bishops in his range of interests.

Even more it was due to the presence of the theologian Spalding himself had selected to represent the American point of view in the preparatory stages, James A. Corcoran.[43] Corcoran reported that the dogmatic commission, having decided to use the *Syllabus of Errors* as the
basis of its work, was bent on the condemnation of "multitudinous"
errors, "in some of which I verily believe the fundamental principles
of our (American and common sense) political doctrines are condemned." A definition of papal infallibility, he added, was a "foregone
conclusion" unless it was opposed by a large number of bishops on
the ground of inexpediency.[44]

Four months before the opening of the council, Spalding sent a
lengthy "Memoranda" to Barnabò for the instruction of the preparatory commissions, claiming that it represented the views of at least
a third of the bishops of the world! Since the intent of the *Syllabus*
was not always obvious, he declared, clear and positive definitions
should be formulated, especially on matters of church and state. Care
should be taken not to reprobate the arrangements that prevailed in
the United States, Great Britain, and Prussia but rather to commend
them as models for those Catholic countries where the church enjoyed
small liberty. The punishment of heretics and resort to the secular
arm were anachronisms best ignored. As for a definition of papal infallibility, would not an implicit definition, he asked, one not "likely
to excite controversies now slumbering," be preferred to an explicit
one? Should there be an explicit one, he concluded, its exercise should
be clearly marked.[45]

At the council Spalding was named by the pope to the congregation
on proposals and elected to the deputation on faith, the two most
powerful bodies in the conduct of the council. Guessing the outcome
of the contest over papal infallibility, he prepared a compromise definition soon after his arrival in Rome.[46] He attempted a neutral stance,
therefore, in the intense lobbying between the "infallibilists" and
"inopportunists," as the proponents and opponents of the definition
were called, though some of his American colleagues would later claim
that he privately encouraged the inopportunists. When it appeared
that the infallibilists had won, he presented his compromise definition,
an implicit one that rehearsed earlier decrees. His attempt, however,
to create a third party ultimately failed. The *zelanti* swept all before
them.[47]

The preparatory commission's schema on the church touching the
points that Spalding had addressed in his Memoranda was at this
juncture distributed for discussion. There can be little doubt that the
American bishops would have rallied under Spalding's leadership to
do battle for American principles and thus play an important role at

Vatican Council I had the debates proceeded as scheduled. Instead the decision was taken to advance the discussion on papal infallibility.

Spalding, as a consequence, was soon embroiled in a *guerre de brochures*. To Bishop Félix Dupanloup of Orléans, leader of those who still opposed a definition, he addressed a letter protesting Dupanloup's use of his compromise definition as evidence of his support of the anti-infallibilist position. Now that inopportunity had been rejected as a viable argument, he proclaimed, one could stand only with the pope or with his enemies. He himself would "never stray from the glorious paths in which our young church in America has followed up to this point with unshaken fidelity."[48] A letter in support of Dupanloup appeared over the signatures of archbishops Kenrick and Purcell, acting also for "several" others. It charged Spalding with inconsistency in his stance on a definition. It denied, moreover, that he spoke for all the American bishops and that in pretending to do so without consulting them he had acted contrary to custom. For the first time in his life, Spalding backed away from controversy. In a letter to Dupanloup that he probably never sent, he declared that with his own "dearly beloved Colleagues" he would have no quarrel.[49] Stung by the charge of inconsistency, however, he released to the press the proposal for an implicit definition he had sent to Barnabò the summer before, noting that it admitted of an explicit one.

In a lengthy defense of his own position that clearly went beyond the argument of expediency, Kenrick quoted a work of Spalding to the effect that papal infallibility was simply an opinion. Spalding had, in fact, changed his views in one important particular. Whereas in earlier writings he had insisted that papal infallibility could be exercised only in conjunction with the bishops, he would now have the pope exercise it of himself "and not from the consent of the Church," as it was defined by the final vote taken July 18, 1870.[50]

The reason for the change he explained in a pastoral issued the following day as "Gallicanism revived." In the course of the council debates, he had come to the conviction that opposition to papal infallibility was rooted in Gallican principles and not in inexpediency. Gallicanism was for him a cancer in the church that had to be eradicated. The principal purport of the pastoral, however, was to explain to American Catholics the true meaning of papal infallibility and to assure non-Catholics that it posed no threat to republican institutions.[51]

The archbishop's return was made the occasion of clamorous protests in both Baltimore and Washington of the "sacrilegious" invasion of Rome that occurred soon after the prorogation of the council. In almost every letter to Rome in the year and three months left to him,

Spalding alluded to past, present, and future efforts in behalf of Pius IX. On the twenty-fifth anniversary of his coronation, Spalding cabled the pontiff: "Grand Jubilee Demonstration in Baltimore—General Communion—Illumination and Torchlight Procession—Hundred Guns—Hundred Thousand People." There were rumors that Spalding would receive the red hat at the next consistory. He died in February, 1872, sustained to the end by his accustomed good humor.[52]

There can be little doubt that had he lived until 1875 he and not John McCloskey of New York would have been the first American cardinal, the ultimate prize that Spalding doubtless coveted. But he had literally worked himself into an early grave. That few were aware of the chronic illness that beset him most of his life—five times he was near death—was a token of the awe in which he was held for his tireless energy.

To his responsibilities as ordinary and *de facto* primate he brought equal quantities of zeal. If he enjoyed greater success in the former role, it was because the time was not ripe for many of the goals he set himself in the latter. The Third Plenary Council was to succeed where the second had failed, legislating a catechism, a university, a special organization for the blacks, and it was to harden into precept (the decree on parochial schools, for example) what the Second had been forced by episcopal timidity to leave as exhortation because Spalding had planted seeds and provided a working model.

None of the incumbents of the premier see has ever seized the reins of power with the eagerness of Martin John Spalding. None, certainly, between John Carroll at the beginning of the century and James Gibbons at the end was as active and influential. Carroll was obliged by the infant character of the church he governed to break new ground. Gibbons would be nudged into prominence by his friends. Few, if any, American prelates excelled Spalding in balancing a per-fervid nationalism with an intense loyalty to the Holy See.

Few exemplified to the degree he did the strengths and weaknesses of the immigrant church—its courage, generosity, loyalty, and piety but at the same time its defensiveness and insularity. Spalding was quite comfortable within the confines of American Catholicism. He made few friends outside the church and rarely graced civic functions by his presence.

One of the most remarkable features of the life of this scion of an old family of comfortable means was the degree to which he identified with the lower class, a fact of which his nephew and biographer, John Lancaster Spalding, boasted:

> [His] great Catholic heart went out in love and sympathy to all—to the
> orphan, to the negro, to the sinful, to the outcast, to the aged, to all who

suffered and had none to pity them. He felt that the poor, above all others, need the church, and that she needs them.[53]

The "great Catholic heart" tempered less admirable traits of character: a touch of vanity, a pinch of spitefulness, and, of course, a measure of ambition.

Spalding would, of course, have seen his advancement as consonant with the progress of church, which in truth it was. Perhaps to a greater degree than any other bishop at midcentury, John Hughes not excepted, Spalding contributed to the shaping of the immigrant church by articulating its attitudes, breathing life into its institutions, and systematizing its discipline. The mold he helped to set would not be broken for a hundred years and more.

CHAPTER
7
James Gibbons of Baltimore

John Tracy Ellis

$\mathcal{H}$e reigned in Baltimore like a king, but he met every man like a comrade."[1] Such was the comment of Canon William Barry, an English priest, who was the guest of Cardinal Gibbons in 1893, a comment that caught the spirit in which James Gibbons conducted his administration of the premier see of the United States from his advent as archbishop in October 1877, at the age of forty-three to his death forty-four years later in March 1921. He was born (July 23, 1834), baptized, ordained, and consecrated in Baltimore, and he died in Baltimore, an identification of which he was proud and a relationship of which Maryland's metropolis was increasingly conscious and in which it took its own measure of pride. This happy circumstance was in striking contrast with that of both Gibbons's predecessor, James Roosevelt Bayley, who never warmed to Baltimore nor ceased to feel nostalgia toward his Diocese of Newark, and Gibbons's second successor, Francis P. Keough, whose longing for his native New England lessened the effectiveness of his regime between 1948 and his death in 1961.

Like all other persons bishops inevitably draw upon their previous experience in carrying out their episcopal duties. What, in brief, were Gibbons's experiences in the years leading up to 1877 that left a lasting impression on his mind and that served to influence and color his career as archbishop of Baltimore? Taken back to Ireland as a child of three, when his family's intended holiday extended over sixteen years, the period of his childhood and young manhood were spent in the village of Ballinrobe, County Mayo, where his parents had grown up and where young James attended the local school and worshiped at Saint Mary's Church amid the simple and humble surroundings of the region. Following the deaths of his father and sister his mother decided to return to the United States in 1853 with her surviving five children. The family settled in New Orleans for the reason that Mrs. Gibbons had such fond memories of her time in Baltimore that she had not the heart to return there without her husband.

In any case, young Gibbons found employment in a grocery store until he decided to study for the priesthood, a decision that had been strengthened when the twenty-year-old youth attended a mission preached by Isaac Hecker and his fellow Redemptorists. Years later Gibbons told Clarence A. Walworth, one of the missionaries, that when he was considering the priesthood, "I heard a sermon from you which gave me an impulse in the right direction."[2] In 1855 he entered Saint Charles College in Ellicott City, Maryland, the Sulpician preparatory seminary, and from there went on to Saint Mary's Seminary in Baltimore from which he was ordained in 1861. After a brief period in parochial work he was made secretary to Martin J. Spalding, archbishop of Baltimore, which entailed among routine tasks making preparations for the American bishops' Second Plenary Council of October 1866. It was at that council that the Holy See was requested to erect fifteen new ecclesiastical jurisdictions, among which was the Vicariate Apostolic of North Carolina; to this office the thirty-four-year-old Gibbons was named in 1868, he then being the youngest bishop in the country, as he was the youngest a year later at Rome among the nearly 700 bishops at the opening of Vatican Council I.

For the nine-year period 1868–1877, the youthful bishop functioned as a typical Catholic missionary in the overwhelmingly Protestant South where his vast jurisdiction both in North Carolina, and in the Diocese of Richmond, to which he was promoted in 1872, had only a scarce Catholic population of widely scattered and generally poor laity, a mere handful of priests, and a woeful lack of diocesan institutions and resources. Moreover, these were the years of Reconstruction, a troubled time for the region that added a further handicap. Many years later Gibbons recalled the situation he encountered upon his advent to North Carolina:

> The night I arrived in Wilmington, there was a torchlight procession of the emancipated slaves, many of them now holding office and domineering over their former masters. If one can imagine an enormous crowd

of negroes, most of whom were intoxicated, all of whom were waving torches in the blackness of the night, one can very easily imagine the first impressions of a new and very young bishop.[3]

What, it may be asked, did Gibbons's nine years on the missions of North Carolina and Virginia contribute to his lengthy tenure of the See of Baltimore? First, they served as a laboratory, so to speak, in which he developed and matured pastoral techniques that he was destined to follow for the remainder of his life, and which accounted in no small measure for his success as a leader. Limitation of space precludes a detailed description and will, I trust, give warrant for the following summary:

1. An instinctive tendency to consult others who, he felt, were wiser and more experienced than himself, a characteristic he displayed even in old age. It was a contributing factor to the widespread confidence that, as time wore on, others came to have in his wisdom and judgement

2. A marked consideration for the feelings of others, especially for those of lower station than himself.

3. A naturally irenic temperament that prompted him to unfailing courtesy toward those of other and of no religious persuasion, a quality that made him an unwitting ecumenist long before that movement had arrived.

4. A generally balanced judgment that weighed all aspects of a problem and that prompted him on occasion to use his authority only as a last resort.

5. A keen intelligence, which he cultivated by wide reading, with a specialty in American constitutional history.

If these characteristics accounted in part for the leadership that Gibbons exercised to an increasing degree as time went on, there were other personal traits that tended to inhibit or to lessen that leadership. He was, for example, singularly unoriginal in his thinking and acting, a quality that, needless to say, had little to do with moral character but was more attributable to the man's temperament and to his ease of mind with the *status quo*. Yet this trait should not be emphasized unduly, for the publication of the *The Faith of Our Fathers* in 1876, a work destined to become the most famous treatise in apologetics in the English-speaking world, was not altogether lacking in originality, even if its contents were traditional and if it had been strongly urged by Father Mark Gross, one of Gibbons's missionary priests. The book grew out of the bishop's experience on the southern missions where he found suitable literature to explain the church's teachings pitifully scarce and so much in demand. True, one does not ordinarily think of authorship as closely related to leadership; but when a book has sold millions of copies and is still selling over a century after its first publication, that fact is not entirely devoid of leadership of a kind.

On the subject of Gibbons's lack of originality it may be said further that bold and strikingly new proposals usually brought an initial hesitation and backing off. That reaction was shown in enterprise that ultimately won out, involved his somewhat reluctant participation, and in the end redounded to his credit by reason of the superior way in which he carried out the leadership role thrust upon him. For example, he was definitely cool toward the idea of a plenary council when in the early 1880's bishops of the Middle West urged a council, a proposal that received the opposition of certain high prelates of the East such as Cardinal John McCloskey of New York. Yet once the council was decided upon and Pope Leo XIII had named Gibbons as apostolic delegate to preside over its sessions, he not only gave it his full support but in the event led the assembly of over seventy bishops with such skill that the Third Plenary Council of Baltimore in November and December of 1884 made him a national figure for the first time. In reminiscing later he confessed his nervousness at the outset: "When I started to read the prayer at the beginning of the first session, my hand trembled violently."[4] His ultimate success in this endeavor can, I think, be understood if it is kept in mind that during the month-long debates Gibbons as presiding officer lived up in spirit to the promise of his opening remarks on the first day:

> For my part I must say in all candor & simplicity that since my return from Rome last March, I have labored in season & out of season in preparing the way for the C[ouncil] while I have studiously avoided to do any thing which wd. trench on the prerogatives of the Prelates or forestall their legitimate action. I hope that in what I have done I have interpreted yr. wishes. If I have in any way transgressed the bounds of propriety, I crave yr. indulgence, & I beg you to ascribe my shortcomings not to any want of regard for yr. sacred rights, but to my youth & inexperience.[5]

Words of that kind spoken in sincerity and carried out in action bespoke leadership of a type to win followers, and that it did quite beyond the council of 1884.

It is the rare human being, indeed, who in the course of his or her life fails to disclose defects both major and minor. To this general rule James Gibbons was no exception. Thus there was a strain of vanity in him that delighted to parade his cardinal's finery in ecclesiastical processions, a minor defect that did no more harm than furnish grist for the mill of his enemies, of whom Bernard J. McQuaid, bishop

of Rochester, was a prime example, one who repeatedly alluded to
the cardinal's vanity and ambition. Yet this vanity never soared to
the level of pride and haughtiness that seriously put others off, as
was true of Gibbons's contemporary, Cardinal William O'Connell of
Boston.

If, as Canon Barry remarked, Gibbons met every man as a comrade,
he could be otherwise when he felt there was reason for distancing
himself from certain individuals. For example, for reasons that were
never altogether clear he did not favor Father Francis Clement Kelley,
the founder of the Catholic Church Extension society, and when Kelley
appealed for support to Secretary of the Navy Charles J. Bonaparte,
a Baltimore-born Catholic who, in turn, asked for Gibbons's advice,
the latter replied, "I would be sorry to see your name associated with
it, at least in its present indefinite form."[6] He took even a stronger
stand against Bonaventure Broderick, Connecticut-born auxiliary
bishop of Havana, who had incurred displeasure in Havana government circles. When, therefore, Gibbons learned of a suggestion that
Broderick be put in charge of a bureau in this country for the collecting
of Peter's Pence, he quickly dispatched a stout protest to Cardinal
Rafael Merry del Val, secretary of state to Pius X, which ended the
idea once and for all.[7]

After weighing the cardinal's qualities, pro and con, I would say
that in the final analysis his major weakness may well have been his
failure in certain delicate and controversial matters to come to a decision and to adhere to that decision once made. The problem arose
from his effort to please the maximum number of those involved, but
his indecision at times ended by causing confusion and doubts all
around. The 1880s was a period when the American hierarchy were
sharply divided over a number of issues among which working out
plans for the Catholic University of America was a notable example.
The division of opinion in the United States was, of course, reflected
in Rome, where the conflicting parties sought support for their respective positions. In this situation it was natural that the Holy See
would look to Gibbons, the sole American cardinal after McCloskey's
death, for guidance, but that guidance was not forthcoming.

The silence from Baltimore drew forth one of the most candid and
courageous criticisms that Gibbons ever received. Writing from Rome
in December 1886 (where he and John Ireland, bishop of Saint Paul,
were then representing certain American interests), John J. Keane,
bishop of Richmond and designated rector of the university, stated:

> We have lately been pouring out our honest indignation at the charge
> that the signatures of the Prelates to the University petition could not
> be implicitly trusted as giving the real sentiment of the signers; but I

cannot help recognizing with what crushing force they can say to us: "Why look, even your Cardinal puts his name to statements & recommendations which he will afterwards take back or modify; if even he will send us important documents, not because he believes them best for the interests of the Church, but in order to please this one or that one, what confidence can we repose in any of these signatures?". . . Even the Holy Father himself has thus intimated his apprehension that your Eminence was uncertain & vacillating in your views as to the University's location, etc.[8]

When researching the life of the cardinal I looked in vain for a copy of his reply to this remarkable letter, but beyond a brief diary entry that simply stated that he had answered Keane, no answer was found. It can be seen, however, that with the passage of time, the blunt criticism brought no break in the close friendship of the two men; and, secondly, one could, I think, thereafter detect a more decisive attitude on Gibbons's part in regard to controversial issues. Both results reflected credibly on the cardinal as a man humble enough to accept criticism from a lifelong friend, as well as to mend his ways, so to speak, in view of that friend's honest appraisal of his weakness.

While on the subject of the university I should mention that as in his initial negative attitude toward the Third Plenary Council, here too he moved from a sentiment of sheer duty with no enthusiasm in the early years to an enthusiasm that made the institution ultimately one of his favorite preoccupations in his role as chancellor. To what does one attribute this marked change of mind? It was due, in my judgment, to a combination of circumstances. His instinctive reluctance to accept change, to which reference has been made, gradually gave way as his basically high intelligence weighed the issues involved to the point where he viewed both the council and the university in terms of service to the church, a factor to which he gave unfailing support. In both enterprises Gibbons observed the wholehearted participation of churchmen whose judgment he had come to value and admire—for example, the participation of John Lancaster Spalding, bishop of Peoria, and John Ireland of Saint Paul in the council; and in the development of the university Spalding and Keane in the early years and later Thomas J. Shahan, who was to become university rector after 1909 and to exercise a decided influence on the cardinal's thinking and action (just as in earlier years that role had been conspicuously filled by Alphonse Magnien, S.S., French-born superior of the Baltimore Sulpicians until his death in 1902.)

As previously mentioned, Cardinal Gibbons's leadership was abetted and advanced by his cultivation of close friends and advisors upon whom he leaned to his profit and whose counsel he sought and followed in many particulars, a trait that has played a significant part in the leadership role of many outstanding figures in both church and state. It would be both tedious and unnecessary to list the names of all those on whom Gibbons depended in one way or another, but in relation to the university the third rector, Denis J. O'Connell (1903–1908), a lifelong favorite, should not go unmentioned. It was during the O'Connell administration that there occurred the bankruptcy of the university treasury in 1904. In the face of this crisis Gibbons the chancellor came forward in a forceful way by pledging everything he had to the cause, and it was this show of strength that, in turn, helped to rally the American bishops to save the institution from collapse. Furthermore, by that time Gibbons's personal charm had endeared him to most of the hierarchy to a degree that in all likelihood it was his appeal as much as it was their concern for the institution that brought their financial assistance. In fact, toward the close of his life so much had the aged cardinal become identified with the Catholic University of America that John J. Glennon, archbishop of Saint Louis, was justified declaring in his sermon at Gibbons's funeral in March 1921, that were the cardinal to speak he would "leave as a heritage, his body to Baltimore, his heart to the University and his soul to God."[9]

In the execution of their duties leaders in every walk of life cannot escape controversial issues about which they must make uncomfortable decisions. For those in the ranks it is easy to be critical of those who lead, whereas for the latter their public stance often entails a painful process that makes them the target of sharp criticism, which may be either warranted or unfair. Cardinal Gibbons shared in both. If the barbs of Bishop McQuaid, his Roman agent, the convert journalist Ella Edes, and others about his ambition to be a cardinal and to take the top post in the American church were often exaggerated and underserved, there were other instances in which criticism of his public stands, or the lack thereof, were near the mark. Let two examples from the 1890s illustrate what is meant.

The steady rise of appeals to the Holy See from priests who felt aggrieved at their bishops' treatment hastened the determination of Rome to have a papal representative here in the United States who might settle many of these disputes and thus make appeals to Rome unnecessary. The Holy See's efforts to establish an Apostolic Delegation in the United States were of long standing and had drawn the steady opposition of most American bishops, whose position James Gibbons strenuously supported from the outset. In fact, he signed a letter on January 4, 1893, that tactfully but strongly expressed the bishops' opposition to a delegate. Ten days later, however, there came a cablegram from Rome that read, "Delegatio Americana creatur. Satolli primus delegatus." In view of this *fait accompli* it was to be expected that further opposition would cease. But it was not to be expected that Gibbons as titular leader of the hierarchy would address a fulsome letter of capitulation to Pope Leo XIII in which *inter alia* he stated:

> Satisfaction has been very general in our ranks, and even those who have been surprised or even piqued by this exercise of your apostolic authority have already been led, or will soon be, by their personal reflection and by public sentiment to change their views and to accept with good grace the decision of Your Holiness, even to rejoice heartily in it.[10]

Given the circumstances and the current opinion in ecclesiastical circles in the United states, this letter sailed dangerously close to violating the truth and misrepresenting the situation. In brief, it was far from being Gibbons's finest hour.

The second episode occurred five years later and was related to the Spanish-American War. On February 15, 1898, the battleship *Maine* was sunk in Havana harbor by a mammoth explosion, an event that greatly heightened the danger of war. At the requiem mass in the Baltimore cathedral for those lost on the *Maine* the cardinal preached. After expressing condolences to the families of the bereaved he declared:

> This nation is too brave, too strong, too powerful, and too just to engage in an unrighteous or precipitate war. Let us remember the eyes of the world are upon us, whose judgment we cannot despise, and that we will gain more applause and credit for ourselves by calm deliberation and masterly inactivity than by recourse to war.[11]

These were admirable sentiments, surely, from the nation's ranking Catholic churchman, who had worked in close harmony with John Ireland, archbishop of Saint Paul, in trying to avert war. Yet when war came in mid-April there was no hint of its unjustifiable character from the cardinal, who some days later, piqued by the slurs of the London *Daily Chronicle* concerning the American Catholics' attitude, stated: "Catholics in the United States have but one sentiment. Whatever may have been their opinions as to the expediency of the war, now that it is on they are united in upholding the government."[12] Too much should not be made of Gibbons's *volte face*, but one might wish that he had shown a more qualified reaction to a war that has been regarded as far from just in the judgment of history.

At this point the reader may well be prompted to ask whether it is not strange to respond to a request to treat Cardinal Gibbons's qualities as a leader by cataloguing his faults and weaknesses. The question would be entirely understandable. Let me explain what I have had in mind by this approach. I spent three years in research for the Gibbons biography, which were followed by three years of writing and an additional year of seeing the work through the press. I would be less than honest were I to pretend that it did not ultimately become a labor of love as I became aware of the man's full stature. Yet throughout I made a conscious effort to be objective and to avoid what I have often characterized as "moonlight and roses history." I can say that the defects enumerated above represent the sum total of the blemishes I uncovered in the man's character and conduct.

Given the extraordinary level of leadership that James Gibbons achieved and sustained for more than a generation in both church and state, I consider the negative features of his lengthy career to have been surprisingly few and not gravely damaging. While he was never submitted to the pressure and scrutiny often visited on churchmen by the media of the 1980s, yet as titular leader of the American hierarchy he was called upon repeatedly to speak in the church's name, sometimes on delicate issues that involved matters of a controversial nature in the public or civil domain, as well as issues of a purely ecclesiastical character. True, at times he hesitated and vacillated, but the remarkable thing was that he ultimately came through without seriously stumbling and without causing lasting embarrassment or injury to the cause he represented. That, it seems to me, was no mean accomplishment, and in what follows I will try to demonstrate how Gibbons brought off his exacting role with a degree of success that up to that time was quite unparalleled in American Catholic circles.

The pattern of leadership that emerged in the life of James Gibbons may be said to have unfolded on various levels, namely, the personal, the diocesan, the national, and the international plane. In assesssing his approach on any of these levels the personal was, of course, involved, and that element may, indeed, account in the final analysis for the success he achieved in all levels. Let me illustrate the personal element by several authentic stories told to me by those who experienced the event at first hand. For example, John M. McNamara, auxiliary bishop of Washington, recounted for me how in his early priesthood he was appointed to a rural parish in southern Maryland before being brought in to Saint Patrick's Church in Washington, the church where Gibbons stayed when he was in the capital. One morning McNamara was asked to serve the cardinal's mass and while doing so was called away by the pastor to go on an errand. At breakfast Gibbons said to him, "You do not know your ceremonies, Sir, you left before Mass was over," whereupon McNamara replied, "If you had not left me so long in the country I might know my ceremonies better."

This story tells us a good deal about Gibbons. Even his young priests felt free to speak to him in his way, knowing they would incur no serious displeasure. In fact, it told me more about the man's approachability, about his not taking himself with undue seriousness than would a lengthy discourse, for McNamara added that his brash words brought nothing more than an amused smile as Gibbons proceeded with his breakfast. The ability to take criticism normally bespeaks a measure of humility, especially when that criticism comes from a subordinate.

On another occasion Monsignor Louis Stickney, rector of the Baltimore cathedral in the last years of Gibbons's life, told me that at one time there was a local fad for youngsters to gather autographs, which brought a steady stream to the door of 408 North Charles Street. One day several black boys appeared, asked for the cardinal's autograph and were sent on their way by Stickney, who said the cardinal was busy. The latter, who had been watching unseen from the stairs above the front door, asked who they were and what they wanted. When Stickney explained, Gibbons said, "Don't you ever do that again. I am as much the archbishop of those boys as I am of any one else." Stickney remarked to me, "It was the most severe rebuke I ever had from him during the years I lived with him." The incident was not a matter of prime importance perhaps, yet it revealed an engaging characteristic of the aged churchman.

Part of Cardinal Gibbons's daily routine included brisk walks through the neighborhood, frequently accompanied by a student from Saint Mary's Seminary on Paca Street. He would often stop and chat with those he met, especially with children. Many years ago I attended a confirmation service at a parish located in what was then called Texas, Maryland. The pastor described for us how a man of advanced age had recently come to ask for instructions to become a Catholic. The pastor welcomed the man but confessed that he was curious as to what had prompted him to take the step so late in life. The reply ran something like this: "I am not sure what has motivated me, but I remember that when I was a child playing in the streets of Baltimore an old man with a cane would come along, stop and speak in a friendly way to us, and he never asked what was our religion. That was your Cardinal Gibbons, and that had something to do with it." Again, not a very striking occurrence, but one that portrays the cardinal in an appealing light.

Here, then, was a highly placed churchman whom it seemed the most natural thing to honor and revere the personal touch, a man of gentle speech and open countenance whose demeanor demonstrated the truth of William Barry's words quoted at the beginning of this essay. If the manner was warm and personal, as it was, it warmed in turn the heart of the recipient and enkindled a respect and regard that for many came nigh to an enduring affection. In short, if Gibbons was always aware of the dignity of his office, that consciousness was never permitted to take on an air of aloofness or disdain for others of whatever social rank. To be sure, it is not possible to be precise about the effects that followed from a source of this kind. But it would, I believe, be the consensus of the majority of humankind that genuine leadership is rarely ever experienced in those devoid of this quality. It might, indeed, be thought the most effectual single quality in Gibbons's role as a leader.

In the ecclesiastical realm few persons are more persistently and consistently under critical scrutiny than ordinaries of dioceses, both from their priests, from men and women religious, and from their laity. James Gibbons was no exception to this universal phenomenon. As archbishop of Baltimore his jurisdiction covered less than 7,000 square miles, a notably smaller area than the states of North Carolina and Virginia, which had been his responsibility before coming to Baltimore in 1877. At that time the archdiocese numbered about 200,000 Catholics who were served by 234 priests with twenty-one parishes in Baltimore proper and eleven parishes in Washington with the remainder in the counties. One of Gibbons's earliest pastoral letters, "Christian Education," stated that there were then (1883) 17,500 students being educated in the Catholic schools on all levels. That the archbishop was conscious of his obligation to the ethnic and racial minorities in his jurisdiction was evident in his welcome to the Sisters of Saint Francis from England who came to staff a foundling home and school for black children, and evident likewise in Gibbons's appeal to the Redemptorist provincial in Vienna for Bohemian priests to care for the increasing number of Bohemians then crowding into Saint Wenceslaus Parish.

The life of a bishop ordinary of a diocese is a ceaseless round of parochial visitations interspersed by ceremonies of ordination, confirmation, dedications, parish jubilees, and anniversaries of one kind or another. Precisely how to weigh a bishop's leadership on the diocesan level in view of these events is not easy. As far as the extant evidence permits one to judge, Gibbons performed these episcopal tasks in a generally satisfactory way. Beyond these routine duties he responded to particular needs, for example, his support, both moral and financial, to Mount Saint Mary's College in Emmitsburg when it encountered grave financial difficulties in 1881, assistance that prompted William Byrne, the president, to tell the archbishop:

> I must avail myself of this opportunity to thank Your Grace for your kind co-operation, generous support and wise counsel in this whole struggle. I hope that neither your patience, charity or indulgence has been ex-

hausted by our proceedings so that I may venture to ask to be allowed to make heavy drafts on them soon.[13]

When a year or more before Gibbons had told Bryne's predecessor at the Mount, "I am warmly interested in its welfare,"[14] he apparently meant it. Nor was he unmindful of Mount Saint Mary's neighboring institution, Saint Joseph's provincial house of the Daughters of Charity, where he visited in the summer of 1882 and urged the sisters to bestir themselves in behalf of the canonization of their founder, Elizabeth Seton. On that occasion he declared: "I would myself very gladly take the initiative, if I had any encouragement from here; the first movement must naturally begin here . . . . You remember too that American canonized Saints are very rare birds, and Mother Seton's name would add another to the very short list."[15] That Seton's canonization had to wait until 1975 was not in any case due to the local ordinary's lack of interest almost a century before.

In the carrying out of his duties James Gibbons was generally careful to consult others before making a decision in disputed matters, a practice he followed on the diocesan level as well as in his capacity as metropolitan of the Province of Baltimore. In the early years it was Edward McColgan, vicar general for twenty years, among others; later it was the Sulpician superior, Alphonse Magnien, on whom Gibbons leaned heavily—so heavily, in fact, as to cause criticism from some of the clergy. Whenever it became necessary to discipline a priest he showed a moderate spirit as, for example, when he advised Archbishop William Henry Elder, archbishop of Cincinnati: "Although we are not obliged, I think it is desirable whenever the nature of the offense will admit of it, to give Pastors of mature years a trial before degrading them to an inferior place. It is well to have the clergy sustain an action when practicable."[16] He could, however, show a stern side when he felt a priest deserved it, as in the case of Father John B. Manley with whom he had agreed on a transfer only to have Manley reverse himself. Thereupon the archbishop wrote:

> Such a sudden change of mind is very annoying to me after having made other arrangements depending upon your transfer, which was made at your own request. You are hereby instructed to remain where you are in Hancock until such time as I can provide another place for you.[17]

As occupant of the premier see and metropolitan of the extensive Province of Baltimore, to say nothing of being chancellor *ex officio* of the Catholic University of America, no small amount of Gibbons's time and energy were channeled into these activities. As metropolitan his was the prime voice in filling vacancies in suffragan sees, for example, when he promoted John J. Keane, one of his pastors, as bishop of Richmond and consecrated him in August, 1878, the first of twenty-three such ceremonies he would perform to set a record up to that time. With the increase of the houses of study of religious orders and congregations at the univeristy he was called upon to ordain priests, and here too Gibbons set a record of having ordained 2,471 priests in his episcopal years.

More, indeed, could be said about Gibbons's leadership on the diocesan level, but two matters must not go unmentioned. It was obvious in 1911 when William O'Connell of Boston was made a cardinal that his star was on the rise in Rome by reason of his friendship with Cardinal Merry del Val, secretary of state. It was a situation that aroused genuine uneasiness in ecclesiastical circles far beyond New England lest the long arm of O'Connell reach out to put men of his choice in other dioceses. With this in mind Gibbons's auxiliary bishop and diocesan consultors wrote him a lengthy letter in which they urged that he seek the appointment of a coadjutor with the right of succession who would be one of his own choosing. The letter was composed with the utmost tact and with emphatic assurance of their high esteem and affection, points that were clearly made when they declared:

> We should be pained beyond expression if our action should give rise in your mind to a doubt of our affectionate loyalty to Your Eminence. Our action is prompted by no disaffection towards your benevolent administration either in the past or in the present. We desire no change. Should you in your wisdom and generosity accede to our wishes, we beg that all jurisdiction and authority be retained absolutely by Your Eminence, and that the Coadjutor be given a vacant parish or provided with a residence at the Seminary.[18]

One could hardly improve on the tone of their message, but it was all quite in vain, for James Gibbons would have no coadjutor. Had he lived to know his successor, the Irish-born Michael J. Curley, bishop of Saint Augustine, Florida, he might well have regretted his failure to respond to the suggestion made to him in 1912. Gibbons and Curley were utterly unlike and, in fact, the latter told me when he gave permission for the use of the archives for the cardinal's biography, "I did not approve of Cardinal Gibbons. When I came here to Baltimore I found the atmosphere saturated with liberalism." No more need be said on that score except to add that when I recounted this for the Baltimore-born Peter L. Ireton, Bishop of Richmond, he quickly replied, "It's a damn lie!"

In the second matter Gibbons not only responded forcefully but manifested about as agitated a state of mind as he showed throughout his whole life. It pertained to the rumors that began to circulate in 1914 that Washington would be cut off from the archdiocese of Baltimore and made a separate diocese. In letters to Pope Pius X, to Merry del Val, and to Cardinal Gaetano de Lai, Gibbons marshaled every possible argument against the division, and while telling de Lai he could scarcely believe such a thing would happen in his lifetime, he revealed a lingering doubt when he added, "If I thought there was any real danger of its accomplishment, I would protest against it with all the earnestness and energy of my soul until my last breath."[19] For so mild a man as Gibbons this was vigorous language, to be sure. And to make doubly certain that his view would prevail, at the age of nearly eighty he went to Rome in the spring of 1914, a trip which his traveling companion, Louis Stickney, told me was made solely for the purpose of heading off a division of his archdiocese. His intervention succeeded; it was only in July, 1939, that Washington was made an archdiocese and not until January, 1948, that it received its first resident archbishop in Patrick A. O'Boyle.

In assessing the cardinal's leadership on the national level one must think in terms of both the ecclesiastical and the civil domains. In the former his influence increased as his fellow bishops came more and more to trust his judgment amid the controversial issues that marked the last two decades of the nineteenth century. For example, when Archbishop Elder sought his counsel on the Knights of Labor, Gibbons wisely advised, "A masterly inactivity & a vigilant eye on their proceedings is perhaps the best thing to be done in the present junction."[20] In the ensuing months the cardinal became convinced of the Knights' innocence insofar as the church's ban on forbidden societies was concerned, and that conviction prompted him to affix his signature to the remarkable letter addressed to the prefect of Propaganda at Rome in February, 1887, strongly opposing their condemnation, a document of the utmost significance for the future of Catholicism in the United States. Gibbons aligned himself with the workingmen who composed the majority of the Catholic community, and in so doing declared *inter alia*, "To lose the heart of the people would be a misfortune for which the friendship of the few rich and powerful would be no compensation."[21] It was a striking stand that endured and set the American church on the right road toward a tradition of social reform. True, in the composition of the letter he had the assistance of John Ireland, John Keane, and Denis O'Connell, but Gibbons alone signed the document.

A few years later when the national rivalry between American Catholics of Irish and German birth or ancestry threatened the unity of the Catholic community, Gibbons's voice was raised in strong condemnation of the ethnic feud when at the conferring of the pallium on Frederick Katzer, archbishop of Milwaukee, in Saint John's Cathedral in August 1891, he preached the sermon and used extraordinary strong terms in denouncing ethnic divisions. Years later he confessed it was one of the most audacious things he ever did, remarking, "When I finished they were aghast, but I think the lesson had its effect."[22] While Gibbons's occupancy of the premier see, and his being the only American cardinal between 1887 and 1911, gave him an advantage over all other bishops, that advantage might well have been dissipated had he not possessed the qualities of prudence, sound judgment, deference for the opinions of his fellow bishops, and a warm and kindly personality that was singularly free from any suggestion of haughtiness or pride.

The combination of these characteristics not only made James Gibbons *facile princeps* among his own fellow Catholics, but they assured him as well of the deep respect of Protestant and Jewish religious leaders such as John G. Murray, Episcopal bishop of Maryland, and others. And what was true of the cardinal's relations with religious persons and groups not of his faith was, equally true of prominent figures in the civic realm. He was immensely proud of his American citizenship and was at pains to say so from time to time, for example, in September 1880, upon his return from a trip of four and a half months in Europe. Preaching in his cathedral on a Sunday shortly after his return he recounted the highlights of his time abroad and remarked, "[I am] proud to own that whatever be the faults and drawbacks of our own system & they are not a few, still I would infinitely prefer to live under our own flag than any Gov. of contin. Europe, for with us liberty is not a name, but a living reality."[23]

That he meant what he said is certain; no one who knew anything about the cardinal of Baltimore would doubt his sincerity in making these periodic proclamations of love for his country and his native city of Baltimore. He constantly urged his own flock to be active citizens and to vote—even when the Nineteenth Amendment to the Constitution was ratified in August 1920, giving women the right to vote, a measure he had opposed. Monsignor Stickney told me that invariably on election day he would urge the members of his household to vote, but he would never disclose to them how he himself would cast his ballot. It was a measure of the cardinal's political wisdom that helped to preserve him from being used by politicians for their own interests. That was conspiciously the case when on the Sunday preceding the national election of November 1912, he urged the cathedral congregation to exercise their duty to vote, but was careful to add: "There are three conspicuous citizens who are now candidates for the Presidency. Whatever may be my private and personal preference and predilection, it is not for me in this sacred pulpit or anywhere else publicly to dictate or even suggest to you the candidate of my choice."[24]

It was political sagacity of this kind that won the cardinal a wide circle of admirers among Americans of all walks of life and of all religious persuasions. It was of a piece with the advice that Gibbons gave when President William McKinley sent for him to ask what he thought of the United States retaining the Philippine Islands after their conquest from Spain in 1898. "Mr. President," he said, "it would be a good thing for the Catholic Church but, I fear, a bad one for the United States."[25] With the exception of Woodrow Wilson, the cardinal was on friendly terms with all the presidents from Grover Cleveland to William Howard Taft, but the relationship was especially close with Theodore Roosevelt. In January 1917, Roosevelt wrote him and paid a striking tribute when he declared, "Taking your life as a whole, I think you now occupy the position of being the most respected, and venerated, and useful citizen of our country."[26]

If there had been any doubt as to the unique standing of Cardinal Gibbons in American life that doubt would have been laid to rest in June 1911, on the occasion of the golden jubilee of his priesthood. Originally suggested by Oliver P. Baldwin, editor of the Baltimore *Sun*, the favorite newspaper of the cardinal, an immense civic celebration was held on June 6 at the Fifth Regiment Armory, which drew a crowd of 20,000 persons headed by the president of the United States, former President Theodore Roosevelt, Chief Justice Edward D. White, members of the cabinet, the Congress, and the diplomatic corps, as well as the governor of Maryland and other Maryland and Baltimore officials. It was an unprecedented gathering for a Catholic churchman, one that remains without parallel. In a series of speeches the cardinal was addressed in tributes that are seldom accorded to any human being, including a graceful speech from James Viscount Bryce, ambassador of Great Britain. President William Howard Taft summarized in appropriate words what constituted a central theme of the day when he praised Gibbons's contribution to the nation by his inculcation of respect for authority, for religious toleration, and for the wholehearted interest he had always shown toward the moral and material welfare of all elements of the population. Taft then declared: "What we are especially delighted to see confirmed in him and his life is the entire consistency which he has demonstrated between earnest and singleminded patriotism and love of country on the one hand, and sincere devotion to his church and God upon the other."[27] As the encomia flowed on from one speaker after another the guest of honor listened quietly. At the end he rose to respond, thanking the vast audience and the speakers and remarking he had been overwhelmed with confusion by the praise of himself. He stated that the speakers had portrayed their subject, not as he was in reality, but as he ought to be, and added: "But I have become so enamoured of your portrait that it shall be the endeavor of my life to imitate and resemble that portrait more and more during the few years that remain to me in this world."[28] It was a fitting close to one of the most memorable days in the long life of James Gibbons.

If the Baltimore civic celebration of 1911 voiced a nation's respect and esteem, the notable celebration of the cardinal's golden jubilee of his episcopacy on February 20, 1919—delayed due to the influenza epidemic of 1918—did the same for his ecclesiastical career. And here the international standing that Gibbons had acquired was evident when Pope Benedict XV sent Archbishop Bonaventure Cerretti as his personal representative for the festivities held at the Catholic University of America in the presence of virtually the entire American hierarchy and the hierarchy of other nations including Louis Cardinal Bégin, archbishop of Quebec. If space allowed much more could be said of Gibbons's leadership on the international plane such as his active participation in the conclave of 1903 when he intervened in company with Francesco Cardinal Satolli in urging the reluctant Giuseppe Sarto, patriach of Venice, to accept election to the papacy to which he finally assented, taking the name of Pope Pius X.

As I look back at the lengthy chapters of my biography of James Gibbons entitled "The Leader of the American Church" and "The International Churchman," I am conscious of how very much of a significant character has had to be omitted on both the national and international aspects of the cardinal's career. One thing of major importance, however, must find a place here, and that was his consistent support of the American principle of separation of church and state. Never was that position more evident than in the sermon Gibbons preached on March 25, 1887, in taking possession of his titular church of Santa Maria in Trastevere at Rome. With graceful remarks on the encyclical of Pope Leo XIII entitled *Immortale Dei* (On the Civil Constitution of States) issued in November 1885, wherein the pontiff had stated that the church can and does flourish under any and all kinds of governments, providing she is allowed to enjoy "the genial atmosphere of liberty," the cardinal then made his memorable defense of the American way when he stated:

> For myself, as a citizen of the United States, without closing my eyes to our defects as a nation, I proclaim, with a deep sense of pride and gratitude, and in this great capital of Christendom, that I belong to a country where the civil government holds over us the aegis of its protection without interfering in the legitimate exercise of our sublime mission as ministers of the Gospel of Jesus Christ.[29]

If these words sound commonplace in the 1980s they were anything but that a century ago when the official teaching of the church still held to the union of church and state. That sermon represented one of Gibbons's finest efforts in making a contribution to both the ecclesiastical and civil order. He closed by thanking Leo XIII for naming him a cardinal which he interpreted as a compliment to the United States in general, to the American hierarchy, the clergy, and the Catholic laity, and he then added: "I presume also to thank him in the name of our separated brethren in America, who, though not sharing our faith have shown that they are not insensible—indeed, that they are deeply sensible—of the honor conferred upon our common country."[30] It was a typical expression from this sincerely irenic churchman whose lifelong conduct had anticipated the ecumenical spirit of Vatican Council II, just as his famous Roman sermon of 1887 had held to the tradition Gibbons had inherited from the first occupant of the see of Baltimore, John Carroll, and all Carroll's successors. This very tradition received a sanction, so to speak, when in December 1965, Pope Paul VI promulgated the Declaration on Religious Freedom; the conciliar document would have delighted the heart of James Gibbons, who had embodied its principles in all that he had said and done through his nearly eighty-seven years in this world.

The leadership exercised by Cardinal Gibbons was demonstrated on the dual plane of his fidelity to the ideals of his church and his country, and the latter was frequently focused on Gibbons's regard for the Constitution. Thus it was fitting that his last published article written a few weeks before he died should have been on that theme. "As the years go by," he said, "I am more than ever convinced that the Constitution of the United States is the greatest instrument of government that ever issued from the hand of man."[31] The twin allegiance of James Gibbons was emphasized by the preacher at the golden jubilee mass of his priesthood, Archbishop Glennon of Saint Louis, who described the role of cardinals of an earlier day and then spoke in words that afford an appropriate conclusion to this essay:

> We may not deny their greatness, their learning, their consecration; but unlike any one member of either group, our Cardinal stands with the same devotion to his country as Richelieu had for France, cultivating a citizenship as unstained as Newman, and while reaching out to a broader democracy than even Cardinal Manning, he still remains pre-eminent in his unquestioned devotion to Holy Church.[32]

CHAPTER
8
John Ireland

Marvin R. O'Connell

$\mathcal{J}$ohn Ireland's reputation for strength and vigor often led people who had never seen the archbishop of Saint Paul to imagine he was an extraordinarily large man physically. In fact he stood five feet nine or ten inches and in his youth was slender and sharp featured. His eyes were slate blue, his mouth wide and thin lipped. With the passage of years his big-boned frame took on flesh, the contours of his face smoothed out, the thick black hair, which he always wore just over the ears, turned to silver, and he assumed the mien and bearing of a portly clerical gentleman. The Celtic ruddy and creamy complexion stayed with him into old age.[1]

Perhaps Ireland's most striking physical characteristic was the timber of his voice, honeyed thunder sometimes and sometimes a throaty growl, but always dominant, clear, and loud, a wonderfully vibrant and resonant instrument that carried to the farthest corner of the largest hall. When he spoke from platform or pulpit, he punctuated his words with swinging arms and a series of stabbing gestures—a trait he inherited from his father—which, instead of detracting from the force of what he had to say, lent it a singular vitality and emphasis.[2]

John Ireland enjoyed renown as an orator throughout his public life. His eloquence, of course, was that of his own day and reflected his own tastes and training. On formal occasions he seldom spoke for less than an hour and always from a text written out in his sweeping longhand or memorized word for word. His somewhat florid homiletic style found its inspiration in Bossuet rather than in the best English models, and its structure—not its literary allusions—clearly showed the influence of the classical Latin Ireland read for pleasure and the French he spoke and wrote fluently from his youth. He consistently paid his audiences the compliments of always being prepared, of never talking down to them, of never avoiding the polysyllabic word if that word was best suited to make his point. In his earliest surviving unpublished sermons, preached during the last years of the Civil War, one finds that Ireland assumed not only his hearers' attention but also their ability to follow a sometimes intricate argument. Once, in 1866, he described the union of Christ with the church as so close "that there is between them a species of assimilation." On another occasion he stressed that the supernatural state "is a gratuitous gift."[3] Such expressions became the ordinary Sunday morning fare of a congregation composed of hod carriers and stevedores and their harried wives, refugees in a harsh new land, few of them able to read and write. But what mattered to John Ireland was that proper dignity be served—the dignity of his message, to be sure, and of himself, but, perhaps most pressing of all, the dignity that belonged to the people who listened to him and who had to learn to reach beyond their natural grasp if they were to fulfill their destiny.

What he conceived that destiny to be, and how he viewed the role he was to play in the process of fulfillment, provide the key to an understanding of Archbishop Ireland's career as a churchman and a popular leader. For Ireland the "immigrant church" was no abstraction, but a reality he encountered every day. For him the United States was not just a geographical location, not just a place of refuge for Europe's teeming masses, but a land of providential opportunity. He walked with his fine head erect among a rootless and harassed people and assured them that America was their country, that they should be proud of it and of themselves, that they needed to fear no hostile ascendancy any more. He said in a great speech in Baltimore in 1884:

> I love too deeply the Catholic Church and the American republic not to be ever ready to labor that the relations of the one with the other be not misunderstood. It is true, the choicest field which providence offers in the world today to the occupancy of the Church is this republic, and she welcomes with delight the signs of the times that indicate a glorious future for her beneath the starry banner. But it is true, also, the surest safeguards for her own life and prosperity the republic will find in the teachings of the Catholic Church, and the more America acknowledges those teachings, the more durable will her civil institutions be made.[4]

This was John Ireland's Americanist evangel, and as he lived it and propounded it for more than half a century he took on in the eyes of his coreligionists and of many others of his fellow citizens a form larger than life.

John Ireland was born on September 11, 1838, in the village of Burnchurch, County Kilkenny.[5] Eleven years later, in the wake of the great Irish Famine, the family emigrated to the United States, where John's father, Richard, found employment as a carpenter first in Vermont and later in Chicago. In the spring of 1852 the Irelands moved on to Saint Paul, Minnesota Territory, then no more than a small river town perched on the edge of the wilderness. A year later the first bishop of Saint Paul, the French-born Joseph Cretin, sent John Ireland to Cretin's own alma mater, the preparatory seminary of Meximieux, near Lyon. He studied classics there for four years and spent four more years at the theologate of the Marist Fathers located near Toulon. He returned home in the summer of 1861 and was ordained to the priesthood on December 22 of that year by Cretin's successor, Thomas Langdon Grace.[6]

Ireland's sojourn in France, which lasted through eight impressionable years of adolescence and young manhood, had a profound affect upon him. During that time he became acquainted with the kind of orderly clerical life that was to remain his life long ideal. He adopted also habits of reading and study that were to be similarly permanent characteristics. When as a mature bishop he founded educational institutions within his own jurisdiction, the model he always invoked was that of Meximieux. By no means unimportant in his later ecclesiastical career was the fluency he acquired during his student days in written and spoken French, a skill that enabled him to deal directly with the officers of the Roman Curia.[7] Ireland remained a francophile all his life, and the high regard in which he came to be held in certain French Catholic circles played a significant role in the Americanist crisis of the 1890s.

The Civil War had begun even before Ireland returned from France, and within months of his ordination the young priest was named chaplain to the Fifth Regiment, Minnesota Volunteer Infantry. He participated in the campaign, which culminated in the Battle of Corinth, fought in Mississippi on October 3 and 4, 1862, and wrote at the time a lively and largely accurate account of that battle.[8] He reminisced often in later life about his military career and indeed tended to romanticize it. Thus, in a memoir of 1892, he characterized "my years of chaplaincy [as] the happiest and most fruitful years of my ministry,"[9] when in fact his period of service had lasted less than ten months. Ireland took great satisfaction in the sobriquet commonly applied to him in Minnesota—"the fighting chaplain of the fighting Fifth"[10]—and when, many years after the war, the story circulated that at a crucial point in the Battle of Corinth Chaplain Ireland had saved the day by distributing cartridges to the soldiers in the line, the old archbishop could not be got to deny it. Brief as it was, John Ireland's army service was in its own way as important in his development as the long years spent in France. Scarcely more than a boy when he joined the regiment, fresh from the contemplative quiet of a French *grand séminaire,* Ireland learned to be a man and to be a priest amid the whine of minié balls and the shrieks of the maimed and dying. He could claim, moreover, a place among the million men who, in their youth, had rallied to save the Union. Like them he had earned the right to wear the badge of an American patriot. "We were the soldiers of Abraham Lincoln," he liked to say. "This the praise we covet; this the memory we yearn to transmit to the coming years."

From the spring of 1863 until the end of 1875 Ireland served successively as curate and pastor of the cathedral parish in Saint Paul. This parochial ministry, with all its usual preoccupations, was carried out during a period of rapid population growth throughout the Upper Midwest: Bishop Grace founded no fewer than sixty-six parishes in his vast diocese during this span of years.[11] Father Ireland, who resided with the bishop in the clergy house next to the cathedral, learned at first hand the skills required to administer a frontier diocese. He was fortunate, moreover, in his tutor. Thomas Grace, a cultivated and relatively well-educated Dominican, was never a leader who initiated policies, but neither would he obstruct a subordinate who did. John Ireland's restless genius, with all its rough edges, thus found an ideal superior in Grace, who gave his gifted younger colleague free rein and always bestowed credit where credit was due.

So it was that, early on, Ireland plunged into a host of endeavors in which he enjoyed the confidence but also the detachment of his ordinary. An instance of this was Ireland's fierce advocacy of the cause of total abstinence from alcohol, a cause to which Bishop Grace, though he routinely condemned the evil of excessive drinking, never subscribed. Ireland, by contrast, placed all his gifts at its disposal, all his energies. He spent a lifetime in the struggle and, in doing so, displayed all the best facets of his character: his straightforwardness, his vigor, his utter fearlessness, his genuine concern for the well-being of his fellows. No means to achieve the end of general sobriety were beneath him or beyond him. He brooked no compromise with the principle that all liquor, whether fermented or distilled or brewed, was poisonous. "Remember," he said once, "if you are what is called a temperate man who takes a glass but never exceeds, your example is worse than that of a drunkard."[12] He began his efforts to promote total abstinence by forming a Father Mathew Society—named for the Irish Capuchin Theobald Mathew, the "Apostle of Temperance," whom Ireland as a boy, had met in Kilkenny—in his own parish (1869), but soon he extended his activities across the state of Minnesota and, before long, across the nation. Indeed, it was due to his fiery oratory on the temperance circuit—his lurid descriptions of the sordid lot of those addicted to drink were particularly memorable[13]—that gained for Ireland his first measure of notoriety outside his own locality.

"Father Mathew of the Northwest" was a nickname in which John took both pride and pleasure. Early in 1875 the notice that another, more formal title was to be bestowed upon him caused him considerably less delight. A year earlier the bishops of the Province of Saint Louis had sent to Rome the usual list of three nominees, or *terna*, for the vacant vicariate of Nebraska. Bishop Grace explained later that he had permitted Ireland's inclusion in third place on the *terna* only as a compliment to a worthy young priest and only with the assurances of his episcopal colleagues that the appointment would never take place. The officers of the Congregation of Propaganda, however, judged the first two nominees unsuitable, and therefore, as the laconic Roman résumé expressed it, "for the Apostolic Vicariate of Nebraska no name remains save that of the priest Ireland, about whom there is, besides, sufficient satisfactory information." Grace hurried off to Rome and laid siege to the palazzo of Propaganda on the edge of the Piazza di Spagna. He expressed his personal displeasure at the turn of events. He warned that Ireland's departure would cause deep resentment in Minnesota and would lead to a host of unspecified troubles. He threatened, finally, to resign. Ireland meanwhile, in a letter addressed to Pope Pius IX, did in fact resign the vicariate. Propaganda finally resolved the problem, to Grace's satisfaction, by appointing Ireland coadjutor bishop of Saint Paul, with right of succession. He was ordained to the episcopal order on December 21, 1875.[14]

Ireland served as Grace's coadjutor for nine years, during which time Catholic population growth and institutionalization continued apace. The two vicariates of Northern Minnesota (1875) and Dakota (1879) were carved out of the diocese of Saint Paul, and, in the terriotry left to him—roughly the southern third of the state of Minnesota—Grace founded fifty more parishes. Schools, hospitals, and orphanages operated under Catholic auspices also came into being in impressive numbers. Ireland's primary job during these years was to help Grace fulfill the usual duties incumbent on a bishop, most of which were religiously significant and therefore important in that sense, but not otherwise remarkable.

One inititative, however, was entirely the coadjutor's own. Ireland had long been convinced that the ideal locale for the Catholic immigrant was the countryside. He had a Jeffersonian vision of a class of sturdy Catholic yeomen who owned and farmed their own land and who thus gained a measure of independence and respectability unattainable by propertyless day laborers. Shortly after his episcopal consecration he announced the formation of the Catholic Colonization Bureau of Saint Paul, at whose disposal the Saint Paul and Pacific Railroad had put 75,000 acres of unoccupied land in southwestern Minnesota. The bureau had been designated as the sole agent in the sale of this property at an average price of six dollars an acre. The agreement with the Saint Paul and Pacific proved to be the first of eleven such contracts Ireland signed with various railroad companies between 1876 and 1881. The result of this effort was a group of ten rural communities, which thrive to this day. The colonization movement in Minnesota prospered because it coincided with the financial interests of the railroads and, no less importantly, because Ireland and his aides set down for themselves attainable goals and tempered their idealism with a hardheaded appreciation of economic realities; with one notable exception—and that a disastrous failure—they brought to their colonies only those who had enough means to survive the deprivations inevitable during the first year or two of settlement on the prairie. That Ireland's bureau had no capital of its own proved, ironically, its secret of success, as the failure of attempts—in which Ireland himself took an active part—to promote Catholic colonization in the West generally by a nationwide appeal for funds amply demonstrated.[15]

As the years passed Thomas Grace increasingly left the chores of diocesan administration to his coadjutor, and, in 1884, on the silver jubilee of his arrival in Saint Paul, the old bishop retired. Thus it was that Bishop Ireland attended the momentously important Third Plenary Council of Baltimore as an ordinary in his own right. During the conciliar sessions he espoused episcopal rights vis-à-vis the lower clergy and the religious orders, commitment to the Indian missions, and, predictably, the cause of temperance. In the debates that occupied the month of November 1884 he was more often than not allied with his friend and comrade in the national colonization movement, John Lancaster Spalding of Peoria. But the greatest impression Ireland made at Baltimore came outside the formal meetings of the bishops. On the evening of November 10, from the pulpit of the Cathedral of the Assumption, he delivered a ninety-minute oration which he called, "The Church—the Support of Just Government." His performance was widely regarded as a rhetorical tour de force, and the modest reputation he had heretofore enjoyed around the United States as a temperance crusader and a colonizer was immensely enhanced by it.[16] The basically simple thesis of the speech—that Catholicism and the American ethos were mutually beneficial and supportive—had long been Ireland's deepest conviction, and it continued to guide his thought and action for the rest of his life.

Also in attendance at the council were other men similarly disposed, and the presence of all of them at Baltimore provided the occasion for the formation of that set of professional and personal associations that would become known later as the "Americanist" party. Among them were James Gibbons, archbishop of Baltimore and soon to be cardinal; John J. Keane, bishop of Richmond and soon to be first rector of the Catholic University of America; and Denis J. O'-Connell, soon to be rector of the North American College in Rome. These were the major collaborators destined to stand with John Ireland in the struggles that lay just ahead.

The legislation of the Third Plenary Council was of extreme importance in the life of the Catholic Church in the United States—a hallmark, indeed—but its passage signaled an end, rather than a beginning, to an era of good feeling among the American bishops.[17] Over the next decade and a half, controversy, increasingly bitter, raged over such issues as the pace of Americanization among immigrant Catholics, particularly Germans; the status of fraternal organizations with psuedomasonic trappings, like the Odd Fellows and the Knights of Pythias; the attitude of Catholics toward public education; and the position to be assumed within the Catholic community by a national university, the founding of which had been mandated by the council. John Ireland held strong views on these and related matters, and, as was his wont, expressed those views with the utmost vigor. Opposed to him within the hierarchy were Archbishop Michael Augustine Corrigan of New York and Bishop Bernard McQuaid of Rochester, the latter hardly less outspoken than Ireland himself. So the parties gradually formed, fluid at first but eventually unyielding: Ireland, Keane, O'Connell, a sometimes reluctant Gibbons, the Paulists, the Catholic temperance forces, and the more intellectually adventuresome clergy on one side; and Corrigan, McQuaid, the Germans (clerical and lay), the Jesuits, and most of the other religious orders on the other.[18]

Given the ecclesiastical realities of the late nineteenth century, however, the battles could not be decisively fought out on American soil. Never before had the papacy's prestige among Catholics stood higher, never before had the theoretical right of the pope to "universal jurisdiction" been more effectively exercised. The result was that the contentious American prelates found themselves competing for favor at the Vatican, where, it was acknowledged by all of them, the final decisions would be reached. Like many an able chief executive officer, the suave and sophisticated Pope Leo XIII, who prided himself on his diplomatic skills, saw his administrative role as that of a kind of referee, without commitment to either faction.

John Ireland's introduction to this world of high policy and, inevitably, of intrigue occurred in 1886. In November of that year he accompanied John Keane to Rome. During their stay there they lodged with Denis O'Connell at the North American College, where James Gibbons joined them later. Keane's formal mission was to secure the approval of the Roman curia for the statutes of the new Catholic University of America, while Ireland, ostensibly on his *ad limina* visit (an official personal report to the Holy See made every five years), was present in support.[19] But, in the midst of the university negotiations, the two bishops almost immediately became embroiled in other problems. They had to rebut a complaint registered at Propaganda by certain influential German-American Catholics, who charged the English-speaking hierarchy in the United States with discrimination.[20] They also had to ward off attempts to secure a Roman condemnation of the Knights of Labor on the grounds that this organization of workers was a species of masonry. By the time the latter crisis came to a head, Gibbons had arrived in Rome to receive his cardinal's red hat, and it was largely thanks to his intervention that the proposed condemnation was avoided.[21] Meanwhile, however, Archbishop Corrigan's opposition to the Catholic University had surfaced, and Gibbons, in despair that without New York the university was bound to fail, might well have abandoned that project had not Ireland energetically protested against "so cowardly a surrender to so unworthy an opposition."[22]

When Ireland, Gibbons, and Keane bid adieu to O'Connell in early April, 1887, they had reason to be satisfied with the results of their Roman sojourn. Ireland had also taken advantage of his presence in the Eternal City to launch another initiative. Saint Paul was suffragan to the metropolitan See of Milwaukee, where German influence was paramount, and Ireland was anxious to head a province of his own. The negotiations with Propaganda continued for more than a year until a papal brief, dated May 15, 1888, named John Ireland first archbishop of Saint Paul, "The resolution of Propaganda, as approved by the Holy Father," he told Gibbons, "[was] just as I had desired— Mgr. O'Connell seconding, of course, with his usual diplomatic skill."[23] The new province embraced the states of Minnesota and North and South Dakota and included five suffragan sees, at the heads of which Ireland, after fierce struggles that lasted another year, succeeded in having appointed protégés of his own. This was the way, O'Connell assured him, that "you can command the future as long as you live."[24] Ireland needed little urging on this point, nor did he ever let his activities in the national or international arena distract him for long from his home base. He tended his own flock out of simple duty, to be sure, but also out of genuine regard and love for the people from whom he had sprung. He entered at the same time into civic life with a zest that made him one of the most popular figures in his city and region.

The greatest single problem facing Ireland locally—and by extension facing all his fellow American bishops, whether friendly to him or not, at the end of the last century—was that of providing education for Catholic children. The issue was particularly volatile, because no institution was so prized among the American populace generally as the public school, while American Catholics, not without reason, had long considered it an agent of the predominant Protestant culture. Catholics therefore had built and financed their own schools, a policy that the Third Plenary Council had confirmed and decreed mandatory in every parish in the country. Archbishop Ireland, with his profound dedication to the process of rapid Americanization, could not but be of two minds about the theory of parochial education, since it was universally acknowledged that the public school was the primary catalyst of immigrant customs and languages. This circumstance indeed brought him into even sharper contention with his German corelgionists, who maintained the most successful parochial schools and unabashedly taught the language of the old country in them. But aside from the theory—and Ireland was never given much to speculation—the financial obstacles in the way of establishing a parochial system that could educate more than a fraction of American Catholic children appeared insurmountable.

These were some of the considerations of the archbishop of Saint Paul when he addressed the convention of the National Education Association meeting in his see city in July 1890. He paid tribute, first of all, to the principle of "the free school of America: Withered be the hand raised in sign of its destruction!" Then he recommended to a mostly hostile audience the plan in effect in Poughkeepsie, New York, whereby the local board of education rented the parochial school building for a nominal sum and conducted secular instruction there through the normal school day, after which the plant reverted to the control of the parish and the same children were taught their catechism by the same teachers.[25] This speech, widely publicized around the country,[26] brought Ireland support from predictable sources but also much hostility from those Catholics who thought such a compromise spelled doom for the parochial schools, and from those non-Catholics who thought it amounted to spending tax monies in support of the Roman religion.

The practical implications of the NEA speech became startlingly apparent the following year, when Ireland was able to introduce the Poughkeepsie plan into two communities in his diocese, Faribault and Stillwater. A veritable pamphlet war followed within the Catholic community. Ireland found it necessary to travel to Rome at the beginning of 1892 to defend himself, and, though by furious lobbying he won vindication of what now came to be called the "Faribault School Plan," he paid a heavy price. The overwhelming majority of his episcopal colleagues sided against him on the school issue, none more violently than Lancaster Spalding, who denounced Ireland to Rome in the harshest terms.[27] The enmity of Corrigan and McQuaid, of the Jesuits, of the German faction—who accused him and O'Connell, not unjustly, of defamation[28]—took on a bitter new intensity. Ireland also had to agree to the establishment of an apostolic delegation in the United States, a scheme long cherished by Leo XIII but opposed by all the other Amerian archbishops, including Gibbons. And, as became clear only later, the pope's support in the school controversy owed less to the principle involved than to Ireland's supposed popularity in certain republican circles in Paris at a time when papal diplomacy was aiming toward improved relations with the French Third Republic.

The hollowness of Ireland's Roman victory was underscored when the agreements he had reached with the school boards at Faribault and Stillwater quickly disappeared without leaving a trace. Meanwhile, the archbishop of Saint Paul drifted upon a sea of other troubles. The apostolic delegate, Francesco Satolli, who first came to America under Ireland's patronage and for the sake of whose mission Ireland sacrificed much good will among his colleagues, gradually grew alienated from him.[29] His relationship with Corrigan was reduced to a growling litany of epithets like "liar" and "hypocrite," and McQuaid publicly attacked him from the pulpit of the Rochester cathedral. His friends Keane and O'Connell were both dismissed from their posts.

Besides enduring these public reverses Ireland had to deal as well with a personal crisis. Since his days as a colonizer he had invested in real estate heavily and, as the events proved, imprudently. The nationwide depression that began in 1893 drove him to the brink of financial ruin. The hundreds of thousands of dollars he admitted having lost were his own, but the rumors that he had played fast and loose with the resources of his diocese persisted and put in the hands of his numerous enemies another stick to beat him with.[30] For more than a decade Ireland avoided bankruptcy only because of the largesse of wealthy friends like Marcus Hanna, Marshall Field, and, especially, the railroad tycoon James J. Hill. For a man who put as much stock as Ireland had in the possibilities of the American dream, and who took understandable pride in pointing to his own career as an instance of the fulfillment of that dream, the collapse of his fortune and the consequent need to beg for assistance exacted a fearful toll. "I am simply crushed down with this load of debt," he told Hill on one occasion. "My power for work is impaired. The responsibilities of my position, in view of a loss of public credit, take from me all peace of mind. . . . There is no other way out of this dreadful crisis into which I have got but your friendship."[31]

The financial moguls who extended him help were by no means indifferent to the archbishop of Saint Paul's consistent advocacy of the Republican party. Indeed, at a crucial moment during the presidential campaign of 1896 Ireland, at Hill's request, gave a strong public endorsement of William McKinley's candidacy.[32] But Ireland might well have done so without any external pressure, because all of his sympathies lay with the party that espoused middle-class probity and imperialism and that, rhetorically at least, reflected his own enlightened views on race relations as well as his dedication to temperance. He took great pride, in any case, in counting among his friends McKinley, Theodore Roosevelt, and Taft. Aware of this circumstance—and overestimating its political significance—the Vatican dispatched Ireland to Washington in April 1898, in hopes that he could help prevent the outbreak of war between Spain and the United States. Though the archbishop pursued this goal with all his accustomed vigor, his diplomatic efforts ended in failure.[33]

That failure was prelude to another. Throughout the summer and autumn of 1898 rumor was rife that the pope intended to issue a condemnation of "Americanism." The immediate occasion for the papal displeasure was the allegation that some French Catholics had adopted certain principles of individual liberty and initiative that they identified as American and that, while acceptable enough in the civil community, posed a serious danger "to Catholic doctrine and discipline." More fundamental, however, was the fact that Pope Leo's prorepublican French policy, in which the archbishop of Saint Paul had played a role since 1892, had collapsed in the wake of the Dreyfus affair. In January 1899, Ireland went determinedly to Rome, but he could not prevent the publication of a censorious apostolic letter. *Testem benevolentiae* was in itself hardly more than a mild rebuke, carefully qualified, and Ireland promptly accepted it. But he remained angry and bewildered "that such a wrong should have been done us— our Bishops, our faithful people, and our whole nature—as to designate . . . by the word 'Americanism' [such] errors and extravagances." Privately he said, "Fanatics conjured up 'Americanism' and put such before the Pope. . . . Who ever 'preferred' natural to supernatural virtues?" This and similar accusations constituted a "nightmare"; they were merely a few bizarre ideas "set afloat in France."[34]

John Ireland was a practical man, not given much—it bears repeating—to theorizing, and he could not see that the dense phrases of *Testem benevolentiae* had anything to do with the church in the

United States as he had known it and had helped to shape it. But, as a practical man, he must have realized that his involvement in so many controversies, reaching their climax in the crisis of 1899, had put out of reach a prize he ardently desired. Yet the dream died hard. As early as 1892 he had begun to count upon being elevated to the college of cardinals, and as late as 1916, when he was seventy-eight, he still harbored hopes for it.[35] His efforts to secure the honor often went to embarrassing lengths, but, even so, he compromised no principle to attain it.[36] How much Ireland's longing for a red hat stemmed from personal ambition or from the purer motive of seeking the highest approbation for his multitude of tasks it is impossible to say; it seems likely that these two motives were always inseparable and not very different in any case.

Ireland's last years were spent in relative serenity. He ventured only once more into the international arena by acting with considerable effect as liaison between the Vatican and the Roosevelt administration in settlement of the vexing church–state problems involved in the American annexation of the Philippines.[37] The contentiousness among the bishops of the United States subsided as the simple passage of time quieted many of their quarrels, and the hand of death did the same. Corrigan died unreconciled to the archbishop of Saint Paul, but in December 1905, Ireland spent a pleasant three days in Rochester as the guest of Bishop McQuaid.[38] Ireland seemed for the most part content to stay at home. Not since the mid-1880s had he devoted exclusive attention to his own jurisdiction, and now it seemed as though he had found a second wind. He had moreover set for himself, with characteristic bravura, one last great project. "I am very busy with many things," he wrote a French friend in 1911, "particularly with my new cathedrals, now journeying fast toward completion."[39]

The two magnificent churches—one in Saint Paul, the other in Minneapolis—were, despite the doubts of skeptics, finished a few years before the archbishop's death in 1918, and they stand today as monuments not so much to Ireland as to the rite of passage in which he was so deeply engaged. The Catholic church in the United States came of age during Ireland's tumultuous career, and it is inconceivable that it should have achieved its maturity without him. No prelate was ever more a man of his times than John Ireland, and yet there lingers a sense that in his weaknesses no less than in his strengths he might have been a man for all times. One is moved at any rate to paraphrase the gospel: There was a man sent from God whose name was John. And when shall we see his like again?

CHAPTER
9
Michael Corrigan: The Conservative Ascendancy

Robert Emmett Curran, S.J.

> N[ew] York is acknowledged at all hands to be the Emporium of the commerce of America, there arriving 50 vessels from all the quarters of the World , whilst there arrive scarce 5 or 10 at any other port, it will increase in extent and population above any other city of the union on account of the local situation for commerce which is unique. N.Y. in the opinion of connoisseurs will be before 15 years another London.[1]

The writer was Anthony Kohlmann, whom John Carroll in 1808 had named as vicar general of the newly established diocese of New York. Now, five years later, Kohlmann was pleading with his Jesuit superior and Carroll not to close the literary institute he had begun for both Catholic and non-Catholic children in the city and not to withdraw the Jesuits to Maryland, "the poorest and most beggarly of the whole union."[2] His appeal to the demographic advantages of New York and the urban future of American Catholicism failed to persuade his superiors, but the Alsatian clergyman's reading of the significance of New York was accurate enough. Kohlmann had seen that, although American Catholicism had been largely confined to the South in the colonial and federal periods, its center was now shifting from the agrarian South to the urban North, and particularly to New York. For the next century and beyond, the church of New York was the most important center of Catholicism in the United States: the largest and wealthiest diocese in the commercial and financial capital of the country, a city in which the Irish, the ethnic group that came to dominate the church in the nineteenth century, early came to power, both in secular and ecclesiastical politics.

In 1813 the city, which had already surpassed Philadelphia as the country's largest, was in a period of economic stagnation brought on by Jefferson's embargo and the War of 1812. The Erie Canal and the mass immigration from Ireland and Germany that followed the Treaty of Ghent in 1815 quickly confirmed Kohlmann's prediction. From 1820 to 1860 the city's population grew from 123,700 to 805,358. New York became the commercial hub of the country and the entry point for the majority of immigrants.

In 1815 there were but 15,000 Catholics in the New York region. Within a few years there were 20,000 in New York City alone. By 1860 it counted over 200,000 foreign-born Irish.[3] As early as the late eighteenth century the Irish were a majority of the ethnically mixed Catholic population. With one exception, every bishop of New York to date has been either Irish-born or of Irish ancestry. The first two were Irish Dominicans, Richard Luke Concanen (1808–1810) and John Connolly (1814–1825), both residents of Rome for nearly forty years when they were appointed. John Carroll had been unable to recommend anyone for the newly established see in 1808. The Holy See, under Irish pressure from Dublin, Lisbon, and Rome itself, appointed Concanen, only to have him die before he could get passage to America in the midst of the war.[4] His Dominican successor became the first resident prelate in 1815. Four decades in Roman seminaries had hardly prepared him for New York. In his ten-year administration he increased the churches from three to sixteen, brought in the Sisters of Charity, and founded an orphanage. But lack of resources, both human and monetary, plagued his episcopacy, as did chronic trusteeism at the two city parishes, Saint Peter's and Saint Patrick's.

Rome continued to select outsiders for the diocese. At the recommendation of Kohlmann, now a professor of philosophy at the Gregorian University, John Dubois, an émigré from the French Revolution, was appointed bishop in 1825.[5] The founder of Mount Saint Mary's College and mentor to Elizabeth Seton, Dubois had all the pastoral experience that Connolly lacked. But he was not Irish. Lay trustees at his own cathedral rebelled after he suspended an Irish priest who had insulted him. Rome finally ordered him to reinstate the priest. Nor was Saint Patrick's unique in its opposition. The genteel, saintly Dubois seemed out of time and place in the rough-and-tumble world of the Age of Jackson. Nativist polemics and attacks (one of his churches in New York was put to the torch in 1831) he bore in dignified silence. He added little materially to the diocese. His greatest accomplishment, the seminary he built at Nyack, was open but a few months in 1834 before being leveled by a fire of suspicious origin. Several strokes led to the appointment of John Hughes as his coadjutor in 1837.

In Hughes man and age met. Twenty years later a Catholic historian judged that "no prelate of the Catholic Church has ever attained in the United States a position such as his."[6] Well-publicized controversies made him the national spokesman for the church and the rights of Catholics. He deftly used nativism, patriotism, the papacy, and power to unify New York Catholics as a loyal but proud minority in an alien society. Saint Patrick's Cathedral, begun by Hughes in 1859, was his legacy in stone.

Alive to the terrible poverty that many of the Irish had found in the cellars and shanties of New York, Hughes worked to improve those conditions through church, state, and private agencies, such as the Saint Vincent de Paul Society, the Irish Emigrant Society, and the Emigrant Industrial Savings Bank. But he opposed the movement to colonize the Irish in rural areas as an impractical solution to their plight in cities like New York. As bad as the Irish might have it in the city, they were utterly unprepared for the complex husbandry that American agriculture required.

The Irish respected power and Hughes used it. If he defended his people like an Irish chieftain, he also ruled like one.[7] Hughes wasted no time in attacking trusteeism. When the trustees of Saint Patrick's removed a catechist appointed by Dubois, Hughes through the ailing bishop threatened to interdict the church. The trustees relented. It was the beginning of the end for an independent trustee system in New York. "I made war on the whole system," Hughes boasted.[8] Every new parish was put in the bishop's name alone. In 1861 church law gave control of parish education to the pastor. A state bill in 1863 made it legal for the bishop to become a corporation *sole*.[9]

Hughes had cut his teeth in the polemical wars as a pastor in Philadelphia. As bishop he continued to defend the doctrines of the church and to criticize the exclusive use of the King James Bible in public schools. Most notorious was his aggressive attempt in 1840 to restore public funding in New York City for Catholic schools, a practice that had been discontinued in 1823. He succeeded in breaking the power of the Protestant-dominated Public School Society, which controlled the funds, but failed to obtain any monies for his own schools. Nativists blamed him for driving the Bible out of the schools. In 1842 the militia had to be called out to turn away a mob attacking his residence. When in 1844 anti-Catholics threatened to repeat in New York the violence that had devastated Philadelphia, Hughes cooly warned the nativist mayor of New York that he would find his city in flames, "become a second Moscow," if a single Catholic Church were touched.[10] New York remained dark. The long-range results were the secularization of the public schools and the development of a separate self-funded parochial school system. By 1850 Hughes was advising his people that "the time has almost come when we shall have to build the school-house first and the church afterward."[11] At his death there were forty-three Catholic schools in New York City.[12]

Enormous institutional expansion took place under Hughes— scores of churches, ten religious communities, a seminary, five colleges, and the first hospital in the state. Centralization of administration increased proportionately with the establishment of a diocesan bureaucracy. In 1850 New York became an archdiocese. By that time four dioceses (Albany, Buffalo, Brooklyn, and Newark) had been created from parts of the territory.

Hughes was determined to establish the loyalty of American Catholics both to Washington and to Rome. He was a fierce defender of the papacy, including its temporal power. He began the special role that New York played in the world of shrinking papal finances with the collapse of the Papal States by sponsoring collections to relieve the beleaguered Pius IX. He also was a major founder of the American College in Rome. In 1861 his prominence and friendship with Secretary of State William Seward led to his mission to France and England as a semiofficial envoy of the Lincoln government to prevent their intervention in the War. That mission may well have prevented Hughes from becoming the first American cardinal.

That honor fell in 1875 to Hughes's successor, the noncontroversial John McCloskey, despite the latter's wish that there be "no cardinal's hat in this country. We are better without one."[13] McCloskey, the first native-born prelate of the archdiocese, doubled the number of schools and brought in sixteen religious congregations to staff them and the other institutions in the growing archdiocesan network, but his administration was essentially a placid interlude between the Hughes and Corrigan administrations.

Michael Augustine Corrigan was a symbol of the rising Irish fortunes in the New York area. His immigrant father had used his wholesale grocery and real estate investments to become reputedly the wealthiest person in Newark. A frail child, Michael did his elementary studies at the private school his godfather conducted in Newark, followed by two years at Saint Mary's College in Wilmington, Delaware. In 1855 he entered Mount Saint Mary's College in Emmitsburg, Maryland, where his excellent memory enabled him to take honors in most subjects. In 1859 he became a member of the first class of the American College in Rome, which had been established to provide a sound theological education for potential bishops. Unfortunately the level of seminary education in the mid-nineteenth century was scarcely better in Rome than in America. Corrigan's perfectionist proclivities found fertile ground in the pious but closed intellectual world of Pio Nono's Rome.

His success in theology led to graduate studies following his ordination in 1863. With a doctorate in divinity he returned to the United States a year later to be appointed director of the seminary at Seton Hall College and professor of dogmatic theology and sacred scripture. In 1869 he succeeded Bernard McQuaid as president of the college, which was experiencing declining enrollments and rising deficits. Along with two of his brothers Corrigan raised sufficient capital to prevent the school from closing. In 1873 he was named bishop of Newark at the age of thirty-four, the youngest prelate in the country.

As bishop he added sixty-nine churches and missions in his seven-year episcopate, a remarkable expansion given the depressed times. Much of this growth and economic improvement was due to the consolidating policies of Corrigan. He successfully secured virtually all the diocesan property in his own name, becoming a corporation *sole*. Corporations for each parish were established, composed of the bishop, vicar general, pastor, and two lay trustees, but the latter, as Corrigan assured a fellow bishop, were "little more than figureheads." Parish visitation became another means of ensuring uniformity in practice. The culmination of this centralization came with the diocesan synod that Corrigan called in April 1878.

When Cardinal McCloskey sought a coadjutor in 1880 Corrigan was chosen by Rome, although he was third on the *terna* that the bishops of the New York Province drew up.[14] McCloskey, his health impaired by periodic attacks of malaria, entrusted the administration of the archdiocese, now numbering some 600,000 Catholics, to Corrigan. Although McCloskey continued to make the key decisions until his death in 1885, Corrigan put his stamp upon the archdiocese. He had an enormous capacity for work. He first made a visitation of all the parishes. He reorganized the bureaucracy of the diocese to make it more efficient in meeting the ever-growing needs of the church in New York. As the ordinary he gave special attention to the school system; seventy-five schools were added and the administration consolidated. He brought twenty-four new communities of religious men and women to the archdiocese. Under his leadership there was a proliferation of charitable institutions, ranging from nurseries to residences for homeless women. These were all brought together within the Association of Catholic Charities in 1902.

Nor did he neglect the new wave of Catholic immigrants in New York. Although he resented Rome's tendency to equate Catholic immigration with Italian immigration and initially opposed the creation of national churches for Italians on the grounds of their scattered pattern of settlement and indifferent practice of religion, he became an early enthusiast for the association of Italian priests that the bishop of Piacenza, Giovanni Battista Scalabrini, formed in 1888 to work with Italian immigrants.[15] Within the year, at his invitation the first Scalabrinians arrived in New York. In like manner Mother Cabrini came a year later. When financial problems plagued the Italian priests in their attempts to found churches, Corrigan proposed that they be assigned to established parishes with separate services for Italians.[16] The Scalabrinians and the other Italian clergy persisted, however, and independent Italian parishes became an important part of the ethnic ministry in New York.

As coadjutor Corrigan used his position in several ways to promote cooperation among the prelates in the eastern dioceses. In 1881 he took the initiative in forming an episcopal board for the financial relief of Mount Saint Mary's College. Similar united action raised an estimated $5 million for Ireland. Corrigan also played the central role in the bishops' successful preservation of the American College from seizure by the Italian government in 1884 and had the title transferred to himself and the other four archbishops of the executive board.

Such collaboration in the early 1880s culminated with the Third Plenary Council in 1884. Despite the growing desire of the eastern prelates for joint episcopal enactment of disciplinary legislation, the pressure for the council came from several western bishops, especially Michael Heiss of Milwaukee and Thomas Grace of Saint Paul. The eastern bishops, such as Corrigan, saw a more pressing need for provincial councils rather than another plenary one, since the needs of the church in such an immense country were too heterogeneous to be met by any national legislation. They also feared that the Vatican would control the council by forcing legislation upon them through their own apostolic delegate.

In May 1883 the Vatican ordered the metropolitans in the United States to come to Rome to prepare for a plenary council. Corrigan represented McCloskey. Despite Roman promises of allowing the Americans great freedom in shaping their own agenda, Corrigan found himself and his fellow prelates "treated somewhat as pupils in a classroom."[17] The Americans successfully resisted certain Roman proposals, including the establishment of cathedral chapters, and modified others, such as the creation of formal parishes with full canonical rights. Corrigan pleaded privately, on behalf of his fellow archbishops, that the Vatican not raise the charge of foreign interference by using the occasion to send a delegate to the United States.[18] Rome finally selected James Gibbons of Baltimore as its delegate for the council. Corrigan's work did not go unnoticed. A Canadian bishop observed after the planning sessions had concluded: "There is a [rumor] in Rome that the Archbishop of Baltimore & Monsig. Corrigan in course of time will be created Cardinals. Both made their mark here."[19]

Corrigan and Gibbons worked closely in preparing the council once they returned to America. Although the Americans had fought the centralizing designs in the original Roman *schemata*, left to themselves they were ready enough for quite specific uniformity in discipline, so long as they were in control. They substantially reduced the authority that Rome had given to the clergy as diocesan consulters. With Corrigan's support, John Lancaster Spalding led a futile fight to eliminate priests from the nomination of bishops. "If priests are given the right of electing," Spalding argued, "the people will also covet it."[20] On the whole, however, Corrigan's role in the council seems to have been that of conciliator, a role that Gibbons played on a larger scale. Both he and Corrigan coordinated the successful effort to preserve the acts of the council from Roman revision.

The council was the high-water mark of unity for the American hierarchy. Within the next three years divisions among the prelates surfaced over such issues as the status of German-Americans and the formation of the Catholic University of America.

The German-Americans resented the growing domination of the American church by the Irish. Since 1872 the numbers of immigrants from Germany had surpassed those from Ireland. German Catholics increasingly felt they were underrepresented in the hierarchy and discriminated against in areas ruled by non-Germans. When in 1885 a Propaganda official promised the president of the *Central Verein* of the United States that the pope would appoint a cardinal protector for German Catholics in America, non-German-American prelates saw an international conspiracy aiming at German domination in the area between Cincinnati, Milwaukee, and Saint Louis, the so-called "German Triangle."

"The more I look at this German current," Richard Gilmour wrote to Corrigan late in that year, "the more I am in fear, and the more convinced that if the tide is not stopped the West is lost, rather, swallowed by the Germans. . . . Our only hope is in you & Boston & Baltimore. We build on *you* largely, & hope you will actively influence the others."[21] Corrigan was much less of an alarmist than those urging him to action. Two years before this, he had encouraged Peter Paul Cahensly to open in the United States a branch of the *St. Raphaels-Verein*, the organization that the wealthy merchant of Limburg an der Lahn had founded to assist German emigrants. At first Corrigan took no steps to attempt to influence Rome beyond responding to a Propaganda query by assuring them that parishes for different ethnic groups, even within the same neighborhood, were an absolute necessity in the United States. When, however, a German-American priest, Peter Abbelen, the vicar general of Milwaukee, formally petitioned Rome for equal rights for German-speaking parishes as well as a vicar general for Germans in dioceses with a large German population and a non-German prelate, Corrigan persuaded Gibbons to convene a meeting of the four East Coast archbishops (Baltimore, Boston, New York, and Philadelphia). The prelates protested to Propaganda that Abbelen was seriously misrepresenting the state of ethnic subgroups within the American church. As Corrigan wrote in a separate letter, if the Germans were entitled to a vicar general, then why not the Poles or the Italians or anyone else? "Let things remain equal—as they are now . . . make no laws in favor of one class only."[22]

Hard upon the heels of the news of Abbelen's memorial came rumors that the Vatican would appoint a German-American bishop, Joseph Dwenger of Fort Wayne, as nuncio. But the letters from the American hierarchy persuaded Propaganda to table the matter of a nuncio as well as any action on the German question. Abbelen returned home with nothing beyond approval for the one thing the Germans already had, independent national parishes.

When six years later Cahensly made his plea for more effective care of all immigrant groups, including national parishes, ethnic societies, and proportionate representation in the hierarchy, Corrigan advised him that his proposal was unrealistic. By this time, however, the growing ideological consciousness regarding the establishment of an American Catholic university made Corrigan and his allies much more appreciative of the conservatism of the German-Americans. Indeed, the German-American prelates had themselves become key allies.

Corrigan had been a member of the original committee of bishops that recommended that the Plenary Council approve the creation of a university. He had believed it would be established at Seton Hall, with the college being sold to the hierarchy for that purpose. Although he apparently went along with the choice of a Washington site when Seton Hall became unavailable, he soon cooled on the prospect and refused to cooperate in any fundraising. In the fall of 1886, two weeks after signing a petition to the Vatican for the establishment, he secretly sought to have the Vatican stop the project on the grounds that it had been hastily approved at the council, would be financially ruinous, and was educationally unrealistic given the state of the American church.

Cardinal Gibbons responded successfully to Corrigan's objections, and the pope approved the university in April 1887.[23] Six months later Corrigan resigned from the board and informed Gibbons that he could allow no fundraising for the institution in his diocese. Two years earlier Corrigan would probably have been better able to deal with the differences that developed over the university. By the end of 1887 the fortunes of the university were entangled with the issue that would dominate Corrigan's world for the next eight years and deeply affect his approach to other major concerns of that period.

The archbishop's decade-long dispute with one of his priests, Edward McGlynn, had the most serious repercussions. Not only did it preoccupy Corrigan, but it was a major catalyst of the conservative movement that he became increasingly identified with by the 1890s. McGlynn was the most prominent member of a dissident group of priests in the archdiocese who had been suspect for their liberal tendencies since the 1860s. In 1883 the priest had publicly espoused the single-tax theory of Henry George as the radical solution for the economic inequities of both Ireland and the United States. Given McGlynn's standing with the working class in New York, George welcomed him as "an army with banners."[24] A warning from Rome drew a promise from McGlynn to refrain from any further political activity.

Cardinal McCloskey took no further action even though McGlynn soon resumed his evangelization for the gospel according to George. When the latter ran for mayor of New York in 1886, McGlynn became a chief supporter and defied Corrigan's order that he immediately stop his campaigning. The archbishop's response was a modest one, a private suspension of McGlynn for two weeks. The archbishop, however, had no intention of letting the matter end there. Two weeks after George finished a strong second in the election, a result that many attributed in large part to McGlynn, the archbishop issued a pastoral letter in which he condemned "certain unsound principles and theories which assail the rights of property."[25] (George admitted the right of private property but denied that land could lose its basic communal character.) If Corrigan was misinterpreting George, his letter was still an extraordinary instance of a Catholic prelate taking a public position on a matter relating to the socioeconomic order. Conservatives in the United States as well as abroad hailed Corrigan for taking the lead in educating the Catholic public on social ethics.

McGlynn kept his silence about the pastoral itself but within the week criticized Catholic charities as band-aid remedies for social injustice and faulted "ministers of the gospel" who preached the virtue of poverty and pie-in-the-sky expectations to the poor.[26] On the basis of this report, Corrigan supended him a second time.

The previous summer the archbishop had appealed to Rome for instructions on how to deal with McGlynn. In subsequent letters Corrigan had accused him not only of disobedience and the teaching of economic principles that amounted to communism, but also of various heterodox opinions about papal authority, the sacraments, and ecclesiastical democracy. Many prelates shared Archbishop Elder's conviction that McGlynn had to be silenced because he was poisoning the people's "ideas of justice, of property, of deference for the church."[27] By December Archbishop Corrigan was pleading for Rome to take action. The pope himself (or someone using the pope's name) ordered the priest to Rome to explain himself. McGlynn pleaded poor health and other excuses for not going. A rebellion of McGlynn's parishioners when Corrigan removed him from Saint Stephen's only worsened the priest's position with ecclesiastical authorities. A second summons to Rome came in May, now with the threat of excommunication. McGlynn stayed in New York, claiming he could not in conscience go. When his excommunication was announced in July 1887, a storm of protest erupted in New York and elsewhere. The *New York Times* saw the case transcending questions of ecclesiastical discipline:

> It brings to the issue, premature perhaps, the Americanizing influence in the Catholic Church and the unbending authority of the hierarchy that has its head at Rome and derives its traditions from the dark ages.
>
> There is no question of Dr. McGlynn's faithful adherence to the doctrines of his church, so far as these pertain to matters of faith and of religious observance. He has shown no spirit of apostasy. . . . But EDWARD McGLYNN is an American, a believer in free institutions, in the rights of the people, and in the duty of the citizens of a republic to do their share to uphold and defend its integrity . . . Archbishop CORRIGAN represents the power of the church and the control of that power which has its source in the Bishop of Rome. . . . This power is antagonistic to free institutions and to the rights of citizens to think and act for themselves even in matters which have no vital connection with religious faith and worship.
>
> It is a question whether the Catholic Church in America is to be Americanized and brought into harmony with the spirit of our institutions or whether it is to Romanize those institutions.[28]

The archbishop and his chancery officials used pastoral letters, clerical loyalty oaths, the transfer of priests, and the penalty of a reserved sin for attending McGlynn's Anti-Poverty Society's meetings in order to break the opposition. The center of resistance was not workers but middle-class clerical and lay Catholics, including many women, who were drawn to McGlynn more to support clerical and lay rights within the church than to embrace particular theories of land reform. Indeed the archbishop came to regard the canonist Richard Burtsell as "the backbone of the rebellion" because of his defense of the canonical rights of both priests and laity. When in 1889 Burtsell buried a woman parishioner who had been a faithful attendant at the Anti-Poverty meetings, Corrigan transferred him upstate.

In order to discredit McGlynn, archdiocesan officials sent to Rome affidavits from several women claiming to have had sexual relations with the priest and charging him with heretical teaching concerning the sixth commandment. The Holy Office subsequently secretly condemned McGlynn for solicitation and "perverse doctrine in sexual matters."[29] That did nothing, of course, to reduce McGlynn's public influence. Prodded by friends in both America and Europe, Corrigan in the fall of 1887 formally petitioned Pope Leo XIII that the Congregation of the Index examine George's major work, *Progress and Poverty*. A year and a half later the Holy Office officially condemned the book but ordered the decision to be kept a secret "in light of the peculiar circumstances."[30] Rome had serious fears that a precipitous condemnation of George might provoke a schism among American Catholic workers, or at least charges of Vatican interference in the civil lives of American citizens.[31] Corrigan then pressed for an explicit declaration regarding the right of private property in order to combat the rising tide of socialism in the United States. When *Rerum Novarum* appeared in 1891, the archbishop and his supporters felt vindicated, since the encyclical condemned "certain obsolete opinions" that denied any individual ownership of land.

A priest who served under Corrigan once wrote that he "was often deceived in his estimate of men, in his estimate of events, in the far-reaching consequences of his own acts."[32] By 1890 events were forcing the archbishop and his friends to turn to Rome in a way that would have startled most of them a decade earlier.

One of the tactics McGlynn's followers had advocated as a means of showing their strength was a boycott of the Peter's Pence, the annual collection in each diocese for the support of the pope. Corrigan knew the significance of showing financial support for the Vatican. As bishop of Newark his Peter's Pence collections had consistently been larger than those of New York. In 1887 special efforts were successfully made to raise the largest amount ever sent from New York, but there was a slight decline in subsequent years from the previous average of nearly $20,000. Under Corrigan the New York Archdiocese had also become a major manager of the Vatican's funds. The archbishop clearly recognized the importance of such a role. When Propaganda made a decision to withdraw the funds in 1889 because of their low growth rate, Corrigan convinced them that their best interests lay in keeping them in New York.

Edward McGlynn initially had no supporters among the bishops. When certain prelates such as John Ireland of Saint Paul and John Moore of Saint Augustine reluctantly attempted to use their influence in Rome in McGlynn's behalf on the grounds that he had been denied due process, their position provided to Corrigan and his colleagues initial evidence of the liberal tendencies that came to be labeled

"Americanism" by the end of the century. To the archbishop of New York and his conservative colleagues, the Americanist movement of John Ireland and the liberal prelates was the natural outgrowth of the clerical radicalism that had first manifested itself in the sixties and that McGlynn had come to personify. By 1890 two distinct blocs were forming within the American hierarchy. The liberal bloc, led by Ireland, John Keane, Denis O'Connell, and to some extent, James Gibbons, had particular strength among the Paulists and Sulpicians, and was in control of two strategic institutions: the American College in Rome and the Catholic University of America. The conservative group, including the German-American prelates and the Jesuits, was larger, with its own valuable connections in Rome and its center in the ecclesiastical Province of New York.

Inevitably Archbishop Corrigan became the leader of the conservative bloc. As early as 1890 he was warning Rome of "the *ultra*-Americanism" of liberals, whom he accused of trying "to rule the destinies of the American Church" by putting their friends into key episcopates throughout the country.[33] Corrigan, McQuaid, and other conservatives were also disturbed that the archbishops had begun to meet annually and take upon themselves the determination of policy for the church in the United States. A few additional archiepiscopal appointments, the conservatives feared, would give control to the liberals. The liberals did attempt to put one of their own in the see of Milwaukee when it became open in 1890, but Rome appointed a German, Frederick Katzer. Other liberal efforts to gain two other sees within the "German Triangle," those of Green Bay and Cleveland, also failed as the appointments went to two German-Americans, Sebastian Messmer and Ignatius Horstmann, both close friends of Corrigan. He also managed to put his secretary, Charles McDonnell, into the see of Brooklyn, despite strong clerical opposition that had the support of Ireland.

Open conflict among the bishops developed over the issue of primary education. Since the abrasive fight between John Hughes and the New York Public School Society, American Catholics had been almost totally stymied in seeking public funds for their schools. James McMaster, the editor of the New York *Freeman's Journal*, had turned the issue of "godless" public schools into a crusade for parochial schools in the 1870s. With the aid of Ella Edes, the veteran American correspondent whose contacts in the Roman Curia made her an important agent for the conservatives, McMaster succeeded in securing the Roman directive in 1876 that became the basis for the legislation of the third Plenary Council. When Archbishop Ireland praised public education as one of the glories of America in an address before the National Education Association in 1890, he touched off a pamphlet war over rights and responsibility in education. At Corrigan's request, the Jesuit René Holaind published *The Parent First,* which contended that the responsibility for education rested with the parent, not the state.[34] To give control to the state was to promote socialism. But the controversy soon centered not on the theoretical issues but an experimental plan that Ireland had implemented in two towns in Minnesota. In a special arrangement between the local parishes and public school boards, the parishes supplied facilities and teachers, and the boards paid salaries and set the regulations. Ironically, Ireland had gotten the idea from a parish in Corrigan's own diocese, a fact the archbishop of Saint Paul was quick to point out. That the pastor of the parish was a close friend of McGlynn only made the experiment seem more mischievous to Archbishop Corrigan and others, who saw it as merely the first stage of secularization.

In response to American protests, a special Vatican commission examined Ireland's plan and found that it could be tolerated "taking into consideration all the circumstances."[35] What *"Tolerari potest"* meant became a new issue. Corrigan was relying on his Roman allies to maintain that it meant nothing more than a reluctant exception to the norm of parochial education. Privately they feared that it would seem to sanction public education as a cheap alternative. Ireland and Gibbons had both warned the pope that to condemn the plan would very possibly lead to a resurgence of anti-Catholicism in the United States. When Corrigan learned of these warnings, he and his fellow bishops of the province wrote Leo that such fears of a backlash against Catholics were without foundation. Leo denied that they had even raised the issue. But Corrigan, pushed by Roman friends who were alarmed at Ireland's rising influence there, would not let the matter die. Thanks to Salvatore Brandi, the Jesuit editor of *Civiltà Cattolica,* he now had copies of the letters in question, which he used to point out to Vatican officials the damning passages and to claim that if Ireland's plan became the norm, the parochial system of education would collapse.[36] An angry pope questioned the archbishop's loyalty to the Holy See. Corrigan's own vicar general, John Farley, thought he had come close to being deposed.[37]

American prelates had longed feared that internal disorder would provide a pretext for Rome to establish a permanent delegation in the United States and thus lessen substantially their independence. Archbishop Francisco Satolli's appointment in 1892 was welcomed by some liberal prelates, like Ireland, who were confident that Satolli would advance their program. Corrigan and his fellow conservatives quickly had their worst fears confirmed as Satolli began to endorse the educational views of Ireland and support clerical dissidents, including McGlynn, whom Satolli judged to have taught nothing contrary to church doctrine.

Corrigan was defiant. He wrote Cardinal Rampolla that Satolli was making the parochial school seem a "utopia of the bishops." Nonetheless, he asserted, "we will not give our Catholics up to the atheistic teacher, to the neutral school."[38] Archbishop Corrigan refused to receive McGlynn back and orchestrated a newspaper campaign against the delegate. With the delegate seemingly the captive of the liberal prelates, many conservatives readily supported Corrigan's bold stand, if not all his tactics. As one Catholic laymen told him, "You have been made, whether you wish it or no, the head and front of the Conservative Catholic party here . . . who are in a vast majority.[39]

Amid reports that the archbishop would be forced to resign because of his opposition to the delegate, Corrigan dispatched his Italian secretary, Gherardo Ferrante, to Rome to represent his position. Ferrante quickly began to win the sympathy of important Vatican officials, including Cardinal Mieceslaus Ledochowski, the prefect of Propaganda. The archbishop now also had some important allies in Rome among the Jesuits, especially Brandi. Corrigan was able to take advantage of the tensions between Propaganda and the Secretariate of State. The latter had been largely responsible for Satolli's appointment but the delegate as well as the American church still fell under the direction of Propaganda. Ireland and O'Connell had hoped to use the delegation as a means of increasing the independence of the American church from Propaganda. Corrigan's opposition to Satolli made him a natural ally of the Sacred Congregation. In supporting Corrigan, Propaganda could help check the larger strategy of the pope and Rampolla to pursue the papacy's *ralliement* policy to gain leverage against the Triple Alliance, especially Italy. Rampolla warned Satolli that Corrigan could cause much trouble for them.[40] In August of 1893 Leo advised Satolli that he make peace with the New York archbishop, and a ceremony of reconciliation followed at Saint Patrick's Cathedral between the two prelates. Thereafter Satolli began to take radically different positions on parochial education, dissident priests, and related matters. The pope declared in a letter to the American hierarchy that the mandate of the Third Plenary Council for a Catholic school in every parish still held.[41] In December 1894, two years after Satolli had restored McGlynn, Corrigan finally gave him a parish, in Newburgh, forty miles up the Hudson.

The McGlynn case had been significant in shaping the divisions that formed among the American hierarchy in the late 1880s and 1890s. By 1895 it was becoming clear that Rome was rejecting the liberal program. The condemnation of three American secret societies was one sign; the encyclical *Longinqua Oceani* another.[42] Within the year Dennis O'Connell and John Keane were removed rectors of the American College and the Catholic University respectively, the victims of growing conservative complaints. As Michael Corrigan explained Keane's removal to a layman, "The leading heresy of the day against the Catholic Church is Liberalism. . . . The Holy See is bound to put down liberalism in teaching. This error had crept into the University through Bishop Keane."[43] The appointment in 1896 of the ultraconservative Sebastiano Martinelli to succeed Satolli was another indication of the changing tide.

When "Americanism" became an international issue in 1897 with the publication of Abbé Felix Klein's translation of Walter Elliott's *Life of Father Hecker*, Corrigan kept his silence. He could afford to. In three Rome-based religious orders, (Jesuits, Dominicans, and Redemptorists) and several key cardinals, including Satolli, he now had more powerful allies at the Vatican than he had ever had. Months before the issuance of *Testem Benevolentiae*, as the Americanists were working feverishly to influence the Roman reaction, Corrigan knew that the expected encyclical would reflect the prevailing hostility there toward Americanism.[44]

As Ireland, Gibbons, and other American prelates denied that American Catholics were guilty of any such heresy as the pope described as "religious Americanism," Corrigan assured the pope that his suspicions of an attempt to form a church in America, "different from that which is in the rest of the world," were well founded. In the name of the New York Province he thanked Leo formally for confronting this creeping "Americanism" through his "infallible teaching."[45]

That the archbishop extended papal infallibility to encyclicals was a clear indication of how ultramontane this conservative leader had become by 1900. In turning so completely to Rome to save the church in the United States from the democratic vision of the Americanists, the conservatives had abandoned the American Catholic tradition that valued a balance between papal loyalty and collegial independence. Given the centralizing policies of Pius IX and Leo XIII, such an outcome may have been inevitable, but both liberals and conservatives ultimately played into Rome's hands. The irony is that neither Michael Corrigan nor John Ireland received the red hat for their efforts.

At his death in 1902 Corrigan left an archdiocese much better prepared to meet the needs of the largest Catholic population in the country. His concern for immigrants, for a learned clergy, for scholarship, and for religious education, had built a lasting legacy in churches, religious communities, a seminary, and in the United States Catholic Historical Society. The underside was the repression of dissidents, loyalty oaths, and pressure tactics that left their own legacy in the memories of New Yorkers. At the national level he had played a key role in both the building and undermining of episcopal collegiality. For two decades after *Testem* the American bishops did virtually nothing as a body. That the Catholic University of America failed to become an intellectual center worthy of its name must also in part be laid at Corrigan's feet. But the most important consequence of his leadership was a Romanization that eventually controlled the hierarchical as well as intellectual life of the American church.

PART THREE

Romanization and Modernization, 1910–1960

For the Catholic church in America the twentieth century was an age of consolidation, shaped by the aftermath of the condemnations of Americanism in 1899 and modernism in 1907. Intellectually, the American church went into a dogmatic slumber. But the bishops of the era were builders and organizers. Immigration continued, especially from eastern and southern Europe, but it was slowed down by the restrictive immigration acts of the 1920s. There was still tension between Catholicism and American society, especially under the presidency of Woodrow Wilson. From the beginning of the century, the Holy See began appointing a new breed of bishops to the key American sees. They depended not upon their nomination by priests of a diocese or members of the hierarchy but upon their friendship with Roman officials. During World War I, the Holy See formalized this procedure by changing the process of nominating bishops and placing more authority in the hands of the apostolic delegate. The result of this was further to diminish the older American tradition of collegiality, despite the establishment in 1919 of the National Catholic Welfare Council (whose name was altered to National Catholic Welfare Conference after 1922).

Bishops tended to concentrate their efforts on their own dioceses.

They expanded their concern for Catholic education to include high schools. Still, they were defenders of the faith in a society that was frequently hostile but to which they pledged their patriotic loyalty. Their princely style gave vicarious identity to a people still struggling to prove they were American. None symbolized this grandeur more than Cardinal William O'Connell of Boston and Cardinal George Mundelein of Chicago. The Boston Irish Catholics reveled in the exploits of their cardinal in tweaking the beard of the Brahman lion. As a "prince of the blood," a title granted to cardinals, and a holder of the Order of the Rising Sun, he alone in Boston was really qualified to greet a Japanese prince, though the commoners had tried to exclude him. The Jesuits at Boston College reveled in his praising their education as so similar to that of Rome, knowing that across the river was another institution, Harvard, that had to be inferior to such an ancient tradition as that represented in the Eternal City.

In an exercise of princely one-upmanship Mundelein was not be outdone. Freshly back from receiving his red hat in Rome, he arranged to have Chicago host the first International Eucharistic Congress held in the United States in June 1926. It was a grand affair. The Pullman Company built special cars, all painted cardinal red. European cardinals were to assemble in New York at the residence of Cardinal Patrick J. Hayes. The train, nicknamed the "Red Special," conveyed ten cardinals, two apostolic delegates, four archbishops, seven bishops, and three policemen across a special right-of-way to a specially built station in Chicago. Not on board was Cardinal Dennis Dougherty of Philadelphia, who informed Mundelein that the Pennsylvania Railroad was providing him with a special car. Cardinal O'Connell arrived by private boat with 500 Boston pilgrims aboard. Part of the congress was held at Mundelein's new seminary, Saint Mary of the Lake, well outside the city. Its Georgian buildings, clustered around an artificial lake, made a statement about the identification of the church with the national culture that would have been the envy of any Ivy League university.

Mundelein was trying to make a statement—a statement about the prominence of the church in the Midwest and about the power of the church in the United States. Such display, he hoped, would counter hostile groups such as the second Ku Klux Klan, which was on the rise and which had made the Catholic church one of its prime targets. In August 1925, it had held a massive parade in Washington, D.C. The Eucharistic Congress was intended as a militaristic display of Catholic might. But Mundelein's plan may have backfired and contributed to the defeat of Alfred E. Smith in the presidential election of 1928.

Not all bishops and not all cardinals were taken with the grandiose style, In New York Hayes, Mundelein's schoolmate at Manhattan College, kept quietly to himself in his see and earned the epithet "Cardinal of Charity." But his administration was not as efficient as that of Mundelein. New York awaited an aggressive leader and got it in Francis Spellman.

But the bishops were far from being all style and little substance. While Catholic intellectual life wallowed in its cultural isolation from the nation, one aspect of Catholic thought remained progressive. Progressive social thought was one of the hallmarks of the American church. In 1919, the bishops had issued the "Program for Social Reconstruction" after World War I. Written by Father John A. Ryan of the NCWC's Social Action Department, it reflected the Progressive Era in involving government in economic, labor, and industrial reforms, but it also provided a basis for a Catholic alliance with many of Franklin D. Roosevelt's New Deal proposals. While Cardinal O'Connell dubbed Ryan, after he became a monsignor, "a Bolshevik in a red cassock," for the most part, the bishops respected, even if they did not like, Ryan and his successor (after a brief interlude filled by Raymond McGowan) George Higgins. They kept the loyalty of the working class, which had been lost to most of the European churches—a point that would be of great significance at Vatican II.

While the bishops in the East and Midwest were bringing more centralized administration to their dioceses, the west was rapidly developing. In 1922, the diocese of Monterey–Los Angeles was divided into the dioceses of Los Angeles–San Diego and Monterey-Fresno. John J. Cantwell, the fifth choice for Monterey–Los Angeles, retained the southern California diocese. In 1936, Los Angeles was elevated to a metropolitan see, and California became the only state with two archdioceses. The sleepy little town of Los Angeles was rapidly overshadowing its northern rival of San Francisco. It was being transformed first by the railroad, then by the automobile, and finally by the airplane into one of the world's leading cities. But its real growth occurred after World War II.

The war again provided the opportunity for the church, composed of so many immigrant groups, to prove its loyalty to the nation. None so identified Catholic identity and American patriotism as Francis J. Spellman, archbishop of New York. The war's end brought forth old and new experiences. On the one hand, there was a renewal of anti-Catholic activity, similar to what had followed World War I. On the other, Catholics flocked to college in unprecedented numbers on the G.I. Bill of Rights. The bishops were still called to be defenders of the faith, but they were beginning to lead a flock in the 1950s that was well educated. Few realized the theological ferment seething beneath the surface of the apparently tranquil postwar years.

In Europe, the "New Theology" was creating intellectual contro-versy. In the United States, John Courtney Murray, S.J., had awakened the problem of religious liberty, which had lain dormant since the condemnation of Americanism. By 1950, he was gaining a number of episcopal supporters, notably Cardinal Edward Mooney of Detroit, Cardinal Samuel Stritch of Chicago, and Archbishop John T. Mc-Nicholas of Cincinnati. By 1954, however, the theological opposition to him was so great that he ceased to write on religious liberty or the separation of church and state. His vindication and that of the Amer-ican tradition would have to wait for Vatican II.

When Pope John XXIII convoked the Second Vatican Council, few American bishops were prepared. Like most Americans, they tended to judge the immediate past as normative of all the past. But they rose to the occasion. Religious liberty was to be their major contri-bution. Cardinal Spellman was to brook the opposition of Cardinal Alfredo Ottaviani and Archbishop Egidio Vagnozzi to have Murray appointed a *peritus* (expert or official theologian) at the council. The Americans were to insist that the council consider religious liberty, though the final version of the conciliar declaration reflected other European influences that richly focused the discussion on the theology of the person. The issue also mobilized them as a group and served as the occasion for them to rediscover episcopal collegiality, so new to them at Vatican II and so characteristic of their predecessors of a century before.

In the postconciliar years, the bishops not only implemented the decrees, sometimes gradually and even hesitantly, but they also began to address issues ignored by their predecessors, like war and civil rights. The public reaction to their pastoral on nuclear arms in 1983 was an indication of the moral leadership they had in a pluralistic nation. The hierarchy, moreover, was still increasing in numbers. In 1961, the Province of Baltimore still stretched to the south all the way to Saint Augustine, the only diocese in Florida. In 1962, the Prov-ince of Atlanta was erected, followed in 1968 by the Province of Miami. Large-scale movement to the Sunbelt and the immigration of refugees from Cuba and Central America were changing the face of the Old South.

CHAPTER
10
The Name That Stood for Rome: William O'Connell and the Modern Episcopal Style

James M. O'Toole

*O*n a bright, early spring afternoon in April 1906, a tall, large-proportioned man strode to the middle of the sanctuary, just behind the altar rail of the Cathedral of the Holy Cross in Boston. Looking out at his audience he saw before him five hundred priests of the Boston archdiocese, the third largest see in Catholic America, there to witness his installation as coadjutor to the city's archbishop. Formerly the bishop of the smaller diocese of Portland, Maine, this man had now returned to his native city in order to assume the position of a generalized helper to Boston's aging leader, Archbishop John Williams, and that of the man who would succeed automatically to the archiepiscopal throne on the older prelate's death. Physically, the two men were hardly a match for one another. Williams, who sat off to one side as the powerfully built younger man took command of the crowd, was thin and spare, troubled by failing eyesight and increasingly feeble on this, the eve of his eighty-fifth year. The younger man was fleshy and substantial, holding himself rigidly erect like a

171

soldier and staring at his listeners with eyes that seemed as though they could penetrate steel. Seldom had the imagery of the passing of one generation and the rise of another been so starkly set forth as it was that afternoon.

Though the ceremony was a religious one, in which all present were enjoined to turn their minds to the things above, an electric tension filled the air. Virtually every priest in the cathedral had long seconded Archbishop Williams's wish that Rome would designate an assistant and successor, but the same nearly unanimous number had hoped to see another face before them that day. This desire had been frustrated two months before, when the Vatican had announced its selection, but the open secret lingered that not everyone was happy with the choice. The speaker wasted no time in coming to this very point in an effort to win over the hostile audience. "Ecclesiastical power and authority," he instructed them, "are derived not from the votes of the clergy or from the suffrages of Bishops, but solely from the Apostolic See." He said that, regardless of the personal preferences of anyone there present or elsewhere, "Rome has made her irrevocable decision," which alone was sufficient warrant: "I believe as strongly as I believe that there is a God that that God has placed me where I am." The matter was closed and settled, and anyone who continued to dispute it risked a terrible sanction. "He who from this day breaks the sacredness of order and harmony in this Diocese will have small claim to the respect of any of us who rule it or labor in it." Lest his hearers misunderstand even these blunt words, the speaker with the full baritone voice and the measured oratorical cadences spelled out the conclusion in so many words: "The past is dead, . . . the future is at the door."[1]

The stern man with the hard message that Tuesday afternoon was William Henry O'Connell. Not yet forty-seven years old, he stood at the midpoint of a long career in American Catholicism, a career that saw him progress from distinctly humble origins to a position of national and international renown. By speaking so directly of the authority of the revivified if still struggling papacy, he sounded the theme that had been and would continue to be his hallmark: reliance on Rome as the living center of the Catholic church, to which every Catholic had to turn with docility and love and without which the church itself had little meaning. By pointing so clearly the way to the future, he also signaled his enduring significance in the long story of American episcopal leadership, namely, as a key figure in the modernization of this ancient church, a process that demanded a new approach and style, one that would make the church a steady and steadying presence in the world of the twentieth century.

Who was William O'Connell, and how had he come to that dramatic moment in Boston's cathedral? A clerical career had perhaps been predestined for him from the outset, for he was born on the Feast of the Immaculate Conception, December 8, in 1859 in the mill city of Lowell, Massachusetts. But for that religious coincidence, however, there was little else that marked him out as different from the other babies born that year to the immigrants who had sought refuge in America from the ravages of the Irish Famine. The youngest of eleven children—half of whom had been born in Ireland, half in America—O'Connell was part of a wholly typical family that had made up part of the first great flood of new immigration since the settlement of the New World. His father, who died when he was only five, and all his brothers worked in the mills or at other trades, though as the youngest, little Will had some advantages. His schooling was extended, and he was the only member of his immediate family to graduate from high school, the only one for whom a college education was even a remote possibility.[2]

The religious coincidence of his birth may or may not have influenced his choice of life's direction, but at the least it combined with the high value and prestige that Irish-American families accorded the priesthood to lead him to the discernment of a religious vocation. An altar boy as a youth, O'Connell later recalled that by the age of fifteen he began to reflect on "the sublimity of this service of God" and to feel "by a gentle attraction, which seemed like nothing else but a mother's love," a call to the priesthood.[3] Acting on this call, he enrolled in Saint Charles's Seminary in Maryland, where his first taste of religious life was hardly a pleasant one. He lasted for two years of study, but then at least temporarily changed his plans. He himself maintained that uncertain health forced his withdrawal from the seminary and his return to Massachusetts, and that may well have been at least partially responsible. Whatever his physical condition, he was certainly a prime candidate for simple homesickness. Complicating those ambiguous feelings was also a form of culture shock that he felt at being plunged into what he took for an aggressively French atmosphere maintained by the Sulpician priests who staffed the seminary. Once back at home, however, he continued his education, and he graduated with an above-average record from the Jesuits' Boston College, the instrument hundreds of local immigrant sons like himself were using to advance their families and their fortunes.

More mature now, he returned to his pursuit of the priesthood, securing a place at the American College in Rome. Coincidentally founded on the very day of his own birth in 1859, the college had been established for the purpose of developing an American Catholic clergy that would drink deeply of the Roman spirit, *Romanità*. William O'Connell was an apt pupil, and he readily adopted that view as his own. "The Roman mind is the Church's mind and the mind of Christ," he would later say, reflecting on his first exposure to the city that styled itself "eternal" and that considered itself the capital of the world, both secular and religious. "The Roman mind is neither Italian, nor French, nor German, nor American. It is catholic, . . . it truly represents the world. . . . That, undoubtedly, is the unique gift of Christ to the See of Peter."[4]

Earlier American priests and bishops had had a clearer sense of the distinctive nature of the American church, and they were generally unafraid of emphasizing that distinctiveness. Without challenging their loyalty to the church, they had a greater sense of the limitations on Roman authority. John Carroll, for example, denied neither the primacy of the pope nor the pontiff's real and symbolic significance as the embodiment of universality and unity in the church. He nevertheless looked with a jaundiced eye on the more exaggerated "claims which Rome has always kept up, tho universally disregarded."[5] Boston's own first bishop, John Cheverus, had expressed similar views, writing a letter to a local newspaper in 1800 specifically rejecting as so much Protestant slander the charge that Catholics considered the pope infallible. "To believe the Pope infallible is no part of our Creed," Cheverus wrote; "no Roman-Catholick ever pretended that he is."[6] From the very beginning, William O'Connell and other members of his clerical and episcopal generation expressed a radically different view from this, one in which loyalty and obedience to the Vatican and to its growing administrative bureaucracy in all things was of paramount importance. The young seminarian from Boston was smitten from the very first by "the great universal atmosphere of Rome," and he developed what he himself later identified as an "innate Roman and Catholic sense."[7] These attitudes, formed and fixed early, were to become the repeatedly sounded themes of O'Connell's entire career.

Following his ordination in the summer of 1884, O'Connell returned to America for the routine life of a priest. He served successively in two parishes—one in a quiet country town, the other in the midst of Boston's teeming, ethnically diverse West End—before taking the first giant step of his career, securing appointment as rector of his alma mater, the American College. A measure of personal ambition may well have played a role in this, vaulting him, one of thousands of ordinary priests in the United States, into this prominent position. Rumors circulated at the time and persisted later that, on hearing that the selection process for the rectorship was deadlocked, Father O'Connell took a quick train to Baltimore to lobby Cardinal James Gibbons and the other American archbishops who had the power to make the appointment.[8] Regardless of the circumstances of his selection, the post brought him back to his beloved Rome for the five years from 1896 to 1901, during which time he befriended powerful church officials, demonstrated his ultramontane loyalty, charmed the growing American circle in the Eternal City (Protestant and Catholic alike), and prepared himself for even greater advancement in the century that was just beginning.

That promotion came with his designation as bishop of Portland early in 1901, a post that he embraced as affording him the opportunity to establish a "tighter and stronger link of union and attachment to the Holy See" on the part of American Catholics.[9] Equally important was the opportunity the post gave him to acquire administrative experience in managing the affairs of a small, though geographically dispersed, diocese, making eventual advancement to a larger see the more likely. Though he himself later admitted that overseeing diocesan affairs in Maine was "never excessively absorbing," he set about his task with an energy that would later seem characteristic.[10] He established the practice of closely monitoring the affairs of his parishes and of church-related schools and charitable institutions, keeping an especially tight control over the expenditure of money. Possessed of no particularly sophisticated financial or administrative ability, he concentrated his concern on the avoidance of debt and on a cautious pay-as-you-go approach to church development. "We shall have to see by the amount you can raise that a clergyman can be supported in a fitting manner," the bishop told a group of laymen petitioning for a new parish in a coastal town. "While I am happy to organize distinct parishes, I must in duty see to it that such parishes will be self-supporting."[11] Those laymen did not get their parish until well into the tenure of O'Connell's successor, a sign of the hesitancy and conservatism that marked the young bishop's brief tenure in Maine. While the state's Catholic population grew by nearly 15 percent in O'Connell's few years there, he created only three new parishes, preferring instead to expand the number of mission stations attached to already-existing churches.[12]

If O'Connell was cautious in managing the temporal affairs of his diocese, however, he was more anxious to develop an active, outgoing public image and style for himself as bishop. Catholics were a distinct minority in Maine, but O'Connell quickly established himself as a highly visible public figure. Later claiming that he had set as one of his goals the desire "to lead our good people forward in the estimation of the people who often are prone to misunderstand us," the bishop embarked on a sustained effort of openly demonstrating the Catholic presence in the Yankee stronghold.[13] He led a religious procession through the streets of Portland, a first in the city's history, and he redecorated his cathedral in a grand manner. What is more, playing

on his time in Rome to establish himself as a cosmopolitan, he befriended the Yankee Protestant political, economic, and social leaders
of Maine, joining the exclusive Cumberland Club and taking up "that
most excellent game" of golf by enrolling in a previously all-Yankee
country club.[14] Not forgoing an elaborate personal style that included
a Roman-like retinue of a valet, a housekeeper, a driver, and an Italian
singing-master for his cathedral choir, O'Connell quickly achieved
the kind of status he hoped for. "His personal popularity here promises
to overflow all church barriers and take in all his fellow citizens,"
one local newspaper said of him, while another congratulated him
on having "won the respect and esteem of the community."[15] By de-
liberately creating an unabashed public persona, one in which the
members of his flock could vicariously participate, he was making a
clear statement about the improved circumstances of Catholics in
America. At the same time, he was advancing the development of a
modern style of episcopal leadership, one in which Catholic bishops
were public men in the community at large as much as they were
spiritual shepherds of their own people.

This aggressive, relentlessly public stature made O'Connell a leading candidate to succeed Archbishop Williams in the more important
venue that was the archdiocese of Boston. For many years, observers
both in the church and outside it had known that a successor to Williams, who had governed the metropolitan see since 1866, would need
to be chosen and that the name of the selection would possess a significance that was not merely local. The appointment would come at
a critical time for the American church and would be understood as
a bellwether for the future. Pope Leo XIII had denounced Americanism
only a few years before, rejecting views such as those that had been
expressed by bishops like Carroll and Cheverus and taking to task
those who sought a peculiar identity for the church in the United
States. This condemnation notwithstanding, liberal and conservative
members of the hierarchy still struggled with one another for control
of the future direction of American Catholicism. Though the principals
in this struggle came largely from other cities—Archbishop Michael
Corrigan of New York led the conservative, Roman faction; Archbishop John Ireland of Saint Paul led the liberal, American group—
Boston quickly became their battleground. If Ireland and his supporters were successful in securing the appointment for their favorite,
who was Bishop Matthew Harkins of Providence, a more open, American course might be charted. If Corrigan and his allies triumphed,
Catholicism in America would be tied ever more closely to the Roman
model, outlook, and program. William O'Connell assumed an active
role in this struggle, not only by aligning himself with Corrigan but

by emerging, in part through vigorous self-promotion, as the conservative champion.

The selection process dragged on for several years, with active campaigning on both sides. Harkins's backers emphasized their strength, namely, the overwhelming support of the priests of the Boston diocese and the other bishops of New England. O'Connell and his friends relied more heavily on their behind-the-scenes influence at the Vatican, an influence that only increased with the election of Pope Pius X in 1903. The Portland bishop was not reluctant to engage in political infighting or to encourge his friends to do the same; nor was he demure in emphasizing the larger ecclesiastical issues that were at stake. Claiming that he was the victim of an Americanist plot to keep out of consideration "any name which stood for Rome, for Roman views and for Roman sympathies," he told the papal secretary of state dramatically that "Boston is at this moment in the balance between Rome and her enemies" within the church.[16] Such blunt language was not lost on the Vatican, which ended the period of speculation and maneuvering in January 1906 by announcing its selection of O'Connell, a man whom one priest approvingly called "preeminently the best exponent of the Holy See in these parts."[17] The door slammed shut on the Americanists. It was this selection and the lingering dissatisfaction it caused among the Boston clergy that brought O'Connell and his priests to their tense confrontation in Holy Cross Cathedral on that April day.

Thus, O'Connell owed his promotion to the rank of leader of this major Catholic center to his unflinching policy of *Romanitá*. By embracing his role as the name that "stood for Rome," he attained a power and influence at home and abroad that had never been approached by his predecessors. By constantly repeating the theme of Roman supremacy, he accustomed American Catholics to thinking in similar terms and to accepting papal triumphalism as one of their most characteristic beliefs. Becoming archbishop of Boston in his own right on Williams's death in August 1907, he began to play out on a larger stage the same public role he had experimented with in Maine, and he achieved correspondingly larger success. The newspapers embraced him as continually "good ink," and the timing of his return to Boston seemed propitious, coinciding as it did with the election of John F. Fitzgerald, the first of the great Boston Irish ward heelers, as mayor of the commonwealth's capital city. A new age seemed to be dawning, one in which the once-despised Catholics began to solidify their hold on the former Yankee bastion, a new age graphically presented in the advent of new leaders.[18] O'Connell recognized this seismic shift, and he expressed it when he presided over the celebration of the centennial of the founding of the Boston diocese in 1908, declaring flatly that "the Puritan has passed; the Catholic remains. . . . The child of the immigrant is called to fill the place which the Puritan has left."[19] No one represented Catholic arrival and intention to remain better than O'Connell himself, and his upward course seemed as if it would go on indefinitely. In 1911, he was given the red hat of a cardinal, a further sign of official approval.

For all his rapid success and power, however, O'Connell was to fall victim to a series of events that brought his practical influence within the church to an early end. His triumph was real, but his authority was short-lived. The first shock hit him with the death of Pius X in 1914. Racing to Rome for the conclave to choose a successor—where he would surely have voted for the Spaniard Cardinal Raphael Merry del Val, Pius's willing second in the vigorous repression of modernism and O'Connell's chief patron at the Vatican—O'Connell arrived too late to participate. The election of Benedict XV ushered in a new regime, one in which control of the church passed to other figures who were wary of the Boston cardinal. So firmly had O'Connell defined himself as a member of one particular faction in Vatican politics that, when that faction fell from power, he found his own importance measurably reduced both in Rome and in America. Owing to his rank, his advice was still routinely sought in such matters as the appointment of new bishops, but it was seldom taken. In time, he lost even the power to choose his own auxiliaries, an ironic note for a man who had so successfully managed his own rise.[20]

O'Connell continued to make an effort at influencing church affairs, but he found little support on either side of the Atlantic. Bishop Louis Walsh, his successor in Portland who was to become an archnemesis, wrote New York's Archbishop Patrick Hayes in 1919, decrying the Bostonian's various "machinations" but adding, "I . . . never had any fear, for he is well known in Rome."[21] Worse, O'Connell's credibility was further damaged by an extended financial and personal scandal in his official household. Though the details of this affair, which involved the cardinal's nephew, never became widely known to the general public, the lingering troubles led to O'Connell's near-total ostracism from his fellow bishops. Cincinnati's Archbishop John McNicholas minced no words on the subject, telling the apostolic delegate: "Many of us older bishops who know him do not believe him; we do not trust him; we consider him a most dangerous Prelate."[22] As advancing age gave him unchallenged seniority, O'Connell would claim the title of "dean of the hierarchy," even though he was enduringly hostile to the National Catholic Welfare Conference, fearing that it infringed on the powers of individual bishops. Not even his ostentatious presiding over the annual meetings of the American bishops in the 1920s and 1930s, however, could hide the fact that he was almost wholly bereft of friends and supporters in the church.

Foreclosed from playing the role of chief figure and power broker for the American church as a whole, O'Connell directed his energies closer to home and concentrated on Boston. This concentration he applied both to the internal affairs of his archdiocese and to the emerging role of Catholics in the larger society. To the management of the parishes and institutions of Catholic Boston O'Connell turned his typical energy and the techniques of close supervision with which he had experimented in Maine. He saw himself as a reformer, imposing "the maximum of unity and efficiency" on an entity that resembled a large modern corporation as much as a church organization.[23] Carefully constructing for himself the image of a manager-shepherd, an image also adopted by such other American prelates as Chicago's George Mundelein and, later, New York's Francis Spellman, O'Connell seemed to exercise a tight control over all aspects of church life. No pastor could spend more than a hundred dollars for any purpose without first obtaining the cardinal's permission, for example, and the activities of all priests and nuns were closely scrutinized. O'Connell created an efficient chancery office machinery that was openly intended "to take complete cognizance" of all archdiocesan affairs.[24] The members of the rising Catholic middle class, who were moving beyond their immigrant status and into the professions, were assuming positions in the world of affairs, and it seemed appropriate that their leader too be a man of this world in advancing the things of the next one.

The simplicity of this picture of a disorganized church on the brink of collapse saved through the intervention of a hardheaded cardinal archbishop masked a more complex reality. The archdiocese of Boston was neither so badly off before O'Connell instituted these strict measures nor so completely changed by them. Though the cardinal later recollected that, on his arrival, many archdiocesan institutions were in "an almost incredible state of disorganization," with bankruptcy knocking on every door because of years "without any sort of supervision or inspection," in fact most parishes and charitable agencies were at his arrival already stable and successful.[25]

Like most nineteenth-century prelates, Archbishop Williams had employed a more decentralized model for presiding over his archdiocese. The rapid growth of the Catholic population and the equally speedy expansion of church institutions and services to meet that population's needs had made rigid central control cumbersome and inefficient. As a result, in Boston and elsewhere a great deal of local autonomy was permitted. Without denying the authority of the archbishop, pastors freely followed their own policies and determined their own priorities based on the demand of local exigencies. Occasionally, there could be differing views, but such differences were tolerated in a system that allowed for subsidiarity, leaving local decisions in local hands. In Cambridge in the 1880s, for example, two pastors came to very different conclusions on the question of parochial schools, and they argued about it openly in speeches and in print. One of them, Father Thomas Scully of Saint Mary's parish, vigorously promoted the development of separate Catholic schools. Another, Father John O'Brien of Sacred Heart, opposed the idea with equal vigor, proudly proclaiming that he would never build a school in his parish (though he eventually did) and even serving a term on the Cambridge school committee.[26] Archbishop Williams found no threat to his own position in such local differences, and he left his priests largely alone to make these decisions themselves.

From the first O'Connell sought to check such autonomy. Extrapolating on the local level his Roman view of the church, in which all power was concentrated at the top and only sparingly parceled out to those below, he demanded an apparently firm structure that made his will and activity the measure of all churchly things. In fact, his success at enforcing this vision was more limited. Though he talked the language of a centralized, absolute monarchy, the reality he lived with was basically feudal. Power remained decentralized, and Catholics—whether priests, nuns, or even the laity—who were disposed to resist the cardinal's centralizing advances and were willing to be brave in the face of his admittedly intimidating personality could generally get their own way. O'Connell's rigorous administrative procedures looked more harsh, inflexible, and transforming than they actually were.

Examples of Catholics who found the means to prevail in disputes with their leader, even in the face of the cardinal's active suspicion or opposition, abound. In the late 1920s, a pastor in the solidly Catholic neighborhood of Dorchester submitted plans for a new rectory, which O'Connell rejected out of hand as being too elaborate, suggesting instead a more modest structure. Biding his time for about a year, the pastor submitted a second set of plans which called for a house that was precisely one foot smaller in each of its dimensions and that cost approximately the same as the original, and this time his proposal was readily approved.[27] The Sisters of Saint Joseph, the principal teaching order of the archdiocese, successfully headed off the cardinal's plan to have them open a retreat house in 1921, a work sufficiently far removed from their traditional duties to arouse their considerable opposition. In 1934 they blocked O'Connell's attempt to interfere in their election of a new superior.[28] A Catholic laywoman, the journalist Frances Sweeney, even survived a personal interview with the "arctic" O'Connell and continued to hector him in print for his (to her mind) insufficient efforts to promote interethnic and interreligious understanding.[29] O'Connell was sometimes able to get his own way in things both little and great through sheer intimidation of submissive subordinates. He appropriated one pastor's pet parrot, to which he had taken a fancy during a parish visit, and he drove home from another priest's funeral in the departed's shiny new automobile; he also successfully acquired a substantial sum, previously earmarked for a school that would never be built, from a parish treasury.[30] Like a European monarch on progress through his kingdom, O'Connell possessed almost unlimited theoretical authority, but like that monarch he frequently had to accommodate himself to local centers of authority that would not yield to his attempts to bend all archdiocesan institutions to his will.

The gulf between the rhetoric and the reality of O'Connell's efforts to remake Catholic Boston in his own image and likeness calls into question any facile conclusion that he, or indeed his entire generation in the episcopacy, was able to consolidate his power so readily as historians have sometimes supposed. In fact, the old dynamics of church life proved remarkably resilient. O'Connell was unable, for example, to enforce centralized banking or systematic control of parish finances on any of his pastors, a significant omission from any allegedly complete administrative system. He was also unable to restrict the tenure of pastors in their autonomous parish benefices, a triumph for central authority that Boston's archbishops would not achieve until the reign of O'Connell's more approachable latter-day successor, Cardinal Humberto Medeiros, in 1972.[31] Decades of talking the language of an all-powerful center with docile and compliant fringes may have paved the way for the center's eventual success, but the change came slowly, and O'Connell did not live to see it. Like life itself, the historical reality of O'Connell's episcopal leadership and program was not always as neat or straightforward as he may have wanted it to be. Rather than constituting the "dawning of a new era," therefore, his time at the head of Boston Catholicism was more of a transition period, combining aspects of a modern, streamlined organization with the older, feudal world of the church in which authority was always acknowledged but not always deferred to.[32]

If the cardinal was not as successful as he had hoped to be in controlling church affairs at home or abroad, however, he did achieve significant results in remaking the public image of, and in changing the nature of public expectation for, Catholic bishops in the United States. By constantly presenting himself as the leader and spokesman for his emergent flock and by maintaining contact with other public figures, he set a standard of behavior that was emulated by bishops of his own time and since.

From his earliest days in Boston, he had never been shy about consorting with the powerful: kings, presidents, governors, mayors, and leaders of finance, industry, and the arts. Such contacts were surely heady stuff for the boy from Lowell, but they were more than just personal megalomania or social climbing, since they also performed a valuable service for the Catholic community as a whole, providing a reinforcement of their own achievements. "A broad interpretation of his function as a Catholic prelate," said the Boston writer Henry Robinson of the thinly veiled character in his novel *The Cardinal*, enabled O'Connell "to accept the friendship of men who ruled society, created its opinions, and took its praise or blame with Jovian unconcern. His ear was sought, his favor solicited, his judgment valued in matters extending far beyond the administration of his Diocese."[33] For Boston's Catholics, O'Connell's triumphs were their triumphs, his successes theirs. When he visited the White House or received medals of honor from European monarchs or stole the show at the levees arranged by Isabella Stewart Gardner, the doyenne of Boston society, at her Renaissance palace on Boston's Fenway, O'Connell represented thousands of Catholics who would never experience those thrills themselves but who were advancing far enough to covet them secretly.[34] Full social acceptance was still years away, but O'Connell's public behavior seemed to hasten it, and he was accordingly supported and even cheered in the kitchens and parlors of South Boston and Roxbury. He himself knew of the important symbolic role he could play in Catholic self-assertion, and he was always ready to highlight it. When elevated to the cardinalate in 1911, at a conclave in which the archbishops of New York, Paris, London, and Vienna were similarly honored, he had observed pointedly that "even in the smallest hamlet of the farthest East today Boston [and Catholic Boston in particular] is known as never before, honored as never before."[35]

Such visibility and position, both real and metaphoric, gave O'Connell a power that his predecessors had never possessed, a power he exercised regularly and easily. As the natural spokesman for what was assumed to be a monolithic and unchanging "Catholic position," he gave voice to opinions on a range of social and political issues. In politics he was a potent force, competing for influence with John F. Fitzgerald (who had risen quickly but peaked early) and the rascally James M. Curley. Under the golden dome of the Massachusetts State House, O'Connell was referred to simply as "Number One," and a word from him was generally sufficient to settle any question. When a Curley-backed measure for a state lottery seemed destined for easy passage in 1935, an O'Connell remark in the morning papers caused half the legislature to change its mind, sending the bill down to lop-sided defeat by sunset. His active involvement against referenda changing the child labor laws in 1924 and the birth control laws in 1942 proved decisive among the electorate as a whole. Even when he was misquoted he was powerful: an anti-Curley newspaper cleverly printed one of the cardinal's speeches out of context on the morning of election day 1937, making it appear that O'Connell had actively endorsed another candidate. Curley and others held this maneuver largely responsible for the flamboyant mayor's defeat.[36]

Nor did social and cultural matters escape the cardinal's notice, and O'Connell delivered himself of a host of opinions that were widely reported and accorded significant weight. His denunciation of Pro-hibition in 1926—like most Catholic prelates he favored (if he did not always practice) voluntary abstinence rather than compulsory pro-hibition—attracted national attention, as did his 1932 condemnation of modern music, especially the "crooners," whom he adjudged to be purveyors of "immoral slush."[37] He warned against the questionable morality of the motion picture industry, and he denounced women who used too much makeup or wore open-toed shoes. He publicly ridiculed the science of Albert Einstein and the literature of H. G. Wells and George Bernard Shaw, and he found the psychology of Sig-mund Freud not merely wrong but positively dangerous. His sense of the standards of proper behavior was simple and innocent, and if it seems quaintly old-fashioned today it was in its own time seriously expressed, intended, and accepted.[38]

What is more, his positions in that age of paramount Catholic cer-tainty in all things were recognized and appreciated beyond the bounds of his own church. An unsympathetic intellectual observed that "his Catholicism has always been militant," while Boston's lead-ing Republican newspaper praised him for being "such a steady and steadying figure in the community while the nation is in a state of flux."[39] The modern world was perhaps taking its toll elsewhere in society, but in William O'Connell's Catholicism all remained calm and self-assured. By embodying this sense of Catholics' being "so cer-tain and set apart," he provided the kind of leadership his people seemed to demand, and if they did not feel warmly about him per-sonally they still embraced his authority. He was, like Robinson's fictional counterpart, "a peremptory man with a stiff Irish neck," though most people would also have agreed with the novelist's im-mediate appreciation: "he's a perfect father."[40]

O'Connell had a very long tenure as leader of the archdiocese of Boston, serving from his controversial accession in 1907 until his peaceful death in April 1944 at the age of eighty-four. He had held that position during a time of great change—two world wars, a depression, significant shifts in the direction of the political and social life of his diocese and of the country as a whole—but through it all he had been, as the Boston newspaper reported, a "steady and steadying" figure. His life and career had a relentless consistency. From the beginning he was the principal Romanist of his episcopal generation, serving both to symbolize and advance that position in the church in the United States. Even after circumstances had deprived him of the influence and power he sought to exercise in the highest councils of the church, he was still the embodiment of the belief that the phrase "American Catholic" meant nothing, while the phrase "Roman Catholic" meant virtually everything. Before his reign, another option had seemed possible; after it, the matter was no longer open for discussion. By glorying in the supreme spiritual authority of a papacy that had entered the nineteenth century very much on the skids but had emerged from it triumphant, O'Connell was at once the beneficiary and the avatar of the American Catholic belief that it was possible to be fully loyal to the pope and fully loyal to one's own country at the same time. For his people he expressed that integrating force, and his long tenure accustomed them to thinking in those same terms, embracing that vision as their own.

At the same time, his deliberate playing of a public role set the modern standard of behavior for succeeding generations of bishops, who were now expected to be not just the leaders of their own church, appearing only (or even primarily) at church-related affairs. Rather, bishops were now to be public men, not removed from the center of society but active in the whole range of life's activities. Their authority was to be not narrowly religious but broadly moral. What they had to say on any subject was noteworthy simply because they said it. For the Catholics of the archdiocese of Boston, O'Connell created this position for himself at the critical time, the period when they were emerging from their status as despised outsiders to that of full participants and even determinants of public life. For the Catholics of the nation as a whole, who would see one of their own—a man whose parents the cardinal had married—elected president fewer than two decades after O'Connell's death, O'Connell prepared the way for their snatch at the brass ring of acceptance. The cardinal had always been stern and imposing, more respected than loved, but he nonetheless offered his people a clear vision of themselves. Even if that vision is no longer so clear today, his own accomplishment is not diminished.

CHAPTER
11
Bishops on the Fringe: Patrick W. Riordan of San Francisco and Francis Clement Kelley of Oklahoma City

James P. Gaffey

*T*he lodestars of episcopal leadership in Catholic America during the last century have been the cities of the East and Midwest. With few exceptions, students of American bishops have concentrated on churchmen in Baltimore, New York, Boston, Chicago, Saint Paul, Saint Louis, and Philadelphia. Fortunately, however, recent studies like the prizewinning biography of Archbishop Jean-Baptiste Lamy by Paul Horgan have recalled the prodigious and complex activity in which bishops have engaged on the "fringes" of Catholic America.[1] This chapter will study two bishops whose dioceses were, like Lamy's Santa Fe, distant from the power centers of their respective generations. Together, their tenures extended some fifty years around the turn of the twentieth century, bridging the era of immigration and that of Romanization. Despite differences in temperament and locale,

Archbishop Patrick W. Riordan of San Francisco (1884–1914) and Bishop Francis Clement Kelley of Oklahoma City (1924–1944) were forceful domestic leaders and acute observers of national and international trends. A comparison of their views and work reflects a subtle transition of style and perspective; and as representatives of the Far West and Southwest, these two men may serve to complete the picture of episcopal leadership already well provided for in Catholic historical literature.

Regardless of the obvious differences in time and place, the early lives of the two men bring to light several connections between them, a surprising continuity of background. Both had been born in the maritime provinces of Canada, Riordan in New Brunswick in 1841 and Kelley in Prince Edward Island in 1870, and both were children of Irish families who had migrated before the disastrous famine in Ireland. In time these two Canadians took circuitous routes to Chicago. After Riordan's birth his family had returned to Ireland, where hardships forced their return to North America, and this time they chose to settle in Chicago, where Patrick was educated and ordained, taught in the diocesan seminary, and became a pastor. Kelley's detour to the Windy City, however, was more fortuitous. Having received his schooling on Prince Edward Island, he joined the Diocese of Detroit, where he championed the home-mission movement and in 1905 founded the Catholic Church Extension Society to aid missionary projects in rural America. A year later—at Riordan's suggestion, the only known time in which their lives intersected—Kelley made the key decision of his life by moving the society to Chicago, where it reached a larger corps of benefactors and where it has since flourished for over eighty years.[2]

Chicago was more than a coincidental crossroads where both men were eventually named bishops—Riordan in 1883 and Kelley in 1924—and dispatched to their remote sees. Both were profoundly influenced by the unique spirit and strength of this community. During his episcopate in San Francisco, Riordan attributed his success as a shepherd and an administrator to the sense of religion and enterprise he had inherited in Chicago. Returning in 1899 from a visit to Rome, he called on his former home city, where he publicly expressed his debt for the lessons he had learned there, describing it as "the greatest, the most progressive, and most catholic city . . . in the world."[3] Kelley likewise built the Extension Society upon the special advantages that Chicago offered. It was the first major population center in the country that was genuinely interested in the rural ministry supported by the society. By papal decree, the society's chancellor was its archbishop, whose position by its very nature commanded respect from other members of the hierarchy. And from the beginning the society's paneled offices were positioned in the heart of the financial district where it rapidly took on the appearance of a well-run, prosperous business.[4]

This common affiliation with Chicago was a two-edged sword. While the city brought the benefits of a great Catholic and commercial center, it introduced the two men to their first partisan activity as priests and to the explosive factionalism within the clergy. Only four years after ordination, Riordan had involved himself in promoting the removal of James Duggan, the fourth bishop of Chicago, on the grounds of mental instability. In the course of this development, the young priest was associated with a party of clergy whom some viewed as rebels with "Garibaldian tendencies" and who included Riordan's own uncle, a pastor of a downtown parish in Chicago. The tragic situation ended with Duggan's retirement in 1869, but not until Riordan had seen his beloved uncle die in the state of clerical suspension and himself, along with his friends, scattered to remote parishes.[5] Kelley, who had joined the Chicago archdiocese, fared as poorly. Always an outsider, he had offended leaders of the Chicago clergy when he was granted special privileges by the Extension Society's first chancellor, Archbishop James Quigley. The alienation deepened when, upon Quigley's death in 1915, Kelley championed as successor his friend Peter Muldoon, bishop of Rockford. His open advocacy of Muldoon's candidacy focused a steady underground smear campaign from his enemies, who were dubbed by one observer as "stilletto men," wielders of the notorious "Chicago knife." "They hold you guilty of one unpardonable offense," Kelley was told. "You came in a stranger and got close to the throne."[6]

Canada and Chicago were not the only links binding these two men. Though 1,626 miles separated their sees, there existed certain striking similarities between them. Both bishops viewed their dioceses as immense and isolated. "We are . . . cut off from the great life of the nation," said Riordan of San Francisco in 1903, "by two ranges of Mountains, the Rockies and Sierras, and a vast desert intervening, that we seem to belong to a Foreign country."[7] Kelley expressed much the same sentiment when he observed of Oklahoma twenty-seven years later, "I live in a State of magnificent distances, with a Diocese half as large as Italy."[8] Both men, furthermore, succeeded European-born bishops who had founded the dioceses in which they worked. Joseph Sadoc Alemany was the first archbishop of San Francisco. A native of Spain, he had served indefatigably for thirty-one years, governing a territory that embraced parts of northern California and Nevada and all of Utah. By the time of his retirement in 1884, his faithful were concentrated in the city of San Francisco, where they numbered 150,000 but where priests were in short supply, one for nearly every

5,000 Catholics, and where the parishes were in a dilapidated state
of repair.[9]

Kelley's episcopal predecessor was the Belgian-born Theophile
Meerschaert, who had labored in Oklahoma for thirty-three years.
His jurisdiction comprised the entire state of Oklahoma, some 70,000
square miles, which required the bishop to be in nearly constant motion for parish visitations. At first, Oklahoma's population resembled
that of pioneer California. The lure of oil had brought thousands with
get-rich-quick schemes just as the specter of gold had drawn miners
to the mother lode a generation earlier. In time, however, the population of California had stabilized as the economy matured and di-
versified, whereas in Oklahoma Kelley's Catholics migrated contin-
uously in and out of the state, and the majority of those remaining
were scattered in small towns and farms, never exceeding three percent of the state's population.[10] Two cities graced his landscape.
Oklahoma City was the center for the "old settler" Catholics who had
allowed their parishes to deteriorate; and in the east lay Tulsa, where
wealthier Catholics in the oil industry provided well for their parishes
but were too provincial to take responsibility for much else.[11] On the
horizon in both dioceses, when Riordan and Kelley took the reins,
there loomed a financial crisis. The diocesan debt in San Francisco,
Riordan calculated soon after his arrival in 1883, was $600,000; and
the usual sources of income were inadequate to service it.[12] Kelley
likewise felt that he had inherited a see on the edge of bankruptcy.
Though endowed with assets valued at $2 million, the diocese had
accumulated a debt of over $1 million. This prompted him to confide
to his future successor this piece of advice: "If they ever try to make
you a Bishop look carefully at the ledger before accepting; but I am
afraid they won't give you time to see the ledger."[13]

In this way, Riordan and Kelley, though belonging to two generations divided by World War I and two distinct regions of the country separated by the old lands of Mexico, emerge from settings start-
ingly similar. Canadians by birth, seasoned in the church of Chicago,
they took on provincial assignments where they were the first North
Americans to rule, and they were sufficiently successful as to have
had the successors of their choice. Together, their episcopates span
some five decades, a lengthy period that marks a full quarter of the
entire life of the American hierarchy dating from John Carroll. Despite
differences in disposition and resources, they faced together domestic
challenges of distance, organization, clergy, and civic responsibility,
along with responding to the current trends and issues prevalent
across the nation and abroad. A comparison of these two "fringe"
bishops may allow us to sight some traces of the subtle transition
undergone in vision and priorities as episcopal leadership in Catholic

America evolved from the age of James Gibbons to the age of William O'Connell.

The first focus of comparison is the infrastructure of diocesan organization. Archbishop Riordan brought with him the strong hand of administration that he had displayed as a pastor in Chicago, where he had built after the fire of 1871 one of the largest and most splendid churches. A man with keen financial sense, he began immediately to liquidate the diocesan debt, and within four years reduced it by more than 80 percent. The next task was to build a new cathedral. Ever since 1854, San Francisco had been served by what is now called "Old Saint Mary's," an edifice that Archbishop Alemany had built on the edge of the young city soon after taking up his residence. Through the years, however, his cathedral had become engulfed in the Chinatown district, a sprawling ghetto that teemed with poverty and vice and prevented the cathedral from serving as a center of Catholic life. Riordan, less then a year after his installation, announced in 1885 that he had awarded a contract for excavating a site far from the old cathedral, and he developed a systematic plan to collect funds for the project. Six years later he dedicated the new edifice to Saint Mary of the Assumption in elaborate ceremonies that reflected the importance of this enterprise and that included his Louvain schoolmate, Bishop John Lancaster Spalding of Peoria, as preacher. Designed by two Chicago architects, Riordan's cathedral was not an extravagant or innovative building, but it was functional, providing a spacious interior that accommodated a congregation of 3,000 and was designed with the absence of pillars to give an unobstructed view of the altar and pulpit. Its exterior—a red brick façade with two flanking towers and an imposing flight of forty granite stairs—vaguely resembled his old parish church. Officially known as "Modern Romanesque," it differed entirely from the styles of other churches in the city, and it was not long until it was described in some less-reverent circles as a model of "Chicago Gothic."[14]

Riordan's second cornerstone was the establishment of a seminary, a venture more complex than the building of a cathedral. In an abortive effort to develop a native clergy his predecessor had experimented with a theologate staffed by the Marists, but the lack of mature students with a proper academic background and the lack of steady financing and a convenient campus had reduced this undertaking to ashes.[15] Riordan learned from Alemany's failure and carefully planned the foundation of a preparatory seminary which in time would evolve into a theologate. He first recruited the Sulpicians, a renowned community of diocesan priests specializing in clerical formation who were at first reluctant to come to the Far West. Next he raised substantial sums for an endowment and constructed a handsome building on a perfectly situated site, a oak-filled meadow only thirty-two easy miles from San Francisco and virtually adjacent to the newly founded Stanford University, whose trustee Mrs. Jane Lathrope Stanford anonymously built and furnished the seminary chapel. The project progressed slowly but steadily. In only a decade after the opening of Saint Patrick's Seminary in 1898, Riordan's dream was fulfilled when he ordained the first priest who had received the full course at Menlo Park. Since then, the institution, described by Riordan as his "crowning work," continues to be one of the important professional schools for western clergy.[16]

Kelley's predecessor, like Archbishop Alemany in San Francisco, had left a legacy of not only an opportunity for endless work but also a weak infrastructure to support it. As a Chicago priest Kelley had had, in addition to his successes in fund-raising for the Extension Society, eight years' experience in running a parish, but unlike Riordan he had had no conspicuous success. When he left his parish in Wilmette, Illinois, for Oklahoma in 1924, he had failed to clear the debt and to build the school that had been planned; and, worse, he had allowed his parishioners to become alienated from supporting any archdiocesan projects, including Archbishop Mundelein's new seminary, Saint Mary of the Lake.[17] Hence, it comes as no surprise to discover that in Oklahoma Kelley posted no more than a tolerable record as an administrator. A one-time diocesan fund drive launched two years after his arrival enabled him to avert bankruptcy during the depression, but it was not until domestic prosperity arrived, brought on by World War II, that the diocese was close to liquidating its indebtedness. The ongoing support of Kelley's chancery was another financial thorn, and at first he was able to raise no more than two-thirds of what was required for diocesan administration. This chronic shortage of capital compelled him frequently to use his personal income from book royalties and lectures to make up the difference.[18]

Equally frustrating was Kelley's attempt to build a preparatory seminary. In 1928 a site was developed on the edge of Tulsa, and the city's most prominent pastor was appointed rector. Despite these promising beginnings, the enterprise collapsed when irreconcilable differences arose between bishop and rector; Kelley was unable to recruit a faculty and to raise the necessary funds, and at times he appeared all too ready to abandon his commitment. Within three years the diocese was forced to sell the incomplete facility at less then a quarter of its value.[19] The seminary project best revealed Kelley's managerial style as sometimes mercurial and inconsistent. After two decades of episcopal rule he produced no program or institution that encouraged Oklahoma youth to join the diocesan priesthood. The true flowering of the native secular clergy in his state awaited his successor.

While Kelley had no need to build a cathedral in Oklahoma City, he succeeded brilliantly in providing an extraordinary church for his second city, Tulsa. Like Riordan, he favored a Chicago architect, but unlike Riordan's choices, Kelley's designer was an innovative genius. Barry Byrne, a pupil of Frank Lloyd Wright and a central figure in Catholic architecture in America, was the leading force among ecclesiastical designers in checking the spread of traditional design churches such as Byzantine-Romanesque. Seven years with Wright had taught him that a church was basically a "holy enclosure" and should be planned from the "inside out." His radical view that the needs of the interior determined the external mass and shape had freed him from imitating antique styles and aligned him with the budding liturgical movement. With Kelley's personal encouragement, those ideas were integrated in the building of the Church of Christ the King in Tulsa. Completed in 1927, the graceful, chaste building drew rave reviews from designers, including Wright, and was featured in general reference works like the *Encyclopaedia Britannica* as a model of a functional contemporary church.[20] Kelley's triumph as a manager in this undertaking was less in being the perfect client than in playing the enlightened patron who provided opportunity to an artist of major importance.

Besides building institutions, a vital element in diocesan infrastructure is the relationship between the bishop and his clergy. Riordan appeared to have earned general respect and cooperation in the ranks. The only tension vaguely recorded between him and his priests as a whole centered on the new seminary. The majority of San Francisco clergy were Irish-born and trained. Combining the spirit of the adventurer and the hardy zeal of the missioner, they had proved themselves indispensable to the church in the Far West. At first, however, they did not approve of any institution that promoted a native clergy, and preferred that the archdiocese maintain its historic dependence upon the young Celts being trained abroad. With a patrician's restraint, Riordan won over these critics, dedicating the school to the patron of Ireland and scheduling clergy retreats regularly on its campus. Eventually, this subtle tactic won them over to their archbishop's "crowning work."[21]

In his dealings with problematic individuals Riordan was less compassionate. One of these was Peter C. Yorke, the eloquent polemicist who defended the church against all series of nativist attacks in the mid-1890s. For more than a year, Yorke responded to wave after wave of anti-Catholicism, publishing lengthy defenses in the daily press, his replies bristling with facts, threatening his antagonists with a thoroughness of research and with a pungency of expression that withered all opponents. In time, when Yorke's public statements became uncontrolled, Riordan reacted by removing him as editor of the diocesan paper without a public word of disapproval, and granted him a leave of absence. Yorke never knew the depth of his superior's annoyance until he returned to San Francisco a year later and discovered that no assignment awaited him and that as an unattached priest he had to arrange his own appointment as a curate.[22]

This indirect manner of censuring an intelligent but controversial subordinate was effective. In later years, Yorke rose to defend trade unionism, Irish independence, and other causes, but his influence was forever crippled. Complete rehabilitation had to wait until the final years of Riordan's episcopate. It is little wonder, then, that during the negotiations for a successor to the Archdiocese of Chicago in 1902— a period that coincided with Yorke's humiliation and canonical limbo in San Francisco—some clergy in the Midwest eyed Riordan cautiously as a stern "disciplinarian."[23]

While Riordan enjoyed the general affection of his clergy, Kelley by contrast fumbled at winning over the Oklahoma priests. Unfortunately, he set an unnecessarily strident tone at the beginning of his episcopate when he inaugurated his fund drive to clear the diocesan debt. In rallying his pastors, he warned: "I don't want any excuses and I won't take any," and in an indiscreet display of authority, he concluded his appeal with words that chilled clergy across the state: "I am not signing Francis C. Kelley to this letter. I am signing it simply Your Bishop."[24] The root of this and other ill-advised outbursts was Kelley's persistent ambivalence toward his clergy. While he esteemed the heroic Europeans, he nursed strong reservations about their usefulness, a conspicuous tendency that injured morale. Their age, for one thing, alarmed him. When an older priest expressed interest for work in Oklahoma, Kelley discouraged him with the retort: "I have all the relics I can handle with two-thirds of my clergy over fifty."[25] A more serious complaint he had concerned difficulties in language. When Kelley's predecessor recruited in European seminaries, he did not require his respondents to possess skill in English, and this deficiency led Kelley to report to Rome that these priests could do little beyond sacramental celebrations in Latin.[26] Such lack of respect and sympathy bred a similar reaction in his priests, which poisoned any true collaboration during most of his episcopate.

If Kelley's eminence lay not in astutely managing his scarce physical resources and personnel, one might expect better results from his tested ability as America's premier home missionary to conceive and articulate a pastoral vision that would blueprint the evangelization of his state. His twenty-year episcopate encompassed two apostolic campaigns. The first occurred between 1924 and 1929, during which his neighboring bishop in Arkansas expected to see Oklahoma emerge as "the model missionary Diocese of the country."[27] The campaign sparked a "scatter-shot" ministry, exploring a variety of techniques in reaching non-Catholics and lapsed Catholics as well as whites and every minority in the state. Though Kelley's summons to action was inspired and comprehensive, his execution was erratic—in his own words, "hit and miss."[28] The key to this gulf between promise and performance was a narrow focus on convert-making as the essence of the missionary apostolate. Under him, significant inroads were made within the non-Catholic population, but the responsibility to hold and confirm the neophytes was a task that failed to interest him deeply.

This peculiar inconsistency surfaced early in Kelley's pastoral vision and was to weaken it throughout his episcopate. The second campaign followed in the 1930s with another eye-catching flurry of activity across the state, much of it novel and original, including the first American endorsement of the Young Christian Workers. Privately, however, Kelley admitted that these operations produced no more than a stalemate in reaching the non-Catholic majority. In the grimmest passage of his quinquennial report of 1939, he was forced to acknowledge no visible progress after fifteen years since his arrival, and went on to describe "the whole work of the Church of Oklahoma as having scarcely begun."[29]

Although Riordan enjoyed greater success than Kelley in anchoring the infrastructure of this diocese, both made monumental contributions to their civic communities. In 1906, the greatest earthquake in California's history shook San Francisco to its foundations. After three days of fighting to contain the fires, some 200,000 were homeless and nearly five square miles of the city were destroyed. As thousands of refugees were evacuated, reports circulated that the city's spirit had been crushed. After surveying his stricken see, Riordan played a historic role in restoring it. "We shall rebuild," he urged. "We must restore confidence."[30] His most celebrated moment occurred at a public meeting of civic leaders. While they were still stunned by the enormous losses and the ruins smoldered only blocks away, the archbishop delivered the most stirring appeal of his life, quoting in impressive tones the words of Saint Paul, "I am a citizen of no mean city, although it is in ashes." He went on:

> Almighty God has fixed this as the location of a great city. The past is gone, and there is no use lamenting or moaning over it. Let us look to the future and without regard to creed or place of birth, work together in harmony for the upbuilding of a greater San Francisco.[31]

These words galvanized the distraught community. Those present at this event recalled his appeal as "the most inspiring address heard," providing the compelling phrase needed to arouse the city to a renewal of hope and an immediate program of rebuilding.[32]

Kelley's major community service consisted in spearheading the reform of higher education in Oklahoma, a phase in his life that earned him the highest respect at all levels of state government. In 1932, he proposed the integration of public and private colleges, hoping at first to renew the "culture of spirit" in a state that prized engineers and scientific farmers and perhaps to rally the slipping enrollment in Catholic institutions. When he urged that all colleges join the Greater University of Oklahoma, secular educators saw this as a call to end the futile independence of Oklahoma's scattered colleges and to systematize public higher education. The proposal proceeded through a labyrinth of nine years of political hurdling, which included three state administrations and an amendment to the state constitution that established the plan in 1941 but dropped private colleges from the statewide system, allowing them, however, to become "coordinated" with it.

Kelley's civic involvement was thus crowned by the creation of the Oklahoma State Regents for Higher Education, which eventually took control of twenty-five tax-supported institutions. More than anyone, he had committed two governors to bringing order to collegiate life in Oklahoma. During the deliberations he was seen as the most imaginative thinker, researching alternative forms of schooling and never allowing limitations in law and partisanship to confuse what was essential to education. Though he was unable to penetrate the constitutional barrier against private colleges, he took this loss gracefully and continued to work for the state until an acceptable plan was produced.[33]

If one looks beyond local affairs, one can see even greater differences between Riordan and Kelley in their agenda and attitude. National leadership among the bishops of Riordan's generation had polarized into two parties. One was sympathetic to the spirit of Pius IX, assuring the faithful of the changelessness of their faith and condemning the liberal trends of the day. Among its American spokesmen were Archbishop Michael A. Corrigan of New York and Bishop Bernard McQuaid of Rochester. The other party was less dogmatic and more attuned to the conditions of a modern democracy and to the progressive spirit of the pontiff of its day, Leo XIII. Its partisans were known as the "Americanizers," and they included Cardinal Gibbons of Baltimore, Archbishop John Ireland of Saint Paul, Archbishop John Keane of Dubuque, and Bishop John Lancaster Spalding of Peoria, Illinois.

Riordan's general reaction to the key national issues revealed his sympathy with the Americanizers. From afar, he observed in 1887 the acrimonious dispute between Archbishop Corrigan and Father Edward McGlynn, an articulate champion of social reform and disciple of the single-tax theory of Henry George. Despite Corrigan's charges that McGlynn was a socialist, Riordan asked Keane to intercede in Rome on the priest's behalf, adding:" At heart he is all right, though he may be imprudent and obstinate."[34] While encouraging ethnic parishes in San Francisco, Riordan stood in the same year alongside Gibbons, Ireland, and Keane in denying the accusations of German-American leaders that the Irish-dominated hierarchy in America had oppressed non-English-speaking Catholics.[35] A few years later, he joined Gibbons in his opposition both to Rome's establishment of a permanent apostolic delegation, on the grounds that it was a threat to the collegial tradition of the American hierarchy, and to Rome's condemnation of secret societies on the grounds that it was an unnecessary precaution against religious indifferentism.[36]

Riordan's loyalty to the Americanizers, however, was not a blind and mindless allegiance. As time went on, he tired of the controversies and questioned some of the positions taken by his comrades. In 1890, when Ireland announced his willingness to allow some of his schools to come under the partial jurisdiction of local public-school authorities, Riordan was an uncompromising advocate of the separate parochial school system. He broke ranks with his Minnesota friend over this issue and aligned himself with Eastern conservatives like Corrigan, deploring Ireland's ceaseless public agitation over this question.[37] Riordan mellowed further toward the conservatives when, after Corrigan died in 1902, he sealed a personal friendship with the New Yorker's chief ally, Bishop McQuaid. This bond between San Francisco and Rochester had a double impact. First, it would be from McQuaid's own seminary faculty that in 1907 Riordan would choose his successor, Edward J. Hanna.[38] Second, Riordan admired McQuaid's apostolic spirit, especially his attempt to establish a Catholic college at Cornell University. This pioneering project helped inspire Riordan's foundation in 1910 of Newman Hall for Catholic students at the University of California at Berkeley.[39]

The final test of his loyalty to old comrades centered on the fortunes of the Catholic University of America, a national institution profoundly dear to its chancellor, Cardinal Gibbons. In its early days, Riordan had given his suppport by allowing general collections in his western diocese and offering to enroll as graduate students such promising priests as Peter C. Yorke. By the turn of the century, however, Riordan had lost faith in the school. Its financial woes persisted, some caused by what he considered to be a criminal mismanagement of funds.[40] Worse, in his view, was the university's total neglect of making formal provisions for a retiring university rector, and it was Riordan's unexpected task to help arrange honorable exits for the first three rector-bishops. When Keane left the university and after 1897 languished at the Curia in Rome, Riordan devoted three years in helping to have him appointed to an American archdiocese.[41] Three years later, after the term of Keane's successor, Bishop Thomas Conaty, had expired, Riordan accepted him as a suffragan and engineered his appointment to the diocese of Monterey–Los Angeles.[42] When the third rector, Bishop Dennis O'Connell, chose not to extend his term of office in 1908, Riordan with some reluctance took him to San Francisco as auxiliary.[43] These haphazard arrangements had so strained Riordan's commitment to the university that at one time Gibbons justifiably feared his desertion. However, though discouraged and disillusioned, Riordan nevertheless did not bolt, more out of personal friendship with the cardinal than out of a conviction to support what he felt to be a perennially troubled institution.

Kelley's involvement in the national issues of his generation followed a different route from that of Riordan's, a simpler one that touched principally upon two issues only but a more intense one that showed Kelley as a significant force in policy-making. As bishop, the founder of the Extension Society remained primordially committed to the home-mission movement. Unlike prelates who came to power in Riordan's age, Kelley's closest friendships were formed not through a sharing of an ecclesiological vision, but simply through former association from Chicago days at the Extension Society—Bishops Emmanuel B. Ledvina of Corpus Christi, William D. O'Brien of Extension, and Kelley's eventual successor in Oklahoma, Eugene J. McGuinness. This unconditional dedication to the movement also led Kelley as bishop to advocate related causes such as the formation of the American Board of Catholic Missions (ABCM). He had long been convinced that a portion of revenues collected nationally for the foreign missions should be distributed among the struggling missions in this country. His dream materialized in his first year as a bishop, when the newly formed ABCM was empowered to distribute 40 percent of mission revenues. Significantly, in its first fifteen years this agency of the American hierarchy dispensed to the home missions more than $12 million in undesignated gifts.[44] It is no exaggeration to acknowledge Kelley as the principal force in providing this mechanism whereby Catholic America could extend itself to the critical needs at home which had been so long neglected.

The other national issue of importance that occupied Kelley was the question of how to assist the persecuted church in Mexico. Modern anticlericalism in that country dates from 1913, when civil war erupted among several factions, unleashing the first of several waves of religious persecution. As Extension president, Kelley had become involved when refugees poured over the border into the American Southwest, where his society supported several missions. This crisis transformed him into a major defender of the Mexican church. In the years that followed, he published articles and booklets, helped to provide relief for refugees, and lobbied the Wilson administration to force Mexico to give guarantees of religious liberty. His patronage in these early years would earn him the title of Mexico's "Guardian Angel."[45]

His devotion to this cause did not cease after his appointment to Oklahoma. As bishop, he engaged in two campaigns to awaken American public opinion regarding the tragedy across the southern border. He first produced in 1926 the original draft of a pastoral letter on Mexico authorized by the hierarchy. The carefully argued document did not persuade Americans to support the church in Mexico, but it gave to the Mexican hierarchy a welcome expression of support. "It is consoling," Mexican bishops wrote, "to have some one sympathize with us when we are in trial and tribulation, to plead for us when we are accused and defamed, to defend us when we are injured, and to uphold us when we are discouraged!"[46] No individual deserved this expression of gratitude from the Mexican episcopate more than their brother in Oklahoma.

As the turmoil in Mexico continued, Bishop Kelley published in 1935 *Blood-Drenched Altars*, a book of more than 500 pages presenting a history of Mexico from a Catholic perspective. Drawing only mixed reviews in the secular press, it was no more successful in arousing public opinion in America than the bishops' pastoral letter had been. However, it was instrumental in committing the American hierarchy to its most sustained program of Mexican relief and to its guaranteeing the future of the Mexican church as an institution. Influenced in large part through Kelley's writings, the American bishops undertook the support of an interdiocesan seminary in Montezuma, New Mexico, where for thirty-five years nearly three thousand Mexican students matriculated in a safe setting far from government interference. As the principal American founder of this unique school, the Oklahoman had initiated one of the most extraordinary Catholic experiments in North America, one that brought two national hierarchies into an unusual and long-term partnership and that provided more than 500 priests for dioceses in Mexico.[47]

Episcopal leadership travels along three paths. It first deals with domestic, or diocesan, issues, and, second, it sometimes records an impact in national affairs and policy. The third dimension is the bishop's personal and professional relationship with the Holy See and those who represent it, a bond that is known popularly as *Romanità*.

Neither Riordan nor Kelley was an unorthodox or disobedient bishop, but this fact should not prevent one from noticing the spirit in which they greeted and implemented Vatican decisions, from assessing their views as to what was appropriate for the Vatican in its exercise of authority, and from reviewing their responses to any effort in Rome to centralize its authority by trimming the rights of national bodies of bishops and making individual bishops more directly responsible to the Curia, a process known as Romanization.[48]

Riordan revealed his willingness to criticize Vatican policy early in his episcopate when he opposed the establishment of a permanent apostolic delegation in 1894 and a year later again opposed the condemnation of secret societies. It was, however, the pontificate of Pius X that brought out more clearly his indisposition to subscribe to the earliest traces of Romanization. On viewing this pontiff's election in 1903, Riordan sensed that the advances made under Leo XIII would be halted and that the new secretary of state would be the chief instrument of stalemate or of reaction. "We shall have a weak and colorless administration," Riordan confided to Bishop John Lancaster Spalding, "and no attempt to settle the great difficulties that beset our progress. The appointment of Merry del Val is to my mind the key-note to the whole administration."[49] His worst fears materialized three years later when the ultramontane William O'Connell was named coadjutor archbishop of Boston. This major development might be said to have inaugurated the process of Romanization in America, because O'Connell's appointment was made without the recommendation of a single American bishop but rather through the intervention of Vatican officialdom, most probably O'Connell's close friend Cardinal Merry del Val. This circumvention of normal procedure in filling a diocese prompted the angry Riordan to charge: "Such an appointment is a national scandal. I do not see any use in holding meetings and sending money across the Atlantic when no attention is paid to the proceedings of the Bishops and the Archbishops."[50]

While faithfully orthodox, Riordan's theological horizon was broader than the narrow focus taken by the Vatican, especially after its condemnations of modernism in 1907. This complex movement had arisen before the turn of the century mainly from the application of new critical methods to the study of Scripture and the history of dogma, but Pius X proscribed it because some leaders were inclined toward agnosticism and relativism. Three years before the papal decree, however, Riordan had chanced upon *The Soul's Orbit*, a book by the leading English-speaking modernist George Tyrrell, S.J., who was already under investigation for heresy. Finding the book valuable and suggestive, Riordan wondered privately why it had not been made available to the general public. In the following year, Tyrrell's future dimmed further as he faced the prospect of expulsion from the Jesuits and failed to gain admittance as a secular priest into the archdioceses of Westminster and Dublin. When Riordan learned of his canonical limbo, the archbishop invited him to San Francisco, a generous invitation that Tyrrell declined with the remark that as he awaited some type of censure he would not risk embarrassment for "one so kind as your Grace has proved."[51] Even after the final condemnation, Riordan confided to a friend regarding the tragic Tyrrell that "There is a place for him and plenty of work for him to do in the great Church of Christ."[52]

Riordan was given a more involved and intimate view of the Vatican's fear of modernism when he elected to defend Edward J. Hanna, the man whom he had chosen in 1907 to succeed him. A theologian in the Rochester seminary and a candidate for the coadjutorship in San Francisco, Hanna was accused of heresy because of articles on the human knowledge of Jesus in which he suggested possible limitations in Jesus's awareness and opened to discussion and debate the common teaching of theologians that as man Christ possessed full knowledge from birth. During the awkward investigation of Hanna's orthodoxy, Riordan refused to abandon the theologian and remained constant even after his candidacy had been disqualified by the Curia. The archbishop's fidelity was rewarded five years later when Hanna was sent to San Francisco as auxiliary.[53] Evidently, Riordan had no misgivings about leaving in his place a leader whose reputation has been solidly tainted in Pius's Rome.

Whereas *Romanità* left scarcely any trace on Riordan's character, Kelley surrendered to it early and fully. His first important act as the Extension Society's founder in 1910 was to have the society named a pontifical institute. This arrangement gave Extension a special union with the Holy See, awarding it a cardinal "protector" to be named by the pope and guaranteeing that the society's president would likewise be a papal appointee. The principal figure who engineered this plan was Cardinal Merry del Val, whom Kelley idolized all his life. In addition, the first and only cardinal protector appointed was Sebastiano Martinelli, a former apostolic delegate to the United States and one of the leading proponents of Romanization in the Curia.[54] So strong was Kelley's sense of canonical independence during the pontificate of Pius X that later in the same year he flagrantly ignored the collegial procedures of the American episcopate. In an attempt to get a national collection for the home missions, he appealed directly and individually to the bishops without consulting Cardinal Gibbons, the dean of the hierarchy. This bold effort made the gentle Gibbons *"simply furious,"* according to one observer, who told Kelley that the cardinal did not appreciate the Extension Society's "underhand methods."[55]

Kelley's desire to acquaint the Catholic public with the Holy See led him to promote greater exposure in the media of the inner operation of church government. The papacy had been virtually cloistered since the loss of the Papal States. Not since 1870 had popes made public appearances, not even imparting their blessing from an open balcony at Saint Peter's. This seclusion, Kelley feared, would obscure these leaders to the majority of the faithful who were unable to attend the select audiences within the walls of the Vatican. Under his editorship, *Extension Magazine* regularly advocated the restoration of papal independence and even took pains to acquaint its readers with the Curia through a rare series of articles and photographs describing the major figures and departments. In 1913, Kelley considered making a motion picture that would contain scenes with Pius X, but that project collapsed when the pontiff firmly declined to be filmed under any conditions.[56]

Kelley's appointment to Oklahoma did not diminish his resolve to promote the presence of the Holy See in America. Encouraged by H. L. Mencken to write his memoirs, Kelley published in 1939 his best-known book, *The Bishop Jots It Down*. A product of five years' work, this life story not only recorded the milestones of his career but also revealed for the first time to a mass audience the humanity of the church, notably at its highest levels. Anecdotes abound, fresh and flawlessly structured. The most engaging ones render the Vatican as managed by wise and benevolent churchmen who were never too occupied to greet a stranger. A typical passage runs thus:

> The cardinals in Rome are the ears of the Church, trained to listen and learn. No one with anything of importance to say can claim that he went to Rome and was denied a hearing. A witty Texas bishop said, "If you want justice go to Rome. But before you go be sure that it is justice you want."[57]

Another passage reinforcing the same theme projects the author's intention into even sharper relief. At the last minute, while the book was in galley proof, Kelley inserted a paragraph recounting a chance meeting twenty-five years earlier with Monsignor Eugenio Pacelli, who was a rising member of the papal bureaucracy when Kelley first encountered him but who was, on the eve of the publication of this autobiography, the newly elected pontiff Pius XII. In a frantic effort to introduce this pope to the American reader, Kelley embellished the brief, almost forgotten, episode, describing the young monsignor as "tall and thin, graceful in carriage, and with a face that might be that of a saint."[58] While the book gave Kelley his greatest chance to reach the mass market, selling nearly 15,000 copies—"Very few American books touch that figure," Mencken observed, "or anything like it"—it also provided outsiders a seldom-seen glimpse into the heart of Roman Catholicism.[59]

Riordan and Kelley in two generations and in different "fringe" settings traveled along three avenues of episcopal leadership. As a diocesan leader, Riordan was an unqualified success, fortifying his infrastructure with sound finances, a new cathedral and a seminary, and a motivated clergy, and rising to meet his city's greatest disaster as its leading citizen. Kelley's domestic record was poor, except in giving a visionary's touch to a pastoral plan for Oklahoma and to a novel church in his wealthiest city. As a civic leader, however, he rose above the introversion common to religious minorities and participated mightily in the educational improvement of his state. On the national scene, Kelley's record is more impressive than Riordan's. Though Riordan contributed thoughts and encouragement from afar on the great issues of this day, there is no single monument outside his diocese that bears his name, whereas Kelley's enduring work for the home-mission movement produced the ABCM and led the American hierarchy into its noble performance on behalf of the Mexican church.

While Riordan and Kelley score differently on local and national levels, it is on the level of their relationships with Rome that one best sees the key difference between the two generations. Riordan was an inside member of the "old guard" of the hierarchy, an ally of Gibbons and the liberal wing who appreciated the rights of a national episcopate and watched with suspicion any infringement upon a prerogative. Though junior to him by only thirty years, Kelley was entirely Romanized, a development that dates from the pontificate of Pius X when the Vatican nurtured the beginnings of his work at the Extension Society and that concluded in the era of Pius XII, who gently relieved him of his burdens in 1944. Together, these two bishops gave a half-century of service on the "fringes," and it is ironic that, close as they were in background, they demonstrate the succession of opposite generations of episcopal leaders in Catholic America.

CHAPTER
12

The Beginning and the End of an Era: George William Mundelein and John Patrick Cody in Chicago

Edward R. Kantowicz

*W*hen Cardinal George William Mundelein of Chicago was buried on October 6, 1939, the administrator of the archdiocese declared all three and a half million Chicagoans, Catholic and non-Catholic alike, honorary pallbearers. So closely had the cardinal identified himself with his adopted city (he came from New York) that this unusual gesture seemed perfectly appropriate. Mundelein's influence extended far beyond Chicago, however, to Rome and Washington. The eulogist at his funeral noted: "Cardinal Mundelein was not a man to confine himself to the sacristy, but, exercising his franchise as a free American citizen, he played a man's part in public life." A *Chicago Tribune* col-

umnist styled Mundelein "the most influential Catholic in the world
. . . next to the Pope." Both Mundelein's contemporaries and later
observers have concluded that the Chicago cardinal "put the Catholic
Church on the map" in the United States.[1]

Forty years and three archbishops later, Cardinal John Patrick
Cody was laid to rest on April 29, 1982. Hundreds of dignitaries and
thousands of mourners attended the splendid obsequies for Cody, but
nonetheless a cloud seemed to hover over the proceedings. Controversy
had swirled about Cody's seventeen-year stewardship of the Chicago
archdiocese. Many observers believed that both Pope Paul VI and Pope
John Paul I were on the verge of removing him in 1978 when death
felled them both. The *Chicago Sun-Times* revealed in 1981 that the
United States attorney had instructed a grand jury to investigate
Cody's diversion of funds to a woman who turned out to be his stepcousin. The eulogist at Cody's funeral delivered an eloquent address
on the Christian meaning of death, but he barely mentioned the deceased cardinal. Chicagoans seemed more relieved than saddened by
Cardinal Cody's death.[2]

Why the vast difference in reputation between those two cardinals,
whose administrations in Chicago spanned nearly half the twentieth
century? The simplest explanation is that Mundelein ushered in the
beginning of a distinct era in church history and identified himself
with it, whereas Cody came at the end of that era and, unfortunately
for him, outlived it. Mundelein's administration marked a rising sun,
Cody's signaled sunset. There were important differences in management style and personnel policy between the two men as well, but
in order to understand the contrast between them, we must first de-
lineate the beginning and the end of their era.

CONSOLIDATING BISHOPS AND AN ERA OF INSTITUTIONAL MATURITY

The years from about 1910 up to the Second Vatican Council of the
1960s mark a distinct period in American Catholic history, though
this has been insufficiently noted by church historians.[3]

Prior to the turn of the century, American Catholicism was weak
and disorganized. Catholic bishops had their hands full simply building churches and schools for the millions of immigrants pouring into
America and had no time for fine points of administration. The laity
took the initiative in shaping their own brands of immigrant Catholicism, priests were often undisciplined and always independent-
minded, American Catholics lacked status and respect both in Rome
and in America. Roman authorities considered the United States a

mission territory as late as 1908, and in 1899 the pope condemned a vague set of doctrines he called "Americanism." American Protestants, for their part, feared and mistrusted the Catholic church as an un-American invader of the republic. American Catholics were too Roman for the native Protestants but also too American for Rome.

Then in the years surrounding World War I, a generation of American-born but Roman-trained bishops came to power in the largest urban dioceses of the United States. Men such as Cardinal William O'Connell in Boston, Cardinal George Mundelein in Chicago, and Cardinal Francis Spellman in New York were "consolidating bishops" who, like their counterparts in business and government, saw a need for greater order and efficiency. They centralized and tightened the administrative structure of their dioceses and put them on a firm financial footing; they built the beginnings of a national Catholic administration in Washington; and they tied American Catholicism more closely to headquarters in Rome.

The consolidating bishops also gained new respect for the American Catholic church, both in Rome, where their financial support became the Vatican's mainstay, and in the United States, where their highly visibly leadership bolstered the self-image of American Catholics and earned the grudging respect of non-Catholics. The careers of O'Connell, Mundelein, and Spellman spanned the entire period from the turn of the century to Vatican II. Their leadership and that of similar bishops in other cities brought the American Catholic church to institutional maturity and earned for it self-confidence and power at home and in the Vatican.[4]

This period of institutional maturity and satisfied self-confidence ended with astonishing swiftness after the Second Vatican Council, when priests, nuns, and laity openly challenged their bishops and then left the church in droves. Yet, for about forty years, from 1910 to 1960, the American church seemed monolithic and unchanging. Having overcome the administrative disorder and psychological insecurity of an immigrant church, the Catholic community in the first half of the twentieth century felt fully Catholic and fully American—an enormous achievement for the leadership of the consolidating bishops. Their leadership had many facets, but three aspects of their episcopal style—Romanism, triumphalism, and centralization—will illuminate the comparison between Mundelein and Cody.

ROMANISM, TRIUMPHALISM, AND CENTRALIZATION

Born in 1872 in New York City, George William Mundelein entered priestly studies for the Brooklyn diocese, whose bishop, Charles

McDonnell, handpicked him for a Roman education. Mundelein studied at the Urban College of the Propaganda from 1892 to 1895 and was ordained in Rome by Bishop McDonnell on June 8, 1895. One acquaintance he made in the Eternal City, John Bonzano, proved crucial to his later career. A few years older than Mundelein, Bonzano later served as rector of the Urban College and, more important, as apostolic delegate to the United States from 1912 to 1922, where he was instrumental in Mundelein's appointment to Chicago.[5]

Mundelein remained a thoroughgoing Romanist all his life. In 1907 he wrote an essay defending the pope's condemnation of modernism, a Latin literary effort that earned him entrance into the ancient Roman Academy of the Arcadia. As archbishop of Chicago, he made the Peter's Pence collection a top priority, raising over $120,000 per year in the 1920s, more than the entire American church had collected at the turn of the century. When he built a new major seminary for Chicago, he chose early-American, neoclassical architecture for the façades, but he designed the seminary rules from Roman models. The interior of the seminary library was patterned after the Barberini Palace in Rome and the focal point of the seminary plan centered on a Roman obelisk with a statue of the Virgin atop it. Under Mundelein's leadership, the Catholic church in Chicago became American on the outside but Roman to the core.[6]

The cardinal cultivated a special relationship with Pope Pius XI, who appreciated Chicago Catholic financial support and encouraged Catholic Action social experiments. Each of the major consolidating bishops—O'Connell, Mundelein, and Spellman—was close to a particular pope, O'Connell to Pius X, Mundelein to Pius XI, and Spellman to Pius XII. Mundelein's special relationship to the pope who reigned during most of his administration in Chicago earned him a reputation as a "kingmaker," with a decisive voice in the naming of American bishops.

Mundelein conducted all his public activities with an imperial flair, which is nowadays called triumphalism. Affecting the manner of a Renaissance prince, he collected old coins and manuscripts, purchased gigantic paintings from the school of Rubens and Titian, and assembled a collection of famous men's autographs. Clerical wags referred to him as the "late Cardinal Mundelein" for he often arrived slightly late at a public ceremony, sweeping in swiftly for maximum effect with horns blowing and police sirens blaring.

Mundelein believed that the church should "go first class," in order to overcome its immigrant defensiveness.[7] He hired the best law firm in the city to defend the church's interests and worked with the speaker of the Illinois House of Representatives as his personal agent in the legislature. When he built his new seminary, Saint Mary of the

Lake, he designed a lavish plan, sprawling over a thousand acres, with a private golf course and lake. Each seminarian enjoyed his own room with a bath. Mundelein provided first class facilities for his seminarians, then demanded a lot in return. He expected them to be giants—physically, intellectually, spiritually.

The high point of Mundelein's triumphalism came in 1926 when he brought the International Eucharistic Congress to the United States for the first time. Prelates and pilgrims gathered from all over the world at the lakefront Soldier Field from July 20 to 24. Then, on the final day, close to one million worshipers attended an outdoor procession at Mundelein's seminary outside the city. The Chicago Catholic newspaper *The New World* cautioned its readers: "Let there be no mistaking the fact that the Eucharistic Congress is no endeavor to demonstrate strength. There is no thought behind it of a flaunting of vast numbers before non-Catholics." Yet a "flaunting of vast numbers" is precisely what Chicago's Eucharistic Congress accomplished. It was a flamboyant, slightly arrogant proof that American Catholics had arrived.[8]

Such triumphal display may seem like megalomania, but it was more than personal vainglory. Mundelein was trying to carry a whole institution—a whole generation of immigrant outsiders—upward with him. Acutely aware that Catholics in America lacked self-confidence and social status, he tried to burnish the image of the Catholic church. Triumphal display carried risks. It could, and probably did, evoke Protestant fears of the church's foreign and antirepublican connections. Yet, on the other hand, Americans love spectacle and they frequently fawn over royalty. In a country without a royal family, cardinal princes filled a psychological vacuum and raised the status of the Catholic minority.

Mundelein, however, earned his greatest accolades not for ceremonial excess but for businesslike management.[9] The cardinal centralized fundraising for Catholic Charities and other causes and levied assessments on the parishes to finance the seminary and the Eucharistic Congress. He took all crucial brick-and-mortar decisions away from the individual pastors. Before a pastor could build, he had to negotiate a nine-step bureaucratic process that included the bishop's approval of the architect, a full discussion of the parish finances by the board of consultors, and the constant supervision of the project by a two-man subcommittee of consultors. He removed a handful of priests from parish work and named them diocesan directors for charities, schools, cemeteries, and the missions, thus creating the beginnings of an administrative bureaucracy in the chancery office.

In order to shift capital internally within the archdiocese, Mundelein used his corporate bonding power to create a central banking mechanism. Legally constituted as a corporation sole, the Catholic Bishop of Chicago had the power to issue bonds. Mundelein required parishes that showed a surplus to invest the money in Catholic Bishop of Chicago bonds, and then he loaned this money to poorer parishes at a low rate of interest. In effect, he had created a diocesan bank that shifted money from wealthy parishes to those in need and permitted rational planning and management. Cardinal Spellman of New York is often credited with devising the first central bank in a Catholic diocese, but Mundelein's system predates Spellman's by twenty years.[10]

Centralized management put the Catholic church in Chicago on a firm financial footing and gained the respect of American businessmen. The archdiocese's credit survived the depression intact, and Catholic Bishop of Chicago bonds rarely dropped below par. There was an oft-repeated comment, variously attributed either to Julius Rosenwald of Sears, Roebuck or Frederick Eckert of Metropolitan Life as well as to other business leaders, that Mundelein missed his calling by going into religion rather than business.

Thirty-five years younger than Mundelein, John Patrick Cody grew up during the heyday of the consolidating bishops and apprenticed with one of their number, Archbishop John Glennon of Saint Louis.[11] Born in Saint Louis in 1907, Cody entered the seminary at age thirteen, receiving an even more thorough Roman indoctrination than Mundelein had. He spent nearly ten years in Rome, first as a student at the North American College from 1927 to 1931, then as vice rector of the college and staff member of Cardinal Pacelli's Secretariat of State from 1932 to 1938. One of his fellow workers in the Vatican Secretariat was a young papal diplomat named Giovanni Montini. Later, as Pope Paul VI, Montini would assign Cody to Chicago, name him a cardinal, then hesitate indecisively over the possibility of removing him. Cody liked to joke about his closeness to Paul VI: "Whenever the Pope sees me, he always reminds me that I was ordained a bishop seven years before he was."[12]

Indeed, Cody's Roman training brought him rapid ecclesiastical advancement. Archbishop Glennon recalled him to Saint Louis in 1938 to serve as his personal secretary. Cody then became chancellor of the Saint Louis archdiocese in 1940 and auxiliary bishop in 1947. The Roman authorities moved Cody frequently before finally assigning him to Chicago. Between 1954 and 1965 he served in three different dioceses—Saint Joseph, Missouri; Kansas City, Missouri; and New Orleans, Louisiana. In each case, he started out as coadjutor to an aging bishop, then swiftly ascended to full authority as ordinary.

Cody had already proved his complete Romanism and his primary loyalty to the church before he was consecrated bishop. In February 1946 he accompanied Archbishop Glennon to Rome when the ailing elderly prelate belatedly received a cardinal's red hat. After the conclave, Glennon retired to his boyhood home in Ireland to die, posing Cody with a thorny dilemma. Cody's mother also lay mortally ill at this time, so he had to choose which deathbed to sit by, Cardinal Glennon's or his mother's. He chose the cardinal's. On March 9, 1946, Glennon died with Cody at his side; that very same day, Mrs. Mary Cody was buried in Saint Louis.[13]

Once appointed to Chicago, Cody continued the imperial style of his predecessors. Indeed, he stage-managed a triumphal entrance into the Windy City worthy of a prince or a president. To the surprise of his advisors, Cody decided to travel from New Orleans to Chicago by train, not by air. He set off with the mayor of New Orleans aboard, then picked up the mayors of Saint Louis and Kansas City along the way. South of Chicago, he changed trains and made the final run into Union Station flanked by Chicago Mayor Richard J. Daley and Illinois Governor Otto Kerner. Thousands of priests and nuns, with flag-waving schoolchildren, cheered him at each stop.[14]

Cody's physical appearance also seemed a throwback to a more imperial age. The *Chicago Tribune* called him, tactfully, "a man of great scale," and the *New York Times* described him as "a man who might have been a Notre Dame tackle in the Rockne days but has since lost his battle with the scales." The archbishop liked to assert his authority in the time-honored Chicago practice of demonstrating "clout." The editor of the archdiocesan newspaper reported that "He would boast about being able to get his plane in—if he was coming in and planes were all stacked up, he could get the plane he was aboard landed ahead of the others at O'Hare. . . . If he wanted something, he could always find people to do it."[15]

Cody also continued and completed the work of bureaucratic centralization and administrative consolidation that Mundelein had begun. Mundelein's immediate successors had not much changed the administrative structures of the Chicago archdiocese. Cardinal Samuel Stritch (1939–1958) was a gregarious, outgoing person who gave speeches and shook hands but left administration to his chancellor and vicar general, men handpicked and trained by Mundelein. Cardinal Albert Meyer (1958–1965) was so preoccupied with the proceedings of the Vatican Council in Rome that he had little time to make changes in Chicago. But Cody hit the city like a whirlwind, summarily dismissing a handful of old pastors and proceeding to shore up the central bureaucracy of the archdiocese.

He instituted life and health insurance plans for priests, funded a pension plan for both lay and clerical employees, and organized a personnel board to standardize appointment procedures. He greatly expanded the number of central archdiocesan agencies, housing them under one roof in a downtown office building. Not even his official newspaper was certain how many new offices and agencies he opened, but it was "at least sixteen," the newspaper reported.[16]

Cody's administrative improvements were overdue, and his Roman imperial style was no different from that of Mundelein or dozens of other bishops; but, unfortunately for him, times had changed. To put the matter bluntly, a rotund potentate in red robes, exercising personal prerogative and centralized authority, seemed out of place in the Age of Aquarius and the era of democratic reform in the church.

Shorty after Cody's arrival in Chicago, an ad hoc group of younger clergy formed a coordinating committee that led to the founding of the Association of Chicago Priests (ACP) on October 24, 1966. This unofficial body representing several hundred Chicago priests avoided the word "union," but it acted much like one, constantly pressuring Cody on personnel matters and demanding consultation with him on major policy decisions. The high point of ACP militance came on June 15, 1971, when the association, by a narrow vote, censured Cody and all his auxiliary bishops for failing to represent adequately the Chicago clergy's views on celibacy at the annual meeting of the U.S. bishops.[17]

It is not hard to imagine what Cardinal Mundelein would have done to a group like the ACP. He would have disbanded it immediately and exiled its leaders to parishes in steel mill and coal-mining towns. Cody broke off all contact with the ACP after its censure vote, but he took no reprisals against individuals. As Father John Fahey, who later delivered the eulogy at Cody's funeral, once remarked: "This is a rough era to be in a position of authority in the Catholic Church."[18]

CODY CHANGES WITH THE TIMES

The archdiocese of Chicago seemed to have come full circle. Mundelein was sent to Chicago in 1915 to impose discipline on a fractious, unruly group of priests with a tradition of rebellion against their bishops.[19] He succeeded in disciplining them and instilling a remarkable esprit de corps. Yet, after the Second Vatican Council, Chicago's priests became restive and assertive again, unwilling to defer to authority unquestioningly. Even if John Patrick Cody were an exact clone of George William Mundelein, he still would have experienced difficulties with the clergy of Chicago. But he was not an exact clone of Mundelein. He compounded his difficulties with a secretive, obsessive style of management. Yet, in fairness to him, we must also admit that Cody did change with the times in some areas, advancing far beyond Mundelein on some important policy matters.

In 1970 Cardinal Cody laid aside one of the more visible tokens of triumphalism, Illinois license plate No. 1, which had traditionally been assigned to the archbishop of Chicago since Mundelein's day. Cody characterized the No. 1 plate as "ostentatious." Thereafter, the secretary of state of Illinois assigned the first license to the wife of the governor.[20]

More important, Cardinal Cody completely reorganized the major seminary, replacing the old rector, greatly liberalizing the rules, and reforming the curriculum. He enthusiastically promoted the ordination of married men to the permanent diaconate and thus created the largest corps of married clergy in the Roman church. He implemented the liturgical reforms of the Second Vatican Council and thoroughly renovated Holy Name Cathedral in the spirit of the new liturgy. Not content simply to turn the altar around, Cody's architects stripped away nearly all devotional pictures and graven images from the cathedral, leaving it starkly modern and bare, much like a Protestant church. Characteristically, the ACP complained about the $3 million cost of the cathedral renovation, avowing that the money might have been better spent on social action or charity. They did not, however, object when Cody deposited $12 million into the priests' pension account to compensate for unfunded liabilities.[21]

Cody's most strikingly progressive actions, however, came in the field of race relations. Cardinal Mundelein had been socially and politically liberal, openly supporting Franklin Roosevelt's New Deal, defending the rights of labor unions, and encouraging the activities of Bishop Bernard J. Sheil, Monsignor Reynold Hillenbrand, and many other social action pioneers. But Mundelein had a blind spot on race relations. He admitted early in his administration that he felt "quite powerless" to change racial segregation in his city, and he accordingly assigned all black Catholics to a handful of segregated parishes conducted by missionary priests. By employing missionaries to deal with the blacks, Mundelein succeeded in ignoring them.[22]

Cody had experienced the folly of a similar policy in his own archdiocese of Saint Louis, where archbishop Glennon was even more segregationist than Mundelein, and the scandal of racial exclusion in the Saint Louis Church delayed his election to the College of Cardinals until he was virtually on his deathbed.[23] Cody learned this lesson well and vigorously promoted desegregation of Catholic churches and schools in all the dioceses he headed. In New Orleans he had earned a national reputation for racial liberalism and personal courage in the cause of desegregation.

Cody was named coadjutor to New Orleans archbishop Joseph

Francis Rummel on August 14, 1961. The following spring, Rummel issued an order decreeing that all parochial grammar schools and high schools would be desegregated in September. It is unclear whether Rummel or Cody made the decision, but Cody took the blame for it as an "outside agitator." He also took the responsibility for implementing the decision; for the ailing, nearly blind Rummel, having excommunicated three archsegregationists, petitioned Rome to relieve him of authority. Cody was named apostolic administrator in June 1962; and in September of that year he courageously defied pickets and protests in pushing Catholic school desegregation to a successful, and largely peaceful, conclusion.[24]

Cody continued support for the civil rights movement in Chicago. He met privately with Martin Luther King, Jr., on February 2, 1966, to discuss King's upcoming northern city campaign; and at a July 10 mass rally in Soldier Field, he sent an auxiliary bishop to read what King's biographer has called a "surprisingly strong message of support." He participated personally in a "summit conference" with Mayor Daley and Dr. King to work out procedures for ensuring order on King's open housing marches in Chicago.[25]

Later in Cody's administration, Chicago priests criticized the cardinal for closing some inner city schools and consolidating black parishes. One priest even called Cody an "unconscious racist." This was the most unfair charge ever leveled at Cody. He may have been abrupt and undiplomatic in the way he proposed parish consolidation, but the work of consolidation needed to be done and has been carried on vigorously by his successor. Furthermore, Cody was not abandoning inner city parishes. Throughout his administration, he allocated approximately $3 million per year in subsidies to about fifty black and Hispanic parishes. In 1976, he also established a "twinning" or "sharing" program, whereby wealthy white parishes held monthly collections for a "sister parish" in the inner city.[26]

Significantly, when Cardinal Cody came under attack in 1981 from the *Chicago Sun-Times* for alleged improprieties and misuse of funds, the first group to openly defend him was the Black Catholic Clergy of Chicago. Black priests held a news conference at Holy Angels church on September 16, 1981, and Rev. George Clements announced that the group was grateful for the "spiritual and material support" the cardinal had given to black parishes. The black clergy sponsored a support rally for Cody on September 18 at the International Amphitheatre. Thousands of black schoolchildren cheered as Cody accepted a plaque at the rally.[27]

Cardinal Cody did not neglect the inner city. In fact, just the opposite was true—he neglected the suburbs. From the start of his administration in Chicago, he declared a moratorium on construction of suburban Catholic schools. A rational bureaucratic management would have gradually withdrawn resources from the inner city, which was no longer Catholic, and applied them to the increasingly Catholic suburbs. Cody did not do this; and, as a result, a whole generation of Catholic parishioners is growing up without Catholic schooling. This may well be the most permanent effect of Cody's stewardship in Chicago.[28]

AN INSECURE AUTOCRAT

Cardinals Mundelein and Cody shared a general style of leadership— Romanist, triumphalist, centralizing—but a closer analysis reveals that their management techniques and their choices of subordinates differed greatly. These differences in respect to process and people ultimately account for the great disparity in their reputations.

Mundelein was an authoritarian manager. He laid down the law to his clergy and enforced it vigorously. He made large plans and drove them forward single-mindedly. He always remained the boss, and he swiftly demoted anyone who failed to live up to his standards. Yet he was not an autocrat, for he never tried to do everything himself. Mundelein delegated authority extensively and chose his subordinates wisely. He not only permitted subordinates to take responsibility, he demanded it; he would not let them pass major decisions back to him. If his subordinates proved able and competent, they might go for months or even years without seeing him. He did not look over their shoulders.

Mundelein even tolerated divergent personalities and competitive management styles. For example, his auxiliary bishop and vicar general, Bernard J. Sheil, was constantly hatching new social action schemes before yesterday's plans were finalized, and he rarely counted costs or consequences. Mundelein gave Sheil his head, but he also hemmed him in with cautious, conservative priests such as Monsignor Robert Maguire, the chancellor. As long as Sheil and Maguire battled each other in private, he let them fight it out, hoping that somehow the result would be a plan both visionary and practical.[29]

Cody, on the other hand, hated to delegate authority and thus lose control, especially control over money. He insisted on signing all checks for more than two dollars, he read every piece of incoming and outgoing mail at the chancery office, and he personally sent birthday and anniversary cards to hundreds of priests and lay acquaintances. Journalists compared him to the insecure Captain Queeg in the novel *The Caine Mutiny*. Queeg was so obsessed with trying to figure out who stole the strawberries that he neglected his duty and never noticed the growing mutiny on his ship. So too, Cody immersed himself in trivial details, often letting more important matters pile up and ignoring the disaffection of his clergy.[30]

The subordinates with whom Cody surrounded himself tended to be yes-men, cronies, or soulless bureaucrats. He purchased diocesan insurance through a Saint Louis broker, David Dolan Wilson, who was the son of his stepcousin, the woman to whom he allegedly diverted large sums of money. His closest lay financial advisor, Francis O'Connor, was also a Saint Louis friend.[31] Even when these subordinates made the right decisions, the manner in which they acted lost respect for the archdiocese.

Cody's secretive, obsessive management is partly explained by his background. He had served in the delicate post of coadjutor bishop on three separate occasions, and he certainly must have observed how painful it was for the aging and infirm bishops whose authority he was taking over. Finally on his own in a major see, he probably wanted to ensure that no one ever took over from him. Hence his obsession with total control of detail. Ironically, his insecure, autocratic management techniques nearly produced the result he most feared.

The history of Cody's pet project, the Catholic Television Network of Chicago (CTN/C), aptly illustrates the various strands of his administrative style and how this style differed from Mundelein's. The concept of the Catholic Television Network, linking all the parishes of the Chicago archdiocese, was a brilliant idea, fully in accord with the Second Vatican Council's decree on modern communications. When Cody opened the four-channel, closed circuit network on February 3, 1975, it was not the first such Catholic media facility but clearly the largest and most ambitious.[32] The concept, then, was visionary, a proof of Cody's ability to move with the times.

Yet the way Cody executed the CTN/C plan was clearly old school. He announced the project to the Priests' Senate (a canonical consultative body mandated by Rome, not to be confused with the ad hoc ACP) in January 1974 as a fait accompli, without any request for consultation or advice. When priest senators questioned the $4 million investment in studio equipment, Cody replied: "Let me worry about the money, you just give it your blessing."[33] His response resembled a saying in the Vatican: *Roma locuta est, causa finita est* (Rome has spoken, the case is closed).

Furthermore, Cody made abysmal personnel choices to run CTN/C. Charles Hinds, the station manager, moved CTN/C away from its prime mission of religious programming and devoted most of the studio resources to production of TV commercials. Father James Moriarty, the priest-director at the station, failed to stop this deviation from the primary mission. Despite the growing commercialism,

CTN/C still required an annual subsidy averaging $1.2 million between 1975 and 1981. Finally, Cardinal Cody's successor, Joseph Bernardin, commissioned a consultant's study of CTN/C which concluded sharply: "Clearly, the original intentions concerning primary function have been lost along the way—actually, quite some time ago. The commercial production has become virtually an end in itself. And, apparently, not a profitable one, even in just a commercial sense, for the Archdiocese."[34]

It is interesting to speculate how Cardinal Mundelein might have managed CTN/C. Actually the cardinal contemplated the founding of a similar Catholic radio station in the 1920s, but he abandoned the idea "due to the flatness of our purse."[35] Mundelein rarely risked the church's money on projects that were peripheral to the church's primary mission of worship, education, and charity. Had he gone ahead and found the project straying from its religious purpose, he would have fired the lay manager (and possibly sued him) and exiled the priest director to North Chicago for life.

Four dusty red hats hang from the ceiling in the sanctuary of Holy Name Cathedral, fading pennants of past glory, like NBA championship banners in the Boston Garden. George Mundelein was the "First Cardinal of the West," the first American named a cardinal from a city west of the Appalachians; and each of his successors in turn has been nominated to the College of Cardinals. Yet John Patrick Cody's hat will be the last to hang in the cathedral, for Pope Paul VI terminated the custom as an unnecessary bit of triumphalism. Four hats—Mundelein's at the beginning, Cody's at the end—symbolize an era in church administration.

Neither Mundelein nor Cody was well loved by priests or people. Each was too aloof and authoritarian for that. Yet Mundelein was universally respected by priest and layman, Catholic and non-Catholic. His imperial style served an important purpose: it put the Catholic church on the map. When I was interviewing priests for my biography of Cardinal Mundelein in the mid-1970s, I found that most priests would rather gossip about their present archbishop, Cody, than reminisce about Mundelein. To my astonishment, I discovered that not a single priest I talked to—from the youngest "Young Turk" to the most elderly monsignor—expressed any respect for Cody.

I have a hunch why Cardinal Cody, at the end of an era, failed to win the respect of his clergy. He seems to have lost track of the distinction between ends and means. Mundelein, for all his authoritarianism and triumphal display, always used money and power as means to an end, the advancement of his church and its spiritual mission in America. Cardinal Cody, whose administration came along when the church was well established in Chicago, seems to have pursued power largely for its own sake. The former editor of *The Chicago Catholic*, A. E. P. Wall, has stated that he believes Cody was an agnostic, uninterested in God or religion but only in the material, institutional apparatus of the church.[36] This is an extreme, and unverifiable, assertion, but it points to a possible truth. Cody mistook the means that Cardinals Mundelein and Glennon had employed for ends in themselves.

Cardinal Cody manipulated the structure of power and authority that Cardinal Mundelein had painstakingly constructed forty years earlier. But the structure had become a hollow shell. An era had ended.

CHAPTER
13
Francis J. Spellman: American and Roman

Gerald P. Fogarty, S.J.

*F*rancis Joseph Spellman was born on May 4, 1889, in Whitman, Massachusetts, the first of five children of William and Ellen (Conway) Spellman. He was an American, not an Irishman, he insisted, for his parents, though of Irish ancestry, were both born in Massachusetts. But he was an American of a different stripe.

After graduating from Fordham College in New York in 1911, Spellman went to the North American College in Rome as a seminarian for the archdiocese of Boston. He earned his doctorate in theology from the Urban College of Propaganda and was ordained a priest on May 14, 1916. Study at the Urban College could be an important step in an ecclesiastical career if a student was ambitious, for the professors were predominantly Italian diocesan priests destined for service in the Curia. Spellman took advantage of this opportunity and cultivated his professors, especially Francesco Borgongini-Duca.[1] Although Spellman was intensely conscious of being American ever after, he also represented the zenith of the Romanization that had characterized the hierarchy from the turn of the century.[2] American and Roman were the attributes of his career as the most influential American Catholic prelate of his age. But in order to rise to prominence he had to overcome many obstacles, foremost among which was his ordinary in Boston, Cardinal William Henry O'Connell.

216

For reasons not altogether clear, Spellman and O'Connell developed a strong antagonism from the beginning. Spellman was also frequently at odds with the cardinal's nephew and chancellor, Monsignor James P. E. O'Connell, who had been secretly married since 1913 and was ordered dismissed from the priesthood in 1921.[3] As a young priest Spellman was given a series of temporary and insignificant assignments—two years in a parish, four years working to increase the circulation of the diocesan newspaper, *The Pilot*, two more years on the chancery staff, and then archivist for the archdiocese and part-time proofreader for *The Pilot*. But he kept up his Roman connections. In 1923, he translated into English two books by Borgongini-Duca. This drew him praise from Archbishop Giovanni Bonzano, the apostolic delegate to the United States hierarchy, and the recommendation of Borgongini-Duca that O'Connell name Spellman a monsignor. The cardinal bluntly replied that Spellman did "not yet have a position to be raised to the purple."[4] Spellman now sought to gain such a position.

In 1925, Spellman accompanied Boston pilgrims to Rome, nominally as the secretary to Bishop Joseph Anderson, the auxiliary of Boston. While there, he arranged to be appointed as director of the Knights of Columbus playgrounds in Rome, subject to the Extraordinary Affairs of the Vatican Secretariat of State. His diary records his growing friendship with a number of prominent people—Nicholas and Genevieve Brady, American Catholic millionaires residing in Rome; Enrico Galeazzi, a Vatican engineer; and especially Eugenio Pacelli. Late in 1929, Spellman recorded his delight that Pius XI had named Pacelli to succeed Cardinal Pietro Gasparri as Secretary of State.[5] Now Spellman began to receive a number of important assignments. In 1931, for example, Pius XI issued the encyclical *Non Abbiamo Bisogno,* condemning Fascism. Because the Fascists had suppressed the church press, Pacelli had Spellman smuggle the letter out of Italy to Paris where it was printed and distributed by the Associated Press and United Press.[6]

In 1932, Spellman was named auxiliary bishop of Boston—though O'Connell had not asked for an auxiliary. The appointment and consecration in Saint Peter's Basilica were rich in symbolism. Borgongini-Duca designed an original coat of arms for Spellman—the Santa Maria of Columbus on an azure field. Pius XI gave him his motto—*Sequere Deum.*[7] He was consecrated on September 8 by Cardinal Pacelli, assisted by Borgongini-Duca and Archbishop Giuseppe Pizzardo, another former professor. He wore the same vestments Pacelli had worn at his own consecration by Benedict XV. Romanization and Americanization had been wed.

Spellman's appointment as auxiliary of Boston was ironic. In 1906,

O'Connell had been named coadjutor archbishop of Boston, though his name had not been on any *terna*. He owed his rise to his close friendship with Cardinal Raffaele Merry del Val, secretary of state to Pius X. Now he was receiving an auxiliary bishop, though certainly not the one he would have chosen. Before leaving Rome, Spellman received assurances from Pius XI that he would probably succeed O'Connell.[8] As soon as the appointment was announced, however, he reported, in telegraphic style, "[O'Connell has] issued long statement to papers minimizing my honors. If I am asked to comment I shall say Cardinal perfectly right."[9] "But," he added later, "we are starting in fine."[10] On September 27, Spellman boarded the *Rex* in Genoa for the voyage to Boston. While still at sea, he received a curt telegram: "Welcome to Boston. Confirmations begin on Monday. You are expected to be ready. Cardinal O'Connell."[11] The reception in Boston was colder still. "Mass at cathedral," Spellman noted, "Cardinal not here to receive me. Mons. Burke gave me my instructions, said I was to live in Seminary."[12] It was the beginning of a seven-year ordeal that was well known to his fellow bishops.

In December 1932, Archbishop John T. McNicholas, O.P., of Cincinnati wrote Pizzardo that Spellman seemed "happy despite the unnecessary trials to which he has been subjected since his return. I am sure his love for the Church and his devotion to the Holy See will make even his present uncongenial surroundings profitable to him."[13] Within a few years, McNicholas's words would be filled with a certain irony when both he and Spellman were candidates for the archdiocese of New York.

Spellman remained without assignment and continued living in the seminary. In March 1933, he received word that Pius XI intended to name him coadjutor archbishop with right of succession. He subsequently learned, however, that Cardinal Pietro Fumasoni-Biondi, former apostolic delegate to the American hierarchy, opposed the appointment, lest O'Connell think him responsible.[14] In the meantime, Spellman had decided to demand a parish, Sacred Heart in Roslindale, which had been recently vacated.[15] Again, he was thwarted. On April 6, he received a letter from Cardinal O'Connell appointing him pastor of Sacred Heart in Newton Center, Massachusetts. It was "couched in peremptory tones," said Spellman, but, "I replied frankly accepting it but saying I would prefer to remain where I am if I couldn't get Roslindale."[16] O'Connell had made sure to specify that Spellman was to be a "Removable Parish Priest."[17]

Spellman was to remain in Newton Center for the next six years, while the tension with the cardinal grew. In the fall of 1933, O'Connell was summoned to Rome to discuss the situation.[18] He described his audience with Pius XI as "the best . . . he had had with anyone of the four popes he knew." This seemed "to be excessive," thought Spellman, "but we shall see."[19] Still, there was no noticeable change in the cardinal's attitude toward his auxiliary.

Spellman handled the difficult situation by being as deferential and independent as possible. His diary became his confidant for recording his relations with the cardinal. On one occasion, he recalled, the "Cardinal spoke to us and his most striking phrase was that even if a Bishop bought a bishopric he is still a bishop. And he might have added the same truth applies to a Cardinal."[20] The strain between them was open. In November 1934, Spellman attended his first meeting of the American hierarchy. O'Connell presided at the morning session. "I met him for the first time in months," Spellman wrote, "& kissed his ring before everybody."[21]

Under O'Connell's repressive regime, Spellman's only solace was maintaining his Roman friendships and building new ones with Americans. He sprinkled his diary with references to letters received from Pacelli and other Roman prelates. He also recounted his growing friendship with Joseph P. Kennedy, through whom he came to know James Roosevelt and later the president himself. He was gaining national prominence, and he gained even more as a result of his role in the visit of Cardinal Pacelli to the United States.

Early in August 1936, his longtime acquaintance Mrs. Brady telephoned Spellman from Paris that Cardinal Pacelli was coming to America as her personal guest. Spellman wanted to make sure the cardinal's trip was not a mere vacation—but his maneuvers destroyed his friendship with Mrs. Brady. He wrote several letters to Rome and gained Galeazzi's assurance that "my suggestions are being followed."[22] Just what these suggestions were, he did not record, but they may have pertained to Charles Coughlin, the popular radio priest in Royal Oak, Michigan, who was then challenging the Roosevelt administration. Spellman had already told Archbishop Amleto Cicognani, the apostolic delegate, of "President Roosevelt's displeasure with Father Coughlin."[23] On September 27, he met with Cicognani, who said he could do nothing about Coughlin. Spellman thought Cicognani "could at least rebuke [Bishop Michael J.] Gallagher [of Detroit] or demand that he keep Coughlin in Detroit." "I think that he is weak and frightened," he continued, "and being sure that he is suspicious and too cautious I did not tell him of Cardinal Pacelli's visit."[24] Though he kept Cicognani ignorant of the visit, he made sure to tell Roosevelt about it the next day at a meeting at Hyde Park, where they also discussed Coughlin.[25] By the end of September, Pacelli's visit was public knowledge.

For Spellman this visit would be an emotionally trying time. While Pacelli's ship was still out at sea, Spellman made a radio telephone call to him and then dispatched a letter to Galeazzi warning him "of the dangers of following the Duchess [Brady] to [sic] closely & ignoring the Cardinals."[26] Somehow, his memorandum of the telephone call and his letter to Galeazzi seemed to have fallen into Mrs. Brady's hands. On October 8, when Spellman joined Cicognani, Cardinal Patrick Hayes of New York, and Mrs. Brady to meet Pacelli's ship at quarantine, Mrs. Brady attacked Spellman, "aided and abetted by Cardinal Hayes and Apostolic Delegate."[27] Bad feelings persisted. The next day, he went to Hayes and Cicognani "to ask my lost memorandum card back. Both denied having it or knowing anything about it." Sometime later, he added: "They are both liars & so is Mons. [James Francis] McIntyre [Chancellor of the Archdiocese of New York]"[28] Spellman's introduction to the New York ecclesiastical scene was most inauspicious.

Despite the tension accompanying Pacelli's arrival, Spellman triumphantly escorted him to his parish in Newton Center and then traveled with him on a trip that took them from New York to Philadelphia, Baltimore, and Washington, and then by chartered plane to Cleveland, South Bend, Chicago, Saint Paul, San Francisco, Los Angeles, Saint Louis, and Cincinnati.[29] Both gained national exposure, and Spellman took pains to show the cardinal his influence in the American church. And the best was yet to come—a meeting with the president.

One of the purposes of Pacelli's visit was to establish more direct contact between the United States and the Holy See; indeed, a year earlier Joseph Kennedy had expressed optimism that Roosevelt would pave the way for such contact. Cicognani was kept ignorant of these negotiations[30]; as soon as Pacelli's visit became public knowledge, Cicognani was instructed through conventional channels to arrange a meeting between the cardinal and the president. For this purpose he enlisted the aid of Father John Burke, C.S.P., secretary general of the National Catholic Welfare Conference. Burke had just about completed the arrangements for a meeting at the White House when Cicognani learned, to his considerable annoyance, that Spellman had already arranged for Pacelli to meet Roosevelt at Hyde Park.[31] The meeting was to take place on November 5, two days after Roosevelt won election to his second term of office. Spellman seemed at last to realize he had upstaged the pope's official representative to the hierarchy and, at the last moment, tried unsuccessfully to have Cicognani invited to the meeting.[32] Yet Cicognani may not have missed very much after all. When news of the meeting became public, the press speculated that diplomatic relations would be on the agenda, but Spellman, who was present for the meeting, recorded nothing in his diary.

For several months after the Roosevelt-Pacelli meeting, Spellman reported several additional overtures on diplomatic relations. Roosevelt, however, undertook a different initiative with Cardinal George Mundelein of Chicago, long a supporter of his New Deal. At a luncheon at the cardinal's residence in Chicago in October 1937, Roosevelt expressed his "intention," as Mundelein told Cicognani, "to send a special envoy to the Vatican."[33]

Spellman, in the meantime, seemed to be unaware of Mundelein's involvement and continued to keep Pacelli informed of his own negotiations, principally through James Roosevelt. He apparently implied that diplomatic relations were imminent, for in November, Pacelli responded: the Holy See always required [that its nuncio] be recognized as the Dean of diplomats of the same grade." The practical procedure to arrive at the establishment is simple," he went on. "It would be enough that the Government express a desire so that everything can be easily prepared."[34] For several more months, Spellman proceeded to keep Pacelli abreast of his discussions and the headway he thought he was making with the president.[35] Early in 1938, however, his overtures on diplomatic relations became intertwined with an event that directly influenced his career.

On September 4, 1938, Cardinal Hayes of New York died. Spellman knew that he was a candidate for the important see. "The battle is certainly starting soon," he wrote, "but with all the opposition I believe it is impossible."[36] On September 9, he attended Hayes's funeral, at which Mundelein presided. Afterward, he conferred with the cardinal about both his candidacy for the archdiocese of New York and diplomatic relations.[37] In October, he attended the annual bishops' meeting in Washington and then dined with Roosevelt. Next, he attended the Eucharistic Congress in New Orleans where Mundelein presided as legate. Spellman journeyed to New York to see Cicognani off on his way to Rome to report on the congress. Mundelein himself had delayed a day to stay the night at the White House. Because Cicognani monopolized most of Mundelein's time, Spellman had only a five-minute conversation with the cardinal. As the ship set sail, Spellman reflected: "It was funny, the Delegate, Bishop [Stephen] Donahue and I standing on the dock. The Cardinal must have laughed as he looked at us."[38]

Just what Mundelein thought about Spellman's candidacy remains uncertain; Galeazzi reported that he displayed a "good disposition."[39] But Mundelein was later known to have favored the transfer of Archbishop Joseph Rummel to New York. Filippo Bernardini, former professor of canon law at the Catholic University and then nuncio to Switzerland, expressed amazement to Cardinal Dennis Dougherty of Philadelphia that "a man of 'sound mind' " such as Mundelein could possibly think of recommending Rummel, a German-born prelate, for New York as the world moved toward war.[40] For Dougherty, such a choice was dangerous in light of Germany's ambitions, and his answer was simple: "Deutschland über alles."[41] Indeed, Rummel's German birth may have been sufficient reason to prevent his appointment. But there were other candidates for New York.

Bishop Donahue, the administrator of the archdiocese, remained the favorite local candidate. Archbishop Edward Mooney of Detroit was also mentioned. But the strongest contender was Archbishop John T. McNicholas, O.P., of Cincinnati. Late in November, Spellman heard that the archbishop was "cleaning his desk preparing to go to N.Y. as Archbishop."[42] McNicholas had, in fact, received unofficial word of his appointment from friends in Rome and confided the information to his secretary, Clarence Issenmann.[43] But other events were to intervene.

On February 10, 1939, Pius XI died. On the third ballot at the conclave, the cardinals elected Eugenio Pacelli, who took the name Pius XII. If other American prelates owed their rise to their friendship with Roman patrons, Spellman now had the most powerful of them all. For the new pope, it was also imperative that the archbishop of New York be on good terms with the president of the United States, and Pacelli knew McNicholas was not.[44] Still, Pius XII delayed making the appointment. Early in April, Spellman, perhaps alluding to O'Connell, Mundelein, and Dougherty, noted "that three cardinals are against me going to New York." He added, "That is one reason why I should think I might go."[45] O'Connell, just back from the conclave, told him: "The Holy Father asked for you and asked if you were cooperating with me." Spellman said he did "not understand the query and consider[ed] it superfluous."[46] Finally, on April 12, he received word from Cicognani that he had been appointed archbishop of New York. He intended to fly to Washington from which he would cable Rome: "Father, if it be possible, let this chalice pass from me." But inclement weather canceled the flight, so he cabled Cicognani his acceptance.[47]

Only on April 24 did the Holy See publicly announce Spellman's appointment. The first person he notified outside his family was Roosevelt. Then he went to see Cardinal O'Connell. "It was quite an interview," he recalled.

> He was very nice. Of course he knew the past and also the immediate past and I knew the past and also the immediate past. I gave out a statement which was well received. . . . He gave out a statement to the newspaper men speaking better of me than I had ever heard him speak of anyone in my life. It was quite a contrast to the statement issued when I was made a bishop six years ago.[48]

Before leaving Boston, Spellman had one further interview with his former ordinary. It was a "pleasant cordial visit," he noted. "He advised me not to be "so humble." "That doesn't get you anywhere." I said to myself "O, Yes!" He advised me to make some changes in the personell [*sic*] of those about me. I am satisfied so why make changes.[49]"

O'Connell was not alone in suggesting that Spellman make some changes in the archdiocesan staff. Cicognani had recommended reassignments in the seminary adminstration and in the chancery office.[50] Among these administrators was the chancellor of the archdiocese, Monsignor McIntyre, with whom Spellman had developed friction during Pacelli's visit in 1936. It was apparently McIntyre who traveled to Newton Center soon after Spellman's appointment to offer his resignation. "Retaliation," Spellman responded, "is a luxury I have never been able to afford."[51] But Spellman could distinguish between personal feelings and respect for professional competence, and soon made McIntyre his auxiliary bishop.

On May 23, 1939, Spellman was officially installed as the archbishop of New York, with Bishop Donahue as the celebrant of the mass. He had been given ten tasks to accomplish. Several pertained to the finances both of the archdiocese and of other institutions. But one task in particular illustrated that, while he gave the impression of being an efficient and aloof administrator, he could also display great pastoral sensitivity. This was the approach he took to the restoration to the active ministry of Bishop Bonaventure Broderick.

American born Bishop Broderick was named auxiliary bishop of Havana after the Spanish-American War. In 1905, he was appointed collector of the Peter's Pence collection for the United States through his friendship with Cardinal Raffaele Merry de Val. Cardinal James Gibbons of Baltimore, however, his credentials revoked. Without means of support, except for a pension from the Archdiocese of Havana, Broderick moved to Millbrook, New York, where he purchased a farm and later operated a gasoline station. In 1933, Cicognani had been told to work on his restoration, but it was Spellman who succeeded. In September 1939, Spellman arranged to pay a visit to Millbrook and then have the pastor quietly drop him off at the bishop's residence. In a moving letter to Cicognani, Spellman recounted his offer of assistance to the old man. Within a few days, Broderick wrote on stationery bearing his episcopal coat of arms to accept Spellman's offer. In December, he was named the chaplain of the Frances Schervier Hospital in New York city.[52]

Spellman, meanwhile, was still working on diplomatic relations between the United States and the Holy See. Roosevelt had already made the unprecedented gesture of sending Joseph P. Kennedy, then ambassador to the Court of Saint James, as his personal representative to the coronation of Pius XII. The president's ally in the church had up to this time been his friend Cardinal Mundelein, but Mundelein's unexpected death on October 2, 1939, closed that avenue of diplomacy. Spellman was now the American prelate with whom Roosevelt would have to deal and he lost no time in taking the initiative.

The State Department was already urging Roosevelt to establish a diplomatic mission at the Holy See. Roosevelt, however, preferred a more limited "special mission" to the Vatican to coordinate efforts to care for refugees. On October 24, he discussed this matter with Spellman at the White House. The next day, through Cicognani, Spellman informed Cardinal Luigi Maglione, the secretary of state, that Roosevelt intended to establish a special mission to aid refugees while Congress was adjourned between November 3 and January 5. Such a mission would not require congressional appropriations, he explained, and the president had already suggested appointing either Myron C. Taylor, former chairman of the United States Steel Corporation, or Breckinridge Long, former ambassador to Italy, as his emissary. When the response came on November 28, however, it was not to his liking. Cicognani wrote: "The Holy Father has learned of the report with pleasure and hopes that Your Excellency as well as I will make opportune overtures to the President, that he may carry out his proposal."[53] In short, Cicognani was implying that he and Spellman *jointly* take the initiative with Roosevelt.

Spellman took matters into his own hands. He immediately wrote to Roosevelt requesting another meeting with him. He then completely revised Cicognani's original letter to him. His revision focused on Pius XII's enthusiasm and claimed that the Pope had left to Spellman alone the initiative of dealing with the president. It stated: "The Holy Father received with great satisfaction the information that the President desires to appoint a mission to the Holy See to assist in the solution of the refugee problem and to treat other matters of mutual interest." The pope was now reported to have been "particularly pleased to know that the President has the intention of establishing this mission soon after the adjournment of Congress and before January 5, 1940." Spellman was to convey to the president the pope's "expression of deepest appreciation . . . and to say that he believes and prays that the resumption of relations between the United States and the Holy See will be most propitious, especially at the present time."[54] Spellman's version made it clear to Roosevelt that the pope thought this "special mission" was but a step toward full diplomatic relations. Above all, Spellman alone was to approach the president.

On December 7, Spellman left for Washington. First, he successfully gained Cicognani's signature for the letter. Then he went to the White House. "The President was wonderful to me," he recorded.

> Luncheon lasted 1 hour and a half and he agreed to recognize Vatican and send either Myron Taylor or Harry Woodring as Ambassador. He agreed to make announcement himself at Xmas as my letter from the Delegate which I left with President was sufficient to give official assent of the Holy See. It was a wonderful day.[55]

Whether Spellman wished again to upstage Cicognani or wanted to prod Roosevelt into action after four years of discussion by giving a clear sign that the Holy See would accept a "special mission," his tactic was successful. On December 24, 1939, Roosevelt announced that he was appointing Myron C. Taylor as his "personal representative" to Pope Pius XII.[56]

At the end of 1939, Spellman was also named the vicar for the armed forces of the United States. He immediately had Father John O'Hara, C.S.C., president of the University of Notre Dame, appointed as his auxiliary bishop for the vicariate. His dual role as Archbishop of New York and military vicar launched him into national and international prominence. Moreover, he further sought to ingratiate himself with Roosevelt. One opportunity presented itself with the transfer in December, 1939, of Archbishop Samuel Stritch from Milwaukee to Chicago as Mundelein's successor.

Roosevelt had made no secret that he would like to have seen Bishop Bernard Shiel, Mundelein's auxiliary, succeed to Chicago. He had, moreover, heard that Stritch supported Coughlin and was unsympathetic with the New Deal. The president originally had requested that Myron Taylor, his representative in Rome, discuss Stritch with Pius XII, but then he decided to approach Spellman about the matter. Early in 1940, Spellman phoned Stritch and then wrote him about his problematic attitude toward Roosevelt's policies. Stritch replied in writing, denying the accusations and declaring his support for the president's general policies. To inform the Vatican of the president's reservations and Stritch's response to those reservations, Spellman forwarded a copy of Stritch's letter to Galeazzi. In what may have been a breach of confidentiality, he sent the original letter to Stritch to Roosevelt, who was, in any case, assuaged.[57]

Spellman's first year in office had been successful, but the specter of the harsh Boston years came back to haunt him. On March 12, 1940, he was to receive the pallium and thereby become fully invested with authority as metropolitan of New York. Cardinal O'Connell, perhaps in a sign of reconciliation, had agreed to impose tha pallium on him, but Cardinal Dougherty had declined an invitation. Four days before the ceremony, however, O'Connell excused himself because of a sore throat. Spellman then had to phone Dougherty and persuade him to preside at the ceremony.[58]

Despite O'Connell's final insult, Spellman's stock continued to rise. In May 1941, he wrote Pius XII that, if the archbishop of Lima cooperated in reducing his New York debts, "the good Lord will have helped me to have solved all of the ten major problems that the Delegate told me existed in New York prior to my coming, problems— some of them of many years standing." He told Pius of his election to the administrative board of the National Catholic Welfare Conference, where he found, even when he disagreed, "Thus far the other Bishops have accepted my viewpoint." He did not mention to the pontiff that Mooney, Stritch, and McNicholas were the dominant figures in the NCWC. Instead, he deftly singled out for praise the bishops he himself had chosen. O'Hara was "a most extraordinary man," while McIntyre was "invaluable to me" and "a devoted exemplary priest and one of the ablest bishops of the U.S."—the latter so valuable that Spellman recommended him as his successor. He also had strong praise for Richard J. Cushing, who had succeeded him, with his strong recommendation, as auxiliary of Boston.[59]

As the United States moved toward war, Spellman became the personification of Romanization and Americanization. As early as the summer of 1940, a Fascist journal attacked him as the "agent of Jews in America" and the financial supporter of the Holy See's anti-Fascist attitude.[60] During the war, he closely identified Catholicism and American patriotism. His poem "The Risen Soldier," for instance, made a dying American soldier a Christian martyr.[61] He now had even more frequent contact with Roosevelt.

After Roosevelt met at Casablanca with Winston Churchill and General Charles de Gaulle in January 1943, Spellman gained Roosevelt's permission to make the first of what later became annual visits to American troops overseas. The president asked him to confer with him at the White House before departing. On February 4 they met, and Roosevelt placed at Spellman's disposal all the resources of the armed forces he might require. Two days later, Maglione requested that Spellman also visit the Vatican. With White House approval of this additional journey, Spellman was now to travel through enemy territory.[62]

The reason for the United States government's cooperation with this unusual venture soon became evident. On February 12, Spellman arrived in Madrid and had an audience with Franco to explain American intentions in the war. As Spellman informed Roosevelt, he believed the only pro-Axis feeling remaining in Spain was due to fear of communism. He sought to assuage this by noting that Stalin had

signed the Atlantic Charter and had stated that Russia had no desires
"to possess any non-Russian territory or to impose its form of government on any nation."[63] To keep the Fascist-leaning Franco neutral,
nothing could have been more useful to Roosevelt than to have as his
emissary a Catholic archbishop and one who also enjoyed the confidence of the Vatican.

On February 20, Spellman arrived in Rome and remained until
March 4, but neither to his diary nor to his authorized biographer
did he confide what he discussed or with whom he met.[64] Other
sources indicate that he probably met with several Italian government
dignitaries. Even to Roosevelt, Spellman did not reveal the content
of his conversations with Pius XII other than to convey the pontiff's
greetings and deep appreciation for Myron Taylor. He did, however,
report on the strong anti-German sentiment of the Italian people who,
he thought, were looking forward to an American liberation and would
immediately make peace, were it not for Mussolini and the danger
of the Germans bombing Rome.[65]

Leaving Rome, Spellman visited North Africa, the Middle East,
and the Holy Land. He interrupted his schedule to fly to London to
attend the funeral of Cardinal Arthur Hinsley, archbishop of Westminister—and to be the guest of the Churchills for lunch. In Egypt,
he intervened to gain the release of Italian priests and religious who
had been interned by the British. In Istanbul on May 14, he met for
the first time Archbishop Angelo Roncalli, then the apostolic delegate
to Turkey and later Pope John XXIII, who reported that the reputation
of the Holy See was enhanced because the highly regarded Archbishop
Spellman had stayed with him. Spellman was then scheduled to go
to the Far East and meet with Chiang Kai-shek, but he was forced to
return immediately to New York. The Allies bombed Rome on July
19.[66] With this first of two bombings of Rome, the issue of declaring
Rome an open city would strain relations between Roosevelt and
Spellman.

Spellman arrived back in Washington on August 1. Some journalists speculated that he had some role in an attempt to overthrow
Mussolini.[67] But he and other members of the hierarchy were now
walking a thin line between wanting to carry out the Holy See's wishes
to prevent any further bombing of Rome and wishing not to appear
unpatriotic or critical of Roosevelt's policy. He waited a full month
before seeing Roosevelt.

On September 2, Roosevelt asked Spellman to meet him and
Churchill at the White House. The military situation was changing
rapidly, as first Italy surrendered to the Allies and then German troops
occupied Rome. The Eternal City was now a military target. On September 15, Spellman was again at the White House together with

Mooney and Stritch. They urged Roosevelt to declare Rome an open city. He agreed to establish a twenty-mile free zone around Rome, provided the Germans respected it. "It will be O.K," recorded Spellman, "if he keeps his promise. I am glad the three of us went."[68]

For the next few months, the Holy See relied upon Spellman to have Roosevelt keep his promise. But relations between the president and the hierarchy, already strained, were further strained by four bombing raids on the papal villa at Castel Gandolfo between February and June 1944. After the second bombing, Spellman wrote Roosevelt a strong letter of protest. The villa, he said, contained no German soldiers, but only "helpless and homeless people." In view of this situation, he announced that he felt compelled to make a public statement.[69] As the occasion for his public protest, Spellman chose the annual memorial mass for the Knights of Columbus at Saint Patrick's Cathedral on George Washington's Birthday. Deploring the American attack on "the territory of a neutral state," he prayed "that, as Britain once spared the Holy City of Mecca, military ingenuity will overcome 'military necessity,' which would destroy the Eternal City of Rome, the citadel of civilization."[70] This was strong criticism from an archbishop who had long regarded himself as such a close friend of the president.

The bombing of Rome ceased to be an issue on June 4, 1944, when Allied troops entered the city. Pius XII again sent for Spellman. Before departing for Rome, Spellman gained Roosevelt's promise not to use the city as a military base.[71] On July 28, Spellman had the first of several audiences with the pope. He also met with officials of the United States government, the Italian government, and the Vatican. But his description of the pope was perplexing; on August 4, he noted, the pontiff "wept" during their audience.[72]

On August 14, Spellman left Rome to begin visiting American troops, only to be summoned back to Rome five days later. On August 20, he found Pius XII "restless and nervous." The next day, the pope was still "nervous," and, Spellman added, "He doesn't want me to go away."[73] One reason for the pope's nervousness was the deteriorating health of Cardinal Luigi Maglione, his secretary of state, who died on August 22. On August 26, Spellman again left Rome to visit the troops in England, France, and North Africa. A month later, he was back in Rome. Cushing, he noted, had just become archbishop of Boston to succeed O'Connell, who had died in April. But Spellman learned that the pope also had plans for him. "I was asked today," he recorded on September 28, "about the position of Secretary of State. I said I was indifferent, that I would leave New York, family or anything else if the Holy Father thought I could serve in any place for the Church."[74] For the next year, the State Department received reports that G.B. Montini had assured Bernardini that Spellman would be the new secretary of state, unless he himself declined the office.[75] This possibility, however, was never to be realized.

World War II had made Spellman well known to a host of American and foreign political, military, and ecclesiastical leaders. On April 12, 1945, however, Roosevelt died, and Spellman never developed quite the same close relationship with the new president, Harry S. Truman. In May, Germany surrendered to the Allies, and on August 7, the United States ushered in the age of nuclear war by dropping the first atomic bomb on Hiroshima. The next day, Spellman received a request from Henry Luce, president of Time-Life, Inc., and Joseph Kennedy "to ask if I would ask President Truman for 5 or 6 day truce to give Japan 'a chance to surrender.' "[76] Why Luce and Kennedy thought Spellman had such influence with Truman is unclear. If he did act on their request, he was unsuccessful, for on August 9, the United States dropped a second atomic bomb on Nagasaki, and Japan sued for terms of surrender. Spellman was in the White House when Truman formally accepted the terms. He described the scene:

> John L. Sullivan accompanied me to President Truman. It was an historical meeting. Secretary of State [James] Byrnes came in with document to be sent to Japan accepting Proviso to retain Emperor & President read it to me. Saw Secretary [James] For[r]estal [Secretary of the Navy] and [Robert] Hannegan [Postmaster General]. James Byrnes very nice to me too and Leo Crowley.[77]

The war was over at last. Thereafter, Spellman's influence with some of the leaders of postwar United States was enhanced by his elevation to the college of cardinals. On February 18, 1946, Pius XII held his first consistory, delayed as a sign of mourning because of the war. In addition to Spellman, three Americans received the red hat: Mooney of Detroit, Stritch of Chicago, and John J. Glennon of Saint Louis, who, however, died before returning to the United States. Of the three American cardinals in office when Spellman became archbishop of New York, only Dougherty of Philadelphia still lived. In the coming years, Spellman was frequently seen as the most powerful American prelate, but, in fact, he never came to dominate the American hierarchy.

Spellman had mentioned to Pius XII in 1941 that he had been elected to the administrative board of the National Catholic Welfare Conference. The inner circle of the NCWC, however, was composed of Mooney, Stritch, and McNicholas, each of whom alternated the chairmanship every year from 1937 to 1950. Each of them had reason to resent Spellman's power and quite consciously to resist it by forming the "Hindenburg line," as they called their attempt to prevent the extension of his influence beyond the East.[78] Only once did he manage to cross the line. In 1947, McIntyre, who a year earlier had become coadjutor archbishop of New York without right of succession, became the second archbishop of Los Angeles.

In the East, however, Spellman dominated. In the spring of 1947, Galeazzi urged him always to write to the pope as well as the delegate about episcopal nominations. "Try to do so for Baltimore," he counseled, "it is too important, and whenever you have some specific elements for an appointment your friend here [Pius XII] should be supplied with all reasons, and considerations in regard to your proposals, so that he might with full conscience give instructions against possible different advices from Biltmore [the code name for the apostolic delegation, taken from its former address]."[79] Spellman needed little such encouragement. Although it is difficult to determine his role in the appointment of Francis P. Keough as archbishop of Baltimore, the new archbishop of the nation's oldest see was no threat to his influence. For the see of Washington, formally separated from the administration of the archbishop of Baltimore in 1947, Spellman's director of Catholic Charities, Patrick A. O'Boyle, was named the first archbishop. In 1951, O'Hara, who had become bishop of Buffalo in 1945, succeeded Dougherty in Philadelphia. Thus Spellman was responsible for reshaping the American hierarchy in the East, at least in the 1950s.[80]

While Spellman had his opponents among the bishops, especially in the Midwest, he continued to be the most prominent spokesman on several postwar issues. His wartime patriotism was superseded by his cold war anticommunism. In 1949, he publicly accused the leaders of the union of grave-diggers in Catholic cemeteries of being associated with communists, because the union was affiliated with the CIO. After the grave-diggers had been on strike for six weeks, he brought in seminarians to dig graves. The issue ended only when the union voted to sever its relationship with the CIO and join the AFL.[81] His anticommunism also led him to embrace the controversial Senator Joseph R. McCarthy.[82]

Spellman also made himself the champion in a campaign against a more traditional foe—the anti-Catholicism that emerged in the postwar years. In 1949, he entered the lists against Eleanor Roosevelt, who had written a column in favor of a bill pending in the House of Representatives that prohibited aid to parochial schools. Spellman publicly accused her of anti-Catholicism and of "discrimination unworthy of an American mother." The well-publicized controversy ended only when he paid Mrs. Roosevelt a visit at Hyde Park.[83]

Anti-Catholicism also provided part of the context ending Spellman's "special mission" to the pope. In January 1950, Myron Taylor resigned as Truman's personal representative to Pius XII, but the United States did not formally notify the pope that the mission was abolished. Spellman, nevertheless, continued to work for the establishment of diplomatic relations. In the fall of 1950, Truman nominated as "ambassador to the Vatican" General Mark Clark, who had no chance of gaining approval of the Senate Foreign Relations Committee. After Clark voluntarily withdrew his name, Truman made no new nomination. In 1953, Spellman reported to Pius XII that Senate opposition made impossible the confirmation of any ambassador. This report drew from G. B. Montini, Pius XII's substitute secretary of state, the strong criticism that

> "the Holy See cannot remain indifferent to the unreasonable and unreasoning attitude of non-Catholics in the United States. In connection with this matter of diplomatic relations and on other occasions in the recent past, there have been repeated, vulgar, bitter and entirely unjustified attacks against the Holy See, with unwarranted deductions and unmerited conclusions that are scarcely compatible with the 'freedom' of which the United States claims to be the champion and guardian.

He concluded with the rebuke:

> I cannot conceal it from Your Eminence that it is felt here that such attacks on the part of non-Catholics did not arouse an adequate reaction on the part of the Catholic community in the United States, that neither orally nor in the press has there been a sufficient response or any particularly authoritative voice raised in defence of the Holy See.[84]

Spellman expressed "surprise and pain" that Montini thought the American church had not responded adequately to anti-Catholic attacks. He had kept the Vatican informed of American Catholic efforts in this regard by sending clippings and news accounts, he wrote, but he now enclosed a packet of documents "to save your Excellency from any inconvenience in locating them in the Vatican archives." He reminded Montini of the role he and the American hierarchy had played in mobilizing Italian-Americans to write their relatives in Italy to vote against the communist party. He felt a particular "poignancy of grief" at the charge because "the Hierarchy, the clergy and the faithful of the United States are second to the people of no country in the world, I repeat, of no country in the world, in their devotion to the Vicar of Christ."

As evidence for this devotion, he asserted that "more precious" than the $200 million in money and supplies distributed through the Catholic War Relief Services during the previous ten years were "the numbers of religious men and women from the United States who are leaving their homeland to bring the Gospel of Christ to the pagan world, and even to countries assumed to be almost entirely Catholic."[85]

Across the top of his copy of the letter, Spellman wrote that he never received any reply. His sharp exchange with Montini, however, must be seen in the context of a series of letters in which the Vatican was asking Spellman to do something to counter the charges leveled by Paul Blanshard that Catholicism was incompatible with American democracy. This letter marked the end of Spellman's attempts to promote diplomatic relations. In an interview in 1959, John F. Kennedy, then a presidential candidate, said he was opposed to diplomatic relations with the Vatican, because their establishment would create such divisiveness as to undermine the effectiveness of any ambassador to the Holy See—a position he reiterated in his speech to the Houston Ministerial Association during his campaign in 1960. Although Spellman was no longer actively engaged in pursuing diplomatic relations, he nevertheless gained from one of Kennedy's associates an explanation for his opposition to the cause that Kennedy's father had promoted since 1935.[86]

The year 1958 was a year of transition for Spellman. In October his patron, Pius XII, died. Spellman attended the conclave that elected John XXIII, Angelo Roncalli, whom he had met in Istanbul during the war years. The previous May, Cardinal Stritch had died in Rome, and on October 25, Cardinal Mooney also died in Rome, just before the conclave. Spellman was now the senior cardinal in the American Church—a position that gave him the right to preside over meetings of the bishops, the position that Cardinal O'Connell had held for twenty-three years. The position became yet more important in December, when John XXIII named Cicognani, apostolic delegate to the American hierarchy since 1933, a cardinal. Though Spellman had frequently acted like a quasi-delegate since his days as auxiliary bishop of Boston, he had gradually worked out a modus vivendi with Cicognani. The new delegate, however, was Archbishop Egidio Vagnozzi, with whom Spellman was not on good terms. It was ironic that, though Spellman was a theological conservative, he would take a liberal stance on a number of issues at Vatican II in part because Vagnozzi opposed them.

On ecumenism, Spellman took a pragmatic approach, based as much on friendship as on theology. On Christmas Day, 1959, when he was visiting American troops in Turkey, he accepted an invitation to meet Patriarch Athenagoras, former metropolitan of New York. Immediately afterward, he flew to Rome to meet with John XXIII and other Vatican officials to present the patriarch's "views to His Holiness and see if some reunion were possible."[87] He found the pope most open, but Cardinal Domenico Tardini, then the secretary of state, less than enthusiastic. Tardini altered Spellman's draft of a letter to Athenagoras and insisted that the cardinal send it out himself from New York. No meeting was to take place between the patriarch and John XXIII. Four years later, after Paul VI had met with Athenagoras in Jerusalem, Spellman recounted his earlier role to Vagnozzi. Because of Tardini's deletion of "a few sentences from my letter," he wrote, "I must say the letter as expurgated was not as cordial as I would like and was not conclusive."[88] Precisely what Tardini deleted is not known, but Spellman seemed clearly to believe that a meeting between the pope and patriarch could have occurred earlier.

Spellman had remained aloof from the theological debates on religious liberty and the biblical question that had divided the American Catholic theologians in the 1950s. Here was where Vagnozzi's opposition proved to be a disguised blessing for the American church. In 1960, Vagnozzi asked Spellman to withdraw his imprimatur from the Bible Pamphlet Series, published by the Paulist Press, because it did not agree with his perception of legitimate biblical scholarship. Spellman summoned the editor of the series and his own advisers to a meeting and then sent Vagnozzi a strong letter stating that the series was following the norms of legitimate biblical scholarship and that he would not withdraw his imprimature.[89] The cardinal was not about to tolerate the intrusion of a delegate into the affairs of his diocese.

In 1962, when Vatican II opened, Spellman discovered that John Courtney Murray, S.J., the theologian of religious liberty, had been excluded because of the opposition of Vagnozzi and other Roman officials. Asserting his authority, Spellman had Murray made an official theologian of the council. In fact, after Spellman was elected to the presidency of the council, he made more interventions than any other American prelate. In the summer of 1963, he participated in the conclave that elected Montini Pope Paul VI. When he learned that religious liberty was not on the agenda in the fall of 1963, he summoned the American bishops together, had Murray draw up a memorandum, and then signed a petition in the name of the hierarchy to the pope, the presidency of the council, and the moderators to have religious liberty put back on the agenda. Yet he failed to see the theological rationale for episcopal collegiality regarding some of his independent practical actions. At the same time he fought for the council to discuss religious liberty, he spoke against the bishops' role in reforming the Roman Curia. On the theological level, he was a man of action and not of thought.[90]

In the years after the council Spellman became the object of increasing criticism for his support of American involvement in the Vietnam war. In the fall of 1965, Pope Paul VI had made the first visit of a pope to the United States. Addressing the United Nations, he declared "no more war, never again war."[91] The following Christmas, Spellman made his traditional visit to American troops, this time in Vietnam. Upon his arrival, he paraphrased Stephen Decatur's oft-quoted dictum: "My country, may it always be right. Right or wrong my country!"[92] For the first time in history, however, one of the nation's wars had evoked strong American Catholic opposition. Spellman's statement was construed as a blind paean to American patriotism. His long crusade against communism led him to see it as the sole issue not only in Vietnam but also in Latin America. His equally long battle to prove that Catholics were American made him incapable of realizing that patriotism did not necessarily mean obedient service in the nation's wars.

Spellman's death on December 2, 1967, ended the career of one of the most influential Catholic churchmen in the nation's history. His influence within the church had already begun to decline by the time Pius XII died, and other prelates had begun their rise. Like most great men, he was a study in contrasts. Theologically conservative, he was instrumental in gaining an acceptance in Vatican II of religious liberty and in defending biblical scholars. Socially and politically conservative as well, he nevertheless defended priests and nuns who marched in Selma, Alabama, against Vagnozzi's attacks.[93] Other bishops were his peers, but none equaled him in his blending of Roman and American.

CHAPTER
14
Paul J. Hallinan

Thomas J. Shelley

*C*ardinal Joseph Bernardin once pointed out that, when Paul Hallinan became bishop of Charleston, South Carolina, in September 1958, he was an unknown quantity. When he died ten years later as the first archbishop of Atlanta, he was one of the best-known bishops in the United States, and his reputation rested on solid achievements in many areas, despite the fact that he had headed two of the smallest sees in the country.[1] One reason for his prominence was that he welcomed many of the contemporary developments in the church and in American society and tried to shape a balanced and informed response to them. He was generally regarded as a liberal, but he could also have been described as an authentic conservative, for he had an instinctive aversion for extremists on both the right and the left. On almost every issue, from liturgical reform to the Vietnam war, he tried to stake out a centrist position—"the vital Christian center," he liked to call it—where he thought that truth was most often to be found.

There was little in Hallinan's early life to indicate the positions that he would take in the 1960s. However, one characteristic never changed. He was always an immensely likable person, with a genial disposition, a ready smile, and a capacity for making and keeping friends from almost every walk of life. A priest who served with him in his first assignment as a young curate remarked that "for him religion was a happy experience, and he had the ability to communicate that enthusiasm to others."[2]

235

Paul Hallinan was born on April 8, 1911, in Painesville, Ohio, a city of some 5,000 people thirty miles east of Cleveland. He was educated entirely in Catholic schools, first at Saint Mary's in Painesville, and then at Cathedral Latin School in Cleveland; the University of Notre Dame; and the Cleveland diocesan seminary, Saint Mary, Our Lady of the Lake. The religious formation that he received was solid and effective but also narrow and rigid, as it was in most Catholic institutions of that period. At Notre Dame, for example, the undergraduates lived under a semimonastic regime that even most seminarians would find intolerable today. At South Bend, Hallinan also came under the influence of the well-known Father John F. O'Hara, C.S.C., the ubiquitous prefect of Religion, who was an enthusiastic promoter of his own Catholic version of muscular Christianity.

At the time of his ordination on February 20, 1937, there was little to set young Father Hallinan apart from most priests of his generation. He shared their deep faith and commitment to the church, but also their narrow intellectual horizons and intensely individualistic piety. His first assignment—as third assistant at Saint Aloysius parish in the Glenville section of Cleveland—only served to reenforce these attitudes. Saint Aloysius was the quintessential big city parish of that era, with 8,000 active parishioners, two schools, a huge church and an Irish-born pastor who could have starred in *Going My Way*. It was a self-contained little Catholic community whose unquestioned leaders were the parish clergy. Hallinan loved every minute of his five years there, especially his work with the young people of the parish.

When the United States entered World War II, Father Hallinan followed the example of many priests of his age and joined the United States Army as a chaplain. He served with distinction for thirty-two months in the South Pacific, earning a purple heart and several commendations for bravery in combat. It was his first experience as a priest in a non-Catholic environment, and he found it somewhat disconcerting. At times, he said, he needed to be both Thomas Aquinas and Emily Post in order to reconcile the demands of his textbook theology with those of ordinary Christian charity. Back home in the United States, other Catholic clerics—like Archbishop Edward F. Mooney of Detroit and the theologian Father John Courtney Murray, S.J.—were searching for conciliatory solutions to many of the same problems of ecumenism. At this stage in his life, however, Hallinan was much more the disciple of Fathers Joseph C. Fenton and Francis J. Connell, C.Ss.R. "I want no watery faith for my diet," he said, "and I don't intend to feed it to anyone else."[3]

Almost immediately after his discharge from the army, Father Hallinan joined the Newman apostolate, first as a part-time chaplain at Cleveland College, then as director of Newman Clubs for the whole diocese. It was the beginning of the golden age of the Newman movement in the United States. Thanks to the G.I. Bill of Rights, the number of Catholics in secular colleges mushroomed dramatically, and some of the brightest priests in the country joined the apostolate. In these years Newman clubs and Newman conventions were among the liveliest places in the American Catholic church, abuzz with talk of liturgical renewal, the social apostolate, and the latest trends in European Catholic thought. Ten years of this kind of stimulation left its mark on Hallinan, as did his discovery of John Henry Newman, whom he began to read in earnest at this time.

Still another broadening influence was the graduate work in history which he did, first at John Carroll University (where he earned an M.A. degree in 1953), then at Western Reserve University. At the suggestion of John Tracy Ellis, he decided to write his doctoral dissertation on Richard Gilmour, the second bishop of Cleveland. Among other things, the research forced him to read widely in American Catholic history, giving him a perspective on contemporary events that proved to be very valuable. When he finally received his Ph.D. in 1963 as archbishop of Atlanta, he set a record that still stands: the first and only Catholic bishop to receive a doctorate at an American university while he was in office.

In the spring of 1958, after ten years of Newman work, Hallinan was looking for a change of assignment. When asked by his bishop what he would prefer to do, he replied that he would like a year of study at the Catholic University of America and then an appointment to the diocesan seminary to teach church history.[4] Instead, on September 16, 1958, he was appointed bishop of Charleston, South Carolina. On the day of his consecration in Saint John's Cathedral in Cleveland, a murmur went through the crowd as word was passed from one person to the next that, in Rome, the cardinals had just elected a new pope, Angelo Roncalli, who had taken the name of John XXIII.

The diocese of Charleston was ten times the size of the diocese of Cleveland, but it had only a fraction of its Catholic population—30,000 people, or 1.5 percent of the total population of the state of South Carolina. Even these statistics were deceptive, for fully half the Catholics were concentrated in and around three cities: Charleston, Columbia, and Greenville. Only in Charleston county did the the number of Catholics rise above 5 percent. In seven other counties the Catholic population ranged between 1 and 5 percent. In the remaining thirty-six counties, the percentage was less than 1 percent; in four of them, there was not a single resident Catholic.[5]

By contrast, the twenty-nine white Protestant denominations in South Carolina had 3,700 churches and claimed a membership of more than 800,000, or 63 percent of the white population. There was no doubt that this was the Bible Belt, for Protestant clergymen constituted more than 10 percent of all white professionals in the labor force.[6] Remarkably, the Catholic church was able to maintain an institutional presence throughout the state through a network of fifty-seven parishes, of which religious orders staffed twenty-one (including all of the fourteen black parishes). In fact, there were really two Catholic churches existing side by side in the diocese of Charleston. In a few places there were large city parishes that were not very different from their counterparts in the North. Everywhere else, however, there was only a fragile string of rural parishes with their missions and mass stations in out-of-the-way places with names like Walhalla, Moncks Corner, and Ware Shoals.

Later, Hallinan was annoyed when he heard of Catholic tourists from the North who had attended mass at a large Charleston parish and then left for home wondering if South Carolina really was mission territory. He invited them to come back and discover for themselves the other face of South Carolina Catholicism. He described what any tourist would find:

> He will come to a neat, wooden church, shingled roof, seating about eighty people, built probably in the twenties or thirties. Twenty-three parishioners are present—23. The rest are tourists. The twenty-three have come miles for Mass, from homes that are spread out over two or three counties.
>
> The tourist keeps driving. Another fifty miles and he sees a small Catholic church, built recently with faith, good taste, imagination and contributions from all over the United States.
>
> In case of fire, the pastor knows just what he would do. He would carry out the sacred vessels in one hand and his mailing list in the other. If that were lost, his thirty Catholics could never rebuild his beautiful church.
>
> What the visitor does not see, even as he gets deeper into the story of the Carolina missions, is the "Church intermittent." This means the Masses said regularly in privates homes, funeral parlors, scout-rooms, theatres, even garages. For a few minutes each week, Christ becomes present in the most unlikely places. After the Mass is over, the place goes back to its everyday use.[7]

By 1958 anti-Catholic prejudice in South Carolina was far less virulent than it had been in the past, but it was still capable of arousing considerable emotion in certain quarters. A few weeks after Hallinan's arrival in Charleston, an official of a group called Protestants and Other Americans United for Separation of Church and State made a speaking tour of the state. In Charleston he claimed that "Roman Catholicism is the strongest center of the Communist conspiracy," and he predicted that government aid to parochial schools would lead to the curtailment of religious freedom for American Protestants. Hallinan responded immediately through a paid advertisement in the Charleston *News and Courier* in which he expressed shock at "preachers who attack other churches than their own." He invited "Protestants and Other Americans Fearful of the Catholic Church" to visit any Catholic church, school, or hospital in the state to lay their fears to rest.[8]

The last major flare-up of anti-Catholic bigotry in the South occurred in 1960, when John F. Kennedy was the Democratic candidate for president. The president of the Southern Baptist Convention told a Mississippi audience that he would not "stand by and keep my mouth shut, when a man under the control of the Roman Catholic Church runs for the Presidency of the United States." In South Carolina Hallinan got no response when he asked the religious leaders of the state to subscribe to ten principles of fairness formulated earlier that year by one hundred nationally prominent Catholics, Protestants, and Jews. Hallinan's own tactics were to defend the church firmly and aggressively, but without the truculence that in the past has sometimes made Catholic apologetics counterproductive.

Two weeks before the election he noted favorably that some Protestant clergymen had begun to denounce the bigots in their midst, and he declared publicly: "We wish more of them would speak out so that the whole framework of good Catholic-Protestant-Jewish relationships is not wrecked before November 8." At the same time, Hallinan went out of his way to reassure Protestants who were skeptical about the patriotism of American Catholics. He told them "The American Catholic finds nothing in his religion that conflicts with his duty as an American. . . . Dozens of Catholic bishops have declared that no such obstacles exist or could exist." And he added for good measure: "No Pope has ever contradicted them."[9]

By far the biggest challenge facing Hallinan in Charleston was the burgeoning civil rights movement, whose thrust at that moment was to put an end to segregated schools in the South. Four years earlier the United States Supreme Court had outlawed "separate but equal" schools, and, two weeks before Hallinan's installation in Charleston, the Catholic bishops of the United States had declared that they could not reconcile segregation "with the Christian view of man's nature and rights." However, in November 1958, the only integrated school in the whole state of South Carolina was tiny Saint Anne's parochial school, an old rectory in Rock Hill that had been converted into a two-room schoolhouse in September 1954.

Hallinan knew how delicate his own position was. One pastor reported to him the comments that he heard frequently on visits around his parish: "What's the new bishop going to do—mix us up?" At first, Hallinan trod warily, discussing integration privately with his priests but making only veiled references to it in public. At a day of recollection for Catholic women in Charleston, his allusions were so indirect that one nun said: "He talked about integration, but they didn't understand it."[10]

During the spring of 1960, as sit-in demonstrations spread throughout South Carolina, the bishop feared that the situation would deteriorate into serious violence. During the summer and fall, the school situation in New Orleans was the center of attention throughout the South, as a federal judge tried to integrate the city's public schools and the governor tried to prevent it. In Charleston itself, black parents took legal action to force the transfer of black students from overcrowded black schools to underutilized white ones.

It was against this background that Hallinan pondered what to do at the beginning of 1961. Then, on January 3, he received a telephone call from Bishop Thomas McDonough of Savannah, inviting him and Bishop Francis Hyland of Atlanta to discuss the racial situation. The three bishops met in Savannah on January 12 and agreed to issue a pastoral letter on the subject. It was written largely by Hallinan and published at the beginning of Lent by each of the three bishops under his own name. The gist of the letter was that the bishops promised to integrate their parochial schools "as soon as this can be done with safety to the children and the schools . . . [but certainly] not later than the public schools are opened to all pupils."[11]

The reaction to the announcement was less hostile than Hallinan had feared. There were some nasty letters and an abortive attempt to establish a segregated Marian Academy, but no serious opposition. Many people were openly supportive, including Governor Ernest Hollings, who told the bishop: "Were I with your responsibility, this inspiring letter would give me satisfaction that I had done the right thing."[12]

In the meantime, Hallinan tackled the ticklish issue of the admittance policies of the Catholic hospitals in his diocese. Only two of them, Saint Eugene's in Dillon and Divine Savior in York, accepted black patients. The three largest hospitals, Saint Francis in Charleston, Providence in Columbia, and Saint Francis in Greenville, were still all-white institutions. At a meeting with the hospital administrators on February 17, 1959, the bishop told them that "all of us should move toward the full acceptance [of black patients] on the same basis as white." He saw an opportunity to make this wish a reality when the three hospitals began to expand their facilities. He refused to give permission for the expansion programs unless the hospitals agreed to open their doors to black patients, and he explained to one hospital official why he would not back down on this issue. "Last year," he said, "a report was made to me by a woman who was criticized in Confession because she did not have the foetus baptized in a miscarriage, and, when asked by the priest why she had not gone to a Catholic hospital, had to reply: 'I couldn't—I'm Negro.'"[13]

As with school integration, Hallinan tried to steer a moderate and conciliatory course. At Providence Hospital the advisory board balked at immediate integration but agreed to admit blacks at some future date, when it would be possible to provide a separate wing for them. Hallinan reluctantly accepted the compromise because it at least committed the hospital to accepting blacks as a matter of principle. Five months later, additional government money unexpectedly became available, and Hallinan insisted that the hospital honor its commitment. He told a reluctant hospital administrator: "I do not believe that any thinking person would try to justify a Catholic hospital turning away sick people merely because they have black skin."[14] By Christmas all five Catholic hospitals had agreed to accept both black and white patients.

Not everyone was pleased at the pace of Hallinan's integration program. *Time* magazine sneered that his school policy was "Not Later But Not Now." A local black convert expressed his disappointment that Hallinan would not order the integration of Catholic schools until the public schools had done so. "Since when does the Church follow?," he asked the bishop. "I always thought that it led on all moral issues."[15]

On the other hand, knowledgeable southern moderates thought that he had struck exactly the right note. Ralph McGill, publisher of the Atlanta *Constitution*, commenting on the Lenten pastoral of 1961, expressed the opinion that [the three Catholic bishops] "say what many a silent Protestant minister would like to tell his congregation, if he had apostolic authority behind him."[16] Hallinan had told Governor Hollings back in January 1960 that "another governor and another bishop will be around for the final solution of this problem."[17] In fact, it was under Hallinan's successor, Bishop Francis F. Reh, that the Catholic schools in South Carolina were desegregated—without incident. However, by carefully preparing the ground, and waiting for a year or two longer to end a practice that had existed for many decades, Hallinan helped to make integration a success when at last it came.

The bishop of Charleston had no inkling that his stay in the diocese would be so brief. On February 15, 1962, he observed the silver jubilee of his priesthood with a mass in the cathedral and announced that he would like to celebrate his golden jubilee in the same place. The next day, the apostolic delegate, Archbishop Egidio Vagnozzi, telephoned to tell him that Pope John XXIII had elevated Atlanta to a metropolitan see and had selected him as the first archbishop.

His new see was something of a statistical nightmare. Even more than in Charleston, the Catholic population was concentrated in one small area. Atlanta and its suburbs contained fifteen parishes, while the other sixty-nine counties had only fourteen parishes. When the new archbishop conducted a census in 1963, he discovered that 83 percent of the 43,000 Catholics lived in metropolitan Atlanta. Moreover, fully one-quarter of those counted in the census had lived in the archdiocese for less than a year. Diocesan priests were scarce (only thirty-four of them, many Irish-born), but, fortunately, there were also seventy-two religious priests in the archdiocese, and they staffed ten of the twenty-nine parishes. Even in 1971, when the Catholic population had climbed to 56,000, there was not a single resident Catholic in one-third of the counties of the archdiocese. In another third of the counties, the Catholic population was less than 1 percent. One Glenmary missionary, pastor of a rural parish that covered three counties in the northeastern corner of the state, reported that his main problem was the attitude of non-Catholics. "Some of them look upon Catholics not as a different Christian Church," he explained, "but as a different religion like the Moslems."[18]

In Atlanta, however, Hallinan received a cordial welcome from the new mayor, Ivan Allen, Jr. Like many Atlantans, Allen had never met an archbishop and was unsure how to address him, but he shared the general feeling that the Catholic church was honoring his city by making it the seat of an archdiocese. Later Allen said that he had known few men in his lifetime "who fitted into the pattern of a community better than the new archbishop."[19]

Racial tension was running high when Hallinan arrived in Atlanta. Allen said that, at that point, the city "possessed all of the elements that could lead to full-scale racial bloodshed and turmoil."[20] The archbishop faced the issue directly and immediately. On March 29, 1962, at his installation in the Cathedral of Christ the King, he declared that the church must put into practice its own clear teaching on racial justice, and he urged the people of the archdiocese to implement that teaching "with prudence, with courage, with determination." His own actions were as good as his words. Ten weeks later he announced that he would desegregate all Catholic schools the following September. It was far from a snap decision, for he had carefully canvassed the situation before making his move. Nevertheless, he was well aware of the risk involved. To date only one other bishop in the Deep South had dared to do the same, Archbishop Joseph

Rummel of New Orleans, and he had provoked widespread and bitter opposition.

Hallinan's principal fear was that the state government—still officially committed to segregated education—might attempt to end the tax-exempt status of Catholic schools or deprive Catholic teachers of their licenses. In fact, there was hardly a ripple of protest, either from the state government or from local rednecks. The Atlanta *World*, a black daily, commented: "At last, a move on the part of at least one Church to stand up and set an example for the state."[21]

The following spring the archbishop ordered the desegregation of the two Catholic hospitals under his jurisdiction, Saint Joseph's Infirmary in Atlanta and Saint Mary's Hospital in Athens. In the case of Providence Hospital in Columbia, Hallinan had been willing to tolerate a special wing for blacks. Here he insisted on complete integration and announced: "There will be no separated section for any racial group."[22]

As Hallinan's views on integration became bolder, so did his attitude toward non-Catholics. As an army chaplain he had been extremely sensitive to anything that smacked of *communicatio in sacris*, even refusing to join in the antiphonal recitation of the Psalms with Protestants, when he conducted general services. In Charleston, when he attended the funeral of the mayor in an Episcopal church, he ostentatiously said the rosary during the service. In Atlanta, however, under the impact of the Second Vatican Council, he welcomed contacts with Protestants and Jews and accepted invitations to speak in Protestant churches and in the city's biggest synagogue. He urged his priests to imitate his own example and, in 1963, issued detailed ecumenical guidelines for them. By 1966 relations with non-Catholics had improved to such an extent that, for the Week of Prayer for Christian Unity, Hallinan sponsored a series of services with Protestant and Orthodox Christians. A few days before his death, an official of the Methodist church told him: "Were one man chosen, who has meant the most to the ecumenical movement in Georgia, you would be that man."[23]

Hallinan's interest in the Newman movement remained strong even after his elevation to the hierarchy. From 1960 to 1962 he served as episcopal moderator of the Newman Clubs and had the satisfaction of bringing together six separate Newman organizations into one unified Newman apostolate. At the time there were almost six hundred Newman clubs throughout the country and future prospects seemed limitless. "We are at the threshold of an era," Hallinan told the Newman chaplains in December 1960. Unfortunately and unexpectedly, it turned out to be the threshold of an era of unprecedented upheavals on American campuses. Among the many casualties was the Newman apostolate, which disintegrated before the end of the decade. Even as an archbishop, Hallinan was not isolated from the turmoil in academia. After spending $325,000 for a Newman center at the University of Georgia, he asked some students what they thought of it. They told him: "It's one big, fat booboo, Bishop. You should have given the money to the slums." He asked them if they knew who was the first person to say: "It should have been given to the poor."[24]

With the opening of the Second Vatican Council in the fall of 1962, Hallinan suddenly found himself the only American prelate on the Liturgical Commission. When informed of his election, he admitted that he was "surprised, delighted and scared." One problem was his limited command of Latin. At the first meeting of the Commission, Hallinan sat there, as he said, grasping at nouns and verbs, getting only the general drift of the discussion. More serious was his lack of expertise in liturgy. However, once elected to the Commission, he embarked on a crash course of reading and study. Fortunately too, he formed a close personal friendship with Father Frederick McManus, professor of canon law at the Catholic University of America and the only American *peritus*, or expert, on the Liturgical Commission. The two met almost every day, and Hallinan relied heavily on him for advice and suggestions.[25]

Eleven days after the formal opening of the council, debate started on the Constitution on the Sacred Liturgy. It quickly became a litmus test of the mood of the council, with liberals speaking in favor of it and reactionaries in opposition. A particularly sensitive issue for many American prelates was the use of vernacular languages in the liturgy. After Cardinal Francis Spellman of New York and Cardinal James Francis McIntyre of Los Angeles spoke against the vernacular, Hallinan decided to speak in favor of it. When he addressed the council on October 31, he pointedly began by stressing that he was speaking "for many, although not for all," the bishops of the United States. "The liturgy of the Church must be public," he said, "but this can have real meaning for our people only if they can understand enough of it to be part of it."[26]

Throughout the first session of the council, Hallinan fought hard to move the draft *schema* of the Constitution on the Sacred Liturgy through the Liturgical Commission with as few changes as possible. He became increasingly frustrated at the stalling tactics of the president of the Liturgical Commission, Cardinal Arcadio Larraona, C.M.F., an elderly Spanish canon lawyer. Finally he took his complaints directly to Cardinal Amleto Cicognani, the papal secretary of state, who sympathized with him about Larraona. "Can you understand him?," asked Cicognani. "I can't."[27] With only three weeks left in the first session, Hallinan persuaded the Liturgical Commission to revise its modus operandi in order to expedite the work of revising the schema. The pace was still agonizingly slow. With scarcely two weeks left, only the introduction of the Constitution on the Sacred Liturgy had been sent to the floor of the council. Hallinan was anxious to let the council fathers vote on chapter one before they went home, since it contained an endorsement of the use of the vernacular. There was every indication that it would win overwhelming approval, if only it could be sprung loose from the Liturgical Commission.

At this point Hallinan resorted to some good old-fashioned American horse-trading. He put together a petition requesting a vote on chapter one, got 132 American bishops to sign it, and then asked Cardinal Spellman to submit it to the presidents of the council. Vagnozzi got wind of what Hallinan was doing and accused him of behaving like a politician. "It takes one to know one," was Hallinan's reply. He was not sure whether Spellman ever formally presented his petition or not, but ultimately, the efforts of Hallinan and others were successful.[28] With only three days to spare, the council fathers got the opportunity to vote on chapter one and approved it by 1922 to 11.

At the second session of the council, Hallinan pushed for the widest possible use of the vernacular in the administration of the sacraments and (less successfully) in the recitation of the breviary. He also met informally with several bishops from other English-speaking countries to discuss the possibility of a common English translation of the liturgical texts. It was these deliberations in Rome in the fall of 1963 that led shortly thereafter to the creation of I.C.E.L., the International Commission on English in the Liturgy.[29] During this session Hallinan was elected by the United States bishops to their Commission on the Liturgical Apostolate, and he used his new position to urge the American hierarchy to implement the liturgical changes as quickly and as generously as the law allowed.

Sounding a note that he would repeat again and again, he told the bishops that the best way to combat the extremists on the left was for them to plot their own moderate centrist course rather than listen to the alarmists on the right. "Many priests and laymen are fully aware that the adoption of the vernacular is within our immediate authority," he explained at the annual meeting of the American bishops in 1963. "If we only warn them to be patient, if we only tell them what cannot be done, then our influence will be minimal because it will be entirely negative. . . . If we lead and not merely follow, then we will have their confidence, their loyalty and their full cooperation."[30]

Over the next four and a half years, Hallinan never wavered from this stance, basing his position squarely on the principles contained in the Constitution on the Sacred Liturgy. On the other hand, he was equally quick to criticize the arrogance and intolerance of some liturgical enthusiasts. Speaking at the annual Liturgical Conference in 1964, he reminded his listerners that the resistance to liturgical change did not come entirely from "elderly ladies in devotional tennis shoes" or "ecclesiastical generals and admirals retired from clerical reality." "We need zeal for liturgical renewal," Hallinan told the Liturgical Conference, but "we also need tact and courtesy and kindness and persuasion, and all these are the ways of charity."[31] While Hallinan chafed as much as anyone else at the slow pace of liturgical reform in the United States, he would never countenance the antics of some priests who took matters into their own hands and celebrated their own "underground" liturgies. "That is disobedience," said Hallinan, "and disobedience means that I, John Doe, place myself above the living Church."[32]

Shortly after his return from the second session of the council, Archbishop Hallinan suffered the first of a series of severe attacks of hepatitis. In 1964 he spent 270 days in Saint Joseph's Infirmary, and he never really recovered his health. He skipped the next session of the council but attended the fourth and final session, where he spoke on behalf of the Declaration on Religious Freedom. He also submitted two written interventions, one calling for an explicit condemnation of racial discrimination, the other asking for a declaration on the status of women. "In our society," he said, "women in many places and in many respects still bear the marks of inequality." Specifically he urged the council to allow women to act as lectors and acolytes at Mass, to restore the office of deaconess, to encourage women to study theology, and to assure women religious of proper representation on the Roman congregations.[33]

To the extent that his health permitted, Hallinan still remained active in the civil rights movement. When Martin Luther King, Jr., was awarded the Nobel Peace Prize in 1964, the archbishop was one of four civic leaders in Atlanta who sponsored a biracial dinner—the first in the city's history—to honor King. Few white ministers attended the dinner, but Hallinan left Saint Joseph's Infirmary for a few hours in order to make a brief appearance. In March 1965, when he gave permission to six of his priests to participate in the civil rights march from Selma to Montgomery, Alabama, someone called him "that Nigger-loving archbishop." He replied by saying: "If I were not, I would be untrue to my motto: 'That you may love one another.' "[34]

Diehard segregationists enjoyed one last triumph in Georgia politics in November 1966, when they sent Lester Maddox to the statehouse. A month before the election, without mentioning Maddox by name, Hallinan declared that "the devout Catholic cannot support segregation in any way." When asked by reporters whether the statement referred to Maddox, he replied: "It applies to any political candidate with that stand." Affecting to be more hurt than angry, Maddox said: "It sounds like maybe he's been getting instructions from Mayor Allen and Martin Luther King."[35] After Maddox's election, Allen formed a Community Relations Commission in Atlanta. Hallinan promptly agreed to serve on it and helped to settle a bitter dispute between the Atlanta School Board and local black leaders. Despite the precarious state of his health, he continued to take a close interest in the civil rights movement to the very end, calling for open housing in Atlanta only a few weeks before his death.

By 1966 many Americans were shifting their attention from the civil rights movement to the war in Vietnam, where over 400,000 American troops were now stationed. "Most of them are well aware," said Hallinan at the end of 1965, "that, if they were not there, the Communists would be there instead." A year later, however, the archbishop was having serious doubts about the wisdom of American involvement in the war. In October 1966, he and his new auxiliary bishop, Joseph Bernardin, issued a joint pastoral letter (actually written by Bernardin) which gave a cautious and highly qualified endorsement to American intervention in Vietnam but also stated: "We must keep insisting that our leaders fully inform us of the facts and issues involved in the Vietnam War."[36]

As domestic opposition to the war grew stronger and louder, Hallinan tried to maintain an objective and balanced position. In a speech in New York City in February 1967, he came close to issuing an outright condemnation of the war, but then drew back, when antiwar activists tried to associate him with a movement to promote massive resistance to the draft. "I absolutely refused," he explained, "to give my name to pacifism, massive refusal to serve, campaigns to burn draft cards, spill blood or damn the President."[37]

Continued American bombing of North Vietnam in 1967 did nothing to hasten military victory. American casualties continued to increase, and so did the antiwar protests in the United States. Dissatisfaction with the policies of the Johnson administration led an increasing number of Americans to look elsewhere for solutions. Numerous ad hoc committees appeared, each offering its own special panacea. One such group was Negotiation Now, which rejected both escalation of the war and unilateral American withdrawal in favor of a negotiated peace settlement leading to free elections.

Together with three other bishops, Hallinan gave his endorsement to Negotiation Now in the summer of 1967, provoking a storm of protest from local Catholics. Many of the letters that he received were, he said, "savage in their attack, lacking in logic and coarse in language." He defended himself by reminding his critics that he had lived with war for three years in the Southeastern Pacific. "Even then," he said, "when our nation had been attacked . . . and our cause was clear, I found that war is the total of men who die ugly deaths." He was now convinced, he said, that involvement in Vietnam had been a mistake and that the United States was being weakened by "the terrible cost of American lives, the loss of American stature in this troubled world, the honest but hurtful division within American opinion."[38]

Of all the public issues on which Hallinan spoke, the Vietnam War was the one that he found most frustrating. It was the one issue wherein he failed to find the moderate, centrist position that he always favored, but he had plenty of company in the United States at that time, beginning with President Lyndon Johnson, who signaled his own frustration with the war when he announced in the spring of 1968 (four days after Hallinan's death) that he would not seek a second term in the White House.

Routine diocesan administration was not Paul Hallinan's forte, and he sometimes wondered how successful he would be as a pastor in his own diocese. In Charleston he was happy to leave the day-to-day business in the hands of his chancellor, Joseph Bernardin, and he was even happier when, in March 1966, Bernardin rejoined him in Atlanta as his auxiliary bishop. In an age when bishops were often judged by their achievements with brick and mortar, Hallinan did not do badly. After his forty-one months in Charleston, he left that small diocese with nine new churches and chapels either built or planned, four new schools, four new convents, and expanded facilities in ten other schools. In Atlanta he inherited a financial mess, caused largely by the chaotic management procedures and ambitious building program of his predecessor. One of Hallinan's proudest moments in Atlanta was the synod he held in the fall of 1966. It was the first diocesan synod held in this country after the Second Vatican Council, and he anticipated many of the stipulations in the new code of canon law by providing for a detailed and extensive consultation of the laity prior to the formal proceedings.

In Atlanta Hallinan also experienced the beginnings of the parochial school crisis. It was a national phenomenon, with soaring costs and shrinking enrollments affecting dioceses all across the country, but it was especially acute in a small see like Atlanta. The archbishop did what he could to improve the financial health of his own system, but, in the spring of 1966, he publicly aired his doubts about the future of Catholic schools in dioceses like his own. "We cannot continue to build and operate Catholic schools by an across-the-board assessment on all Catholics," he said, "only to close our doors to many because of increased tuition and a single academic standard that works against the average student."[39]

At the beginning of 1968 Hallinan's health suddenly deteriorated, and he died on March 27 from a combination of severe hepatitis and diabetes. He was only fifty-seven years old, but he had lived through one of the most turbulent periods in American Catholic history. By this time, many clerics of his generation had been angered and bewildered by the winds of change swirling around them. They often reacted by digging in their heels and trying to preserve (or recreate) the church of their youth, the church as it had once existed in places like Saint Aloysius parish in Cleveland and in countless other parishes like it all across the country. No one loved that world more than Hallinan, but by the time he became a bishop he was realistic enough to appreciate that that world was only one stage, and necessarily an ephemeral one, in the evolution of American Catholicism. Neither in Charleston nor in Atlanta did he allow nostalgia for the past to blind him to the realities of the present or the possibilities of the future. His friend, the Benedictine liturgist Aelred Tegels, said of him: "He loved tradition . . . but he understood very deeply that tradition is a living thing and that it requires, not precludes, change."[40]

Paul Hallinan found the Second Vatican Council an exhilarating experience precisely because it confirmed and enhanced his own developing vision of a dynamic rather than a static church, a church capable of almost infinite adaptation to new needs and new circumstances without detriment to its own integrity or its own divine mission. One of Hallinan's close associates in Atlanta described him as a person who "was never a child of the status quo: he always wanted to know if things could work better."[41] Most remarkable of all, perhaps, was the fact that, the older he got, the more pronounced this attitude became. At a time in life when most men become increasingly conservative and intolerant of change, Hallinan remained the genial optimist, convinced that out of the turmoil and upheavals of the 1960s would emerge a revitalized Catholic church and a more democratic American society.

Notes

Introduction

Abbreviations

AANY   Archives of the Archdiocese of New York
ASV   Archivio Segreto Vaticano
ColLac *Collectio Lacensis*
DAUS   Delegazioni apostolica degli Stati Uniti
SS   Segretaria di Stato

1. Robert F. Trisco, "The Variety of Procedures in Modern History," in *The Choosing of Bishops*, ed. William W. Bassett (Hartford, Conn., 1971), 33–38. See also John Tracy Ellis, "On Selecting Bishops for the United States," *The Critic* 27 (1968–1969):44–45.
2. Peter Guilday, *The Life and Times of John Carroll: Archbishop of Baltimore (1735–1815)* (New York, 1922), pp. 354–355.
3. Carroll to Antonelli, Apr. 23, 1792, in *The John Carroll Papers*, ed. Thomas O. Hanley, S.J., 3 vols. (Notre Dame, Ind., 1976), 2:32–33.
4. *John Carroll Papers* 3:132.
5. James Hennesey, S.J., *American Catholics: A History of the Roman Catholic Community in the United States* (New York, 1981), 96.
6. For Conwell's negotiations with Bonaparte, Prince of Canino and Musignano, see Conwell to Bonaparte, Apr. 13, 1829; Apr. 18, 1829; Apr. 18, 1832. Bishop Luigi del Gallo Roccagiovine, a descendant of Charles Bonaparte, graciously provided me with copies of this correspondence in his possession.
7. Patrick W. Carey, *People, Priests, and Prelates: Ecclesiastical Democracy and the Tensions of Trusteeism* (Notre Dame, Ind., 1987), 69–70.
8. ColLac 3:33.
9. Whitfield to Wiseman, Baltimore, June 6, 1833, Archives of the English College (microfilm, University of Notre Dame).
10. ColLac 3:42.
11. Ibid., 58, 71, 88, 102.
12. Ibid., 40–42.
13. Ibid., 115.

14. Ibid., 117.
15. See Gerald P. Fogarty, S.J., "Church Councils in the United States and American Legal Institutions," *Annuarium Historiae Conciliorum* 4 (1972):93n.
16. ColLac. 3:146.
17. On the role of a chancellor, see John Edward Prince, *The Diocesan Chancellor: An Historial Synopsis and Commentary* (Washington, 1942), 38–39.
18. James F. Connelly, *The Visit of Archbishop Gaetano Bedini to the United States of America (June 1853–February 1854)* (Rome, 1960), 275–277,
19. AANY, Barnabò to Hughes, Rome, Jan. 21, 1861.
20. Carroll to Grégoire, June 4, 1811, in *The John Carroll Papers* 3:149–150. See also James Hennesey, S.J., "An Eighteenth Century Bishop: John Carroll of Baltimore," *Archivum Historiae Pontificiae* 16 (1978), 195–197.
21. Hugh J. Nolan, ed., *Pastoral Letters of the American Hierarchy, 1792–1970* (Huntington, Ind., 1970), 51–52.
22. Francis Patrick Kenrick, *Theologia Dogmatica*, 2nd ed., 4 vols. (Baltimore, 1858) 1:227–228. The first edition appeared in 1838 and does not differ in this passage.
23. *Concilii Plenarii Baltimorensis II., in Ecclesia Metropolitana Baltimorensi, a die VII., ad diem XII. Octobris, A.D. MDCCCLXVI., habiti, et a Sede Apostolica recogniti, Acta et Decreta* (Baltimore, 1866), 41.
24. Peter R. Kenrick, *Concio in Concilio Vaticano habenda et non habita* (Naples, 1870), 40. The entire text is also given in Joannes D. Mansi, *Sacrorum Conciliorum Nova et Amplissima Collectio* (Leipzig, 1926), 5, pp. 458.
25. Gerald P. Fogarty, S.J., "Archbishop Peter Kenrick's Submission to Papal Infallibility," *Archivum Historiae Pontificiae* 16 (1978), 211–212.
26. Frederick J. Zwierlein, *The Life and Letters of Bishop McQuaid*, 3 vols. (Rochester, 1926), 2:63.
27. DS, 3112–3116.
28. Peter Guilday, *The Life and Times of John England, First Bishop of Charleston: 1786–1842*, 2 vols. (New York, 1927), 2:85; Thomas F. Casey, *The Sacred Congregation de Propaganda Fide and the Revision of the First Provincial Council of Baltimore (1829–1830)* (Rome, 1957), 55–63.
29. Paul Horgan, *Lamy of Santa Fe: His Life and Times* (New York, 1975), 241–242. Other papers in the archives of the Archdiocese of Santa Fe make it clear that Martinez claimed to be an irremovable pastor.
30. ColLac 3:308, 311–312. For a fuller explanation of this, see Robert Trisco, "Bishops and Their Priests in the United States," in *The Catholic Priest in the United States: Historical Investigations*, ed. John Tracy Ellis (Collegeville, Minn., 1971), 130–132.
31. *Concilii Plenarii Baltimorensis II . . . Acta et Decreta*, 57–58.
32. For the best treatment of this, see Trisco, "Bishops and Their Priests," 150–197.
33. ColLac 3:162.
34. Ellis, "On Selecting Catholic Bishops," 46.
35. *Concilii Plenarii Baltimorensis II . . . Acta et Decreta*, 73.
36. Ibid., 54–55.
37. Gerald P. Fogarty, *The Vatican and the American Hierarchy from 1870 to 1965* (Stuttgart, 1982; Wilmington, Del., 1985), 9–13.

38. Fogarty, *Vatican*, 17–19.
39. *Acta Sanctae Sedis* 12 (1879), 88–89.
40. Fogarty, *Vatican*, 28–30.
41. Ibid., 30–34.
42. Zwierlein, 2:470.
43. Fogarty, *Vatican*, pp. 50–53.
44. *Ibid.*, 65–80.
45. *Ibid.*, 120–124.
46. ASV, SS, 241, "Missioni straordinarie," busta, Sept. 1892, Satolli to Rampolla, New York, Nov. 18, 1892.
47. Fogarty, *Vatican*, 124–127.
48. On the establishment of the delegation and its impact on episcopal appointments, the best treatment is Robert Wister, "The Establishment of the Apostolic Delegation in the United States of America: The Satolli Mission, 1892–1896," (H.E.D. diss., Gregorian University, Rome, 1980).
49. Fogarty, *Vatican*, 143–194.
50. AANY, Edes to Corrigan, Rome, Jan. 6, 1900.
51. AANY, Edes to Corrigan, Rome, May 17, 1901. For the Portland succession, see Fogarty, *Vatican*, 195–196.
52. O'Connell to Merry del Val, Portland, Apr. 17, 1904, quoted in James Gaffey, "The Changing of the Guard: The Rise of Cardinal O'Connell of Boston," *Catholic Historical Review* 59 (1973), 230.
53. ASV, DAUS, Liste Episcopali, 73, Patrick Supple to Gotti, Cambridge, Mass., Apr. 17, 1904.
54. *Acta Sanctae Sedis* 41 (1908), 425–440.
55. ASV, DAUS, Liste Episcopali, 149, meeting of diocesan consultors and rectors, Chicago, July 16, 1915; meeting of bishops of the Province of Chicago, Chicago, July 16, 1915.
56. Ibid., Bonzano to archbishops, Washington, Aug. 18, 1915.
57. Ibid., Dunne to Bonzano, Peoria, Sept. 21, 1915.
58. Ibid., Messmer to Bonzano, Milwaukee, Sept. 1, 1915; Gibbons to Bonzano, Baltimore, Sept. 1, 1915; O'Connell to Bonzano, Boston, Aug. 26, 1915.
59. Ibid., Bonzano to De Lai, Oct. 23, 1915 (copy).
60. Ibid., Bonzano to Gasparri, Washington, Mar. 27, 1916 (copy); see also Bonzano to De Lai, Washington, Feb. 16, 1916. For a summary of the succession to Chicago, see James P. Gaffey, *Francis Clement Kelley & the American Catholic Dream*, 2 vols. (Bensenville, Ill., 1980), 1:151–155, and Hugh J. Nolan, "Native Son," in, *The History of the Archdiocese of Philadelphia*, ed. James F. Connelly (Philadelphia, 1976), 343–344.
61. AANY, Mundelein to Hayes, Chicago, Apr. 20, 1919.
62. See Fogarty, *Vatican*, 208.
63. ASV, DAUS, Liste Episcopali, 150, Bonzano to Farley, Washington, Dec. 26, 1915.
64. Ibid., Farley to Bonzano, New York, Dec. 27, 1915.
65. Ibid., Gasparri to Bonzano, Rome, Mar. 9, 1916; Bonzano to De Lai, Washington, Apr. 13, 1916; Gasparri to Bonzano, Rome, June 22, 1916; De Lai to Prendergast, Rome, Oct. 7, 1916 (copy).
66. Ibid., Mundelein to Bonzano, Chicago, Dec. 11, 1916.
67. Ibid., Muldoon to Bonzano, Rockford, Feb. 18, 1917; consultors of Rockford to Bonzano, Rockford, Mar. 28, 1917; De Lai to Bonzano, Rome, May 5, 1917; Muldoon to Bonzano, Rockford, June 3, 1917; Bonzano to De Lai, Washington, June 4, 1917.

68. Ibid., Donald A. MacDonald to Bonzano, Victoria, Jan 4, 1917.
69. Ibid., Gasparri to Bonzano, Rome, Aug. 26, 1917; Bonzano to Hanna, Washington, Sept. 3, 1917 (draft); Hanna to Bonzano, San Francisco, Sept. 10, 1917; De Lai to Bonzano, Rome, Sept. 17, 1917.
70. *Acta Apostolicae Sedis* 8 (1916), 400–404.
71. ASV, DAUS, Liste Episcopali, 175, Meagher to Bonzano, New York, Jan. 9, 1917.
72. Ibid., 195, Bonzano to De Lai, Washington, Feb. 28, 1918.
73. Ibid., Bonzano to Dougherty, Washington, Feb. 5, 1919.
74. Ibid., 174, Bonzano to De Lai, Washington, Nov. 10 and Dec. 23, 1919.
75. Fogarty, *Vatican*, 61–63.
76. ASV, DAUS, "Stati Uniti," Ryan to Martinelli, Philadelphia, Mar. 14, 1898.
77. Ibid., Ireland to Martinelli, St. Paul, Mar. 24, 1898.
78. Gabriel Andianyni, "Friedrich Graf Revertera, Erinnerungen," *Archivum Historiae Pontificiae* 10 (1972), 268.
79. Fogarty, *Vatican*, 184.
80. ASV, DAUS, Rutheni, Hongelmuller to Falconio, Bar Harbor, Maine, June 3, 1906. Merry del Val to Falconio, Vatican, Aug. 1, 1906. This file contains the reports and correspondence concerning Hodobay's mission.
81. Ibid., Gotti to Falconio, Rome, Mar. 8, 1907.
82. See Bohdan P. Procko, "Soter Ortynsky: First Ruthenian Bishop in the United States, 1907–1916," *Catholic Historical Review* 58 (1973), 513–533.
83. For a fuller treatment of this, see Gerald P. Fogarty, S.J., "The American Hierarchy and Oriental Rite Catholics, 1890–1907," *Records of the American Catholic Historical Society* 85 (1974), 17–28.
84. ASV, DAUS, Liste Episcopali, 149, Mundelein to Bonzano, Brooklyn, Jan 2, 1916.
85. Fogarty, *Vatican*, 211–213.
86. See Elizabeth McKeown, "The National Bishops' Conference: An Analysis of Its Origins," *Catholic Historical Review* 66 (1980), 565–576.
87. ASV, DAUS, Liste Episcopali, 215, Bonzano to De Lai, n.p., May 12, 1921 (copy).
88. Fogarty, *Vatican*, 219–224.
89. Ibid., 224–228.
90. Ibid., 276–277.
91. Vincent A. Yzermans, *American Participation in the Second Vatican Council* (New York, 1967), 382.
92. Ibid., 383.
93. Ibid., 385.
94. Ibid., 384.
95. Archives of the Archdiocese of Baltimore, Cardinal Sebastiano Baggio to Shehan, Rome, May 22, 1974.
96. Joseph Ratzinger, "The First Session," *Worship* 37 (1963), 534.
97. See Gerald P. Fogarty, S.J., "Public Patriotism and Private Politics: The Tradition of American Catholicism," *U.S. Catholic Historian* 4 (1984), 1–48.
98. On the role of religious orders and the care of Italian-Americans, see Silvano M. Tomasi, C.S., "Scalabrinians and the Pastoral Care of Immigrants in the United States, 1887–1987," *U.S. Catholic Historian* 6

(1987), 153–164; and Mary Elizabeth Brown, "Italian and Italian-American Secular Clergy in New York, 1880–1950," ibid., 281–300.
99. Fogarty, *Vatican*, 340.
100. Thomas J. Reese, "The Selection of Bishops," *America* (1984), 65–72.

Chapter 1   An Eighteenth-Century Bishop: John Carroll of Baltimore

1. John Adams, *Works*, 10 vols. (Boston, 1856), 9:355.
2. John Adams, Samuel Adams, and James Warren, *Warren-Adams Letters*, 2 vols. (Boston, 1917), 1:207.
3. Ellen Hart Smith, *Charles Carroll of Carrollton* (New York, 1971), 31.
4. Thomas O'Brien Hanley, ed., *The John Carroll Papers*, 3 vols. (Notre Dame, Ind., 1976), 1:6–25. Subsequent references to this collection, hereafter called J.C.P., will be by volume and pages only. Standard studies of Carroll and John Carroll Brent, *Biographical Sketch of the Most Reverend John Carroll* (Baltimore, 1843); Peter Guilday, *The Life and Times of John Carroll, Archbishop of Baltimore, 1735–1815* (New York, 1922); Annabelle M. Melville, *John Carroll of Baltimore, Father of the American Hierarchy* (New York, 1955); John Gilmary Shea, *The Life and Times of the Most Reverend John Carroll, Bishop and First Archbishop of Baltimore* (New York, 1888).
5. J.C.P. 1:26–31.
6. Carroll to O'Leary, Baltimore, J.C.P. 1:224–225. The editor estimates that this undated letter was probably sent in 1787.
7. Carroll to Plowden, London, October 4, 1790 J.C.P. 1:475. Charles Plowden (1743–1821) was father minister of the Great College at Bruges in 1773. He was later master of novices (1803) and provincial and rector of Stonyhurst (1817–1821) in the English Jesuit Province.
8. Carroll to Plowden, Rock Creek, June 29, 1785, J.C.P. 1:192.
9. Carroll to Plowden, Rock Creek, February 27, 1785, J.C.P. 1:169.
10. Carroll to Plowden, Maryland, February 20, 1782, J.C.P. 1:65.
11. Ibid., 66.
12. J.C.P. 1:59–63.
13. J.C.P. 1:71–77.
14. Carroll to Diderick, Baltimore, July 25, 1788, J.C.P. 1:322.
15. J.C.P. 1:78.
16. Carroll to Joseph Berington, Maryland, near George-town, Potowmack River, July 10, 1784, J.C.P. 1:148
17. Leonardo Cardinal Antonelli to Carroll, Rome, June 9, 1784, in Donald C. Shearer, ed., *Pontificia Americana: A Documentary History of the Catholic in the United States, 1784–1884* (Washington, 1933), 58–59. Standard for this period is Jules A. Baisnée, *France and the Establishment of the American Hierarchy: The Myth of French Interference* (Baltimore, 1934). See also C. R. Fish, "*Documents Relative to the Adjustment of the Roman Catholic Organization in the United States to the Constitutions of National Independence,*" *American Historical Review* 15 (1910):800–829; and Edward I. Devitt, "*Propaganda Documents, Appointment of the First Bishop of Baltimore,*" *Records of the American Catholic Historical Society of Philadelphia* 21 (1910):185–236.

18. Carroll to Plowden, Rock Creek, September 18, 1784, J.C.P. 1:141.
19. Carroll to Doria Pamphili, n.p., November 26, 1784, J.C.P. 1:153 (English text); 154 (French text).
20. Carroll to Thorpe, Maryland, near George-town, February 17, 1785, J.C.P. 1:163. Thorpe (1726–1792) was Roman agent for English and American ex-Jesuits, and himself a former member of the English Jesuit Province.
21. Carroll to Antonelli, Maryland, February 27, 1785, J.C.P. 1: 169–174 (English text); 175–179 (Latin text). The Articles of Confederation, agreed to in the Continental Congress on November 15, 1777, and ratified by Maryland, the last state to do so, on March 1, 1781, were the fundamental law of the United States until 1788. The pertinent section of Article VI read: ". . . nor shall any person holding any office of profit or trust under the united states, or any of them, accept of any present, emolument, office or title of any kind whatever from any king, prince or foreign state . . ." More to Carroll's point would have been to cite Article XLII of the New York State constitution of 1777, which required that those wishing to become citizens of that state "abjure and renounce all allegiance and subjection to all and every foreign King, Prince, Potentate and State, in matters ecclesiastical as well as civil." A similar oath in New York, demanded of all officeholders, barred Catholics from public office there from 1788–1806 (John Webb Pratt, *Religion Politics and Diversity: The Church-State Theme in New York History* (Ithaca, 1967), 95, 107, 123–125). In colonial times the Maryland laity, headed by Charles Carroll II (of Annapolis), had protested both to the English Jesuit provincial and to the vicar apostolic of the London District against appointment of a vicar apostolic in America. Their argument was that such a move would break the law and provide a pretext for persecution. See Thomas Hughes, *History of the Society of Jesus in North America, Colonial and Federal*, 4 vols. (New York, 1907–1917), Text, 2:591–592.
22. Carroll to Plowden, Rock Creek, February 27, 1785, J.C.P. 1:168.
23. Carroll to Plowden, Baltimore, October 12, 1791, J.C.P. 1:524.
24. Carroll to Farmer, n.p., J.C.P. 1:155–158. Farmer (1720–1786) came to America c. 1751 and ministered in New York and New Jersey as well as at Philadelphia. In 1768 he was elected to the American Philosophical Society and in 1779 became a trustee of the University of Pennsylvania.
25. J.C.P. 2:76. Alexander Natalis, *Selecta Historiae Ecclesiasticae Capita*, 24 vols. (1676–1686), was a favorite sourcebook for Carroll.
26. Carroll to Plowden, Maryland, April 10, 1784, in Hughes, *Documents* 1, 2:602–603; Carroll to Farmer, loc. cit., p. 157 n. 24
27. Carroll to Thorpe, Maryland, near George-town, February 17, 1785, J.C.P. 1:162–163.
28. Carroll to Berington, Rock Creek, September 29, 1786, J.C.P. 1:218–219.
29. Carroll to Plowden, Baltimore, March 20, 1789, J.C.P. 1:351.
30. J.C.P. 1:279–280 (English text); 280–282 (Latin text). Robert Molyneux (1738–1808), an Englishman, was later first superior of the restored Society of Jesus in the United States and president of Georgetown College. John Ashton (1742–1815), Irish ex-Jesuit, was procurator general of the clergy.

31. Carroll to Antonelli, J.C.P. 1:285–286 (English text); 290 (Latin text).
32. Carroll to Plowden, Rock Creek, September 18, 1784, J.C.P. 1:151.
33. Carroll to Farmer, n.p., n.d., J.C.P. 1:156–157.
34. Ibid., p. 158.
35. J. Digges et al. to the Gentlemen of the Southern District, n.p., n.d., estimated by the editor to have been distributed in January, 1787; Carroll was a signer, J.C.P. 1:226.
36. Carroll to Plowden, Rock Creek, January 22, 1787/Baltimore, February 28, 1787, J.C.P. 1:241.
37. Carroll to Thorpe, Maryland, near George-town, February 17, 1785, J.C.P. 1:164.
38. Carroll to Antonelli, Maryland, February 27, 1785, J.C.P. 1:173 (English text); 178 (Latin text).
39. Carroll to John Hock, Baltimore, September 15, 1788, J.C.P. 1:329 (English text); 331 (Latin text). According to Carroll Hock was "Ecclesiastical Counsellor at Mainz, Pastor of B.V.M. Collegiate Church, canon and scholar at St. Maurice's" (Ibid., p. 330 n. 1). Carroll later (2:242) described him as "an officious ecclesiastic" and reported in 1798 that he "is now, or at least was lately at New York, having been obliged to fly his country privately." He complained that Hoch (as he now spelled the name) had not made his presence known and that he had heard of his being in the United States only by accident. Carroll to a Pennsylvania Lawyer, George Town, August 24, 1798, J.C.P. 1:243–244.
40. Carroll to Antonelli, July, 1790, on the high seas, J.C.P. 1:448 (English text); 450 (Latin text). Carroll wrote this letter en route to Europe for his episcopal consecration. He completed it in London, July 30, 1790. Carroll had serious problems in Philadelphia with German laity who asserted a *jus patronatus,* and he was dissatisfied with many of the German priests who came to America. For the atmosphere in the Cisrhenane region at the time, see R. R. Palmer, *The World of the French Revolution* (New York, 1972), pp. 238 ff.
41. Carroll to Plowden, Maryland, March 1, 1788, J.C.P. 1:274. Graessl (1753–1793), a contemporary of Johann Michael Sailer in the novitiate of the Bavarian Jesuit Province, arrived in Philadelphia in 1787 and was nominated in 1793 by Carroll to be coadjutor bishop, but died soon after in a yellow fever epidemic.
42. Carroll to Plowden, Rock Creek, June 29, 1785, J.C.P. 1:192.
43. Carroll to Plowden, Rock Creek, July 11, 1786, J.C.P. 1:213.
44. J.C.P. 1:228, 230.
45. Carroll to Diego de Gardoqui, n.p., April 19, 1788, J.C.P. 1:297–298.
46. Carroll to Plowden, Rock Creek, September 18, 1788, J.C.P. 1:151, 152. Franklin made an almost casual note of the appointment in his private journal for July 1, 1784: "The Pope's Nuncio called, and acquainted me that the Pope had, on my recommendation, appointed Mr. John Carroll, Superior of the Catholic Clergy in America, with many of the Powers of a Bishop." The Nuncio had also told him that Carroll would probably soon be made a titular bishop and asked advice on a venue for the episcopal ordination. Franklin recommended Quebec as convenient and assured the Nuncio that the fact of its being in an English province was no problem, so long as ordination by the local bishop would give him no authority over the ordinand. "He

said, not in the least; that when our Bishop was once ordained, he would be independent of the others, and even of the Pope; which I did not clearly understand ." Albert Henry Smyth, ed., *The Writings of Benjamin Franklin*, 10 vols. (New York, 1905–1907), 1:359.

47. Carroll to James Madison, Baltimore, November 17, 1806, J.C.P. 2:534–535. Madison (1751–1836), known in American history as an advocate of strictly interpreted separation of church and state, answered in two letters, both dated November 20. In the first he explained the "scrupulous policy of the Constitution in guarding against a political interference with religious affairs" and left matters to Carroll, saying that he and President Thomas Jefferson were sure that an ecclesiastic would be chosen who was possessed of "a due attachment to the independence, the Constitution and the prosperity of the United States." The second, more personal, letter, expressed Madison's hope that Carroll would be placed permanently in charge of the Louisiana church. John Tracy Ellis, ed., *Documents Of American Catholic History*, 2 vols. (Chicago, 1967), 1:187–188.

48. Carroll to Daniel Brent, Baltimore, March 3, 1807, J.C.P. 3:11–12.
49. Carroll to John Ashton, Baltimore, April 18, 1790, J.C.P. 1:435–537.
50. Garrett Sweeney, "The 'Wound in the Right Foot': Unhealed," in *Bishops and Writers: Aspects of the Evolution of Modern English Catholicism*, ed. Adrian Hastings (Wheathempstead, 1977), pp. 225, 228–231. Only in 1884 did the Holy See claim universal right of appointment, a claim repeated in the canon law codes of 1918 and 1983. Involvement of province bishops in choosing or nominating their colleagues-to-be was a nineteenth-century United States innovation without precedent in the church's practice, which became paradigmatic for the universal church. Ibid., pp. 216–217.
51. Carroll to William O'Brien, Baltimore, May 10, 1788, J.C.P. 1:309.
52. Carroll to Plowden, Baltimore, November 12, 1788, J.C.P. 1:332.
53. Carroll to Antonelli, April 23, 1792, J.C.P. 1:32–33 (English text); 38–39 (Latin text).
54. Carroll to Plowden, Baltimore, April 30, 1792, J.C.P. 2:39.
55. Carroll to Antonelli, n.p., June 17, 1793, J.C.P. 2:95 (English text); 98 (Latin text).
56. Carroll to Antonelli, July 3, 1794, J.C.P. 2:117 (English Text); 118 (Latin text). Graessl died in the fall of 1793. The apostolic brief appointing him bishop of Samosata was dated January 14, 1794.
57. Carroll to Antonelli, Philadelphia, October 15, 1794, J.C.P. 2:129–130 (English text); 130–131 (Latin text). Neale, one of three brothers active in the ministry at the time, was born in 1747, had entered the Jesuit order in 1767, spent the years 1780–1783 as a missionary in present-day Guyana, returned to Maryland in April 1783, served as pastor in Philadelphia, and was president of Georgetown College, 1799–1806. Consecrated as coadjutor in 1800, he succeeded Carroll as second archbishop of Baltimore, 1815–1817.
58. Carroll to Plowden, Baltimore, October 12, 1791, J.C.P. 1:524.
59. Carroll to Stefano Borgia, Baltimore, February 14, 1804, J.C.P. 2:435 (English text); 437 (Latin text).
60. Carroll to Michele Cardinal di Pietro, June 17, 1808, J.C.P. 3:27–28.
61. Carroll to Troy, Washington, September 28, 1808, J.C.P. 3:69–70; Carroll to Plowden, Baltimore, December 5, 1808, J.C.P. 3:72. John

Troy, O.P., had been prior of San Clemente in Rome and was arch-bishop of Dublin 1789–1823.

62. Carroll to Strickland, Baltimore, December 8, 1808, J.C.P. 3:74–75. William Strickland (1731–1819) became president of the English Academy at Liège in 1783 and was later procurator of the English Jesuit Province.

63. The Resolutions are dated November 15, 1810, J.C.P. 2:132.

64. Carroll to the Bishops et al., Baltimore, August 23, 1814, J.C.P. 3:291–292.

65. Carroll to Neale, Baltimore, September 27, 1814, J.C.P. 3:295–296.

66. Carroll to Lorenzo Cardinal Litta, Baltimore, November 28, 1814/January 5, 1815, J.C.P. 3:303–304 (English text); 306 (Latin text). The English text confuses New York (which is in the Latin) with New Orleans.

67. Carroll to Flaget, Baltimore, August 12, 1815, J.C.P. 3:353–354.

68. Loc. cit., n. 65, 303. Maréchal (1768–1828) eventually became coad-jutor archbishop in 1817, but succeeded to the see before his con-secration in December of that year.

69. Carroll to Troy, n.p., n.d., J.C.P. 3:312.

70. Carroll to Plowden, n.p., June 25/July 24, 1815, J.C.P. 3:338–340. Mil-ner and Murray had both gone to Rome as agents for the Irish bishops in an effort to secure withdrawal of the February 16, 1814, rescript signed by the secretary of Propaganda, Monsignor Quarantotti, which favored Grattan's emancipation proposal of 1813.

71. Carroll to Litta, Baltimore, July 17, 1815, J.C.P. 3:344 (English text); 346 (Latin text).

72. Carroll to Neale, Baltimore, July 5, 1801, J.C.P. 2:353. Neale's younger brother, Francis (1756–1837) was pastor of Holy Trinity Church, Georgetown.

73. Carroll to Garnier, Baltimore, November 24, 1811, J.C.P. 3:161.

74. Carroll to Berington, Rock Creek, September 29, 1786, J.C.P. 1:218. An initial enthusiasm for Berington (1743–1817) waned quickly, and Carroll was soon writing of him as shallow and impatient, sarcastic and impious, "unwitty and very irreligious."

75. Carroll to O'Leary, Baltimore, n.d., estimated by editor as 1787, J.C.P. 1:225.

76. Carroll to Grégoire, n.p., September 9, 1809, J.C.P. 3:105. Henri Gré-goire (1750–1831) had become constitutional bishop of Blois in 1791. He remained a staunch opponent of Roman polity and of the con-cordatory settlement of church affairs in France. Carroll in an earlier letter (J.C.P. 3:18) refers to him as "abbé Grégoire," but writes to him always as "My Lord."

77. Carroll to Grégoire, n.p., June 4, 1811, J.C.P. 3:149–150. Two volumes of Grégoire's *Histoire des sectes religieuses* appeared in 1810.

78. Carroll to Heilbron, Baltimore, October 13, 1789, J.C.P. 1:388.

79. Carroll to Holy Trinity Congregation, Baltimore, December 2, 1789, J.C.P. 1:396.

80. Carroll to the Congregation of Trinity Church, February 22, 1797, J.C.P. 2:201–203.

81. Carroll to Antonelli, on the high seas, July, 1790, J.C.P. 1:447 (English text); 450 (Latin text).

82. The *Address* is reprinted in J.C.P. 1:82–144. The section on the locus

of infallibility is on pp. 104–105. Wharton (1748–1833) had a prominent subsequent career as an Episcopalian clergyman in the United States. He had been before his return in 1784 chaplain to the Roman Catholic community in Worcester, England.

83. Carroll received episcopal orders August 15, 1790, in the chapel on the grounds of the estate, Lulworth Castle, of Thomas Weld, Sr. (1760–1810), father of the later Cardinal Thomas Weld, brother-in-law of the wife of George IV, Mrs. Fitzherbert, and one of England's greatest landowners. Carroll had been chaplain in 1773–1774 to Henry, 8th Lord Arundell of Wardour (d. 1808), and he considered that position "the very best place in England." Carroll to Plowden, Maryland, February 28, 1779, J.C.P. 1:53). Charles, 7th Lord Clifford of Chudleigh (1750–1832), was Arundell's son-in-law.

84. Carroll to Plowden, London, September 2 and September 7, 1790, J.C.P. 1:454–459. Butler (1750–1832) was the moving spirit of the Catholic Committee and the Cisalpine Club.

85. Carroll to Petre, London, August 31, 1790, J.C.P. 1:452–453; Carroll to Plowden, London, September 7, 1790, J.C.P. 1:459.

86. Carroll to Arundell, London, October 4, 1790, J.C.P. 1:474; Carroll to Troy, London, October 3, 1790, J.C.P. 1:472.

87. Carroll to Plowden, White-Marsh, February 3, 1791, J.C.P. 1:491. Reeve (1733–1820), Carroll's senior by a year at the Watten novitiate, wrote *A View of the Oath Tendered by the Legislature to the Roman Catholics of England*, London 1790.

88. Carroll to Plowden, London, September 2, 1790, J.C.P. 1:454.

89. Carroll to Plowden, White-Marsh, February 3, 1791, J.C.P. 1:491. Geddes (1737–1802) was a protégé of Lord Petre, who subsidized his biblical researches. He called himself "a Protesting Catholic, but no papist," and denied the pope any "jurisdictive power" beyond the confines of the Papal State, leaving him only a primacy of rank, precedence, and "superinspection." For a recent view, see Bernard Aspinwall, "The Last Laugh of a Humane Faith: Dr. Alexander Geddes, 1737–1801," *New Blackfriars* 58 (July 1977):333–340.

90. Ibid.

91. Carroll to Plowden, Baltimore, March 20, 1815, J.C.P. 3:330.

92. Carroll to Farmer, n.p., estimated by editor as December, 1784, J.C.P. 1:156.

93. Carroll, *Address to Roman Catholics*, J.C.P. 1:105.

94. Ibid., J.C.P. 1:106

95. Carroll to Dominick Lynch and Thomas Stoughton, Rock-Creek, January 24, 1786, J.C.P. 1:203–206. Lynch (1754–1825) and Stoughton (1748–1826) were brothers-in-law, partners in the importing business, and trustees of St. Peter's Church in New York City. Stoughton also served as Spanish consul at New York.

96. Carroll to Plowden, Rock-Creek, May 26, 1788, J.C.P. 1:311.

97. Carroll to Kernan, n.p., August 15, 1805, J.C.P. 2:485.

98. Carroll to Trustees of Saint Mary's Church, Baltimore, August 16, 1814, J.C.P. 3:290.

99. Carroll to Berington, Maryland, near Georgetown, Potowmack River, July 10, 1784, J.C.P. 1:148–149.

100. Carroll to Berington, Rock-Creek, September 29, 1786, J.C.P. 1:219.

101. Carroll to O'Leary, Baltimore, n.d., estimated by editor as 1787, J.C.P. 1:225.

102. Carroll to Plowden, Rock-Creek, June 4, 1787, J.C.P. 1:253–254.
103. Carroll to Coghlan, Maryland, June 13, 1787, J.C.P. 1:254–255.
104. Carroll to Plowden, Rock-Creek, June 29, 1785, J.C.P. 1:193. Joseph (misidentified by the editor as Thomas, his brother) Reeve's *The History of the Old and New Testament*, a translation from the French, was published in 1785 at Philadelphia by C. Talbot.
105. *The Holy Bible*, the first American edition of the Douai-Rheims version, from Bishop Challoner's 1763–1764 second edition, was originally scheduled to come out in forty-eight weekly numbers. The first was published on December 19, 1789, but then the entire Bible was brought out on December 1, 1790. Carroll's first letter of encouragement to Carey on his project was dated Baltimore, January 30, 1789, J.C.P. 1:348–349, and they corresponded regularly thereafter. Matthew Carey (1760–1839) was a leading publisher who had briefly edited the *Freeman's Journal* and *Volunteer's Journal* in Ireland; settled in Philadelphia in 1784 and edited the *Pennsylvania Herald*, the *Columbian Magazine*, and *The American Museum*, the last the most influential news magazine of the day.
106. The British attack on Baltimore took place on September 12–14, 1814. Carroll circularized "our Catholic Brethren in this city, during the present state of alarm and danger, often to implore the powerful aid and protection of our heavenly Father over ourselves and fellow-citizens, and those particularly, who must now leave their homes and families for the common defense." J.C.P. 3:293. On October 20, he joined in the civic thanksgiving day "for our merciful deliverance from the dreadful evils with which we were threatened by the hostile attack of the British fleet and army." J.C.P. 3:299.
107. Carroll to Troy, March 21, 1810, J.C.P. 3:III, 115.

Chapter 2   Louis William DuBourg

1. Arranged in the order of their arrivals, they were: John Dubois, New York, August 1791; Benedict Joseph Flaget, Bardstown, and John Baptist David, Mauricastro, March 29, 1792; Ambrose Maréchal, Baltimore, June 24, 1792; Louis William DuBourg, Louisiana and the Floridas, December 14, 1794; and John Cheverus, Boston, October 3, 1796.
2. Previous sources disagree. DuBourg in his own hand wrote, "I was born on January 10, 1766."
3. At Saint-Sulpice during the Old Regime the major seminary for nobles was called the *grand séminaire*, while that of commoners was the *petit séminaire*.
4. *L'Ami de la religion et du roi*, 57(1828), 150.
5. His brothers Louis and Pierre-François with three younger relatives had arrived in Baltimore from Saint-Domingue in the summer of 1793. Sulpicians from the motherhouse in Paris had begun Saint Mary's Seminary in Baltimore in 1791.
6. Bishop Carroll gave as two of the disagreements: DuBourg's discontent with the directors' new regulations, and anti-French sentiment.
7. Detailed accounts of Saint Mary's College in DuBourg's time are found in Joseph William Ruane, *The Beginnings of the Society of St. Sulpice*

in the United States, 1791–1829 (Baltimore, 1935), 95–158; Annabelle M. Melville, *Louis William DuBourg* (Chicago, 1986) 1: *passim.*

8. Carroll to Maréchal, February 12, 1812, Letterbook, 1799–1815, Sulpician Archives, Baltimore, (hereafter SAB).

9. For DuBourg's role in founding Mount Saint Mary's, see Melville, *DuBourg* 1:168–174.

10. Annabelle M. Melville, *Elizabeth Bayley Seton* (New York, 1951), pp. 119–121. The date was probably November 9, 1806. She had entered the Catholic church on March 14, 1805.

11. Annabelle M. Melville, *Jean Lefebvre de Cheverus* (Milwaukee, 1958), pp. 100–110, gives an account of the part the Boston priests played in Mrs. Seton's conversion and vocation.

12. Melville, *DuBourg* 1:163.

13. Ibid., 2:762, citing DuBourg to Margaret George, January 17, 1826.

14. Ibid., 2:933.

15. Sedella to [Sir], December 9, 1808, Wilson Collection of Saint Louis Cathedral Papers, Historic New Orleans Collection.

16. Flaget to Garnier, December 15, 1810, Sulpician Archives Paris.

17. Carroll to Maréchal, February 12, 1812, Letterbook 1799–1815, 100, Archives Archdiocese of Baltimore (hereafter AAB).

18. *Carroll Papers* 3:191–192. For a detailed account of Carroll's involvement with Louisiana, see Annabella M. Melville, "John Carroll and Louisiana, 1803–1815, *Catholic Historical Review* 64 (Oct. 1968): 64:398–441.

19. Olivier to Carroll, December 5, 1812, 6-A-15, AAB.

20. Melville, *DuBourg* 1:286–288.

21. George Dargo, *Jefferson's Louisiana* (Cambridge, Mass., 1975), pp. 7–11.

22. *Carroll Papers* 3:197.

23. Olivier to Carroll, July 1, 1809, 6-B-10, AAB.

24. DuBourg to Carroll, February 28, 1813, 3-E-7, AAB.

25. Ibid.

26. DuBourg to Carroll, July 2, 1814, 3-E-10, AAB.

27. Ibid.

28. DuBourg to Carroll, n.d., 3-E-11, AAB.

29. Carroll to DuBourg, February 7, 1814, *Carroll Papers* 3:258.

30. Melville, *DuBourg* 1:308–309.

31. DuBourg landed in France on July 12, 1815, and departed from there on July 1, 1817.

32. Pius VII wrote in DuBourg's behalf to secure Ursulines, Christian Brothers, and Jesuits for Louisiana. The first two papal pleas bore results.

33. Litta to DuBourg, June 7, 1817, DuBourg Family Papers, Paris.

34. Melville, *DuBourg* 1:380.

35. The two men were Felix de Andreis and Louis Bighi, recruited in Rome, the former from the Vincentian house Monte Citorio, and the latter from the Gregorian college.

36. Félicité de Lamennais, *Correspondence Générale*, 4 vols., ed. Louis Le Guillou (Paris, 1971) 1:343–344.

37. *Le Moniteur Universel*, n. 148, May 28, 1826, reporting the speech given on May 25, 1826.

38. Melville, *DuBourg* 2:535.

39. Ibid., 1:368–372.
40. Ibid., 2:507–535.
41. Ibid., 2:534.
42. Ibid., 2:562–563.
43. Ibid., 2:564.
44. Ibid., 2:563–565.
45. Ibid., 2:623–634.
46. Ibid., 2:667–673.
47. Ibid., 2:752–759.
48. Fenwick was proposed for Philadelphia, Cincinnati, Detroit, New York, and Boston. Bruté was proposed for Saint Louis, Louisiana, Alabama-Florida, and Boston. Fenwick eventually became the second bishop of Boston in 1825, while Bruté became the first bishop of Vincennes in 1834.
49. Melville, *DuBourg* 1:366.
50. Ibid., 2:644.
51. Ibid., 2:663.
52. John Tracy Ellis, "Selecting American Bishops," *Commonweal*, March 10, 1967, 643–649.
53. DuBourg to Maréchal, May 7, 1819, SAB.
54. A detailed account of DuBourg's efforts to secure a coadjutor is given in Melville, *DuBourg* 2:547–553; 667–678.
55. The two parishes served by older priests were Saint Jacques and Pointe-Coupée.
56. Melville, *DuBourg* 2:783.
57. Ibid., 2:729–730.
58. An account of these years appears in Melville, *DuBourg* 2:775–962.
59. Three were French: John Baptist Blanc, brother of Antoine Blanc; John Mary Odin, who succeeded Antoine Blanc as archbishop of New Orleans; and Eugene Michaud. The three Italians were: John Audizio, Lawrence Peyretti, and John Caretti.
60. Edward J. Hickey, *The Society for the Propagation of the Faith: Its Foundation, Organization, and Success, 1822–1922* (Washington, D.C., 1922), pp. 10–23.
61. *Annales de l'Association de la Propagation de la Foi* 1(1825): 462, L. W. V. DuBourg to Louis DuBourg, March 13, 1823.
62. Carroll to Litta, October 10, 1815, *Carroll Papers* 3:363.

Chapter 3   Benedict Joseph Flaget: First Bishop of the West

Abbreviations

AAB   Archives of the Archdiocese of Baltimore
ASCN   Archives of the Sisters of Charity of Nazareth
ASLA   Archives of the Archdiocese of St. Louis
AUND   Archives of the University of Notre Dame
LC/BC   Lyons Collection at Bellarmine College, Louisville

1. J. Herman Schauinger, *Cathedrals in the Wilderness* (Milwaukee, 1952), p. 197.
2. John Tracy Ellis, "A Historian's Foreword," *Catholic Directory* (Louisville, 1979), p. 4.

3. Stephen Badin, *Origine et progrès de la mission du Kentucky* (Paris, 1821), p. 15.

4. Flaget to Sulpicians of Paris, February 12, 1820. AUND.

5. Quoted in Charles Lemarié, *Mgr. Flaget: Le Patriarche de l'Ouest*, 3 vols. (Angers, 1982–1883), 3:33.

6. Ibid., pp. 312–314.

7. Among the sources that provide a lengthy background of early Kentucky Catholicism are to be noted: Clyde F. Crews, *An American Holy Land: A History of the Archdiocese of Louisville* (Wilmington, 1987); Sister Mary Ramona Mattingly, S.C.N., *The Catholic Church on the Kentucky Frontier to 1812* (Washington, 1936); and Ben Webb, *The Centenary of Catholicity in Kentucky* (Louisville, 1884). Unless otherwise noted, general information on the course of the history of the archdiocese, and its first bishop is drawn from the Crews text, *passim*.

8. John B. Boles, *Religion in Antebellum Kentucky* (Lexington, 1976), p. 52.

9. Alistair Cooke, *America* (New York, 1974), p. 131.

10. Crews, *American Holy Land*, p. 77.

11. Ibid., pp. 35ff.

12. For a clear, concise review of the Dominican versus secular conflict of spiritualities, see Boles, pp. 62ff. Boles writes: [The Kentucky diocese] "was a vast teritory, with problems to match its promise." Ibid., p. 65.

13. Ibid., p. 66.

14. The primal biography of Flaget is that of Martin John Spalding, *The Life, Times and Character of Bishop Flaget* (Louisville, 1852). The basic facts of the bishop's life are drawn from Spalding, *passim*, unless specially noted. The more recent work of Lemarié (n. 5) is excellent, but is currently available only in French.

15. Lemarié, *Mgr. Flaget*, 1:66.

16. Spalding, *Flaget*, p. 100.

17. Presentation to Cardinal Fransoni. 1836. ASCN. Letter Book 2.

18. Flaget Diary, January 1814. There are now only three known extant journals: that of 1812 at AUND; that of 1814 in the Cathedral Museum of Louisville; and that of 1815 at the Louisville Chancery. The 1814 work is available in English translation typescript at ASCN. The edited excerpt here reads in broken, episodic phrases and words; this is frequently the style of these journals.

19. Spalding, *Flaget*, pp. 236ff.

20. Ibid., p. 350.

21. Ibid., p. 189.

22. Ibid., p. 362.

23. Ibid., p. 363.

24. Webb, *Centenary*, p. 376. Crews, *American Holy Land*, pp. 113–114.

25. Spalding, *Flaget*, pp. 275–278.

26. Crews, *American Holy Land*, p. 73.

27. David to Bruté, September 16, 1811. AUND.

28. Flaget to Bruté, April 15, 1817. AUND.

29. Flaget to Eccleston, April 8, 1849. AAB.

30. Flaget to Bruté, August 25, 1811. AUND.

31. Flaget Diary. April 19, 1812.

32. *Catholic Advocate*, January 1, 1842.

33. Spalding, *Flaget*, p. 174. Here is an example of a case in which Spalding in writing his biography had access to some of the diaries that were subsequently lost.
34. Roman Journal of Flaget. ASCN.
35. Crews, *American Holy Land*, p. 104.
36. Robert Trisco, *The Holy See and the Nascent Church in the Middle Western U.S.* (Rome, 1962), p. 389.
37. Flaget to Bruté, August 25, 1811. AUND.
38. Crews, *American Holy Land*, pp. 122–123.
39. Ibid., pp. 94ff.
40. Presentation to Cardinal Fransoni. 1836. ASCN. Letter Book 2.
41. John A. Lyons, *Bishops and Priests of the Diocese of Bardstown* (Louisville, 1976), p. 97.
42. Crews, *American Holy Land*, pp. 79–80.
43. Spalding, *Flaget*, p. 114.
44. Lemarié, *Mgr. Flaget*, 2:254.
45. Spalding, *Flaget*, 186–187.
46. Ibid., p. 246.
47. Crews, *American Holy Land*, p. 79.
48. Ibid., p. 61.
49. William Howlett, *Old St. Thomas* (St. Louis, 1906), pp. 17ff.
50. Crews, *American Holy Land*, p. 83.
51. Flaget to Kenrick, January 22, 1833. AAB.
52. Flaget to Bruté, December 27, 1833. AUND. Flaget to Kenrick, January 22, 1833. AAB.
53. Webb, *Centenary*, pp. 354, 356.
54. Flaget to Rosati, February 3, 1833. ASLA.
55. Reynolds File. LC/BC.
56. Spalding, *Flaget*, p. 326.
57. Lyons, *Bishops and Priests, p. 11.*
58. Spalding, *Flaget*, pp. 241–243.
59. Ibid., p. 216.
60. Flaget to Chambige, May 9, 1835. Duplicate letter Book 21:24–26. ASCN.

Chapter 4   John England: Missionary to America, Then and Now

1. For basic information about the life of England, see Peter Guilday, *Life and Times of John England, 1786–1842* (New York, 1927); see also Joseph L. O'Brien, *John England, Bishop of Charleston: Apostle to Democracy* (New York, 1934); and Dorothy F. Grant, *John England, American Christopher* (Milwaukee, Wisc., 1949). For writings of England, see Sebastian G. Messmer, *The Works of the Right Reverend John England, First Bishop of Charleston* (Cleveland, 1908); Ignatius A. Reynolds, *The Works of the Right Reverend John England, First Bishop of Charleston* (Baltimore, 1849); Hugh P. McElrone, *The Works of the Right Rev. John England, Bishop of Charleston, S.C.* (Baltimore, 1884; New York, 1894, 1900). For ecclesiology of England, see Peter Clarke, *A Free Church in a Free Society: The Ecclesiology of John England, Bishop of Charleston, 1820–1842: A Nineteenth Century Bishop in the Southern United States* (Rome, 1981; Hartsville, S.C., 1982); Virginia Lee Kaib, "The Eccle-

siology of John England, The First Bishop of Charleston, South Carolina, 1821–1842" (Ph.D. diss., Marquette University, 1968). For an examination of England's intellectual and constitutional tradition, see Patrick Carey, *An Immigrant Bishop: John England's Adaptation of Irish Catholicism to American Republicanism* (Yonkers, N.Y., 1982). For England's church–state theology, see Richard W. Rousseau, S.J., "Bishop John England and American Church–State Theory" (Ph.D. diss., Saint Paul University, 1969). For bibliography of England's published writings, see Clarke, pp. 526–531. For documents on England and England-related documents in the Propaganda Fide Archives and the Archives of Irish and English Colleges, Rome, see Finbar Kenneally, O.F.M., *US Documents in the Propaganda Fide Archives: A Calendar* (Washington, D.C., 1966–1981), vols. 1-7 and Index.

2. Guilday, 1:453–473.
3. Ibid., 2:48–67; for text see Messmer, 7:9–43.
4. See Anne Francis Campbell, O.L.M., "Bishop England's Sisterhood, 1829–1929" (Ph.D. diss., Saint Louis University, 1968).
5. Guilday, 2:270–313; Rousseau, pp. 263–290, and "Bishop John England: 1837 Relazione to Rome on His Haitian Mission," *Archivum Historiae Pontificiae* 11 (1973), 269–288.
6. Clarke, pp. 437–440; Richard C. Madden, *Catholics in South Carolina: A Record* (Lanham, M.D., 1985) pp. 389–391.
7. John England, *The Roman Missal, Translated into the English Language for the Use of the Laity, To Which Is Prefixed an Historical Explanation of the Vestments, Ceremonies, etc., Appertaining to the Holy Sacrifice of the Mass* (New York, 1822; Philadelphia, 1843, 1861, 1865, 1867).
8. John England, *The Laity's Directory to the Church Service, for the Year of Our Lord MDCCC-XXII* (New York, 1822). The Calendar in this directory was revised by John Power, but it was published by the publisher of England's *Missal* and intended to accompany the Missal, with a view to facilitate the use of the same (*Directory* 5). From an examination of its contents it would seem that the *Directory* must be considered England's work although it has not been previously attributed to him.
9. Guilday, 1:343–379, 480–501; Clarke, pp. 227–312.
10. Carey, pp. 11–26.
11. J. G. Murtagh, "Australia," *New Catholic Encyclopedia* 1:1086; Clarke, pp. 416–420.
12. Thomas England, *Life of the Rev. Arthur O'Leary* (London, 1822).
13. Letter of England from Bandon, September 1, 1820, State Papers, Dublin Castle, *State of the Country Papers* (1820, p. 775), Ref#429-2182/21.
14. For England on slavery, see Clarke, pp. 389–406, 476–478; John Francis Maxwell, *Slavery and the Catholic Church: The History of Catholic Teaching Concerning the Moral Legitmacy of the Institution of Slavery* (London, 1975), pp. 110–111.
15. Clarke, pp. 463–475.
16. "Diurnal," June 17, 1821, *Records of the American Catholic Historical Society* 6 (1895):53.
17. Messmer, 7:194.
18. Letter to William Gaston, May 17, 1821, *Records ACHS* 18 (1907), p. 368.

19. Messmer, 7:204.
20. Quoted in Guilday, 2:76–78.
21. *Records ACHS* 8 (1897), p. 462.
22. Messmer, 7:101.
23. *Records ACHS* 6 (1895):44.
24. Ibid., 19 (1908):155–158.
25. Corcoran was the first native South Carolina priest; he taught at the Charleston Seminary, was editor of the *Miscellany*, was the one theologian sent by American bishops to assist with the preparatory work of Vatican I, taught at St. Charles Seminary, Philadelphia, and was founding editor of *American Catholic Quarterly Review*. See J. J. Hennesey, "Corcoran, James Andrew," *New Catholic Encyclopedia* 4:319–320.
26. Hewit, taught by Corcoran at the Charleston Seminary, was associate founder and second superior general of the Paulists and managing editor of the *Catholic World*. See J. J. Flynn, "Hewit, Augustine Francis," *New Catholic Encyclopedia* 6:1092–1093.
27. Records ACHS 8 (1897):323–324.
28. One of these women beginning the Ursuline community in Charleston was a postulant, Harriet Woulfe, who founded Saint Joseph's Ursuline Convent, Springfield, Ill. The address of Bishop England given in 1835, when Miss Woulfe received the Ursuline habit, was reprinted in *Half a Century's Record of the Springfield Ursulines* (Springfield, Ill., 1909), pp. 1–34.
29. *Laity's Directory, 1822*, 116. For text of the constitution of the Book Society, see pp. 116–120.
30. Messmer, 7:281.
31. Ibid., p. 275.
32. *Miscellany*, August 25, 1838, cited in Guilday, 2:160; ibid., pp. 160–166 for account of the Brotherhood.
33. Richard C. Madden, "History of the Diocese of Charleston" (Unpublished manuscript) 7, "John England, American Christopher," pp. 62–63, n. 68; Clarke, pp. 201–202.
34. Kevin Condon, C.M., *The Missionary College of All Hallows, 1842–1891* (Dublin, 1986), 32–34; Clarke, 426–434.
35. R. M. Wiltgen, "Liberia," *New Catholic Encyclopedia* 8:713–714; Martin J. Bane, *The Catholic Story of Liberia* (New York, 1950), pp. 25–53; Edmund M. Hogan, *Catholic Missionaries and Liberia: A Study of Christian Enterprise in West Africa, 1842–1950* (Cork, 1981), pp. 12–22.; Clarke, pp. 451–459.
36. Records ACHS 8 (1897):319.
37. Ibid., p. 316.
38. Quoted in Thomas F. Casey, *The Sacred Congregation of Propaganda Fide and the Revision of the First Provincial Council of Baltimore, 1829–1830*, (Rome, 1957) p. 76.
39. Records ACHS 8 (1897):458.
40. Messmer, 7:156.
41. *Constitution of the Roman Catholic Churches of the States of North Carolina, South Carolina and Georgia; Which are Comprised in the Diocese of Charleston and Province of Baltimore, U.S.A.* (Charleston, 1826). For text of the 1841 constitution, see Reynolds, 5:91–108, and Patrick Carey, *American Catholic Religious Thought* (New York, 1987), pp. 74–92.

42. *Constitution*, p. 25.
43. Ibid., p. 28.
44. Ibid.
45. Ibid., pp. 29–30.
46. Ibid., p. 40.
47. Records ACHS 19 (1908):108–109.
48. Guilday, 2:480.
49. *Constitution*, p. 31.
50. Ibid., pp. 34–35.
51. Ibid., p. 35.
52. Ibid.
53. Messmer, 7:213–214.
54. Ibid., p. 217.
55. Ibid., p. 118.
56. Peter Guilday, *A History of the Councils of Baltimore (1791–1884)* (New York, 1932), p. 102.
57. Messmer, 7:89.
58. Ibid., p. 201.
59. Anson Phelps Stokes and Leo Pfeffer, *Church and State in the United States* (Westport, Conn., 1975), pp. 252–253.
60. Andrew Greeley, *The Catholic Experience: An Interpretation of American Catholicism* (Garden City, N.Y., 1967), p. 277.
61. Sydney E. Ahlstrom, *A Religious History of the American People* (New Haven, Conn., 1972), p. 538.

Chapter 5 John Baptist Purcell: First Archbishop of Cincinnati

1. The Cincinnati *Penny Post* published an "Extra" on the occasion of the death of Achbishop Purcell, July 4, 1883. Although it has some minor inaccuracies, this Extra is the best contemporary account of Archbishop Purcell and the Purcell family. The most reliable and the only scholarly treatment of John Baptist Purcell's early life is Anthony H. Deye, "Archbishop John Baptist Purcell of Cincinnati: Pre–Civil War Years" (Ph.D. diss., University of Notre Dame, 1859).
2. This certificate is now in the archives of the Archdiocese of Cincinnati (hereafter referred to as AAC).
3. *Penny Post* Extra, July, 1983.
4. Original in the archives of Mount Saint Mary's Seminary, Emmitsburg (hereafter referred to as AMSMS).
5. For a detailed account of Purcell's years as a student and a teacher, cf. Deye, "Purcell: Pre–Civil War Years," pp. 12–55.
6. Cardinal Pedicini to Résé, December 22, 1832, archives of the University of Notre Dame (hereafter referred to as AUND).
7. F. P. Kenrick to Rosati, Nov. 5, 1832, cited by John H. Lamott, *History of the Archdiocese of Cincinnati 1821–1921* (New York, 1921), p. 71. Cf. also England to Rosati, Jan. 14, 1833, in *Illinois Catholic Historical Review* 9 (1962/27):269–271.
8. England to Whitfield, May 14, 1833, archives of the Archdiocese of Baltimore (hereafter referred to as AAB).
9. England to Purcell, Feb. 25, 1833, AUND.
10. The details of Purcell's trip to Cincinnati and of his installation are

described in a journal that he kept for several months after his appointment as bishop. The original journal is in AAC and a published version edited by Sister Mary Agnes McCann is in *Catholic Historical Review* 5 (July–October, 1919):239–253.

11. For the early years of Fenwick and Young in Ohio, cf. V. F. O'Daniel, *The Right Reverend Edward Dominic Fenwick* (Washington, D.C., 1920), chaps. 11 and 12.

12. Lamott, *Archdiocese of Cincinnati*, pp. 37–38.

13. Cited in Lamott, p. 38.

14. Fenwick to Rev. P. Portier, Surrey, England, Dec. 1, 1831; cited in Lamott, p. 65.

15. Bishop Purcell's Journal, AAC.

16. Purcell to England, Oct. 9, 1834; printed in *Records* of the Am. Cath. Historical Soc. 8 (1897):472–473.

17. Deye, *Purcell: Pre–Civil War Years*, pp. 100–120.

18. A complete set of the *Transactions of the Western Literary Institute and College of Professional Teachers*, 9 vols. in 8 (Cincinnati, 1833/41), is at the library of the Cincinnati Historical Society. Vol. 4 deals with the 1836 meetings.

19. Campbell made his challenge public in the Cincinnati *Gazette* on Dec. 12, 1836. Purcell's acceptance appeared in the same paper on Dec. 15.

20. Originally published as *A Debate on the Roman Catholic Religion between Alexander Campbell and Rt. Rev. John B. Purcell* by J. A. James & Co. (Cincinnati, 1837), the proceedings were reprinted several times throughout the nineteenth century.

21. *A Debate*, p. 197.

22. Ibid., pp. 337–338.

23. Ibid., p. 23.

24. Ibid., pp. 357–358.

25. Cincinnati *Gazette*, Jan. 24, 1837.

26. England to Purcell, July 1, 1837, AUND.

27. For a study of the Germans in Cincinnati during most of Purcell's tenure, cf. Joseph M. White, "Religion and Community: Cincinnati's Germans *1814–1870* "(Ph.D. Diss., University of Notre Dame, 1980).

28. Charles Cist, *Cincinnati in 1841* (Cincinnati, 1841), pp. 37–38.

29. Ibid., p. 270.

30. *The Ohio Guide* (New York, 1940), 79.

31. Guido A. Dobbert, "The Disintegration of an Immigrant Community: The Cincinnati Germans 1870–1890" (Ph.D. diss., University of Chicago, 1965), p. 18.

32. Bishop Purcell's Journal, AAC.

33. *Catholic Telegraph*, Oct. 10, 1834.

34. "Regulations for the Administration of the Temporal Affairs of German Catholic Parishes in Cincinnati." A copy of these regulations with Purcell's signature is in AAC.

35. Cf. White, "Religion and Community," pp. 211–214.

36. A printed copy of this letter is in AAC.

37. *Catholic Telegraph*, Nov. 23, 1850; Purcell to Kenrick, Oct. 10, 1858, AAB, and Purcell to McCaffrey, Sept. 7, 1858, AMSMS.

38. A more thorough study of Purcell's relations to the German Catholics will be published in M. Edmund Hussey, "John Baptist Purcell: Irish Archbishop of a German Church," Roger Daniels, ed., *Cincinnati's Immigrants* (Urbana, Ill., in press).

39. The development of Purcell's thought on this issue is documented in Anthony H. Deye, "Archbishop John Baptist Purcell and the Civil War" (M.A. Thesis, University of Cincinnati, 1944).

40. *Catholic Telegraph*, Oct. 11, 1838.

41. Cincinnati *Commercial*, April 22, 1861, and Cincinnati *Enquirer*, April 24, 1861.

42. Cincinnati *Daily Commercial*, Sept. 2, 1862; Cincinnati *Daily Gazette*, Sept. 2, 1862; *Catholic Telegraph*, Sept. 3, 1862.

43. *Catholic Mirror*, Sept. 30, 1862.

44. Deye, "Purcell and the Civil War," p. 35.

45. *Catholic Telegraph*, July 15, 1863.

46. Bull of Indiction convoking the council, cited by Cuthbert Butler, *The Vatican Council, 1869–1870* (Westminster, 1962), p. 69.

47. Purcell to Spalding, Feb. 29, 1868, AAB.

48. Cf. Judy Olberding, *A Study of the Factors That Contributed to the Non-Infallibilist Position of Archbishop John Baptist Purcell at Vatican I* (M.A. thesis, Athenaeum of Ohio, 1975).

49. *A Debate*, p. 23.

50. Ibid., p. 171.

51. James J. Hennesey, *The First Council of the Vatican: The American Experience* (New York, 1983), pp. 54, 100–101, 110.

52. Ibid., pp. 177–178.

53. The complete (Latin) text of Purcell's speech is in J. D. Mansi, *Sacrorum Conciliorum Nova et Amplissima Collectio*, vol. 72, coll. 365–370.

54. New York *Herald*, Aug. 11, 1870.

55. Lynch to Purcell, Aug. 16, 1870, AUND; Rosecrans to Purcell, Aug. 16, 1870, AUND.

56. Cincinnati *Daily Gazette*, Aug. 23, 1970.

57. Hennesey, p. 308.

58. Richard E. Randolph to Purcell, Aug. 25, 1870, AAC.

59. The bankruptcy is detailed in M. Edmund Hussey, "The 1878 Financial Failure of Archbishop Purcell," *The Cincinnati Historical Society Bulletin*, XXXVI (Spring, 1978):7–41.

60. Sister Mary Monica OSU, *The Cross in the Wilderness* (New York, 1930), p. 285.

61. Memorial of Creditors to Pope Leo XIII, Aug. 24, 1880, AAC.

Chapter 6   Martin John Spalding

1. M. J. Spalding to R. M. Spalding, Rome, June 12, 1834, AAB, 39B-U-10.

2. Sebastian G. Messmer, ed., *The Works of the Right Reverend John England, First Bishop of Charleston* (Cleveland, 1908), 6:174–178.

3. J[ohn] L[ancaster] Spalding, *The Life of the Most Rev. M. J. Spalding, D.D., Archbishop of Baltimore* (New York, 1873), pp. 18–35, hereafter cited as Spalding, *Life*.

4. Thomas W. Spalding, *Martin John Spalding: American Churchman* (Washington, D.C., 1973), pp. 28–52, hereafter cited as Spalding, *Spalding*.

5. Ibid., pp. 87–120; Adam A Micek, *The Apologetics of Martin John Spalding* (Washington, D.C., 1951).

6 *Brownson's Quarterly Review*, Last Series, 2 (1874):113.

7. For the Louisville years, see Clyde F. Crews, *An American Holy Land: A History of the Archdiocese of Louisville* (Wilmington, Del., 1987), pp. 108–147.

8. Spalding, *Spalding*, pp. 53–54.

9. Spalding, *Life*, pp. 151–154, 200–205; Peter Guilday, *A History of the Councils of Baltimore (1791–1884)* (New York, 1932), pp. 167–188.

10. Spalding to Kenrick, Louisville, July 18, 1853, AAB, 32A-N-7.

11. Crews, *Holy Land*, pp. 127–128.

12. See Frank Luther Mott, *A History of American Magazines, 1741–1850* (New York, 1930), pp. 371, 716–717.

13. Crews, *Holy Land*, pp. 138–147; Spalding, *Spalding*, pp. 70–73.

14. David Spalding, ed., "Martin John Spalding's 'Dissertation on the American Civil War,' " *Catholic Historical Review* 52 (1966):66–85.

15. AAB, Spalding journal, pp. 87–88.

16. Spalding, *Spalding*, pp.148–150.

17. Spalding to Johnson, Baltimore, July 31, 1865, AAB, Spalding Letter-book 1:146.

18. Spalding, *Spalding*, pp. 168–172.

19. *Catholic Mirror* (Baltimore), January 6, 1866.

20. Spalding, *Life*, pp. 288–94; Cyril Marcel Witte, "A History of St. Mary's Industrial School for Boys in the City of Baltimore, 1866–1950" (Ph.D. diss., University of Notre Dame, 1955), pp. 1–28.

21. For Spalding's controversy with the Sulpicians, see Christopher J. Kauffman, *Tradition and Transformation in Catholic Culture: The Priests of Saint Sulpice in the United States from 1791 to the Present* (New York, 1988), pp. 147–151.

22. Daniel T. McColgan, *A Century of Charity: The First Hundred Years of the Society of St. Vincent de Paul in the United States* (Milwaukee, Wisc., 1951), 1:212–215, 268–276.

23. Joan Marie Donohoe, *The Irish Catholic Benevolent Union* (Washington, D.C., 1953), p. 4n.

24. Spalding, *Life*, pp. 337–342.

25. *Catholic Mirror*, July 15, 1865.

26. Spalding had imbibed a strain of Jansenism from his boyhood mentors, particularly Father Charles Nerinckx. See Spalding, *Spalding*, pp. 5, 79, 180.

27. Robert F. McNamara, *The American College in Rome, 1855–1955* (Rochester, 1957), pp. 149ff.

28. Among other demonstrations of leadership not mentioned in this chapter were Spalding's attempts to prevent a condemnation of the Fenians and the formation of an American battalion to fight for the pope. Spalding, *Spalding*, pp. 245–250, 255–260. As bishop of Louisville, he was also the principal founder of the American College of Louvain. Ibid., pp. 64, 66, 74–77.

29. *Pastoral Letter of the Most Rev. Martin John Spalding . . . Promulgating the Jubilee, Together with the Late Encyclical of the Holy Father, and the Syllabus of Errors Condemned* (Baltimore, 1865).

30. Spalding, *Spalding*, pp. 240–243.

31. Ibid., pp. 194–205.

32. Spalding to McCloskey, Baltimore, October 9, 1865, AANY, A-22.

33. Spalding, *Spalding*, pp. 203–224.

34. Spalding to Cullen, Baltimore, December 10, 1866, archives of the Archdiocese of Dublin.
35. Purcell to Spalding, Cincinnati, September 7, 1864, AAB, 35-Q-11.
36. Spalding, *Spalding*, pp. 201, 205, 216, 250–251.
37. Spalding to Barnabò, Baltimore, August 15, 1869, APF, Congressi 22:1116r.
38. See John Tracy Ellis, *The Life of James Cardinal Gibbons: Archbishop of Baltimore, 1834–1921* (Milwaukee, Wisc., 1952), 1:486–546.
39. APF, Acta 235:712v–713v.
40. See Robert Trisco, "Bishops and Their Priests in the United States," in John Tracy Ellis, ed., *The Catholic Priest in the United States: Historical Investigations* (Collegeville, Minn., 1971), pp. 111–292, especially pp. 141–194, and Nelson J. Callahan, *A Case for Due Process in the Church: Father Eugene O'Callaghan, American Pioneer of Dissent* (Staten Island, N.Y., 1971).
41. Spalding, *Spalding*, pp. 265–278.
42. Ibid., pp. 331–339; Clyde F. Crews, "American Catholic Authoritarianism: The Episcopacy of William George McCloskey, 1868–1909," *Catholic Historical Review* 70 (1984):560–580.
43. James Hennesey, "James A. Corcoran's Mission to Rome," *Catholic Historical Review* 48 (1962):157–158.
44. Ibid., pp. 160–165.
45. Spalding to Barnabò, Baltimore, August 15, 1869, APF, Congressi 22:1115r; Memoranda pro Concilio Oecumenico, AAB, 39-M-6.
46. Spalding, *Life*, pp. 387–396.
47. See James Hennesey, *The First Council of the Vatican: The American Experience* (New York, 1963).
48. Spalding, *Life*, pp. 396–403.
49. Spalding, *Spalding*, pp. 304–309. The other American supporters of Dupanloup were Bishops Bernard McQuaid of Rochester, Edward Fitzgerald of Little Rock, Michael Domenec of Pittsburgh, and Augustin Verot of St. Augustine, the last two suffragans of Baltimore. Hennesey, *Vatican*, p. 207.
50. Spalding, *Spalding*, pp. 315–318.
51. Patrick Carey, *American Catholic Religious Thought* (New York, 1987), pp. 24–30, 151–173.
52. Spalding, *Spalding*, pp. 326–328; Spalding, *Life*, pp. 449–460.
53. Spalding, *Life*, p. 376.

Chapter 7   James Gibbons of Baltimore

1. William Barry, *Memories and Opinions* (London, 1926), p. 203.
2. Gibbons to Walworth, Baltimore, April 27, 1888, letter in possession of the writer.
3. James Cardinal Gibbons, "My Memories," *Dublin Review* 160 (April 1917):167.
4. Allen Sinclair Will, *Life of Cardinal Gibbons, Archbishop of Baltimore* (New York, 1922), 1:248.
5. Archives of the Archdiocese of Baltimore (AAB), 78-T-3, Gibbons's handwritten account of his greeting to the bishops, November 7, 1884.

6. Library of Congress, Bonaparte Papers, Gibbons to Bonaparte, Baltimore, October 28, 1905.

7. AAB. Gibbons to Merry del Val, Baltimore, March 16, 1905, copy.

8. "Bishop Keane's Admonitions to Cardinal Gibbons, December 29, 1886," *Documents of American Catholic History*, ed. John Tracy Ellis 4th ed. (Wilmington, Del., 1987), 2:439–440. That Gibbons had been lukewarm, to say the least, toward the university project from the beginning was all too obvious. His ambiguity in that regard was clear, for example, when he told Richard Gilmour, Bishop of Cleveland: "If I were to consult my feelings & personal comfort I would have the project abandoned. It has been to me a source of anxiety and care since the close of the council. If the enterprise succeeds, as I hope it will, it will redound to the glory of God & of our faith in this country" (archives of the Diocese of Cleveland, Gibbons to Gilmour, Baltimore, February 15, 1888).

9. John Tracy Ellis, *The Life of James Cardinal Gibbons, Archbishop of Baltimore, 1834–1921*, Reprint (Westminister, Md., 1987), 2:632. The reprint of this work originally published in 1952, was suggested by the writer's friend, Monsignor George G. Higgins, and the suggestion generously adopted by John J. McHale of Christian Classics, Inc.

10. AAB, 91-D-12, Gibbons to Leo XIII, Baltimore, January 30, 1893, copy in French in Alphonse Magnien's handwriting but bearing the signature of the cardinal.

11. *Church News* (Washington), March 5, 1898.

12. *Washington Post*, May 4, 1898.

13. AAB, 76-0-2, Byrne to Gibbons, Emmitsburg, March 7, 1882.

14. Archives of Mount Saint Mary's College, Gibbons to John McCaffrey, Baltimore, October 2, 1880.

15. Archives of Saint Joseph's Central House, Emmitsburg, Annals, August 3, 1882.

16. Archives of the Archdiocese of Cincinnati (AAC), Gibbons to Elder, Baltimore, February 1, 1882.

17. AAB, Gibbons to Manley, Baltimore, September 26, 1888, copy.

18. Archives of Saint Mary's Seminary, Roland Park, Owen Corrigan, auxiliary bishop, et al., to Gibbons, Baltimore, April 20, 1912, copy.

19. AAB, 109-W, Gibbons to De Lai, Baltimore, May 1, 1914, copy.

20. AAC, Gibbons to Elder, Baltimore, May 6, 1886.

21. Gibbons to Giovanni Cardinal Simeoni, Rome, February 20, 1887. For a critical edition of this letter, see Henry J. Browne, *The Catholic Church and the Knights of Labor* (Washington, D.C., 1949), 365–378. The quoted passage will be found on p. 374.

22. Quoted in Will 1:530.

23. AAB 75-1-5, text of the sermon given on September 12, 1880, in the archbishop's own handwriting.

24. James Cardinal Gibbons, *A Retrospect of Fifty Years* (Baltimore, 1916), 2:214.

25. Will 2:611.

26. AAB, 114-P, Roosevelt to Gibbons, Oyster Bay, New York, January 5, 1917.

27. See *History of the Great National Demonstration Held in Baltimore, June the Sixth, 1911 in Honor of Cardinal Gibbons to Commemorate the Fiftieth Anniversary of his Priesthood and the Twenty-fifth of of his Elevation to the Cardinalate* (Baltimore, 1911), 45–47, for the text of Taft's speech.

28. Ibid., pp. 58–61 for the text of Gibbons's response.
29. *Catholic Mirror* (Baltimore), April 2, 1887.
30. Ibid.
31. *Catholic Review* (Baltimore), February 19, 1921.
32. Baltimore *Sun*, October 16, 1911.

Chapter 8   John Ireland

1. Compare the official photograph of 1915 in the files of the Minnesota Historical Society with that taken in 1862, in the files of the *Catholic Bulletin* (St. Paul).
2. John Ireland's inherited physical characteristics can be gleaned with some difficulty from reminiscences of members of his family. See Ann Thomasine Sampson, ed., "The Ireland Connection" (Oral History Project, Sisters of Saint Joseph, Saint Paul, 1982), 2–4, and Clara Graham, *Works to the King: Reminiscences of Mother Seraphine Ireland* (St. Paul, 1950), pp. 13–16. More scholarly are Patricia Condon Johnston, "Reflected Glory: The Story of Ellen Ireland," *Minnesota History* 48 (1982), 13–14, and Helen Angela Hurley, *On Good Ground* (Minneapolis, 1951), pp. 85–88. See also Hurley's plausible if somewhat diffuse and imaginative reconstruction in "John of St. Paul" (unpublished typescript, Minnesota Historical Society), pp. 1–18.
3. In Archives of the Archdiocese of St. Paul, Minnesota (hereafter cited as AASP/M), Ireland papers, there are about thirty manuscript sermons and lectures dated between 1862 and 1871, and a similar number undated (but certainly delivered before 1876).
4. John Ireland, "The Church and Civil Society," in *The Church and Modern Society*, 2 vols. (St. Paul, 1904), 1:29–65.
5. The standard biography has been James Moynihan, *The Life of Archbishop John Ireland* (New York, 1953). Another useful treatment is James M. Reardon, *The Catholic Church in the Diocese of St. Paul* (Saint Paul, 1952), pp. 213–435. Much incidental information is available in the various scholarly works of John Tracy Ellis, Thomas T. McAvoy, Patrick H. Ahern, Colman J. Barry, and Gerald P. Fogarty.
6. There has been some confusion about the exact date of ordination. Compare Moynihan, p. 6, with Reardon, pp. 157, 229, 697–698.
7. John Lancaster Spalding of Peoria learned this lesson early and shared it with Ireland. See AASP/M, Ireland papers, Spalding to Ireland, Rome, January 21,1883.
8. *St. Paul Press*, November 1, 1862.
9. James P. Shannon; ed., "Archbishop Ireland's Experiences as a Civil War Chaplain," *The Catholic Historical Review*, 39 (1953):305.
10. For example, *Minneapolis Tribune*, September 2, 1886.
11. Reardon, pp. 613–627.
12. Quoted in *Northwestern Chronicle* (Saint Paul), January 13, 1872.
13. Among many possible examples, see AASP/M, Ireland papers, "The Saloon" (April 6, 1888).
14. Archives of Propaganda, Acta, 243 (1875), pp. 283–285, and AASP/M, Ireland papers, Ireland to Pius IX and to Grace, Saint Paul, April 22, 1875.

15. The definitive study is James P. Shannon, *Catholic Colonization on the Western Frontier* (New Haven, Conn., 1957).

16. Retitled in the printed version. See note 4, above.

17. Thomas T. McAvoy, *The Great Crisis in American Catholic History* (Chicago, 1957), p. 10, calls the council "the last great manifestation of unity of the Catholic bishops in the nineteenth century."

18. I purposely eschew use of the terms "liberal" and "conservative" on the grounds that in this context they are virtually meaningless.

19. Gerald P. Fogarty, *The Vatican and the American Hierarchy from 1870 to 1965* (Stuttgart, 1982), p. 41, astutely observes that among Ireland, Keane, and O'Connell "it was difficult, if not impossible at times, to determine who led and who followed."

20. For the so-called Abbelen affair, see Colman J. Barry, *The Catholic Church and German Americans* (Milwaukee, Wisc., 1952), pp. 63–69.

21. The definitive study is Henry J. Browne, *The Catholic Church and the Knights of Labor* (Washington, 1947).

22. Archives of the Catholic University of America, Keane papers, "Chronicles of the Catholic University of America from 1885," p. 19.

23. Archives of the Archdiocese of Baltimore, Ireland to Gibbons, Saint Paul, May 7, 1888.

24. AASP/M, Ireland papers, O'Connell to Ireland, Rome, August 7, 1888.

25. AASP/M, Ireland papers, Nilan to Ireland, Poughkeepsie, June 23 and 27, 1890.

26. John Ireland, "State Schools and Parish Schools," *Church and Modern Society* 1:221–232.

27. Archives of Propaganda, New Series, 74 (1895):90–537.

28. For the so-called Cahensly affair, see Barry, pp. 139–152.

29. The definitive study is Robert J. Wister, *The Establishment of the Apostolic Delegation in the United States of America: The Satolli Mission, 1892–1896* (Rome, 1981).

30. Secret Vatican Archives, Apostolic Delegation, U. S., Ireland to Rooker, Saint Paul, May 23, 1896.

31. James Jerome Hill Library, Saint Paul, Hill papers, General Correspondence, Ireland to Hill, Saint Paul, April 27, 1893.

32. James Jerome Hill Library, Saint Paul, Hill Papers, General Correspondence, Hill to Hanna, Saint Paul, September 30, 1898 (copy).

33. For the latest treatment, see John Offner, "Washington Mission: Archbishop Ireland on the Eve of the Spanish American War," *The Catholic Historical Review* 73 (1987):562–575.

34. *Osservatore Romano*, February 22, 1899, and Ireland to Deshon, Rome, February 24, 1899, quoted in McAvoy, 281.

35. AAB, Ireland to Gibbons, Genoa, June 5, 1892, and AASP/M, Ireland papers, Gasquet to Ireland, Rome, September 29, 1916.

36. See, for example, Maria Longworth Storer, *In Memoriam: Bellamy Storer, with Personal Reminiscences of President McKinley, President Roosevelt and John Ireland, Archbishop of St. Paul* (Boston, 1923).

37. AASP/M, Ireland papers, Rampolla to Ireland, the Vatican, May 2, 1901.

38. Frederick J. Zwierlein, *The Life and Letters of Bishop McQuaid*, 3 vols. *(Rochester, 1925)*, 3:251.

39. Archives University of Notre Dame, Klein papers, Ireland to Klein, Saint Paul, December 7, 1911.

Chapter 9   Michael Corrigan: The Conservative Ascendancy

1. Georgetown University Special Collections [herafter GUSC], Catholic Historical manuscript collection, 5.2, memorandum of Anthony Kohlmann [1813?].
2. GUSC, Maryland Province Archives, 204–P–6, Kohlmann to John Grassi, April 26, 1814.
3. Jay P. Dolan, *The Immigrant Church: New York's Irish and German Catholics, 1815–1865* (Baltimore, 1975), pp. 11, 22.
4. James Hennessey, S.J. *American Catholics: A History of the Roman Catholic Community in the United States* (New York, 1981); Florence D. Cohalan, *A Popular History of the Archdiocese of New York* (Yonkers, N.Y., 1983), pp. 21–24.
5. Richard Shaw, *John Dubois: Founding Father* (New York, 1983), pp. 107–108.
6. Henry DeCourcy, *The Catholic Church in the United States*, trans. and enl. John Gilmary Shea, 2nd rev. ed. (New York, 1857), p. 449, quoted by Dolan, *Immigrant Church*, p. 9.
7. The phrase is Jay Dolan's. See *Immigrant Church*, p. 165.
8. Henry Browne, "The Archdiocese of New York a Century Ago: A Memoir of Archbishop Hughes, 1838–1858," *Historical Records and Studies* 39–40 (1952):139, quoted by Dolan, *Immigrant Church*, p. 164.
9. Patrick W. Carey, *People, Priests, and Prelates: Ecclesiastical Democracy and the Tensions of Trusteeism* (Notre Dame, 1987), p. 53.
10. Quoted by Richard Shaw, *Dagger John: The Unquiet Life and Times of Archbishop John Hughes of New York* (New York, 1977), p. 197.
11. Hughes, Pastoral of 1850, quoted by Bernard Meiring, *Educational Aspects of the Legislation of the Councils of Baltimore, 1829–1884* (New York, 1978), pp. 110–111. Some historians have suggested that a less aggressive prelate than John Hughes (the original ecclesiastical boss in America) might well have fared better in the attempt to secure justice for Catholics in New York City. The Catholic record elsewhere in such attempts does not favor this interpretation. John England's newspaper, the *U.S. Catholic Miscellany*, read the signs of the times quite accurately in commenting on the outcome in New York in 1841. "We do not think it likely," it stated, "that a public body can be found in the United States which does not, without its own consciousness or suspicion, think and act under the influence of great prejudice against Catholics, their claims, their rights, their principles, their religion, and their politics." *(U.S. Catholic Miscellany* 20, no. 34 (1841), quoted by Meiring, *Educational Aspects*, pp. 109–110).
12. Cohalen, p. 56.
13. Quoted by Margaret Carthy, O.S.U., *A Cathedral of Suitable Magnificence* (Wilmington, Del., 1984), pp. 39–40.
14. McCloskey apparently promoted him with Roman authorities, over the first choice, Patrick Lynch of Charleston, who had served as an envoy to the Holy See for the Confederacy.
15. M. Francesconi, *Inizi della Congregazione Scalabriniana, 1886–1888* (Rome, 1969), cited by Silvano M. Tomasi, C.S., "Scalabrinians and the Pastoral Care of Immigrants in the United States, 1887–1987," *U.S. Catholic Historian* (Fall, 1987), p. 258.

16. Secret Vatican Archives, Apostolic Delegation of the United States, Corrigan to Francisco Satolli, New York, May 11, 1893, quoted by Tomasi, "Scalabrinians," p. 262.
17. Archives of The Archdiocese of New York (hereafter AANY), Corrigan to McCloskey, Rome, November 18, 1883. The archbishop had long before come to resent Rome's condescending attitude toward Americans. *"They don't want to be instructed by us, or any other outside barbarians,"* he once told McQuaid (archives of the Diocese of Rochester [hereafter ADRo], Corrigan to McQuaid, Newark, September 26, 1878).
18. AANY, Corrigan to McCloskey, Rome, December 14, 1883.
19. Archives of the Archdiocese of Toronto, J[ames] J. Carberry, O.P., to Lynch, Cork, February 11, 1884, quoted by John Tracy Ellis, *The Life of James Cardinal Gibbons, 1834–1921* 1:220.
20. *Acta et Decreta Concilii Plenarii Baltimorensis habita a die IX Novembris usque ad diem VII Decembris A.D. MDCCCLXXXIV*, Thirteenth private congregation, November 24, 1884, pp. lii–liii.
21. Archives of the Diocese of Cleveland, Gilmour to Corrigan, Cleveland, January 14, 1886.
22. AANY, Corrigan to Simeoni, New York, December 27, 1886, abstract.
23. Archives of the Catholic University of America, John Keane, "Chronicles of the Catholic University of America from 1885," 19–20.
24. Quoted by Stephen Bell, *Rebel, Priest, and Prophet: A Biography of Edward McGlynn* (New York, 1937), 22–23.
25. Pastoral Letter of the Fifth Diocesan Synod of the Archdiocese of New York, printed in the *Freeman's Journal*, November 27, 1886.
26. *New York Daily Tribune*, November 26, 1886.
27. AANY, Elder to Corrigan, Cincinnati, August 28, 1882.
28. January 24, 1887.
29. AANY, unclassified, Corrigan to [Cardinal Lucido Parocchi], New York, October 12, 1888, copy.
30. AANY, Simeoni to Corrigan, April 9, 1889, printed.
31. AANY, C-16, McDonnell to Corrigan, Rome, January 19, 1888; ibid., same to same, February 12, 1888; ibid., same to same, January 29, 1888. Archbishop Corrigan had headed the episcopal committee that prepared a report on prohibited societies for the Third Plenary Council. The committee recommended that unions that sought a closed shop and/or used violence be included among the interdicted societies. Corrigan himself had no doubt that a Roman ruling against the Knights of Labor in Canada applied equally to the United States. He intended to make a public announcement to this effect in the fall of 1886. When Terence Powderly, the Grand Master Worker, subsequently assured the hierarchy that the Knights were opposed to boycotts and closed shops, a majority of the archbishops found that the Knights warranted no condemnation. But Corrigan's abstention, as well as the negative votes of two fellow prelates, forced the matter to Rome, where Cardinal Gibbons made his historic intervention in the Knights' behalf. To Corrigan unions seemed the institutionalization of socialism. They seemed breeders of violence, a threat to the rights of private property and the freedom of the individual.
32. John Talbot Smith, *The Catholic Church in New York: A History of the New York Diocese From Its Establishment in 1808 to the Present Time* (New York, 1905), p. 416.

33. AANY, Corrigan to [Cardinal Camillo Mazzella], New York, November 7, 1890, copy.

34. Archives of the Roman Curia of the Society of Jesus, Maryl. 11-1, 36 Campbell to Anderledy, Washington, Dec. 17, 1891, quoted by Gerald Fogarty, *The Vatican and the American Hierarchy from 1870 to 1965* (Stuttgart, 1982), p. 70.

35. Ledochowski to Ireland, Rome, April 30, 1892, quoted by Daniel F. Reilly, O.P., *School Controversy* (Washington, 1943), pp. 160–162.

36. AANY, Corrigan to Parocchi, New York, June 9, 1892, Italian copy.

37. AANY, Farley diary, September 24, 1892, copy.

38. AANY, Corrigan to Rampolla, New York, December 16, 1892, copy.

39. AANY George Keiley to Corrigan, Atlanta, December 24, 1894.

40. Archives of the Secretariat of State in the Secret Vatican Archives, Rampolla to Satolli, Rome, June 14, 1893, quoted by Robert James Wister, *The Establishment of the Apostolic Delegation in the United States of America: the Satolli Mission, 1892–1896* (Rome, 1981), pp. 189–190. The pope had also decided that McGlynn had not given "adequate reparation" for the scandal he had given. (Archives of the Apostolic Delegation in the United States of America, Diocese of New York 11, Leo XIII to Satolli, Rome, August 14, 1893, quoted by Wister, *Establishment of Apostolic Delegation*, pp. 178–179.

41. Leo XIII to Gibbons and the archbishops and bishops of the United States, quoted by Reilly, *School Controversy*, pp. 226–230.

42. Brandi, by now Corrigan's chief collaborator in Rome, was at least partly responsible for the letter, as he divulged to the archbishop (AANY, Brandi to Corrigan, Rome March 13, 1895).

43. AANY, Corrigan to L.P. diCesnola, New York, November 28, 1896.

44. AANY, Brandi to Corrigan, Rome, October 12, 1898.

45. Thomas T. McAvoy, C.S.C., *The Great Crisis in American Catholic History, 1895–1900* (Chicago, 1957), pp. 292–293.

Chapter 10 The Name That Stood for Rome: William O'Connell and the Modern Episcopal Style

1. *Sermons and Addresses of His Eminence, William Cardinal O'Connell* (Boston, 1911), 3:9–17; hereafter called *S&A*.

2. O'Connell's family life and early years are described in detail in James M. O'Toole, "Militant and Triumphant: William Henry O'Connell and Boston Catholicism, 1859–1944" (Ph.D. diss., Boston College, 1987), pp. 9–15, and in Dorothy G. Wayman, *Cardinal O'Connell of Boston: A Biography of William Henry O'Connell, 1859–1944* (New York, 1955), pp. 8–21. O'Connell himself also provided a stylized and somewhat romantic account in his autobiography, *Recollections of Seventy Years* (Boston, 1934), pp. 1–17; hereafter called *Recollections*.

3. *Recollections*, p. 47.

4. Ibid., p. 132.

5. Carroll to Ashton, April 18, 1790, *John Carroll Papers*, ed. Thomas O'Brien Hanley (Notre Dame, Ind., 1976), 1:437. For an extended discussion of Carroll's ecclesiology, see James Hennesey, "An Eighteenth Century Bishop: John Carroll of Baltimore," *Archivum Historiae Pontificiae* 16 (1978):171–204.

6. Cheverus to *The Telegraph*, May 20, 1800, Cheverus Papers, Archives, Archdiocese of Boston (hereafter called AABo), 1:20.

7. *Recollections*, p. 161.

8. *Boston Journal*, December 30, 1903. On O'Connell's priestly career and his appointment to the college rectorship, see O'Toole, "Militant and Triumphant," pp. 25–39.

9. O'Connell to Ledochowski, December 28, 1901, quoted in James Gaffey, "The Changing of the Guard: The Rise of Cardinal O'Connell of Boston," *Catholic Historical Review* 59 (1973):228.

10. *Recollections*, p. 221.

11. O'Connell to Vose, November 23, 1901, Chancery Letterbooks, Archives, Diocese of Portland (hereafter called ADP).

12. *Catholic Directory, 1901* (Milwaukee, Wisc., 1901), p. 460; *Catholic Directory, 1906* (Milwaukee, Wisc., 1906), p. 527.

13. O'Connell to "M," undated, O'Connell Papers, AABo 1:8. This letter, purporting to be a contemporary account of his thoughts and actions, is in fact a later fictional creation. It was intended for inclusion in a successor volume to the *Letters of His Eminence William Cardinal O'Connell, Archbishop of Boston* (Cambridge, Mass., 1915), which are also later falsifications. On the spurious nature of these letters, which all previous writers have accepted as genuine, see James M. O'Toole, "'That Fabulous Churchman': Toward a Biography of Cardinal O'Connell," *Catholic Historical Review* 70 (1984):39–40. Despite their compromised status, these letters may be treated as memoirs.

14. O'Connell to Flagg, August 25, 1902, Chancery Letterbooks, ADP. On O'Connell's campaign of heightened visibility, see Wayman, *Cardinal O'Connell*, pp. 94–103.

15. *Bangor Commercial*, August 23, 1901; *Bangor News*, July 5, 1902.

16. O'Connell to Merry del Val, April 17, 1904, quoted in Gaffey, "Changing of the Guard," 230. O'Connell's active campaign for the Boston appointment is also described in detail in O'Toole, "Militant and Triumphant," pp. 89–118.

17. Cummins to Falconio, April 18, 1904, Apostolic Delegate USA Files 4:73/1, Archivio Segreto Vaticano, Rome.

18. On the rise to power of Fitzgerald and its significance for the local Catholic community, see Doris Kearns Goodwin, *The Fitzgeralds and the Kennedys* (New York, 1987), pp. 92–129.

19. *S&A* 3:132, 137.

20. John Tracy Ellis, *Catholic Bishops: A Memoir* (Wilmington, Del., 1983), pp. 72–73.

21. Walsh to Hayes, April 21, 1919, Hayes Papers, Archives, Archdiocese of New York, microfilm reel #1, 0–7.

22. McNicholas to Cicognani, no date but 1935, Apostolic Delegate Files, Archives, Archdiocese of Cincinnati. The only complete account of the scandal and O'Connell's loss of authority and influence within the church is in O'Toole, "Militant and Triumphant," pp. 177–233. See also Ellis, *Catholic Bishops*, pp. 72–73.

23. Robert H. Lord et al., *History of the Archdiocese of Boston in the Various Stages of its Development, 1604 to 1943* (Boston, 1944), 3:501; hereafter called *HAB*.

24. *Recollections*, p. 301. The chapter in O'Connell's autobiography on his administrative "reorganization of the archdiocese" (ibid., pp. 270–309)

is the longest in the book, giving some sense of the important role this effort had in the cardinal's own estimation. For other accounts of this managerial style, see Wayman, *Cardinal O'Connell*, pp. 143–150, and Robert A. O'Leary, "William Henry Cardinal O'Connell: A Social and Intellectual Biography" (Ph.D. diss., Tufts University, 1980), pp. 107–148.

25. *Recollections*, pp. 271, 270. On the myths and realities of O'Connell's administrative activities, see O'Toole, "Militant and Triumphant," pp. 146–176, 234–273.

26. On the differing approaches to this subject, see James W. Sanders, "Boston Catholics and the School Question, 1825–1907," *From Common School to Magnet School: Selected Essays in the History of Boston Schools*, ed. James W. Fraser et al. (Boston, 1979), pp. 43–75. See also Donna Merwick, *Boston Priests, 1848–1910: A Study of Social and Intellectual Change* (Cambridge, Mass., 1973), pp. 112–116, and *HAB*, 3:80–84.

27. See the correspondence between the Reverend John Harrigan and the chancery office, 1928–1929, Parish Files, AABo 11:24–25. See also James W. Sanders, "Catholics and the School Question in Boston: The Cardinal O'Connell Years," in *Catholic Boston: Studies in Religion and Community, 1870–1970*, ed. Robert E. Sullivan and James M. O'Toole (Boston, 1985), p. 137.

28. On the question of the retreat house, see the entries of June–October 1921 in the Motherhouse Annals, Archives, Sisters of Saint Joseph (Brighton, Mass.). On the disputed election of 1934, see the correspondence June–December 1934 in the Apostolic Delegate Files, AABo.

29. Sweeney's confrontation is described by her protégé, Nat Hentoff, in his memoir *Boston Boy* (New York, 1986), pp. 71–72.

30. On the parrot, see Mitchell to O'Connell, August 4, 1919, and Haberlin to Mitchell, August 9, 1919, Parish Files, AABo 45:1. On the appropriated limousine, see Higgins to Haberlin, October 1, 1917, Wills Correspondence Files, ibid. On the raid on the treasury of All Saints parish, Roxbury, see the memorandum of the Reverend Mark J. Sullivan, April 18, 1931, Parish Files, ibid., 19:13.

31. On the first effort at centralized control of parish funds, see Cushing to pastors, March 29, 1954, Chancery Circulars, ibid., 7:1. On the limitations on pastors' terms, see Medeiros to priests, June 19, 1972, ibid., 12:1.

32. *HAB*, 3:499.

33. Henry Morton Robinson, *The Cardinal* (New York, 1950), p. 514.

34. An O'Connell appearance at Mrs. Gardner's, one in which he distracted attention from the guest of honor, the president of Harvard, is described in Wayman, *Cardinal O'Connell*, pp. 249–250.

35. *S&A*, 3:431.

36. O'Connell's political influence is discussed in James M. O'Toole, "Prelates and Politicos: Catholics and Politics in Massachusetts, 1900–1970," in *Catholic Boston*, pp. 15–42.

37. *S&A*, 11:21.

38. The standard study of the Catholic moral vision of the early twentieth century is William M. Halsey, *The Survival of American Innocence: Catholicism in an Era of Disillusionment, 1920–1940* (Notre Dame, Ind., 1980).

39. Charles J. V. Murphy, "Pope of New England: A Portrait of Cardinal O'Connell," *Outlook and Independent* 153 (October 23, 1929):288; *Boston Herald*, June 9, 1934.

40. The theme of certainty, discussed in Halsey, *Survival of American Innocence*, is elaborated in James Hennesey, *American Catholics: A History of the Roman Catholic Community in the United States* (New York, 1981), pp. 221–233; Robinson, *The Cardinal*, p. 199.

Chapter 11 Bishops on the Fringe: Patrick W. Riordan and Francis Clement Kelley

Abbreviations

AAB	Archives of the Archdiocese of Baltimore
AAOC	Archives of the Archdiocese of Oklahoma City
AASF	Archives of the Archdiocese of San Francisco
ACUA	Archives of The Catholic University of America
ADR	Archives of the Diocese of Richmond
ADRO	Archives of the Diocese of Rochester
APF	Archives of the Congregation de Propaganda Fide
EP	Papers of the Catholic Church Extension Society
SAB	Sulpician Archives in Baltimore
SCAmerCent	Scritture referite nei congressi, America Centrale
UND-MC	University of Notre Dame, Manuscript Collections

1. Paul Horgan, *Lamy of Santa Fe: His Life and Times* (New York, 1975).
2. See James P. Gaffey, *Citizen of No Mean City: Archbishop Patrick Riordan of San Francisco* (Wilmington, Del., 1976), and James P. Gaffey, *Francis Clement Kelley & the American Catholic Dream*, 2 vols. (Bensenville, Ill., 1980).
3. *New World* (Chicago), October 7, 1899, p. 16.
4. Gaffey, *Kelley*, 1:85–93.
5. Gaffey, *Riordan*, pp. 24–39.
6. Gaffey, *Kelley*, 2:142–146.
7. ACUA, O'Connell Papers, Riordan to Denis J. O'Connell, San Francisco, December 28, 1903.
8. AAOC, Kelley to Edmund A. Walsh, S.J., n.p., January 2, 1931, copy.
9. APF, SCAmerCent, Riordan to Giovanni Simeoni, San Francisco, July 24, 1884. See also John Bernard McGloin, S.J., *California's First Bishop; The Life of Joseph Sadoc Alemany, O.P., 1814–1888* (New York, 1966).
10. AAOC, Meerschaert, Third Quinquennial Report (1919; sent to Rome on July 5, 1921), XII, 97, p. 21.
11. AAOC, Kelley to Hugh King, Jr., n.p., November 24, 1926, copy.
12. APF, SCAmerCent, Riordan to Simeoni, San Francisco, July 24, 1884.
13. AAOC, Kelley, Fourth Quinquennial Report (1929), II, p. 13, copy. EP, Kelley to Eugene J. McGuinness, Oklahoma City, August 3, 1926.
14. Gaffey, *Riordan*, pp. 83–86.
15. Leon L. Dubois, S.M., "St. Thomas Seminary at San Jose, California," *Acta Societatis Mariae* 17 (August 15, 1955), pp. 373–382.
16. Gaffey, *Riordan*, pp. 93–103.
17. Gaffey, *Kelley*, 1:186.

18. Ibid., 2:134–135, 254.
19. Ibid., 2:182–190.
20. Ibid., 1:16–17.
21. Gaffey, *Riordan*, pp. 98–103.
22. Ibid., pp. 150–175.
23. Ibid., pp. 374–376. ADR, Hugh P. Smyth to O'Connell, Evanston, July 24, 1902.
24. AAOC, Kelley to the clergy, Oklahoma City, November 13, 1926.
25. AAOC, Kelley to William J. O'Brien, n.p., May 3, 1926, copy.
26. AAOC, Sixth Quinquennial Report (1939) 12:24.
27. AAOC, John B. Morris to Kelley, Little Rock, January 21, 1925.
28. Gaffey, *Kelley*, 2:130.
29. AAOC, Sixth Quinquennial Report (1939) 21, 100, p. 25.
30. SAB, notes of Francis P. Havey, S.S.
31. *San Francisco Call*, April 28, 1906, p. 1.
32. *San Francisco Call*, December 29, 1914, p. 8.
33. Gaffey, *Kelley*, 2:199–224.
34. ACUA, Keane Papers, Riordan to Keane, San Francisco, January 24, 1887.
35. Ibid.
36. AAB, 91-C-2, Riordan to Gibbons, San Francisco, January 18, 1893, telegram; 93-L-1, Riordan to Gibbons, San Francisco, October 2, 1894.
37. UND-MC, papers of William J. Onahan, IX-1-d, Riordan to Onahan, San Francisco, January 12 and February 1, 1893.
38. ADRO, Riordan to McQuaid, San Francisco, April 18, 1907.
39. AASF, Riordan to McQuaid [San Francisco], July 24, 1906, copy.
40. AASF, Riordan to Ireland [San Francisco], March 1, 1911, copy.
41. Gaffey, *Riordan*, pp. 335–341.
42. Ibid., pp. 324–331.
43. Ibid., pp. 304–309.
44. Gaffey, *Kelley* 1:335–336, 348–349.
45. Ibid., 2:3–57.
46. AAOC, minutes of the ninth annual meeting of the American hierarchy, Washington, D.C., September 14 and 15, 1927, p. 7.
47. Gaffey, *Kelley*, 2:92–101.
48. The process of Romanization is brilliantly discussed in Gerald P. Fogarty, *The Vatican and the American Hierarchy from 1870 to 1965* (Stuttgart, 1982).
49. AASF, Riordan to Spalding [San Francisco], November 20, 1903, copy.
50. AASF, Riordan to William Byrne [San Francisco], February 14, 1906, copy.
51. AASF, Tyrrell to Riordan, Richmond, York, December 29, 1905.
52. AASF, Charles A. Ramm to Tyrrell [San Francisco], July 20, 1909, copy.
53. Gaffey, *Riordan*, pp. 281–318.
54. Gaffey, *Kelley*, 1:109–110. Fogarty, pp. 195–198.
55. Ibid., 1:113–114.
56. Ibid., pp. 240–241.
57. Kelley, *The Bishop Jots It Down* (New York, 1939), p. 164. See also Gaffey, *Kelley*, 2:333–348.
58. Kelley, *The Bishop Jots It Down*, p. 174.
59. AAOC, Mencken to Kelley, Baltimore, July 6, 1939.

Chapter 12   The Beginning and the End of an Area: George
William Mundelein and John Patrick Cody in Chicago

1. *Chicago Tribune*, October 3, 1939, pp. 1, 10; October 6, 1939, p. 3; October 7, 1939, p. 7.
2. *The Chicago Catholic*, May 7, 1982, pp. 6–12; Andrew M. Greeley, "The Fall of an Archdiocese," *Chicago* 36 (September, 1987):128–131, 190–192; William Clements, Gene Mustain, and Roy Larson, investigative series on Cody, *Chicago Sun-Times*, September 10, 1981, pp. 1–7; September 11, 1981, pp. 1–5; September 12, 1981, pp. 1–4. The *Sun-Times* charged Cody with nepotism in the purchase of insurance from the son of his stepcousin and also with the diversion of large sums of money to support that stepcousin, Helen Dolan Wilson. It was never stated, but always strongly implied, that Cody was having an affair with Mrs. Wilson. The nepotism is undeniable. Cody did channel substantial insurance business through David Dolan Wilson's agency in St. Louis. Whether this nepotism is improper, however, can be debated. No one ever charged that the insurance purchased was inadequate. Some of Wilson's plans were quite innovative. To paraphrase Mayor Daley, who should the cardinal have given the business to, his enemies? That Cody helped support Mrs. Wilson, a childhood friend whose widowed father had married Cody's aunt, has also been clearly established by investigative reporters. The crucial question, however, is whether Cody gave Mrs. Wilson his own money, which would be perfectly legal, or diverted church funds to her, which would violate the church's tax-exempt status. This has never been established nor has it been proven that Cody had an affair with Mrs. Wilson. The U.S. Attorney dropped all investigations after Cody's death.
3. Too many surveys of American Catholic history lump the early twentieth century in with the nineteenth century, characterizing the whole span of years from the 1830s to the 1960s as the immigrant period. See, for example, James Hennesey, *American Catholics* (New York, 1981). Fortunately, the most recent survey history, Jay P. Dolan, *The American Catholic Experience* (New York, 1985), recognizes the first half of the twentieth century as a period with distinct characteristics.
4. These points are developed in Edward R. Kantowicz, "Cardinal Mundelein of Chicago: A 'Consolidating Bishop'," in *An American Church*, ed. David J. Alvarez (Moraga, Calif., 1979), pp. 63–72; and Edward R. Kantowicz, "Cardinal Mundelein of Chicago and the Shaping of Twentieth Century American Catholicism," *Journal of American History* 68 (1981):52–68.
5. For background on John Bonzano, see Brendan A. Finn, *Twenty-Four American Cardinals* (Boston, 1947), pp. 309–323. Biographical details on Mundelein are drawn from Edward R. Kantowicz, *Corporation Sole: Cardinal Mundelein and Chicago Catholicism* (Notre Dame, Ind., 1983). See, especially, the chronology of his life on pages ix–xi. The book was based on archival sources and extensive interviews. Comments on Cardinal Cody later in this paper, however, are based solely on the public record, as presented in the secular and religious press, for the Cody papers are not yet open for research at the Archives of the Archdiocese of Chicago.
6. Kantowicz, "Cardinal Mundelein of Chicago and the Shaping of Twentieth Century American Catholicism," p. 52.

7. Ibid., pp. 59–60.

8. Kantowicz, *Corporation Sole*, pp. 166–168; Milton Fairman, "The Twenty-Eighth International Eucharistic Congress," *Chicago History* 5 (Winter, 1976/77):202–212.

9. Kantowicz, *Corporation Sole*, pp. 166–168.

10. The two standard works on Spellman erroneously attribute the invention of diocesan central banking to him. See Robert I. Gannon, *The Cardinal Spellman Story* (Garden City, N.Y., 1962), pp. 249–272; and John Cooney, *The American Pope* (New York, 1984), pp. 95–101.

11. Biographical details on Cody can be found in Joseph B. Code, *Dictionary of the American Hierarchy* (New York, 1964). Charles Dahm, *Power and Authority in the Catholic Church: Cardinal Cody in Chicago* (Notre Dame, Ind., 1981), though not a full biography, is the only book-length study devoted to him. For background on Glennon and Saint Louis, see Nicholas Schneider, *The Life of John Cardinal Glennon* (Liguori, Mo., 1971).

12. *The New World*, July 1, 1977, p. 15.

13. For a reasonably full account of Cody's pre-Chicago career, see *The New World*, July 1, 1977, pp. 13, 25–29.

14. Dahm, pp. 1–2.

15. Jeff Lyon and James Robison, "Cody of Chicago," *Chicago Tribune Magazine*, November 9, 1975, p. 25; *New York Times*, June 17, 1965, p. 20; John Conroy, "Cardinal Sins," *Chicago Reader*, June 5, 1987, p. 14.

16. Roy Larson, "Cody—The Man in the Middle," *Chicago Sun-Times*, September 24, 1978, p. 9; A. E. P. Wall, "Chicago's Cardinal," *The Chicago Catholic*, August 24, 1979, p. 11.

17. Dahm gives the fullest account of the founding and subsequent history of the ACP. See pp. 103–108 for the censure vote.

18. Quoted by Larson, p. 9.

19. Kantowicz, *Corporation Sole*, pp. 6–8, 49–64.

20. *New York Times*, November 29, 1970, p. 47.

21. Dahm, pp. 19–20, 64, 183.

22. Kantowicz, *Corporation Sole*, pp. 203–216.

23. Schneider, p. 164.

24. *New York Times*, April 17, 1962, pp. 1, 16; August 19, 1962, p. 73; September 1, 1962, pp. 1, 20; September 5, 1962, pp. 1, 22; September 6, 1962, p. 22; June 17, 1964, pp. 1, 20.

25. David J. Garrow, *Bearing the Cross: Martin Luther King, Jr. and the Southern Christian Leadership Conference* (New York, 1986), pp. 461, 491, 508; Bill Gleason, *Daley of Chicago* (New York, 1970), pp. 45–46.

26. Dahm, pp. 113–114, 176–180, 227–257; Lyon and Robison, p. 25; Larson, p. 9; "The Sharing Years," *The New World*, May 14, 1976, pp. 2–4.

27. *Chicago Sun-Times*, September 17, 1981, p. 4; *New York Times*, September 17, 1981, II, p. 11; September 19, 1981, p. 8.

28. Dahm, pp. 315–316; Andrew M. Greeley, William C. McCready, and Kathleen McCourt, *Catholic Schools in a Declining Church* (Kansas City, Mo., 1976).

29. Kantowicz, *Corporation Sole*, pp. 150–164.

30. Lyon and Robison, pp. 52–54; Larson, p. 9; Greeley, "Fall of an Archdiocese," pp. 130–131.

31. *Chicago Sun-Times*, September 11, 1981, pp. 1, 3; September 12, 1981, pp. 1, 4.

32. *New York Times*, April 2, 1975, p. 34.
33. Dahm, p. 219.
34. Robert B. Beusse et al., "Observations on the Media Organizations of the Archdiocese of Chicago submitted to Joseph Cardinal Bernardin," *The Chicago Catholic*, September 2, 1983, 1a–8a. I calculated the subsidy amount from the financial reports of the archdiocese printed annually in *The Chicago Catholic*.
35. Kantowicz, *Corporation Sole*, p. 126.
36. Quoted by Conroy, p. 32.

Chapter 13　　Francis J. Spellman: American and Roman

Abbreviations

AABo　　Archives of the Archdiocese of Boston
AACi　　Archives of the Archdiocese of Cincinnati
AANY　　Archives of the Archdiocese of New York
AAP　　Archives of the Archdiocese of Philadelphia
ASV　　Archivio Segreto Vaticano
DAUS　　Delegazione apostolica degli Stati Uniti
FDRL　　Franklin D. Roosevelt Library, Hyde Park, N.Y.
NA　　National Archives, Washington, D.C.

1. Florence D. Cohalan, *A Popular History of the Archdiocese of New York* (Yonkers, N.Y., 1983), pp. 267–268.
2. Gerald P. Fogarty, S.J., *The Vatican and the American Hierarchy from 1870 to 1965* (Stuttgart, 1982; Wilmington, Del., 1985), pp. 195–207, 240–243.
3. ASV, DAUS, Diocese, Boston, 94, Gasparri to Bonzano, Vatican Apr. 30, 1921
4. AABo, O'Connell to Borgongini-Duca, n.p., Apr. 9, 1924 (copy).
5. AANY, Spellman diary, Nov. 24–25, 1929.
6. Ibid., June 30–July 3, 1931. See also Robert I. Gannon, S.J., *The Cardinal Spellman Story* (Garden City, N.Y., 1962), pp. 75–77.
7. AANY, Spellman diary, Aug. 2, 1932.
8. Gannon, p. 86.
9. AANY, Spellman diary, Aug. 8, 1932.
10. Ibid., Aug 10, 1932.
11. Quoted in Gannon, p. 241.
12. AANY, Spellman diary, Oct. 8, 1932.
13. AACi, McNicholas to Pizzardo, Dec. 28, 1932 (copy).
14. AANY, Spellman diary, Mar. 17, Mar. 23, May 23, 1933.
15. Ibid., Mar. 22, 1933.
16. Ibid., Apr. 6, 1933.
17. Quoted in Gannon, p. 92.
18. AANY, Spellman diary, Sept. 22, 1933.
19. Ibid., Sept. 25, 1933.
20. Ibid., Aug 23, 1934.
21. Ibid., Nov. 13, 1934.
22. Ibid., Aug. 6, Sept. 7, 8, 16, 1936.
23. Ibid., Sept. 25, 1936.
24. Ibid., Sept. 27, 1936.

25. Ibid., Sept. 28, 1936.
26. Ibid., Oct. 9, 1936, gives the content of this letter.
27. Ibid., Oct. 8, 1936.
28. Ibid., Oct. 9, 1936.
29. Ibid., Oct. 18–29, 1936.
30. AANY, Spellman to Pacelli, Boston, Nov, 27, 1935 (copy).
31. John B. Sheerin, *Never Look Back: The Career and Concerns of John J. Burke* (New York, 1975), pp. 217–218.
32. AANY, Spellman diary, Nov. 4, 1936.
33. FDRL, PPF 321, Mundelein to Cicognani, Chicago, Oct. 6, 1937 (copy).
34. AANY, Pacelli to Spellman, Vatican, Nov. 26, 1937.
35. AANY, Pacelli to Spellman, Vatican, Feb. 26, 1938. I have treated these negotiations more extensively in my *Vatican and the American Hierarchy*, pp. 248–251.
36. AANY, Spellman diary, Sept. 4, 1938.
37. Ibid., Sept. 9–10, 1938.
38. Ibid., Oct. 29, 1938. See also Fogarty, *Vatican*, pp. 253–255.
39. AANY, Spellman diary, Nov. 8, 26, 1938.
40. AAP, Bernardini to Dougherty, Bern, Dec. 4, 1939.
41. AAP, Dougherty to Bernardini, Philadelphia, Mar. 9, 1940 (copy).
42. AANY, Spellman diary, Nov. 26, 1938.
43. Interview with Bishop Clarence Issenmann, Cleveland, Jan. 8, 1981.
44. See Fogarty, *Vatican*, p. 256.
45. AANY, Spellman diary, April 1, 1939.
46. Ibid., Apr. 3, 1939.
47. Ibid., April 12, 1939.
48. Ibid., April 24–25, 1939. Spellman noted that he was recording the episodes of this period on July 24, after he had actually been installed as archbishop.
49. Ibid., June 29–30, 1939.
50. Ibid., April 17, 1939.
51. Gannon, p. 136.
52. Ibid, pp. 146–151. Gannon publishes the entire text of Spellman's letter to Cicognani.
53. AANY, Cicognani to Spellman, Washington, Nov, 28, 1939.
54. AANY, Cicognani to Spellman, Washington, Nov. 28, 1939 (copy); there is also a draft in Spellman's own hand.
55. AANY, Spellman diary, Dec. 7, 1939.
56. See Fogarty, *Vatican*, pp. 259–266 for a more detailed account of these negotiations and of Taylor's mission.
57. Ibid., pp. 258, 263, 266.
58. AAP, Spellman to Dougherty, New York, Mar. 8, 1940; Dougherty to Bernardini, Philadelphia, Mar. 8, 1940 (copy).
59. AANY, Spellman to Pius XII, New York, May 3, 1941 (draft).
60. Maglione to Cicognani, Sept. 3, 1940, *Actes et documents du Saint Siège relatifs à La Seconde Guerre Mondiale*, ed. Pierre Blet, Angelo Martini, Robert Graham, and Burkhart Schneider, 8 vols. (Vatican, 1965–1980), 4:135–136.
61. Quoted in Dorothy Dohen, *Nationalism and American Catholicism* (New York, 1967), 151.
62. Fogarty, *Vatican*, p. 291. See Gannon, pp. 198–200.
63. FDRL, PSF 185, Spellman to Roosevelt, Seville, Mar. 4, 1943; copy in AANY.

64. Gannon, p. 204.
65. Fogarty, pp. 292–293.
66. Ibid., pp. 293–294.
67. Gannon, pp. 220–221.
68. AANY, Spellman Diary, Sept. 15, 1943. See Gannon, p. 227.
69. FDRL, PPF 4404, Spellman to Roosevelt, New York, Feb. 20, 1944.
70. AANY, attached to Spellman to Roosevelt, New York, Feb. 20, 1944 (draft). See Gannon, pp. 229–239.
71. AANY, Spellman diary, July 4–5, 1944; Gannon, pp. 230–233.
72. AANY, Spellman diary, July 28, 29, Aug. 3, 4, 1944.
73. Ibid., Aug. 20, 21, 1944.
74. Ibid., Sept. 28, 1944.
75. NA, RG 59, DS 866.A.404/7-545, Tittmann to secretary, Vatican, July 5, 1945 (cable).
76. AANY, Spellman diary, Aug. 8, 1945.
77. Ibid., Aug. 11, 1945.
78. Interview with Bishop Clarence Issenmann, Jan. 8, 1981.
79. AANY, Galeazzi to Spellman, n.p., May 15, 1947.
80. See Gannon, pp. 144–146, for a fuller list up to 1959. See also Fogarty, p. 315, for the bishops who owed their rise to Bishop Edward Hoban of Cleveland, especially in the late 1950s.
81. Gannon, pp. 276–282. See also John Cooney, *The American Pope: The Life and Times of Francis Cardinal Spellman* (New York, 1984), pp. 187–195.
82. Donald F. Crosby, *God, Church, and Flag: Senator Joseph R. McCarthy and the Catholic Church, 1950–1957* (Chapel Hill, N.C., 1978), pp. 179–184. See also Gannon, pp. 348–351, and Cooney, pp. 218–30.
83. Gannon, pp. 314–322; Cooney, pp. 176–184.
84. AANY, Montini to Spellman, Vatican, Mar. 12, 1953.
85. AANY, Spellman to Montini, New York, Apr. 17, 1953 (copy).
86. For a fuller treatment of this, see Fogarty, pp. 328–331 and 364–367.
87. AANY, Spellman to "Dear Friends," n.p., dated "Christmas Night," but probably Dec. 27, 1959.
88. AANY, Spellman to Vagnozzi, New York, Feb. 26, 1964 (copy).
89. Memorandum of Niel J. McEleney, C.S.P., Apr. 14, 1960; letter of Myles J. Bourke to author, New York, Feb. 22, 1987.
90. See Fogarty, pp. 390–399.
91. Quoted in James Hennesey, *American Catholics: A History of the Roman Catholic Community in the United States* (New York, 1981), p. 322.
92. Quoted in Dohen, p. 1. See also Cooney, pp. 289–294.
93. AANY, Spellman to Vagnozzi, New York, June 29, 1965.

Chapter 14   Paul J. Hallinan

1. Interview, Chicago, October 3, 1985.
2. Telephone interview with the Reverend Francis Zwilling, Saint Petersburg, January 22, 1986.
3. Hallinan, "My War with Australia," pp. 14–15. This is an unpublished forty-seven-page essay written by Hallinan when he was still in the Southeastern Pacific.
4. ADC, Hallinan to Auxiliary Bishop John Krol, April 5, 1958.

5. *Churches and Church Membership in the United States: An Enumeration and Analysis by Counties, States and Regions* (New York, 1957).

6. Joseph H. Fichter and George L. Maddox, "Religion in the South, Old and New," in *The South in Continuity and Change*, ed. John C. McKinney and Edgar T. Thompson (Durham, N.C., 1965), p. 364.

7. (Cleveland) *Catholic Universe Bulletin*, July 22, 1960.

8. (Charleston) *News and Courier*, December 13, 1958.

9. (Columbia) *State*, October 24, 1960; (Charleston) *Catholic Banner*, July 17, 1960.

10. Diary, January 23, 1959; March 19, 1959.

11. (Charleston) *Catholic Banner*, February 26, 1961.

12. Hollings to Hallinan, February 20, 1961. This letter is in the possession of the Reverend Theodore Marszal, Cleveland, Ohio.

13. ADCh, Hallinan to Sister Maria, O.L.M., June 2, 1960, copy.

14. ADCh, Hallinan to Sister M. Paul Johnston, C.S.A., December 1, 1960, copy.

15. *Time*, March 3, 1961; James E. Sulton to Hallinan, March 9, 1961, Marszal Collection.

16. (Atlanta) *Journal and Constitution*, February 26, 1961.

17. Hallinan, Memorandum of a conversation with Governor Ernest F. Hollings, Columbia, S.C., January 28, 1960, Marszal Collection.

18. (Atlanta) *Georgia Bulletin*, December 7, 1967.

19. Interview with Mr. Ivan Allen, Jr., Atlanta, April 28, 1986.

20. Ivan Allen, Jr., with Paul Hemphill, *Mayor: Notes on the Sixties* (New York, 1971), p. 82.

21. (Atlanta) *World*, June 14, 1962.

22. AAA, Hallinan, Statement of admissions policy of the Catholic hospitals in the Archdiocese of Atlanta, March 28, 1963.

23. AAA, Eugene Carroll, director of public relations for the Methodist church in Georgia, to Hallinan, March 21. 1968.

24. Hallinan, Address to the National Newman Congress, Northern Illinois University, DeKalb, Ill., August 31, 1967. The text is in the possession of Cardinal Bernardin.

25. Diary, October 17, 20, 1962. Robert E. Tracy, *American Bishop at the Vatican Council* (New York, 1966), p. 57.

26. Vincent A. Yzermans, *American Participation in the Second Vatican Council* (New York, 1967), pp. 157–158:

27. Diary, November 7, 1962.

28. Diary, November 23, 26, 27; December 3, 1962.

29. ACUA, Hallinan Papers, Minutes of the meeting of the Episcopal Committee at the English College, Rome, October 17, 1963.
    Frederick McManus traced the origins of I.C.E.L. back even further to a "remote and rather indirect beginning" in October 1962, when Hallinan held an informal meeting with several bishops from English-speaking countries. However, his interest at that time was not a common English text, but cooperation among English-speaking prelates on the Liturgical *schema*. Frederick R. McManus, *ICEL: The First Years* (Washington, D.C., 1981), p. 4.

30. ACUA, Hallinan Papers, Hallinan, Report to the United States Bishops on the Liturgical Apostolate, November 16, 1963.

31. John Gartner, S.S.S., ed., *The Challenge of the Council: Person, Parish, World: Twenty-Fifth North American Liturgical Week, St. Louis, Mo., August 24–27, 1964* (Washington, D.C., 1964), pp. 94–100.

32. *National Catholic Reporter*, February 28, 1968.
33. ACUA, Hallinan Papers, Hallinan, Written intervention on the pastoral constitution *De Ecclesia in Mundo Hujus Temporis*, October 8, 1965. An English translation of most of his text appears in Floyd Anderson, ed., *Council Daybook, Session 4, September 14 to December 8, 1965* (Washington, D.C., 1966), pp. 118–119.
34. *Georgia Bulletin*, March 18, 1965.
35. (Atlanta) *Constitution*, October 6, 7, 1966.
36. War and Peace: A Pastoral Letter to the Archdiocese of Atlanta, October 1966, in *Documents of American Catholic History*, ed. John Tracy Ellis (Wilmington, Del., 1987), 2:696–702.
37. *Georgia Bulletin*, December 21, 1967.
38. *Georgia Bulletin*, September 21, 1967.
39. *Georgia Bulletin*, March 3, 10, 1966.
40. *Worship* 42 (May 1968): 309.
41. Interview with Monsignor Noel Burtenshaw, Atlanta, Georgia, June 18, 1985.

Index